W9-AUB-758

The Basic Vegetarian Food Pyramid

This vegetarian food pyramid is accepted by most nutrition and vegetarian organizations. The additional items on the bottom tier are those I consider to be important for total health for every human being. The best diet in the world can't help us if we aren't in balance with the other necessities in life!

Vegans can use the chart on the back of this card, which includes only vegan fare.

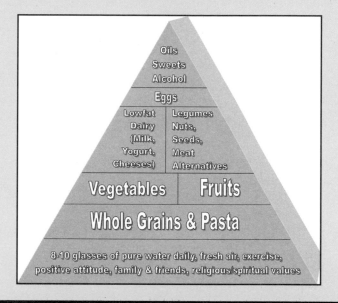

Oils
Sweets
Alcohol

Eggs

Lowfat Dairy (Milk, Yogurt, Cheeses) — Legumes Nuts, Seeds, Meat Alternatives

Vegetables — Fruits

Whole Grains & Pasta

8-10 glasses of pure water daily, fresh air, exercise, positive attitude, family & friends, religious spiritual values

Daily Suggested Servings

Food Group	Servings	What Makes Up a Serving?
Whole grains, bread, cereals, pasta group	6 or more	1 ounce ready-to-eat cereal, 1 ounce of dry cereal, 1 slice of bread, ½ bagel, bun or muffin, ½ cup of cooked pasta or grain
Vegetables	4 or more	1 cup raw or ½ cup cooked vegetables
Legumes, nuts, seeds, and meat alternatives (tofu)	2 to 3	4 ounces of tofu or tempeh, ½ cup of cooked beans, 8 ounces of soy milk, 2 tablespoons of nut butter
Fruit	3 or more	1 piece of fresh fruit, ¾ cup of fruit juice
Dairy (optional)	Up to 3	low-fat dairy is suggested, 1 cup of skim milk, 1 cup of yogurt, 1½ ounces cheese
Eggs (optional)	Up to 3 to 4 per week	1 egg or 2 egg whites
Fats, oils, sweets, salt, and alcohol	Very sparingly	oil, margarine, condiments, cakes, cookies, pies, candy and pastries, beer, wine, and distilled spirits

alpha books

tear here

The Vegan Food Pyramid

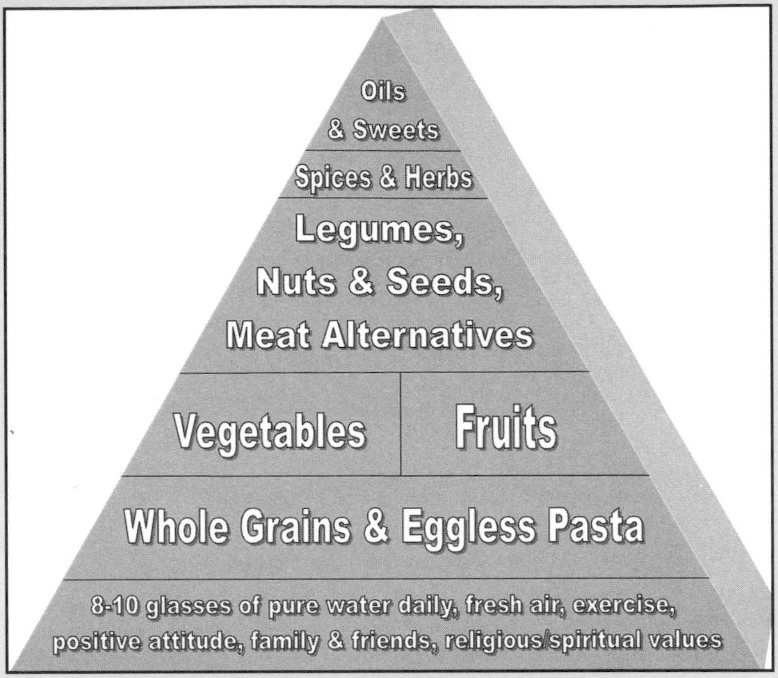

Oils
& Sweets

Spices & Herbs

**Legumes,
Nuts & Seeds,
Meat Alternatives**

Vegetables

Fruits

Whole Grains & Eggless Pasta

8-10 glasses of pure water daily, fresh air, exercise,
positive attitude, family & friends, religious/spiritual values

Note: If you find yourself feeling too weak or getting too thin being vegan, try getting more cooked vegetables, protein, and grains and less fruit and raw veggies. See the opposite side of this card for general serving size suggestions for these vegan foods.

Formula for Whole Health and Happiness

➤ Exercise
➤ Pure water
➤ Herbal nutrition
➤ Proper diet from the vegetarian food pyramids on this card
➤ R&R—rest, relaxation, play time, and your favorite stress-relieving therapy
➤ Positive attitude
➤ Spiritual values
➤ Positive relationships/family/home life
➤ Laughter
➤ Sunshine
➤ Fresh air

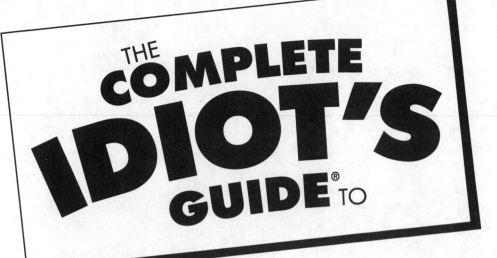

THE COMPLETE IDIOT'S GUIDE® TO

Being Vegetarian

Second Edition

by Frankie Avalon Wolfe

alpha books

A Pearson Education Company

For marketing and publicity, please call: 317-581-3722

The publisher offers discounts on this book when ordered in quantity for bulk purchases and special sales.

For sales within the United States, please contact: Corporate and Government Sales, 1-800-382-3419 or corpsales@pearsontechgroup.com

Outside the United States, please contact: International Sales, 317-581-3793 or international@pearsontechgroup.com

Publisher
Marie Butler-Knight

Product Manager
Phil Kitchel

Managing Editor
Cari Luna

Acquisitions Editor
Randy Ladenheim-Gil

Development Editor
Mary H. Russell

Senior Production Editor
Christy Wagner

Copy Editor
Cliff Shubs

Illustrator
Jody Schaeffer

Cover Designers
Mike Freeland
Kevin Spear

Book Designers
Scott Cook and Amy Adams of DesignLab

Indexer
Sheila Schroeder

Layout/Proofreading
Svetlana Dominguez
Mary Hunt
Bob LaRoche
Gloria Schurick

Contents at a Glance

Contents

Appendixes

Foreword

"You are what you eat," they say, and medical research has now established that the foods and type of diet we consume have a profound effect on our health and well-being. The latest scientific evidence overwhelming supports a healthy vegetarian diet as the best nutritional approach for the prevention and even the treatment of most of the major diseases Western societies face today. Vegetarians have better health than omnivores, and there are many factors in plant foods and plant-based diets that contribute to optimal health. The research shows that vegetarians are less likely to be obese, have less hypertension, less heart disease, less diabetes, and less colon cancer. Vegetarians are only half as likely to suffer from rheumatoid arthritis, kidney stones, and gall stones.

When it comes to achieving optimal nutrition through diet, vegetarians also win hands down. The vegetarian diet supplies more health-supporting, disease-preventing nutrients than nonvegetarian diets. Vegetarians consume approximately two to three times more fiber than omnivores. They consume more antioxidants and phytochemicals that protect against diseases such as cancer, heart disease, stroke, arthritis, and other conditions. Vegetarians have higher folate intakes, which may protect against birth defects and heart disease. And vegetarians consume less of the saturated fat and cholesterol that increase the risk of developing heart disease and some forms of cancer and also avoid heterocyclic amines, which are produced by cooking red meat and linked to an increased risk of cancer.

The question is often asked, "Can't non-vegetarians reap the benefits of a healthy diet by increasing their intake of plant foods and decreasing their meat intake?" Yes, it is true that the more plant foods people incorporate into their diet the healthier they well become. However, the most recent health science research, including the important Adventist Health Study, suggests that vegetarians enjoy even better health than semi-vegetarians who eat meat in limited quantities. The vegetarian diet has so much more to offer when it comes to health and longevity. The ideal diet would be to eliminate the meat, fish, and poultry from the diet altogether and go vegetarian.

Making the change to a vegetarian diet can be difficult at first. For some people it takes a lot of nutrition and culinary education, new recipes and meal plan ideas, and just plain discipline to follow a healthier diet. Frankie Avalon Wolfe has now made it easier to make the change with the help of her book, *The Complete Idiot's Guide to Being Vegetarian, Second Edition.*

The valuable information contained in its pages will give you all the information you need and help make the process easy.

As Frankie points out, "meatless doesn't mean tasteless." You will discover many wonderful, delicious, and nutritious vegetarian foods in these pages that will be pleasing to your palate, as well as many good reasons to try them. Life is made up of the choices that we make. By making the decision to follow a healthy vegetarian lifestyle, you will do more to improve your health and wellness than anything else you could do. The book you now hold in your hands will serve as a tremendous guide and reference for you in your efforts to make the change.

John Westerdahl

John Westerdahl, M.P.H., R.D., C.N.S., is a faculty member and Director of Continuing Education for the American Academy of Nutrition. He is the Director of Health Promotion and Nutritional Services for Castle Medical Center in Kailua, Hawaii, and is the Nutrition Editor for *Veggie Life* magazine.

Introduction

Many business travelers I meet tell me that they would like to eat less meat, or even go vegetarian, if they just knew how. It doesn't take much not to eat meat, but it does takes a little creativity to have a satisfying meal without the use of meat—until you get into the swing of it, of course. This book will serve not only to strengthen your desire to cut meat from your diet (by revealing some things you probably didn't know about what's really between your hamburger buns), but will give you some satisfying, delicious, and nutritionally dense alternatives.

Part 1, "The Beef About Going Meatless," gives you a brief introduction to vegetarianism, where you'll have fun getting oriented to the idea of giving up meat. You can take a light-hearted multiple-choice test to understand how responsive you are to the idea of vegetarianism. You'll see who else is going veg and why.

Part 2, "Eating for Health, Meatlessly," is the educational part of the book, where you'll discover what types of plant-based diets there are. This is where you'll be introduced to the vegetarian food pyramid, supplements to consider as a vegetarian, and all the healthful benefits of many vegetarian staple foods.

Part 3, "Veggin' Out for Your Health," makes the case for being vegetarian for your health. You'll learn how limiting meat is better for your heart, your bones, and your overall physical well-being. This part will help convince you that it is a wise healthful choice for you to be a vegetarian.

Part 4, "Starting Your Meatless Lifestyle," is the practical section, where you'll learn what tofu and other "weird" vegetarian foods look like and how and where to find them. We'll also plan meals together, and I'll give you practical suggestions on making delicious meals and snacks.

Part 5, "Lifestyles of the Rich and Meatless," covers the lifestyle aspects of the new vegetarian and reveals tips on how to travel, dine out, do business, handle social situations, eat for health during pregnancy, raise vegetarian kids, and feed your friends and family enticing veggie meals.

And finally, **Part 6, "Your Choice Affects the World,"** will take your diet a step beyond. You will see the many other reasons that inspire the environmentally concerned, the spiritually or religiously oriented, and the compassionate animal lover to give up animal products. The final chapters reveal some of the behind-the-scenes makings of meat and the needless animal testing for cosmetics and household products, and then offers the vegetarian or compassionate meat-eater some easy ways to choose cruelty-free products.

This book will not only help you eat less meat, but will make your transition fun, simple, and exciting, and will hopefully present you with a few ideas you might not have thought about before. Whether you are just interested in eating less meat overall or you are considering being a pure vegetarian or starting a business in the veg scene, this book will take you as far as you are ready to go.

Now, let's take a look at some nifty illustrated boxes you'll find throughout these pages:

Sprouts of Info

Sprouts of Info boxes include practical tips, tidbits, and miscellaneous pieces of information you can use to make your life easier. Statistics or interesting facts and other useful information on the topic might also be included here.

Lettuce Explain

Lettuce Explain boxes contain definitions for the terms that might not be familiar to you as a new vegetarian. A full glossary of all these terms can be found in Appendix A, "A Veggie Vocabulary."

Steer Clear

Steer Clear boxes are warnings. They give you some things to watch out for and some things to be aware of so that you can make better choices.

Veggie Soup for the Soul

Veggie Soup for the Soul boxes include personal opinions of mine or stories or experiences that I think you might find interesting. (These boxes are a life-saver for authors like me who like to go off on tangents once in a while!) You can get a whole new perspective just by going through the book and reading these boxes.

Acknowledgments

No book gets written without a number of people who make contributions either emotionally to the author or in some other aspect by adding their time, opinions, words of wisdom, and input, whether directly or indirectly. Thanks will always go to my husband first. Thank you for offering to create the figures for this book, and supporting me in such unselfish ways.

Special thanks to Randy Ladenheim-Gil at Alpha Books for your enthusiasm in getting me set to write this edition. I had professional guidance for this book graciously offered by two talented, smart healing women, Ms. Phyllis Light, Nutritional Consultant and Director of Herbal Studies at Clayton College of Natural Health, and Ms. Beth Ellen DiLuglio, Registered Dietician and vegetarian—thank you both for your educational assistance.

I also wish to express my appreciation to the models in the photo in Chapter 15, Chris Varner, Jason Christopher, and friends Becky Torgler, Nancy Holladay, and Townsend Wolfe who so graciously gave up their morning posing in the Boise Co-op for me. What a fun bunch you all are! Thank you Enid for allowing me permission to photograph your dog Oscar (who, by the way, loves fruits and vegetables!), and Gordon and Carol for coming to our rescue when Oscar was being a wiener.

Jane Wolfe, thank you for your most informative editing on the religious aspects of being vegetarian, and thank you Julia Salo at the Doris Day Foundation for your help in Chapter 28. Thank you Christof Ballin, CEO of American Academy of Nutrition, for assisting me in finding a foreword writer for this book, and John Westerdahl—I am flattered to have your foreword in this book, thank you. And Glenn, my long-time friend, your artistic talents are as good as ever. Thanks for the cow cartoon!

And, as always, love and thanks to all of my very dear friends (you know who you are), not to exclude my grandma Fran, the Rents, and my wonderful and tolerant clients who support me throughout my writing and busy, busy scheduling. I need and appreciate all of you. Your love, graciousness, and communication give me comfort and strength to keep producing and doing this work to help you and others. I hope I can give back to you just a fraction of what you give me. (Although you *still* have to buy my books!)

Special Thanks to the Technical Reviewer

The Complete Idiot's Guide to Being Vegetarian was reviewed by an expert who double-checked the accuracy of what you'll learn here, to help us ensure that this book gives you everything you need to know about being a vegetarian. Special thanks are extended to Beth Ellen DiLuglio.

Beth Ellen DiLuglio studied biology, psychology, and nutrition at Wheaton College and received a Master's degree in Human Nutrition from Columbia University's College of Physicians and Surgeons in 1986. She became a registered dietitian in 1987, and a certified nutrition support dietitian in 1990. Beth currently teaches at Palm Beach Community College and is a nutrition support consultant for Cambridge Nutraceuticals, as well as an author of the Florida Dietetic Association's *2000 Handbook of Medical Nutrition Therapy*. She has developed continuing education programs in nutrition support, nutrition and disease, environmental nutrition, and vegetarian nutrition. Beth's quick and easy answer to the vegetarian question is, "I don't eat animals or birds!" and that's an easy start for everyone! Once we all "Kick the Meat Habit" the world will be a cleaner, more peaceful place.

Trademarks

All terms mentioned in this book that are known to be or are suspected of being trademarks or service marks have been appropriately capitalized. Alpha Books and Pearson Education, Inc., cannot attest to the accuracy of this information. Use of a term in this book should not be regarded as affecting the validity of any trademark or service mark.

Part 1

The Beef About Going Meatless

This is the part of the book where I grab your attention and make you want to give up meat for a while. It is an introduction (a meatless appetizer if you will) to why many people give up meat, and it will probably give you more than one interesting reason why you might want to follow that example. It should clear up any misconceptions that you have about vegetarians and their diets. You'll also see that vegetarianism is not meant for the fanatical dieter. This section is written as a balanced, reasonable guide to help you eat better, live better, and feel better, all with little or no meat in your diet.

Chapter 1

Why Eat Less Meat?

In This Chapter

➤ Learn why many are giving up meat

➤ Discover why eating less meat can make you feel better

➤ Use your diet to facilitate other changes

➤ Take a fun quiz to see whether you are a natural vegetarian

➤ Become a new you

Congratulations! You are holding a book that could change your life for the better forever!

There are many reasons you might have picked up this book: Maybe you've met a vegetarian who seems so healthy and vibrant that you are inspired to go meatless for a while yourself. Maybe your 16-year-old just informed you that meat is disgusting and he's going vegetarian, and you need to know what to cook him for dinner. Or maybe you were told by your cardiologist or a concerned significant other to "give up the beef or else!"

This chapter will briefly address many of the reasons for going vegetarian. Then, in later chapters, we'll look at these and more reasons why many give up the meat habit. By the time you're done with this book, you'll have a myriad of reasons to continue with your new way of eating. But first, we're going to walk through the process of making the transition both comfortably and nutritiously into your new diet. No fad diets here—just good old healthy, appetizing, nourishing, scrumptious food, without the meat! Now, let's get on to the meat of this chapter, so to speak.

Why Not Eat Meat?

Let's face it, meat eating is engrained in our society, and vegetarianism isn't for everyone. But millions of folks are either cutting down on their meat consumption or cutting it out completely. Why? There are a variety of reasons, and they can be divided into four broad categories:

1. **Medical- and health-related reasons.** Several conditions are linked to a diet high in animal products, and many are trying to avoid them by going meatless. There are also conditions for which doctors will advise staying away from meat, including irritable bowel syndrome, poor digestive capacity, other colon-related conditions, stroke, heart disease, high cholesterol, gout, arthritis, osteoporosis, obesity, acne, kidney disease, and liver disease.

2. **Environmental and economical concerns.** Those who want to help conserve the earth's natural resources can do so by avoiding meat. I'll also show you in later chapters that by making the change to a whole foods, vegetarian diet, you can save a bundle at the grocery store.

3. **Philosophical, ethical, and compassionate reasons.** Religious and spiritual convictions, ethical concerns over the right to kill animals when alternatives exist, and just plain compassion for other living beings compels many to pass on meat.

4. **Food safety fears.** Fear is a strong motivator, and concerns over Mad Cow disease, food poisoning, hormones, chemicals, antibiotics in meat and animal products, pesticides, and E. coli contamination can be reason enough for many to give up meat.

Whatever your reasons for eating less meat, this book will help to clarify why going vegetarian can be the best decision you've ever made. After you learn about the cons of a meat-based diet, we'll walk through the process of switching to a plant-based diet. I'll also show you how you can live as a healthy, satisfied vegetarian, easily and economically.

Meatless or Vegetarian?

Did someone say vegetarian? Before you meat-eaters get vexed, I want to inform you that this book is also written with you in mind. Although I will be helping you to get comfortable with a more vegetable-based diet, if you still choose to eat meat, occasionally or otherwise, you'll be equipped with information on making better choices when choosing animal products.

You can use this book as a guide for making your diet as healthy and delicious as you want, with or without meat. It is truly designed for anyone who is interested in a more creative and nutritious diet. As a bonus, it will also cover how to live with, work with, or date a vegetarian.

Veggie Soup for the Soul

"It is useless for the sheep to pass resolutions in favor of vegetarianism while the wolf remains of a different opinion."

—Dean Inge (1860–1954), British churchman, in "Patriotism," *Outspoken Essays*

The Many Faces of Meat

Now, before you order that ham and cheese sandwich, hold the ham; let's talk a little about what we mean by *meat*. We will use the term in this book broadly to refer to animal flesh. This includes beef (also known as red meat), wild game of any variety, pork, lamb, fowl (a.k.a. poultry), or any parts thereof, such as liver, tongue, and so on.

Fish or seafood will have its own category, but when I refer to *seafood,* I will mostly be referring to animal life from the waters, such as fish, shrimp, clams, eel, turtles, and so on. Although some plant foods such as dulse, kelp, and other seaweeds also come from the ocean, they aren't considered seafood for our purposes.

Plant food is the main staple for any type of vegetarian—yes, there is a variety. We'll go into all the different types of vegetarian diets in Chapter 3, "Defining Meatless," but for now, you need to know that *vegetarians* are defined as people who eat mainly a plant-based diet and avoid meat.

Lettuce Explain

Meat is the term used throughout this book to refer to foods made of animal and bird flesh or parts. **Seafood** refers to fish and other animal life from the sea. **Vegetarian** means a plant-based diet of vegetables and fruits, nuts, seeds, and grains. Strict vegetarians or **vegans** do not eat meat or seafood or use products derived from or tested on animals.

Time for a Change

Are you ready for a change in your life? Maybe you've moved to a new city, you've started a new family, you have a new spouse, a new job, or you have just retired. Maybe your changes have come in less positive ways, such as recovering from a loss, surgery, or separation of some kind. The good news is that there is always up after down! What a great time to begin anew!

Lettuce Explain

Nutrients are any substance that provides nourishment, such as the minerals that a plant takes from the soil or the constituents in food that keep a human body healthy and help it grow, maintain, and rebuild new tissue.

When you are feeling down about your body or if you aren't feeling the way you want to feel, consider that your body is continually rebuilding itself. For instance, your skin regenerates constantly. You have totally new palms every 24 to 48 hours! Wow! Your body is working on building new muscles, skin, tendons, and bones all the time. Every seven years all of your cells are new, making you a whole new person! Isn't that a concept?

Let me illustrate a bit more. Let's say you are 21 years old. By the time you hit your twenty-eighth birthday, you will be a brand-new woman or man. Not one cell that you had when you were 21 will be present in your 28-year-old body. You'll be a whole new physical person again at 35, 42, 49, 56, and so on, every seven years. See? It's never too late to begin a new healthy lifestyle.

If we are going to build and rebuild, why not rebuild a body on wholesome foods, fresh vegetables, and fruits? *Nutrients* are the elements that we take into our bodies to provide the raw materials needed to build new tissues. Why not give your body the raw materials it needs to build a strong cellular foundation for the next seven years?

Of course, as you age, your body's rebuilding processes naturally slow down. Therefore your body is going to need more and more help along the way. Your internal environment will appreciate it if you lighten the load by lessening your intake of damaging foods and increasing the things that you know are good for you. (And believe it or not, we all have some inherent instincts about what is good and bad for us, although sometimes we choose to ignore them.) But remember, if you don't like your body, you can start right now with some positive changes to ensure that your cells build a new you that you can live with.

Expanding Your Mind

It is going to take a little mental rearranging for you to change your eating habits. In fact most of our eating is just that—habit! Believe it or not, you probably do most of the things that you do and eat most of the things you eat because you have been conditioned to do so. And that's okay! But once you begin to stretch the limits of your thinking, you'll be surprised at the new avenues that will be opened up for you.

One thing about the brain is that it works a lot like a computer, and our thinking is the software. Well, we are going to create some new programs with this book. Once you get used to these new ideas and ways of doing things, you'll have what it takes to reprogram yourself.

Changing your behavior patterns actually creates new *dendrites* in your brain. These are the neural pathways that receive electrical signals from other neurons and conduct signals to the cells. Any new repeated behavior creates new dendrites, making pathways for the new behavior. Before you know it, your dendrites will be so well developed, you won't be able to believe that you once were a meat-eater. And if you follow my nutritional suggestions along the way, you'll soon feel healthier, attain your ideal weight, have more energy, and be better nourished than ever!

Choosing Good Habits

Building new behaviors or brain patterns gives you choice and free will. You will no longer simply go through the motions because of your habits. Let me demonstrate what I mean.

Lettuce Explain

Dendrites are a branched extension of a nerve cell that receives electrical signals from other neurons and acts as a conductor for signals to the cell body. Any new repeated change of behavior creates new dendrites, making new pathways for the new behavior.

Karen is at work, and she's feeling overwhelmed. Her lunchtime comes up, and because of her work-related stresses, she is anxious and irritable. She gets in her car, considers what to have for lunch, and thinks to herself, "Oh heck, I'm just going to run to the fast-food drive-thru and grab a burger and fries." She does, and the sugar, fat, and extra carbohydrates actually do make her feel a bit calmer.

However, she beats herself up at the end of the day because she feels fat, and to make things worse, she's hungry again because the fast-food sugar rush has dropped (most fast food is loaded with hidden sugar). She returns to work the next day and begins the cycle over again. This behavior sets up a pattern linking stress to foods high in sugar and fat. Every time Karen gets stressed, her pattern is to grab something that is not particularly good for her.

So how do we change habits like this? Well, it takes a little bit—okay, a lot—of consciousness. First you have to realize you have a pattern. Then you have to think about the fact that you have options, preferably meatless and healthier ones. Then you can stop, think, and make new choices. Do a little research and find a grocery store that has a wonderful salad bar or a health food store that makes delicious sandwiches. Then you can consciously make a choice to go there when you are stressed, and you'll find that it quickly becomes a new habit for you.

Wouldn't you rather have a habit that leads to better health? Let's go a step further. How about if Karen signed up at a local health club near her job and walked on the treadmill for a half hour during lunch. She'd still have time to grab a salad or smoothie and some nuts and get back to work. This would help her manage the rest of the day with a clearer mind, and this behavior would soon become habitual.

Sprouts of Info

A Burger King Whopper and a regular order of fries totals about 870 calories and contains 54 grams of fat, 21 grams of which are saturated fats. The recommended daily value (DV) for saturated fat is 20 grams. The Recommended Daily Allowance (RDA) for calories, depending on your activity level, age, and sex, is 1,900 to 3,000 daily (for adults).

As you work on programming yourself with these new habits, what once triggered you to grab a candy bar can now trigger a trip to the salad bar. It's simply a matter of training your brain and helping your body get adjusted to new ways of living, eating, and thinking. I'll give you some tips along the way and walk you through until your healthy lifestyle becomes a matter of healthy habits!

Out with the Old

This is a great time for a change, and giving up or cutting back on meat can be an excellent way to start. Consciously reducing your meat intake can help you on your way to new positive changes in your life, your health, your outlook, and your purpose.

One good way to get started is with a cleanse, which involves using herbs or eating specific foods for a short period of time to help clean out your elimination system. Many people give up meat during a cleanse and find they cannot go back to eating it afterward. Cleansing offers you a chance to feel lighter, cleaner, and healthier, and cleansing can often reverse health conditions that have affected you for years. (See the following Veggie Soup for the Soul for a recipe for an excellent herbal cleanse.)

In Part 3, "Veggin' Out for Your Health," we will talk in depth about meat-eating and health conditions, but for now, suffice it to say that once you cleanse and go meat-free for a while, you will notice that all of your tastes begin to evolve. Instead of craving pork chops and bread and butter, you might feel as though you "crave" a fresh spring salad with extra slices of ripe avocado. So this doesn't sound like it could *ever* be you? You might be surprised. Keep reading!

In with the New

Whether you decide to do an herbal cleansing or not, vegetables and fruits are a great way to help clean your system. This is especially true when you are not used to eating a lot of these foods. Sometimes you will experience intestinal gas for the first week or so as you introduce new fibrous foods to your digestive system.

Incorporating fiber and other bowel-cleansing foods into the diet is equivalent to sweeping a dirty concrete floor. In other words, when you begin sweeping up the hard, encrusted dirt from the floor, the dust (intestinal gas) will fly! Eventually, when the basement floor (your intestinal walls) are clean, the dust will settle. Then you will be able to enjoy a cleaner system. Since the intestines are where the body absorbs nutrients, you will also benefit by increasing your body's ability to absorb nutrients from the foods you eat. This has its own benefits.

Veggie Soup for the Soul

To facilitate a body cleanse, it is wise to start with the colon. See your herbalist, if you have one, for a good cleanse or try this colon-cleansing drink for a week or two after you have given up meat.

Each morning, take ...

➤ Two to four capsules of psyllium hulls (pronounced *silly-um*).

➤ Two capsules of cascara sagrada.

➤ Chase it down with a glass of organic apple juice with a tablespoon each of aloe vera and liquid chlorophyll added.

The mixture of supplements will increase your bowel activity, so give it a try over a weekend or on a day you'll be at home to see what your reactions will be.

Meatless and Fancy-Free

Have you ever felt guilty or had health concerns about eating meat? Lots of people do, and those are among the most common reasons for becoming a vegetarian. If you do give up meat, here are some questions you won't need to ask yourself anymore:

➤ Will buying this beef contribute to cutting the rain forests that I've been hearing about?

➤ Is eating this big cheeseburger going to give me a heart attack?

➤ Has this meat been cooked thoroughly enough to kill bacteria that could give me food poisoning?

➤ I wonder whether I have the flu or whether it could have been that chicken sandwich I had yesterday?

➤ Will I be able to chew this nasty piece of gristle or will I have to spit it into my napkin?

In Chapter 24, "Saving Planet Earth," we'll go into more detail on how meat consumption affects the land and environment. In Chapter 8, "Meatless for a Healthier Heart," I'll show you how meat consumption can be related to heart health, and we'll also look at concerns about food safety. But for now, let's continue thinking about change and how you can make the most of it, as we explore more reasons why many are passing on the meat.

So You Want to Feel Healthier?

Many folks are giving up meat for the health benefits. Not that all vegetarians are healthy or even health-oriented, but generally, a well-balanced vegetarian diet includes lots of fresh vegetables, fruits, whole grains, legumes or beans, nuts, and seeds. These foods all have nutritional benefits: They provide roughage, which helps to keep the bowels in shape; they contain a lot less fat than a diet centered around meat products. The fat they do contain is mostly mono-unsaturated fat—the healthiest kind. They also contain health-promoting phytonutrients not found in any animal product.

Therefore, increasing your intake of vegetarian foods is going to give your body benefits. When the body benefits, you feel healthier—and feeling healthier means feeling better.

Sprouts of Info

Vegetarian Times magazine reported that 120 million Americans (that's 46 percent) are reducing their meat consumption, and more than 12 million of these are strict vegetarians.

Don't Follow the Herd

Since most developed countries in the West host meat-centered cultures, living a meatless life is going to make you stand out from the crowd—or most crowds you are in, that is. This can work for you in some positive ways if you want it to, which we'll talk about in later chapters.

No matter what, though, no one likes a smarty-pants. If you choose to go to a clean diet of fresh fruits and vegetables and decide to leave out meat for whatever reason, try not to make others around you uncomfortable. Meat-eating is still a personal choice, and everyone who goes vegetarian will do it when they are ready and not before. Skip to Chapter 18, "Mr. Meat-Free Goes to Work," for more on table manners for the new vegetarian and to get some helpful suggestions on how to handle being invited over for a roast beef dinner.

Being different can force you to be a leader, turn you into a minority, and make you feel slightly more alone. It also can earn you a new sense of confidence because you are doing something you believe in. Making this choice usually requires a certain amount of education, too, and that is what this book is for. Being different, making an educated choice, and sticking to what you believe in require passion and make you a natural leader.

Veggie Soup for the Soul

Don't be a smarty-pants just because you are convinced your way of eating is superior. When you are asked what you eat, for example, avoid saying things like, "I don't eat anything with a face!"—even if it's true. Most of the time, people who ask you are truly ignorant about a vegetarian lifestyle and are interested in your response. A simple, "I eat fresh fruits and vegetables, whole grains, nuts, beans, and seeds, and I feel fantastic," will go farther to help get the positive word out about eating well without meat—even though it's not as funny.

Have you ever thought about why you eat meat? You can take the following quiz and see where you fall in the carnivore spectrum. This might give you a good idea about how easy or difficult changing your habits will be for you.

A Meatless Quiz

Take this quiz to see how passionate you are about eating meat in the first place and to determine how much work this change might be for you. Choose the best answer for each question.

Note: Before you take this quiz, respond to the following statement:

> I'm *only* giving up meat for my health, so let's get on with it! (Yes or no)

If you answered yes, please skip to Chapter 8. Or take the quiz anyway. It can't hurt to have a little fun.

A Meatless Quiz

1. Most pets I've had ...
   a. I've adopted from the pound.
   b. I've named Fluffy.
   c. I've won a blue ribbon for at the state fair—in the beef cattle category.

2. My name is synonymous with ...

   a. A season, animal, flower, or state of being (e.g., Autumn, Bambi, Daisy, Happiness).

   b. My father's or mother's name, what else?

   c. A vehicle, manly state of being, or cut of meat (e.g., Mac, Butch, Chuck).

3. Tofu is ...

   a. Soy bean curd. It's used as a meat substitute.

   b. That stuff my sister-in-law serves. It's not bad.

   c. For sissies.

4. As a child I ...

   a. Begged my dad not to go hunting.

   b. Ate what I was told to eat with no problems.

   c. Helped my folks slaughter the pig for supper.

5. The way I feel about eating meat is ...

   a. I don't eat a lot of it, but what else is there?

   b. I could take it or leave it.

   c. Beef, it's what's for dinner.

6. Choose your response to the following statement: "You can be well nourished, satisfied, and live a robust and healthy life as a vegetarian."

   a. Totally.

   b. I'm open.

   c. Skeptical at best.

7. Finish this sentence: If I stop eating meat I'll feel ...

   a. Better, thinner, and lighter.

   b. The same or better.

   c. Like a shriveled up anemic weakling.

8. A cardiologist is ...

   a. A doctor who deals with the heart.

   b. A specialist my uncle goes to.

   c. The reason I bought this book.

9. When I do eat meat, I usually prefer it ...

   a. Well done.

   b. Medium.

   c. Not far from walking.

10. I view the idea of going meatless as …

    a. A new challenge and a way to improve myself.

    b. Just tell me what to do.

    c. The ultimate acquiescence.

11. The way I feel about vegetables is …

    a. I like/love vegetables.

    b. I can eat vegetables.

    c. They're good for garnishing meat.

Adding it all up:

Score your test by adding up your points for each answer. Then see how you rate.

For every A answer give yourself three points.

For every B answer give yourself two points.

For every C answer give yourself one point.

➤ If you scored 25 to 36 points, you are probably a natural-born vegetarian. You are going to love this new diet right away. You should feel better immediately after eliminating meat from your system. Your acquired tastes for meat will be replaced quickly, and you will soon be on your way to craving salads and brown rice.

➤ If you scored 13 to 24 points, you are the type of person who will eat whatever is put in front of you, so it's just going to take some conscious thought on your part to change what you eat. After the initial adjustment in your shopping, preparing food, and ordering at restaurants, it will be easy because, after all, you are a creature of habit. You probably work best when you have a clear schedule or regime stuck on your refrigerator. See Chapter 17, "Meatless Meals," for a list to get you started. Helping your spouse or partner go meatless with you will also help. In five or six years, when you're ready for another change, look for my up-dated version of this book.

➤ If you scored 3 to 12, you are probably a natural meat-eater and are going to have to approach this change slowly. See Chapter 14, "The First Bite: Where's the Beef?" and start by switching over to the meat substitutes once a week until you get the hang of it. You will probably crave meat once in a while even after you have eliminated it entirely. You may decide to eat meat occasionally, and we'll talk about what your best choices are for that, too. The *good* news is that you are more than likely very adamant about the choices you make. Skeptics and critics are often the best advocates for a cause once we get them to change their minds. So give it a try, and I think you'll be won over by this tasty, healthy, meatless lifestyle.

Reasons for Going Meatless

Meat production, and therefore meat consumption, have an impact on the earth no matter how you look at it. Some of you may be environmentalists and will be happy to know that, yes, your choice to give up meat does help the environment by saving water, making better use of the land, and decreasing pollution. Check out Chapter 24 for more on meat and the environment. In this introductory chapter, I just want to say that your choice does make a difference, and environmental concerns have led many people to either cut down on their meat consumption or go vegetarian altogether.

Steer Clear

The rain forests are critical links in the ecology of the earth. When a rain forest is converted to cattle grazing, the soil is likely to be grazed out within two years, turning a once rich forest into a desert.

Sprouts of Info

Some very well-known spiritual and religious leaders were vegetarians, including Mahatma Gandhi, John Wesley (Founder of Methodism and an English theologian and evangelist), and Ellen G. White (a founder of the Seventh-day Adventist Church).

Spiritual and Religious Connections

Many people decide to go meatless for environmental or health reasons, but there are also some spiritual and religious beliefs that can give you a deeper reason to embrace your new choice. Maybe you can even re-connect with spiritual beliefs you have gotten too busy in life to put into practice. Many people find it much easier to embrace a change if it is connected to a higher value.

Maybe you are part of a religious group or you were raised in a religious family that taught about diet. Many religions restrict meat-eating either altogether or on certain days, and most have restrictions about what types of animals you may consume and even how the meat is prepared.

Many spiritual practices encourage a lighter diet. Some are based on the premise that as our soul evolves, our bodies, needs, and desires become lighter (closer to being spirit-like—as the soul is more ethereal). The idea is that if the body is busy digesting heavy meats and lifeless foods, it is not able to allow the mind to aspire to a higher purpose. It's true that meat takes longer for the body to digest. It really can make some people feel heavier in body and in spirit.

On the other hand, those who need some grounding for their seemingly scattered thoughts can occasionally use a heavy meal to bring them back into reality. Beans are a good alternative to meat for this, as well as nuts and nut butters. We are going to get into the spiritual and religious connections to the diet in Chapter 25, "A Higher Purpose."

Ethical Arguments

Sometimes *ethics* are connected to spiritual or religious beliefs; other times they are not. Atheists have a standard of ethics just as the religiously devout do.

Cutting out or reducing your consumption of animal flesh gives you a chance to look at the big picture and decide if the ethics of it all mean anything to you. If so, you're in luck because, just as a spiritual or religious conviction about your lifestyle can help you not only adopt but also adamantly embrace a lifestyle choice, so can a strong sense of ethics.

Lettuce Explain

Ethics are a system of moral standards or principles.

The Cardiologist Said So

Getting you to lower your fat intake is probably what your cardiologist (if you have one) is most concerned with. The first thing that comes to mind when considering cutting fat is cutting out meat! Not only does reducing the amount of red meat in your diet normally cut your fat intake, it also lightens the load on your digestive system, your kidneys (which help control your blood pressure), your circulatory system, and your liver.

If the main reason you are going meatless is related to a circulatory system condition, feel free to skip right on over to Chapter 8 to read more details about meat and the heart. If you don't care about all that anatomy and are simply taking your cardiologist's (or spouse's) word for it, skip to Chapter 14 to see how you can ease in to this new lifestyle without having to feel resentful.

Steer Clear

Remember that cutting out meat from your diet will naturally reduce your intake of saturated fats, too, unless of course you choose to replace meat with cheese—which *is* high in the fat factor as well. Read on to learn how to be more creative and replace meats with low-fat tasty meat substitutes.

No matter what your reasons for wanting to eat less or no meat, this book will address them, help you through the transition, and make you feel better and live healthier. And remember, when you get compliments on how good you look, recommend this book to others who ask what you've been doing!

The Least You Need to Know

➤ Changing what you eat takes a conscious effort at first but can soon become a healthy habit.

➤ Changing your diet can be a great way to facilitate change in your life.

➤ A balanced vegetarian diet can make you feel lighter and healthier.

➤ Your body is constantly building new replacement cells, which means it's never too late to begin to feed your body better.

➤ People choose to become vegetarians for a variety of environmental, spiritual, and health-related reasons.

Chapter 2

Smokin' the Meatless Myths

In This Chapter

➤ Put your fears about giving up meat to rest

➤ Learn that meatless can be tasty

➤ See how easy it is to get enough protein

➤ Learn why too much protein is unhealthy

➤ Understand how going meatless can fit almost any lifestyle

"Food is an important part of a balanced diet."

—Fran Lebowitz (1950–), *Metropolitan Life,* "Food for Thought and Vice Versa"

Okay, so you've decided you are going to give meatless a try. "What the heck," you think, "sprouts and tofu can't be all that bad, and if I take some protein powder every day, I'll surely get enough protein. And maybe I'll join a vegetarian commune so it'll be easy for me to live and eat this way!"

Well, this chapter is going to show you that you don't have to live in a commune, grow your own food, or supplement your diet with protein powders to live a healthy and happy vegetarian lifestyle. To top it off, I'm going to show you just how interesting—and yes, even delicious—your new diet can be!

Meatless Doesn't Mean Tasteless

Lasagna, spaghetti, burritos, enchiladas, casseroles, stews, chili, burgers, pizza, nachos, stir fry, sandwiches, soups, salads, and pot pies … does this sound like what a vegetarian eats? You betcha! Meatless does not mean tasteless, nor will you starve on a diet that doesn't include meat.

Almost any dish you can think of that contains meat can be made to be just as tasty with the meat removed or replaced. Even restaurant owners are finding value in the fact that they can serve meatless dishes without purchasing any new ingredients.

Think about a taco salad for instance. Most taco salads contain ground beef. But as long as the restaurant serves beans, all you have to do is ask for no meat and extra beans, and you have a satisfying taco salad with corn chips, beans, cheese, lettuce, salsa, sour cream, guacamole, jalapeños, tomatoes, and onions. With all those ingredients you probably won't even miss the beef!

Sprouts of Info

A recent poll taken by the Vegetarian Resource Group showed that over half of the population surveyed (57 percent) sometimes, often, or always orders a vegetarian item when dining at a restaurant!

This meal gives you plenty of protein, fat, carbohydrates, and fiber and can fill you up for the rest of the day. The salsa and tomatoes give you vitamin C, which also helps you to absorb the natural iron content in the meal. Plus you'll be getting servings of grains, legumes, dairy products, and vegetables all in one entree!

So no doubt about it, meatless doesn't mean tasteless. And if I've whetted your appetite for food, you can turn to Chapter 17, "Meatless Meals," for some delicious ideas for vegetarian and vegan meals that you can whip up today.

The Power of Protein

Most of us connect protein with strength, muscle, stamina, and, of course, meat. That's largely because of the early programming we received in school and on TV that told us that meat is the only source of protein. Believe it or not, though, vegetarians can and do get enough protein to survive and even to grow up big and strong. In fact, some of the world's most powerful animals, like gorillas, elephants, and some types of whale, are strict vegetarians. These animals demonstrate that you don't need protein from animal sources to build a strong, healthy body.

Some very active human athletes are vegetarians, too. Among them is the Linda McCartney International bicycling team, which is made up entirely of vegetarians! The cyclers prove that you not only receive strength from a vegetarian diet, but also the stamina required to ride a bike at high speed for long distances!

The average daily requirements (according to the RDAs) for protein are listed in the following table. Remember, though, that there is really no such thing as average. Biochemically, we are all individuals with needs that depend on a variety of factors. These figures will give you some general guidelines to follow, but you'll want to adjust them for your lifestyle, activity level, and state of health. Adult protein needs can be calculated as .8 grams per kilogram or .36 grams per pound body weight.

Category	Grams of Protein Daily
Infants (0 to 6 months)	13
Infants (6 months to 1 year)	14
Toddlers (1 to 3 years)	16
Children (4 to 6 years)	24
Children (7 to 10 years)	28
Preteen male (11 to 14 years)	45
Preteen female (11 to 14 years)	46
Teenager, female (15 to 18 years)	44
Teenager, male (15 to 18 years)	59
Female, healthy, average-sized adult (19 to 50+ years)	46 to 50
Female, pregnant	60
Female, nursing	62 to 65
Male, healthy average-sized adult (19 to 50+ years)	58 to 63

Protein Is as Protein Does

Let's talk about what protein does in your body so you can have an idea of why you need it. When you eat foods containing protein, your body turns the molecules from the food into smaller units known as amino acids, which are essential for building and repairing body tissues such as bone, muscle, hair, and fingernails.

Beyond giving you structure, the amino acids made from proteins also serve as chemical messengers. They help fight infection and aid in bringing oxygen from your lungs to other tissues of the body. Your body requires at least 20 amino acids to function properly. Of the 20, at least 8 are not manufactured by the body and are therefore considered *essential amino acids* that need to be supplied by your diet.

Lettuce Explain

Essential amino acids are amino acids that cannot be manufactured by the body and need to be supplied in the diet. These nine amino acids are lysine, isolecine, leucine, methionine, phenylalanine, thereonine, tryptophan, valine, and histidine.

Veggie Soup for the Soul

Moringa is a common desert tree that produces an herbal supplement with super nutritional value. It includes all the protein of meat (meaning it contains all the amino acids that meat contains), and a single serving has more calcium than four glasses of milk and many other vitamins and minerals. In some countries doctors have been prescribing it to their patients to control diabetes, cure anemia, strengthen weak bones, and prevent malnutrition. It is being promoted in Senegal as part of its national diet. Maybe health really does grow on trees!

So why am I bothering you with all this detail? As a vegetarian, you might want to know a little bit about the protein issue because some objectors to vegetarianism will suggest that you cannot possibly be strong and healthy because you only consume incomplete proteins found in the vegetarian diet. (So if the gorilla example doesn't convince them, try a little science!)

Plus, you'll want to know for yourself that you are going to get everything you need out of your new diet (you will). So bear with me, and I'll put your concerns about protein to rest for good, and you will be equipped to dispel the protein myth!

Sprouts of Info

Research is now telling us that high levels of the amino acid homocysteine in the blood correlate more closely with heart attacks than blood cholesterol levels! Homocystein is generated from the amino acid methionine, which is found in high levels in—guess what—meat!

You Complete Me

An *incomplete protein* is a protein that lacks one or more of the essential amino acids. Incomplete proteins mostly come from plant sources; however, not all plants are lacking in all the essential aminos, and all plant foods vary in which aminos they do have present. Any diet that contains a mixture or variety of foods will complete your proteins.

In simplest terms, you don't have to worry about incomplete proteins because when you eat a food (let's say an apple) that does not have all of the components of a complete protein, these incomplete molecules will basically hang around in your body until you later eat something that contains aminos that are complementary to the aminos in the apple (such as a handful of nuts). After you eat the nuts, the body will take care of the rest.

Complete proteins are proteins that contain all the essential amino acids. Animals and animal products provide complete proteins. Some plant sources, such as soybeans, contain all the essential amino acids and are therefore considered a complete protein too. It is almost impossible not to get enough protein in your diet, even as a strict vegetarian or vegan (those who don't eat dairy products or eggs). If you are concerned anyway, just include a soy-based food in your diet every day, and you are ensured of a whole protein.

Since we weren't created with a calculator in one hand to measure the food value of every item going into our bodies, we shouldn't expect to have to make eating every meal fit into an algebraic equation. So, to ease your mind, there are only two rules you need to remember to get what you need from your meatless diet:

➤ Eat enough.

➤ Eat a variety of foods.

That's all there is to it! To prove how easy and delicious a complete protein can be, here are some good vegetarian choices:

➤ Bean burritos (with or without cheese), served with Spanish rice

➤ Tempeh burger with French fries

➤ Nut butter and jelly sandwich on whole-wheat bread

➤ Stir fry with tofu, mixed vegetables, and brown rice

➤ Vegetarian bulgur chili

➤ Mixed green salad topped with three-bean salad

So the good news for vegetarians is that as long as you are eating a varied diet, you will get complete protein. Now that we've laid the protein myths to rest, let's turn the tables and look at the dangers of too *much* protein in the diet.

Lettuce Explain

An **incomplete protein** is a protein that lacks one or more of the essential amino acids. Most plants contain incomplete proteins, but eating a variety of foods ensures that you'll get full coverage. A **complete protein** contains all the essential amino acids and is found in some plant foods, such as soybeans, and in animal products.

Sprouts of Info

A peanut butter and jelly sandwich on whole-wheat bread provides a nutritionally complete protein combination. However, you don't need to eat these two together in one meal for your body to complete the protein. If you eat a handful of peanuts in the afternoon and a piece of whole-wheat toast later on, your body will figure it out.

Striking a Balance

An average adult vegetarian can more than exceed the daily protein requirement just by eating a lunch of a veggie burger (with or without cheese), pasta salad, and a glass of soy milk! This doesn't include the protein from your oatmeal this morning or your bean burrito this evening!

Steer Clear

Your kidneys play a large role in many functions of the body, including blood pressure regulation, filtering the toxins from the blood, processing vitamin D, and manufacturing certain hormones. Because kidney health is important for your overall health, you want to be good to your kidneys. Too much protein in the diet is not good for them.

However, most health-conscious vegetarians tend to desire lighter fare and gradually lose their taste for lots of high protein foods. The typical vegetarian diet consists of a wide variety of foods, and, therefore, being vegetarian can naturally help you to keep your protein intake level to a healthy medium.

Heavy meat and animal product eaters, on the other hand, easily create problems by getting too much protein since they not only get a great deal of it from meat and other animal products, but also from plants containing protein!

So what's the problem with getting too much protein? To start with, the body can't store it. Therefore, when you eat too much protein, the body has to work hard to process it, break it down, and excrete its by-product through the kidneys. This is a lot of work for the kidneys.

Second, breaking down extra proteins can make the body pH too acidic, which leads to a myriad of other health problems. One of the major contributors to osteoporosis and other bone-loss problems is over-acidity in the body. Consuming protein increases your need for organic forms (plant sources) of calcium (calcium is alkaline, which helps to balance the over-acidic condition). Too much protein in the diet is also a major contributing factor to kidney stones.

Enough Is Enough

In a nutshell, here's what happens. First of all, the body always works to maintain a certain acid-alkaline balance known as pH. When you eat, the protein molecules from your food are broken down in the body and turned into a product that is considered acidic on the pH scale. The body compensates for this extra acid by searching out something alkaline to balance your pH. Calcium is an alkaline mineral, and the biggest source of calcium in the body is in the bones, so the body begins taking the calcium from the bones to calm the acid condition in your blood.

During this process, another problem occurs. In order for your body to utilize the raw calcium being taken from your bones, it needs another element, sodium. Sodium is found primarily in the fluid surrounding the cells in the body, and is essential for fluid and acid-base balance, nerve transmission, and muscle contraction.

Veggie Soup for the Soul

Since the body needs both calcium and sodium to correct an over-acidic condition caused by too much protein consumption, it will rob these items from your body's own stores in the bones, joints, and stomach lining. If you have stomach problems, your sodium levels might already be insufficient to keep the calcium in solution. Calcium that you can't break down or utilize properly is a nuisance to the body and can be a leading factor in painful kidney or bladder stones. The good news? Vegetarians rarely complain of kidney stones.

The biggest sources of sodium in the body are located in the stomach lining and in the joints. Your body has to remove this vital element from these areas in order to utilize the calcium being stolen from your bones. Eventually this will lead to symptoms that can include stiff joints, weakened bones, indigestion, and stomach troubles of all sorts.

A Bad Case of What?

How many people have you heard about who are suffering from osteoporosis or other types of bone deterioration, calcium deposits, dental caries, stomach and digestive troubles, stiff joints, gout, circulatory and blood pressure troubles, or kidney and bladder stones? These all can be directly related to too much protein in the diet!

On the other hand, those diseases related to a lack of protein, such as marasmus and kwashiorkor diseases, are rarely heard of in developed countries. The bottom line is that we all need sufficient protein in the diet to maintain health. The myth is that we need as much as most of us are actually consuming. A vegetarian diet helps to ensure that you will not be getting too much protein.

Who Are You Calling a Vegetable Dip?

Maybe getting enough protein isn't your major concern in all this. Maybe you are worried your buddies are going to think of you as wimpy or different, especially those guys out there from the "real men don't eat quiche" school. Maybe you're worried that you won't know how you are going to handle it. If so, skip to Chapter 18, "Mr. Meat-Free Goes to Work," for more on peer pressure and how to endure it.

The quick answer, however, for dealing with folks who tease you is to remember that people who harass you about your personal choices don't care why you are doing what you are doing. What they care about is that *they* don't look bad for doing something that you chose to avoid! That is the real truth; otherwise, they'd quietly respect your choice.

You will learn a lot about human psychology after you make a change that makes you a little different. You'll learn that people only tease when they feel insecure about themselves, and something about your changes pushes their buttons. Knowing this, you'll know that it is best not to bait these folks with holier-than-thou type comments, which can provoke an uncomfortable situation.

Getting Comfortable

Not that others' insecurities are your problem, but if you don't want to spend the energy debating vegetarian issues, most of the time you can quiet these attacks by saying you are restricting your diet for a time because of some health issues you are working on. Most people are sensitive to personal issues and won't tease you or inquire beyond that. And your true friends are more than likely going to be supportive anyway.

Because many people have preconceived notions about what it means to be a vegetarian, you might want to hold off on any big announcements to give yourself some time to educate yourself and ease in to your vegetarian diet at your own pace. After reading this book, of course, you will have all the information needed to take on any challenge, but since this is still Chapter 2, you might want to lay low until you've read a little deeper.

Not All Vegetarians Are Liberals

You don't have to change your political affiliation to become a vegetarian. You don't have to demonstrate against Lloyd's Furs to skip the ham in your ham and cheese sandwich either. Although many vegetarians have ethical reasons for eliminating meat from their diets, it doesn't mean they all take those feelings to the polls. Vegetarians are libertarians, democrats, and even republicans! Some are liberal and some are conservative.

Steer Clear

Don't brag about your new meatless diet too much until you've educated yourself about your choices and gotten comfortable with your new lifestyle. Then you can announce it to the world!

Sprouts of Info

Don't forget to give thanks to the vegans who started it all. If it weren't for them being different, standing out from the crowd, starting health food stores of their own and getting this trend started, you might never have gotten the opportunity to revel in the joy of tasting an organic, tasty, fresh vegetarian variety platter served to you in less than two minutes flat! Oh, the joys of living in a free country!

But it is true that those of us who live in developed countries where a variety of foods are available do have a choice about what we eat. I believe that we also have the responsibility to make educated choices, both about what we eat and what goes into the foods we choose. Vegetarianism is simply another personal choice we all get to make. It's not for everyone, but it is certainly a viable dietary and even lifestyle choice.

Some Inspiring Vegetarians

Think of someone who has inspired you to eat less meat. Was this person a raving lunatic shouting "Save the cows!" outside a burger joint? Was it a vegetarian who appeared friendly, attractive, in shape, active, and bright-eyed and made you wonder if you might look that good if you went meatless? I bet I can guess your response. Just for fun, take a look at this list of some famous vegetarians and vegans. See if there isn't someone in this list you think highly of.

➤ George Bernard Shaw—philosopher and playwright

➤ Alec Baldwin—actor

➤ Brigitte Bardot—model, actress, and animal activist

➤ Drew Barrymore—actress, vegan

➤ Kim Basinger—actress

➤ Dustin Hoffman—actor

➤ Bryan Adams—rock singer

➤ Brad Pitt—actor

➤ Joan Baez—folk singer

➤ Leonard Cohen—poet and musician

➤ Peter Gabriel—rock singer

➤ Melissa Etheridge—rock singer

➤ Boy George—rock singer

➤ Meatloaf (is that a contradiction or what?)—rock artist

➤ Hank Aaron—baseball great and home run champion

➤ B. J. Armstrong—basketball star

➤ Peter Burwash—tennis player

➤ Andreas Cahling—bodybuilder

➤ Joanna Conway—ice skater

➤ Sylvia Cranston—triathlete

➤ Sally Eastall—marathon runner, vegan

➤ Leonardo da Vinci—artist

➤ Charles Darwin—naturalist

➤ Thomas Edison—inventor

➤ Ralph Waldo Emerson—lecturer, essayist, and poet

➤ Sir Isaac Newton—scientist, astronomer, and mathematician

➤ Plato—philosopher

➤ Nikola Tesla—inventor

➤ Henry David Thoreau—author and philosopher

➤ Leo Tolstoy—philosopher and author

➤ Mark Twain—author, philosopher, and storyteller

➤ Alice Walker—author, vegan

➤ H. G. Wells—author

And this is only a tiny sample of the many, many famous and successful vegetarians. You can see they all have something special, and all have given or continue to give something special back to society. For more info, go online and visit The Vegetarian Pages at www.veg.org. This site has a huge list of famous vegetarians!

It's Easier Than You Think

Did you know that just recently Kraft Foods, the United States's number-one food packager, purchased the makers of the vegetarian Boca Burgers? That means that one of the largest food companies in the world has not only taken notice of a growing meatless market, it has bought into the industry to boot!

Sprouts of Info

In the world of finances and stocks, meat alternatives are considered a high-growth category: They've shown annual double-digit increases for the past five years! This shows a powerful shift in tastes among the average consumer! It also means that we can look forward to more and more interesting and tasty meat-free choices to pick from!

This news means that you will be seeing more and more advertising for meatless prepared foods, meatless frozen foods, vegetarian frozen entrees, and also, of course, the health benefits associated with eating less meat. You won't always have to find a health food store to get these alternative foods, either. More standard grocery stores are carrying them all the time. We'll talk about the benefits of shopping at health food stores later, but not everyone has access to these places, and making meat-free entrees available to more consumers is going to be good news for us all.

Vegetarian Fast Food

Another recent vegetarian news flash includes the roll-out of a new fast-food restaurant chain called Healthy Bites Grill, which will be the first-ever restaurant chain to serve healthful, organic food in the fast-food format. The chain will target densely populated business areas and communities where the fast-food format suits the fast-paced lifestyle.

All these changes mean you won't have to grow your own food to sustain yourself on a vegetarian diet. On the contrary, you will find more and more vegetarian choices at grocery stores, fast-food restaurants, and other eateries. As the trend continues and grows, you will find that it will become even easier to find tasty, satisfying vegetarian food wherever you go. Being vegetarian is getting easier and easier. And it looks as if in the future, vegetarian food will practically be coming to you!

Veggie Soup for the Soul

Recent tests indicate that kids' tastes have a lot more to do with their mental conditioning than not. Blind taste tests showed that soy-based burgers were well received by most students. Then the students tasted the same burgers but were told they were soy beforehand. The kids gave them the thumbs down!

You Won't Even Miss It

Even after being a vegetarian for a while, some people find the aroma of cooking meat appetizing. No doubt about it, there is nothing like the smell of charring flesh, whether you love it or hate it. Unfortunately for those who enjoy this aroma, there is no product you can sprinkle on your tofu to give it that barbecue smell. But I can guarantee that you can cook some veggie meals that will make even a confirmed meat-eater's mouth water.

And here's something else you can look forward to. After you've gone without meat for a while, you might find the smell does nothing for you. Did you ever meet an ex-smoker who can't tolerate being anywhere near smoke? The same thing can happen to the meat-eater, and many seem to lose their affinity for the smell, taste, and texture of meat altogether, as long as their diet is equipped with enough iron, protein, and other nutrients to be satisfying.

But what many people really miss about meat is its texture, and being a texture person myself, I know all about that one! We'll talk about this in Chapter 16, "Cooking at Home," and you'll see that there are some meat substitutes that your teeth might not believe are not meat! So you can have it all, without really eating it all, after all!

The Least You Need to Know

➤ Vegetarians tend to eat a variety of foods, which makes for a flavorful, nutritious, and interesting diet.

➤ Vegetarians who eat a variety of foods get all the protein they need to maintain health.

➤ There are more problems connected with too much protein in the diet than not enough.

➤ Vegetarians come from all walks of life and have a wide range of backgrounds.

➤ Meatless choices are becoming more and more available to everyone.

Chapter 3

Defining Meatless

In This Chapter

➤ Discover the many different ways to go meatless

➤ Learn the term for a vegetarian who eats fish

➤ See what foods a lacto ovo vegetarian eats

➤ Understand what a vegan is

➤ Learn about macrobiotics

Okay, I've given you some reasons to give up meat, and I eased some of your initial fears about being a vegetarian. So what's next? Well, now it's time to learn about the various ways of being vegetarian. You will discover that there are different types of plant-based diets and learn the names that describe these diets and the people who follow them.

By the end of this chapter, you'll be able to speak the language of the vegetarian, and you'll probably begin to form some ideas about what type of diet and lifestyle appeals to you most. So the next time someone asks if you are considering going lacto, you don't have to be offended—you'll know just what he or she means. Read on!

Pescatarians: The Seafood Diet

Have you heard about the seafood diet? You see food, and you eat it! Well, that's not quite the way it is for a *pescatarian*, also referred to as a *pesco vegetarian*. This term describes those who eat a mostly vegetarian (plant-based) diet, but also choose to eat seafood, such as fish.

Lettuce Explain

A **pescatarian,** also referred to as a **pesco vegetarian,** is the term used for a person who eats primarily a plant-based diet but who also eats fish or other seafood. Pescatarians do not eat meat or poultry, dairy, or eggs.

Lettuce Explain

A **lacto ovo vegetarian** is a person who eats no animal flesh but who does consume eggs and dairy products. An **ovo vegetarian** eats no animal flesh or dairy products but does consume eggs. A **lacto vegetarian** eats no animal flesh or eggs but does consume dairy products. **Dairy** includes any animal-milk product, such as cheese, milk, yogurt, and butter.

Because the pescatarian diet includes a flesh product, some vegetarians don't consider this type of diet to be true vegetarianism. Others disagree, and, in any case, it is a mostly plant-based diet.

Pescatarians face many of the same challenges with dining out, going to dinner parties, and staying healthy as pure vegetarians. If you decide to become a pescatarian, you'll have to know what it means so that you won't feel like a fish out of water among other pescos.

Lacto Ovo Vegetarians: Dairy Delicious

Many vegetarians are *lacto ovo vegetarians*. This type of vegetarian eats mostly plant foods but also dairy products and eggs. Strict vegetarians and vegans usually do not consider a lacto or lacto ovo vegetarian a true vegetarian because these diets include animal products.

Nevertheless, lacto and lacto ovo vegetarianism is the most popular vegetarian diet there is. Many people who later become pure vegetarians start out as lacto ovo vegetarians. It can be a transition stage, or it can be permanent, depending on your needs and desire.

To keep this kind of vegetarianism straight, you need to be clear about what counts as dairy (lacto) because some people tend to lump eggs (ovo) along with it. Eggs, however, are not dairy, and have a category of their own. Dairy includes any product derived from animal milk. Examples of dairy foods include …

➤ Cheese.

➤ Ice cream.

➤ Milk.

➤ Yogurt.

➤ Sour cream.

➤ Butter.

The popularity of lacto ovo vegetarianism (or ovo lacto, whichever you prefer), is probably due to the fact that in a fast-paced, grab-a-meal-and-run lifestyle, it is simply easier for most people to accept dairy and eggs among their food choices than to find items that are entirely plant-based.

Vegan alternatives to dairy are becoming more common, though, and, even if you decide to stick with a lacto ovo lifestyle, I'll make sure you know what great alternatives are out there. It might surprise you how tasty many of these dairy-free products can be. You might find that some dairy alternatives taste even better than the dairy-based foods!

Ovo or Lacto?

Lacto ovo vegetarians can also be divided into either category, such as an *ovo vegetarian* who eats eggs but no dairy, or the reverse: a *lacto vegetarian*, who consumes milk products but no eggs.

Are you getting confused? Here's an example that might help. This is what each kind of vegetarian might have for a big Sunday breakfast:

➤ **Lacto ovo vegetarian:** A cheese omelet with hash browns, glass of orange juice, and buttered toast

➤ **Lacto vegetarian:** Hash browns with onions and peppers, topped with melted cheese, a dollop of sour cream, glass of orange juice, and buttered toast

➤ **Ovo vegetarian:** Veggie omelet (no cheese) with hash browns, glass of orange juice, and toast with honey (no butter)

Sprouts of Info

Fortunately, healthful foods are becoming more available. For example, in southern California, almost every street corner has a vegetarian restaurant or, at the least, a restaurant that offers vegetarian or vegan choices. Now, in the United States at least, meatless is becoming more popular, and we are seeing more vegetarian entrées in more and more restaurants.

A Good Egg

I bet you've figured out by now that the term ovo (pronounced *ah-voe*) means egg. Let's talk a little about eggs here to see why the ovo and lacto ovo vegetarians might keep them in their diet.

Some benefits of eggs include …

➤ Eggs are a good source of protein.

➤ Eggs are a whole food and are neatly packaged.

➤ Egg yolk contains lecithin, which is known for its capability to emulsify fat in the diet and to help reduce the cholesterol in your arteries. Lecithin is also a brain food.

➤ Eggs taste good to some people.

Unfortunately, eggs also have a bad side, but we are just learning in this chapter, not judging. If you are considering eliminating eggs from your diet, see Chapter 13,

"High Ho the Dairy, Oh!" for the less sunny side of eggs and for a list of egg and dairy substitutes.

Maintaining Your Friendship with Ben & Jerry

I think the secret reason many vegetarians choose to go lacto ovo is due to the influence of two friendly men from Vermont who make an outrageously good ice cream known as Ben & Jerry's. A strict vegetarian or vegan would, of course, have to forego this pleasure, but ice cream isn't off limits to the lacto ovo vegetarian, and as long as you pick brands that don't have eggs, even lacto vegetarians can enjoy it!

Steer Clear

Lacto vegetarians beware—some ice creams, such as Häagen-Dazs—contain eggs. Check your labels and find a brand or flavor that doesn't contain eggs before you pig out!

Other Terms for Meatless

In addition to these basic kinds of vegetarians, there are all sorts of diets that some people want to include under the umbrella of vegetarianism. Although technically a vegetarian is one who eats a strictly plant-based diet, there's room in this book for all sorts. Let's take a look at some semi-vegetarian labels:

➤ **Pollo vegetarians** are folks who avoid fish and all meats but eat poultry.

➤ **Pesco pollo vegetarians** avoid red meat but eat fish and poultry.

➤ **Psuedo vegetarians** or **semi-vegetarians** are mainly the people this book was written for, and maybe what you are already—a person who has cut back on his or her meat consumption in general but is not a vegetarian (yet).

Beyond the realm of the vegetarian diet, we also find the fruitarian, who consumes only fruits, nuts, seeds, and vegetables whose harvest doesn't kill the plant, and the breatharian, who lives on—guess what? Actually the breatharian philosophy is quite interesting, and I'll touch on it in Chapter 25, "A Higher Purpose," just for your enlightenment. For now, let's stick with eliminating the meat, shall we?

Ronald McDonald or Ronald Vegan?

Although my clever title may have thrown you for a phonetic loop, the term *vegan* is correctly pronounced *VEE-gun*. It is among the strictest forms of vegetarianism and includes products and choices that go far beyond food.

Being vegan is truly a clean way of eating, but it is much more than a diet—it's a lifestyle. Vegans don't eat flesh, seafood, dairy, or eggs, and they do not eat any product derived from animals or insects, such as honey. Some vegans also refuse to eat yeast products.

Veggie Soup for the Soul

Although Argentineans eat more beef than people in any other country, statistics show that beef consumption there fell 12.3 percent from 1990 to 1994. This is due to several factors, including a recession that dropped chicken prices below beef prices. Improving their health seems to be another concern, as it is reported that Argentineans are now exercising more and eating more pasta, salads, tofu, and poultry. And for the first time in Buenos Aires, ethnic restaurants that serve vegetarian fare, including Chinese, Japanese, Indian, and African, are being opened.

Vegans live *cruelty-free* and do not incorporate animal products in any way in their diet or clothing. They follow lifestyle restrictions that exclude the wearing or use of any animal-derived products, such as leather, silk, wool, gelatin, or lanolin.

Choosing a vegan lifestyle is a wonderful ideal, although it is admittedly a more difficult way of life for most people. Living as a vegan forces you to analyze and inspect every purchase you make and every food item you order, and to question everything that comes across your plate. It takes education and lots of effort and creativity, and it's not for everyone.

Sprouts of Info

The term **vegan** was invented by the United Kingdom Vegan Society in the 1940s. The pronunciation *VEE-gun* has also been adopted by the American Vegan Society and is generally the most widely accepted way to pronounce the term.

Letting Go of Leather

I know from experience since I attempted to live as a vegan for a time. I decided to become a vegan after I learned about the typical farming practices used to obtain dairy products and eggs, but I soon found that it was going to take even more effort than I originally signed up for.

I had no problem ordering my shoes and handbags from a company that made only nonleather products (and I'll share some addresses with you in later chapters). I got rid of all my leather goods and wool, traded my down coats for polyester, and eliminated all products that were tested on animals and replaced them with cruelty-free cleaners and cosmetics.

Lettuce Explain

Cruelty-free is a term that refers to a product (household cleaners, cosmetics, toothpaste, and so on) that has not been tested on animals or made with animal derivatives. The phrase "manufactured with compassion" is also used to identify these products.

Lettuce Explain

Casein, also called **caseinate** or **sodium caseinate**, is a milk protein that is used as an additive in some so-called "nondairy" products. Read your labels if you are eliminating all animal products from your diet. **Gelatin** is made from the boiled bones and hooves of animals and is often used to make gel-caps for supplements.

The diet part of the vegan lifestyle was much easier since I was already living as a lacto ovo vegetarian. I replaced cow's milk with soy milk and eggs with egg-replacement powder, and my diet was still very delicious and fulfilling.

However, once I thought I had it all nailed down, I went to a vegetarian society potluck and was told by another vegan that she couldn't eat my dish because it contained soy cheese. I found out that this particular soy cheese has an animal by-product in it called *casein*. Who knew? Then I learned that the encapsulated herbs I was taking were made with *gelatin* capsules. So? I thought, Jell-O is made from gelatin, and Jell-O isn't an animal product. Guess again. Gelatin is made from the boiled hoofs, hides, and bones of animals.

Not So Sweet

Next I was informed that refined sugar products were completely out of the picture because the sugar is filtered through animal bones to refine it. But I couldn't replace sugar with honey because that infringed on the rights of the bees (and I really do think bees are cute!). Needless to say, the list of things I was doing that fell outside the lifestyle of the pure vegan began to grow.

I ultimately decided that I couldn't fully put my money where my mouth was and live a completely vegan lifestyle. I was discouraged by the fact that our society, our foods, and our products are so infiltrated with animal ingredients that I had to remain vigilant practically 24 hours a day to avoid using an animal by-product! It wasn't as simple as being your basic vegetarian and not wearing fur.

I have of course kept my compassion for animals but the pressure of analyzing every detail was too much. I eventually settled into being a lacto ovo vegetarian and finally switched to a lacto vegetarian diet, which made me feel better overall. I came away from the experience with a whole lot of information and some positive choices that were easy to stick to. I sure do admire the drive of the vegan!

Living the Vegan Life

If you look at it another way, living as a vegan can be very simple, if you choose not to get caught up in our fast-paced, traveling, dining-out lifestyle. Many vegans grow their own foods, eat out only rarely, do not eat prepared foods, and are happy to live that way, thank you very much! And if you're fortunate enough to live in an area that has a lot of vegans, like southern California, this lifestyle can be much easier and you'll have more choices for shopping and dining.

Did you ever wonder how some of those famous movie stars are able to live vegan lifestyles? Movie people generally work very hard and lead very busy lives, but then again, many live in cities that offer a variety of food choices. And then, of course, maybe they have cooks that worry about all the food details for them!

Sprouts of Info

This book is oriented toward meat-eaters who are taking their first steps in exploring vegetarianism. For more on the vegan diet and lifestyle read *Compassion: The Ultimate Ethic, An Exploration of Veganism,* by Victoria Moran (Thorsons Publishers Limited, 1985).

Please don't let my story discourage you from going vegan. It is a very clean and wonderful lifestyle if you can manage it. These days it is getting easier to obtain vegan meals, clothing, cosmetics, and herbs, and I'll give you some tips on how to find them.

I'll also help you to learn how to spot hidden animal ingredients in foods where you wouldn't suspect them to be. If you are interested in why vegans choose to practice such a restrictive lifestyle, check out the details in Chapter 27, "The Joy of Being Humane."

Hold the Mayo

Among the most popular foods vegans avoid is mayonnaise, which is made from eggs (lacto vegetarians have to skip it as well). So what do you smear on your sandwich? Well, there's always mustard. If that doesn't do it for you, here are some other suggestions:

➤ **Nayonaise.** A mayo substitute made from tofu.

➤ **Mashed ripe avocado.** It contains good oils for your body and gives some moisture to your bread, like mayo does.

➤ **Tofu.** You can use it to make your own "nay-o-naise" by mixing it in a blender with some lemon juice, a few drops of soy sauce, and some olive oil to make it creamy.

No Honey, Honey

Vegans do not eat honey because it is produced by bees. Instead, they use plant-based sweeteners such as black strap molasses, maple syrup, brown rice syrup, and stevia. See Chapter 4, "A New Food Pyramid," for more on the different types of healthful sweeteners.

Steer Clear

Vegans don't need to worry, but if you are a honey user, remember not to feed it to very young children. Honey sometimes contains minute amounts of bacterial spores that can be fatal to children under the age of 12 months who do not yet have sufficiently developed intestinal bacteria to protect them from it.

Sprouts of Info

Bee honey has antioxidant and antimicrobial properties. It enhances the growth of bifidobacteria, a good bacteria that lives in your body and protects you from harmful foreign bacteria. Unprocessed honey has even been used topically to stop the devastating progression of the flesh-eating bacteria.

Let me stand up for the nutritional benefits of honey, however, and give you some interesting facts on this substance. Honey contains vitamins, minerals, and enzymes. A tablespoon of honey provides 11 mg of potassium, 1 mg of calcium, 1 mg of phosphorus, and trace amounts of iron, zinc, magnesium, selenium, copper, chromium, manganese—and zero fat!

If you choose to eat honey, do your best to purchase raw, unpasteurized, local honey from your own area. Raw honey contains natural enzymes and bacteria that are actually good for you, and they can't survive the high heat of the pasteurization process. (Just remember not to give any kind of honey to children who are less than a year old—their systems aren't mature enough to handle it.)

Unfiltered or strained honey contains some naturally occurring bee pollen, which is a nourishing substance in itself. Bee pollen contains enzymes, vitamins, and minerals and has been used to curb allergies and boost the immune system.

Honey tastes good to most people and provides a more complex sugar to the body than refined sugar does. Refined sugars go directly to the blood stream, forcing the pancreas to release insulin, which gives you a sugar high followed by a sharp low. Honey has some nutritional value, which gives it substance, and it therefore goes through your system just a little bit more slowly than refined white sugar and can sustain your energy a bit longer.

A Raw Look at Macrobiotics

Although a *macrobiotic diet* is not necessarily a vegetarian diet, neither is this book about being purely vegetarian. Therefore, it's only appropriate to cover the various diets that are mostly meatless, and macrobiotics is certainly one of these.

Veggie Soup for the Soul

When you purchase honey or bee pollen produced in your area, you will be taking in the pollen of the flowers and plants that surround you. If you suffer from pollen allergies, you can utilize bee pollen or strained honey in tiny amounts to build up your resistance. However, you need to be very careful with bee pollen and unfiltered honey if you are allergic to bees. Check with your health care practitioner before you experiment on your own.

Forty years ago, Michio and Aveline Kushi from Japan introduced a grain- and vegetable-based diet called macrobiotics to the United States. The philosophy behind it says that the energy of natural foods can be used to bring balance to the body, which restores health. It is based on the principals of yin and yang, which are life force energies. Different foods are categorized as being more yin or more yang, as are different conditions of the body. The idea is that you can help your body back to balance by giving it more yin- or more yang-type foods. When the body is harmonized, it is free of disease.

Those following a macrobiotic diet consume organic (with an emphasis on organic) whole grains, steamed vegetables, and some seafood, although most animal products are excluded. The diet excludes refined products (such as flours and sugars), any processed foods, and those containing chemicals, dyes, and preservatives.

Like veganism, the macrobiotic diet is a lifestyle choice that requires education and dedication. In return, it has rewards: Most folks on a macrobiotic diet claim that it changed their lives by improving their health. Many believe that they have overcome serious illnesses by using this diet. A macrobiotic diet emphasizes whole live foods in well-rounded, balanced combinations. It is also important that they be prepared correctly in order to avoid altering their life-giving properties. Therefore, microwaves, which are believed to change the life force of a food, are forbidden, and cooking over an electric range is undesirable. A gas stove is the preferred method.

Lettuce Explain

A **macrobiotic diet** is based on the Asian concepts of yin and yang, which are life force energies. Different foods containing more yin or more yang are used to restore the body to balance. It emphasizes whole organic foods but is not strictly vegetarian.

Veggie Soup for the Soul

Eventually, as the heavier meat residues leave your body, you will find that you crave meat less. Your tastes will change, and someday you might come back to the chart and say, oh, I guess I've evolved into an ovo vegetarian! But why stop there? If you are feeling good as an ovo vegetarian, maybe you'll consider going vegan, or you might sign up for a macrobiotic cooking class. It's all up to you. The better you feel, the more likely you'll be to work on eating cleaner and more healthful foods.

Mix and Match

Now that we've discussed some diets that involve eating little or no meat, with all their variations, let's sum it all up in a neat reference table. You can use it to help you "find yourself" in the vegetarian spectrum, and it will help you see where you might want to take your diet in the future. And if you invite a guest over for dinner who informs you he's a pesco pollo vegetarian, you can refer to the following table and figure out what not to cook!

Vegetarian Diets

Name	What They *Don't* Eat	What They *Do* Eat
Lacto ovo vegetarian	animal flesh or seafood	eggs, dairy, and plant foods
Ovo vegetarian	animal flesh, dairy	eggs and plant foods
Lacto vegetarian	animal flesh, eggs	dairy and plant foods
Pollo vegetarian	seafood, animal flesh	chicken and plant foods
Pesco pollo vegetarian	animal flesh	fish, poultry, and plant foods
Psuedo vegetarian or semi-vegetarian	reduced meat consumption	mostly plant foods, dairy, eggs, and occasional meats
Pescatarian or pesco vegetarian	animal flesh, fowl eggs, dairy	fish and plant foods
Fruitarian	animal flesh, seafood, dairy, eggs	fruits and vegetables which do not kill the plant when they are harvested, such as apples

Name	What They *Don't* Eat	What They *Do* Eat
Strict vegetarian	animal flesh, seafood, dairy, eggs	plant foods, honey
Vegan	animal flesh, seafood, dairy, eggs, honey, any product derived from an animal such as leather, wool, silk, gelatin, or lanolin	plant foods
Macrobiotic diet	any denatured product (processed food, refined flour, sugar), microwaved food, foods cooked on electric stoves, most animal flesh	whole grains, lightly steamed vegetables, some fresh seafood
Breatharian	food	air

Feel free to mix and match to suit your needs. How about a pesco lacto ovo vegetarian? That would be one who eats seafood, dairy, and eggs, but no animal flesh or fowl. (I'm married to one of these!) The choices are endless. The main concern is that you find a place where you are comfortable making changes in your diet. Maybe you'll want to experiment with the more restrictive ones as your tastes evolve.

Next I'm going to teach you all about the benefits of plant-based foods, and we'll take a look at some of the drawbacks to animal products. That way you'll not only make an educated decision, but you'll also be well-nourished by vegetarian foods along the way. We will take a look at a new food pyramid that does not include flesh products at all and will make sure you are getting plenty of nutrition from the plant kingdom.

The Least You Need to Know

➤ There is a wide variety of meatless or semi-meatless diets you can follow.

➤ A pescatarian does not eat animal flesh but does eat seafood.

➤ An ovo lacto vegetarian eats eggs and dairy products. An ovo vegetarian eats eggs but no dairy; a lacto vegetarian dairy but no eggs.

➤ A vegan is a strict vegetarian who eats no animal products and also does not wear or use them.

➤ A macrobiotic diet is not a vegetarian diet, but involves eating organic whole foods and stresses the importance of balancing yin and yang.

Part 2
Eating for Health, Meatlessly

Now that you've got some good reasons to give up the meat and you understand that you won't starve, you are going to need to see what forms of vegetarianism are available. This section gives you the overview on the "what-else-is-left-without-meat" questions you might have about your new diet, and educates you about the nutrients and benefits found in the plant kingdom. You will certainly see how and why vegetarians can be the healthy minority. This section is going to make you feel good about eating your veggies. Read on, chop, chop!

Chapter 4

A New Food Pyramid

In This Chapter

➤ Learn about the benefits of the staple foods of the vegetarian

➤ Discover how to prepare grains to bring them to life

➤ Understand the value of nuts and seeds in the diet

➤ Use fruit to clean your system

➤ Learn about some healthful sugar substitutes

Now that you know which vegetarian-based diets exist, I want to take you on an exploration of their mainstay—vegetation! When you think vegetarian, don't imagine you'll be deprived of hearty filling meals. You don't have to graze on rice cakes topped with sprouts—ew! No, vegetarianism embraces a plethora of foods from the plant kingdom! We have beans, nuts, seeds, grains, fruits, and, oh yes, vegetables.

If you have a sweet tooth, rest assured that you can have your cake and eat it, too. And since beer, wine, and other spirits are vegetarian, we'll talk about adding that option to your diet healthfully as well. Let's take a closer look at how healthful some of these foods can be so you can get a taste for the benefits you will receive from them!

Beans, Beans, They're Good for Your Heart

You remember that rhyme don't you? Beans, beans, good for your heart, the more you eat, the more you … I don't remember the rest of it. But seriously, could there be any truth to that silly little poem about beans? Are they good for your heart?

Let's spill the beans on the general benefits of legumes:

➤ They provide a good source of fiber.

➤ They are satisfying and can fill you up.

➤ They are low in fat.

➤ They taste good.

➤ They go with just about anything.

➤ They provide a low-fat dietary source of protein.

➤ Added to rice, they provide a complete protein.

➤ In general they are richer in calcium than meat.

We know that lowering your intake of dietary fat and increasing dietary fiber is good, not only for the intestinal tract, but for heart health too. And you probably know that you do need protein to maintain and rebuild muscle tissue, and the heart is a muscle. Beans and legumes provide protein. Given all that, I'd say that beans and legumes really are good for the heart! The more you eat them, the more you … have a healthy heart! Yeah, that's how it goes!

Well-Rounded Proteins

Remember when we talked about proteins back in Chapter 2, "Smokin' the Meatless Myths," and learned how a well-rounded, varied diet contains all the protein your body needs? Well, although most beans (with the exception of soybeans) provide an incomplete protein, you'll get what you need as long as you eat some type of vegetable or other type of grain on the same day to complete the protein.

Keep in mind that it's hard not to get enough protein with a varied diet! As long as you're not eating the same food over and over and over, the plant kingdom will take care of all your protein needs. Beans can work as a replacement for meat in many meals and are great garnished with vegetables or thrown in stews, chili, and casseroles.

Sprouts of Info

To prepare dried beans: Rinse dried beans thoroughly. Remove any tiny pebbles. Put them in a container (crock pots work great) and add water to cover. Soaking at least 10 to 12 hours brings them to life! Now they're ready to cook up in chili, rice and beans, or other dishes.

Beans or Legumes?

The words *legumes* and *beans* are often used interchangeably. There are some technical differences that only farmers care about, but for our purposes, they basically refer to the same thing. Some popular legumes include peas, lima beans, soybeans, lentils, kidneys, garbanzos, navy beans, pinto beans, black beans, and the list goes on.

Technically the legume category also includes peanuts, but because most of us categorize peanuts as nuts, that's where we're going to leave them. (It's like a tomato technically being a fruit instead of a vegetable. Maybe so, but most of us think of and use it like a vegetable!)

Stop the Music!

Because beans are a good source of fiber, they can make you gassy. Fortunately, I know a few tricks of the trade to help eliminate this problem.

Lettuce Explain

The terms **legume** and **bean** are used interchangeably to describe a plant that has edible pods and seeds that are generally eaten cooked.

The outside of the bean contains a sugar substance called hemicellulose, which is chiefly responsible for causing the gas. To get rid of this coating on dried beans, spill off the water after you soak them and rinse them well again with fresh water before cooking them. If this isn't working, try some of the following tricks.

➤ Swallowing a food enzyme or two before consuming beans helps many digest them better. An enzyme supplement may contain varying mixtures of enzymes, including amylase, glucoamylase, and invertase. These help break down the carbohydrates in beans, which helps break down the cellulose in the legume's cell wall. Ask your herbalist, natural health care provider, or the specialist at the store where you purchase supplements for help choosing the best food enzyme for you.

➤ Add a drop or two of Beano to the pot of beans before you eat them. Beano is a commercial product found in most health food stores and super markets that eliminates the gas-producing effects of beans. Warning: Don't take this product if you have an allergy to penicillin.

➤ Chop a large carrot into a few pieces and add it to the beans while they cook, then throw away the carrot before eating the beans. The carrot sucks up the gaseous properties of the beans, and it works great for many.

Some people simply don't experience any gassy effects from beans. Many find that the problem goes away, or at least lessens, as they add more whole foods to their diets and start to eat beans more often. And it can't hurt to hum the little rhyme about beans while you eat … that is, if you can remember how it goes!

Grains for the Brain

Grains are another staple food of the vegetarian diet. They provide starch, roughage, energy, and nutrients if they are prepared properly and eaten in a balanced manner.

Here are some of the benefits of whole grains. They ...

➤ Provide many of the B vitamins.

➤ Are higher in protein, vitamin E, zinc, phosphorus, and phytonutrients than their refined, enriched counterparts.

➤ Are rich in the minerals magnesium and calcium.

➤ Provide fire or heat (energy) for the body.

➤ Contain enzymes when prepared properly.

➤ Are low in fat and help fill you up.

➤ Taste good and go with almost any meal.

➤ Are inexpensive.

Grains come in so many varieties that it would be difficult for you not to find a few you enjoy!

In agricultural terms, grains are considered a cereal crop. Here we want to talk about the benefits of *whole grains* versus refined grains, like those you get in cereal boxes. Sorry, but Fruit Loops and even our beloved Cheerios are not considered whole grains. These cereals are made *from* whole grains, but are refined into a product that must then be enriched with the nutrients that are lost in the refining process.

The Whole Thing

My talented technical editor, dietician Beth DiLuglio, concisely describes whole grains as follows: "Whole grain is literally that: the whole of the grain, without the tougher outer hull removed. Whole-grain products are made from the bran, the germ, and the endosperm. Refined grains are made only from the endosperm." Whole grains can include wheat berries, barley, quinoa, oats, rye, rice, bulgur, and millet. These grains can be purchased in their whole, raw, uncooked state and, with a little preparation, can be brought to life and will provide your body with satisfying nourishment.

When you eat beans and grains, you are feeding yourself starches. Starches make the body warmer. I suggest to my clients that eating should follow nature as closely as possible and should be varied according to the season and your activity levels. For instance, if you live in a place where you have four seasons, you are going to need foods that generate more heat in the winter to help you stay warm.

Have you ever noticed that you usually feel like eating lighter fare in the summer months? That's because heat has a tendency to suppress the appetite, so you can fill up more easily on water-packed foods, such as raw fresh fruits and raw and cooked vegetables, and eat fewer starches and proteins. This type of diet provides many essential minerals and also helps keep you cooler during hot months.

If you are active, you will need more grains for fuel than an inactive person. We'll get into the specifics of customizing your diet in Chapter 6, "Nourishment from the Plant Kingdom." For now, keep in mind all the benefits that whole grains provide.

Too, Too Refined

For a healthful diet, you will want to avoid loading up on *refined grain* products, such as boxed cereal, breads, muffins, cookies, and pasta. When a grain is in its whole state, it contains enzymes, vitamins, minerals, roughage, and other nutrients that are completely lost when they are processed.

The process of taking a wheat kernel, for example, grinding it down to a powdered flour, mixing it with other ingredients, and finally cooking it at high temperatures to make bread turns the grain into a denatured, processed food. Granted, the manufacturers of bread products enrich the bread with synthetic vitamins, but you are still losing a lot of the intrinsic value gained from eating the grain whole.

I am not telling you to give up bread, but don't assume this meets your requirements for whole grains for the day. Make sure you have some variety and take care that some of the grains you eat are whole and live.

Lettuce Explain

Whole grains are most nutritious and contain many vitamins, minerals, and, when cooked correctly, natural enzymes. A whole grain is in its unprocessed state. **Refined grains** are less nutritious than whole grains because of the grinding and heating process. Examples of refined grain products are rolled oats and all refined flours.

It's Alive!

What do I mean by "live" grains? I'm glad you asked! When grains are cooked slowly with low heat (a very simple procedure that I'll explain shortly), the grain comes out of its dormant state and releases enzymes that signal it to grow! It literally comes alive! (We'll discuss the importance of enzymes in Chapter 6.) This in turn activates other nutrients, so when we eat grain in its live state, it is able to give us its life-nourishing properties. Don't believe me? Do your own test. Prepare some grain the way I suggest and then take a few kernels and plant them. If you do it correctly, the kernel will grow into a plant. Now *that's* live food. (It could also put a new twist on the TV commercial for Kentucky Fried Chicken: "Grow kernel, grow kernel!")

Here's the simplest way to prepare live grains. Before you start, make sure you have a quality thermos bottle. Now you're ready.

➤ Choose your favorite grain (my particular favorite is wheat berries).

➤ Rinse the grain with tepid water.

➤ Soak in pure or distilled water 10 to 15 hours (it's best to soak in a dish or jar other than plastic).

Sprouts of Info

If you soak whole grains before you leave for work in the morning and then slow cook them overnight in a thermos, you'll have breakfast waiting for you when you wake up.

➤ Boil some water.

➤ Pour some boiling water into the thermos and let it warm up for about five minutes, then empty it back out.

➤ Fill the thermos about ⅓ full of the soaked grain.

➤ Fill the rest of the thermos with boiling water.

➤ Flip the thermos around a bit to get all the grains exposed to the hot water and set in a warm area for about 8 to 10 hours.

When you get up in the morning, empty the contents into a bowl and garnish however you like. The kernels will be warm and should be popped open like they are smiling at you! You can turn these grains into a sweet breakfast cereal or a hearty meal, depending on the toppings you add.

Nuts and Seeds

Nuts are a plant's shell-covered fruit, and a seed is the actual embryo of the plant, but it doesn't usually have a hard shell. The two are closely related and have similar nutritional values. However, there are differences. Most nuts are rich in protein and minerals. They provide the body with an alternate source of protein and are best eaten raw or in a nut butter form.

A sliced apple dipped in cashew butter makes an excellent satisfying snack. I like to eat a handful of whole raw cashews and a banana after a workout—I get my protein, potassium, and calcium, all of which nourish my structural system. And after you spend an hour working out, it's not a bad idea to give your body the nourishment it needs to rebuild strong muscle tissue.

Good for the Glands

Seeds contain the embryo of the plant and so contain everything they need to nourish a growing baby plant. Seeds are concentrated nutrition and can have a therapeutic value as well.

Because seeds are part of a plant's glandular system, they can also be good for our glandular systems. Pumpkin seeds, high in zinc, have been used as an herbal supplement for men with prostrate troubles. Flax seeds, rich in essential fatty acids (which are covered in Chapter 5, "Supplements for the Vegetarian") are used by many, not only to help clean the bowels, but for all sorts of glandular imbalances, from PMS to endometriosis.

Another popular support for the glandular system is evening primrose oil, which is derived from the seeds of the evening primrose flower (*Oenothera binennis*). Evening Primrose oil is used to help women ease PMS, aid menopausal symptoms, and even to help the pancreas balance blood sugar.

Both nuts and seeds provide these general nutritional benefits:

➤ They feed us essential fatty acids needed for the circulatory system and brain nourishment.

➤ They are rich in protein.

➤ They are concentrated nutrition and therefore can make us feel satisfied.

➤ They have anticancer properties.

Because nuts and seeds contain natural oils, they should be stored in a cool place to preserve their freshness and to protect the oils from turning rancid. Rancid oils are full of free radicals known to cause cancer. So remember, keep your nuts cool!

Take Off Your Coat and Stay a While

A seed is a self-contained unit within a protective coat called a *testa*. The testa prevents the seed from germinating (growing) at inappropriate times. In other words, if you ripped open a bag of birdseed and it scattered across your kitchen floor, the seeds wouldn't automatically start sprouting (wouldn't that be scary?).

Instead, seeds are actually programmed to know when the conditions are just right to begin growth. When they find a place that has soil, water, enough air, and warmth from sunlight, the message goes out and off they go.

That's great if you're a seed. What it means for us is that we need to get around a seed's protective coating, so the best way to eat them is ground up a little, maybe as a nut/seed butter. If nothing else, make sure you chew seeds thoroughly in order to help digest them.

Sesame seed butter is an excellent example of a nourishing way to consume sesame seeds. When the tiny seeds are ground a bit, it breaks the testa

Lettuce Explain

Nuts are the fruit of a plant and usually have a hard shell. **Seeds** contain the embryo of a new plant. You can think of them as the eggs of the plant kingdom.

Lettuce Explain

A **testa** is the protective coating on the outside of a seed that keeps it from germinating until conditions are right. The testa also serves as an enzyme inhibitor and can inhibit our ability to digest them. Therefore it is best to eat your seeds ground up or to chew them thoroughly.

and exposes the nutrients our bodies are looking for. Because most seeds are small, we have a tendency not to chew them very well, and a seed that is not digested goes right through you and offers no nutritional benefit.

Fruit Cleansing

Fruit is such a wonderful food. Fresh fruit is bright and colorful, and bright colors generally make us more cheerful. Fruit is sweet, nice to look at, comes in all different shapes and sizes, and it's nourishing, containing high amounts of water, minerals, vitamins, and enzymes. Plus, it's easily digested.

We use fruit to decorate drinks and other foods, we use fruit to make juices to drink and to sweeten candy, we use fruit skins as natural dyes and their rinds for flavor and nutrients, and we use grapes to make wine. Well, that should make it easy enough for you to incorporate more fruit into your diet, shouldn't it?

And why should you? I'm going to give you just a few of the reasons here. In Chapter 6, you'll find more detail about which fruits to eat and why fruits, when eaten properly, can give you almost all the nourishment you need!

For now you need to know that fruits are the cleansers of the body. Fresh fruits contain elements that are very easy for our body to digest. Food that is quickly digested is quickly eliminated and therefore goes rapidly through the system, cleansing debris from the digestive and intestinal tract along the way. This is what we mean when we say that fruits are cleansing.

This is also why you might get hungry shortly after you eat fruit. Fruit contains fructose, a natural form of sugar. When your blood sugar is increased, it will eventually drop again, triggering hunger. The usable vitamins and minerals contained in fruit are absorbed quickly into the body.

Also, because fruit goes through your system quickly, it basically clears your digestive tract and literally makes way for other foods that are more sustaining. Enjoy fruits, but don't count on them to sustain you unless you have a very clean diet and a system that can survive on frequent snacking on fruit.

Since fruit goes through our system quickly, it is best eaten alone and on an empty stomach. If you are going to eat fruit in the morning, be sure to have something else available to snack on within the next few hours because you will probably be hungry again. A handful of cashews, pumpkin seeds, or raw almonds make a great protein snack an hour or two after you eat a piece of cleansing fruit.

Build Your Body with Veggies

Vegetables are the true staple of all types of vegetarian diets. They provide just about all the nutrients you can conceive of. They contain the build- ing blocks your body needs to survive, as long as you keep your diet varied. If I only had one food group to choose from to live off of entirely, it would have to be vegetables.

You should have as many vegetables as you can on any given day. They should be fresh, they can be eaten raw, lightly steamed, baked, or lightly sautéed. They can serve as a main course as a large salad or as a side dish complementing a bean and grain meal. They can also be creatively designed to make a scrumptious veggie sandwich. Try to get at least one or two raw vegetables daily.

Vegetables are processed through the body more slowly than fruits and therefore are more stabilizing to the body. This makes them a good choice for lunch and dinner, when most people need to concentrate on work. One exception to this rule is potatoes, which are better eaten at dinner or when you have some time to relax and hang out. Potatoes contain a high amount of starch that can make you feel sleepy as you digest it. Could this be the origination of the term "couch potato?"

Sprouts of Info

Some good ways to eat raw veggies include carrot sticks, celery sticks, a veggie sandwich, a cucumber salad, or a big salad with all your favorite raw vegetables. Try mixing lettuce, spinach, cucumbers, sprouts, avocado, and hearts of palm, and while you're at it, throw in some protein, like garbanzo beans, kidney beans, or peas.

Pyramid Schemes

So now we've covered all the wonderful foods that a vegetarian can eat: beans, legumes, grains, nuts, seeds, fruits, and vegetables. Let's take a look at what this new food pyramid looks like. Remember, this pyramid does not contain any of the optional items most of us eat occasionally, such as sweets and alcohol, and it excludes dairy and eggs. You have to admit though, it still looks pretty fulfilling.

Did you know that the original "Basic Four Food Groups" was created, not as a governmental education tool, but as part of an advertising campaign created by the dairy industry? You probably remember seeing this pyramid in your school nurse's office or lunchroom. The original pyramid showed an ideal diet that was very heavy in animal flesh and—surprise—dairy products.

I remember sitting in my high school nurse's office feeling sick one day. As I waited for her, I stared at the food pyramid poster on the wall. The brightly colored photographs showed a pitcher of milk, chunks of cheese, raw meats, and a loaf of white bread, along with a few fruits and vegetables that I barely remember. I wondered how I could be so sick all the time when my diet followed the poster's recommendations to the letter!

The typical pyramid accepted now by the American Dietetic Association (ADA) for vegetarians allows optional eggs and dairy and follows a much different set of guidelines.

*The basic food pyramid
that a strict vegetarian or
a vegan lives by.*

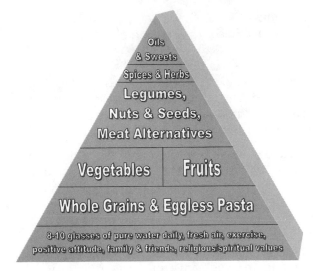

Daily Food Guide for Vegetarians

Food Group	Serving Size	What Makes Up a Serving?
Whole grains, bread, cereals, pasta group	6 or more	1 ounce ready-to-eat cereal; 1 cup of dry cereal; 1 slice of bread; ½ bagel, bun, or muffin; ½ cup of cooked pasta or grain
Vegetables	4 or more	1 cup raw or ½ cup cooked vegetables
Legumes, nuts, seeds, and meat alternatives (like tofu)	2 to 3	4 ounces of tofu or tempeh; ½ cup of cooked beans; 8 ounces of soy milk; 2 tablespoons of nut butter
Fruit	3 or more	1 piece of fresh fruit; ¾ cup of fruit juice
Dairy (optional)	up to 3	low-fat dairy is suggested; 1 cup of skim milk; 1 cup of yogurt; 1½ ounces of cheese
Eggs (optional)	Up to 3 to 4 per week	1 egg or 2 egg whites
Fats, oils, sweets, salt, and alcohol	Use very sparingly	

Here's what the lacto ovo vegetarian food pyramid would look like, following the ADA guidelines:

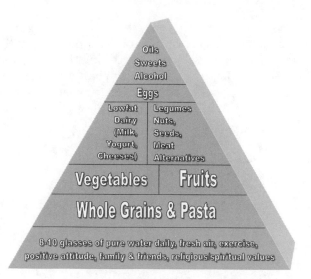

A food pyramid with options for the not-so-strict, or lacto ovo vegetarian. Keeping a balance is the key.

Why Isn't Chocolate a Vegetable?

Sadly for some, chocolate is not a staple food of the vegetarian. Although some recent studies supported by candy bar makers are proclaiming some health benefits for the naturally occurring antioxidants in chocolate and even touting the benefits of caffeine, we cannot let ourselves get carried away. If most of us weren't already consuming too much caffeine and sugar, these studies would be a lot more useful. However, for the chocolate lover in you, here are a couple of facts to help ease your guilt:

➤ Studies show that cocoa powder surpasses both green tea and garlic as a protective antioxidant food, and has concentrations of substances that make up proanthocyanidins, which are found in a herbal supplement known as Pycnogenol, used for its antioxidant properties.

➤ Chocolate contains caffeine, which improves alertness, mental concentration, mood, and overall sense of well-being.

Remember that studies can be presented to make just about anything look valuable, or at least harmless. So if you must eat chocolate, eat it occasionally, for its therapeutic value, of course. Just don't make it a staple food!

Take note here that lacto vegetarians don't have to live chocolate-less! Because most chocolate contains milk products, though, it is excluded from vegan and ovo vegetarian's diets and macrobiotic diets.

Sprouts of Info

The company Sunspire makes a natural candy that is a great replacement for M&Ms. Called Sundrops, they come in plain or peanut varieties, just like M&Ms. The difference is that the chocolate is organic, the color coating is derived from vegetables, and they are sweetened with fruit juice instead of refined sugar. Inquire at your local health food store. Warning: They can be addictive!

Quality in chocolate varies, as does quality in every food, so if you are going to consume it, consider getting quality chocolate from a confectioner. Confectioners that I have talked to (especially when I was living in Belgium and getting the good stuff) seem to love their work and are generally happy to explain to you the chocolate-making process. You might be in for a big surprise once you learn what goes into most commercial chocolates!

The food pyramid most chocolate lovers would like to envision.

Chocolate Syrup

Chocolate Flavored Drinks

Chocolate Flavored Fudge, Pies, Cakes, Pudding, Cookies, Truffles | Chocolate Covered Nuts & Fruit

Solid Chocolate (Belgium, Milk, Dark, White)

What's Wrong with Sugar?

No one says that a vegetarian life can't be sweet! The good news is that over time, the more you fill your diet with wholesome, natural, satisfying foods, the fewer cravings you will have for refined sugar and refined sugar products. Remember, your body will actually evolve, and your tastes will change in response to a cleaner and cleaner diet. Refined white sugar does not contain any nutritional value for our body. If we were to eat a stalk of sugar cane from Hawaii or a sugar beet in its raw state, we would be able to process the sugar contained within it without much trouble. This is because the other nutrients inherent in the whole food would keep all the elements contained in the food in balance for us.

However, sugar is a product that is refined to its purest form and therefore is devoid of the nutrients that help our bodies break it down. When we consume it, the body must come up with its own nutrients, including the B vitamins and many minerals, to utilize the sugar. What eventually happens is that the sugar depletes the body of its own nutrients. This may eventually lead to many forms of illness and disease.

Steer Clear

Chocolate comes from the cocoa bean, which is actually very bitter. To make chocolate into the sweet, tasty treat that we know and love, an abundant amount of sugar has to be added. Sugar not only lacks nutritional value, but also robs the body of nutrients.

54

Don't Fake the Sweetener

So now you know why you shouldn't consume a lot of sugar. "That's okay," you figure, "I'll just use a sugar substitute." Sorry, Charlie, I hate raining on anyone's parade, but I can show you a pile of studies I have collected on the harmful effects of sugar substitutes. One popular variety is actually a petroleum by-product (I never met anyone who had a petroleum by-product deficiency!). The bottom line is that if you are going to consume sweets, please stick to those that contain a natural form of sugar, even if it is refined sugar, and try to avoid the sugar substitutes. Aspartame has been shown in some studies to be damaging to the central nervous system and some consider it a dangerous toxin. Before you put sugar substitutes in your body, consider checking them out by doing some of your own research first.

Gooey Goods

Most of us like and crave sweets at one time or another, so what can we have in place of nutrient-robbing sugar or its potentially toxic substitutes? Here are some choices that not only are sweet to the taste, but contain nutritional properties:

➤ **Honey.** Raw unfiltered is the best because of its enzymes and nutritional value. Refer to Chapter 3, "Defining Meatless," for more on this great food.

➤ **Black strap molasses.** This is an excellent and iron-rich food that is actually a by-product of sugar making and contains all the minerals that are extracted from refined sugar.

➤ **Maple syrup.** This can be used as a sweetener on pancakes, in oatmeal, in coffee (if you are used to adding sugar to coffee) and to sweeten homemade soy or rice milk.

➤ **Brown Rice Syrup.** This sweetener is made from brown rice, and contains some vitamins and minerals.

➤ **Barley malt.** This sweetener comes in powder or syrup form.

➤ **Stevia.** We'll talk about that next.

Stevia: A Good Choice

Stevia (*Stevia rebaudiana*) is an herb whose leaves are used to make a sweetener and flavoring agent. It is about 300 times sweeter than refined sugar, so one or two drops equal the taste of a teaspoon of white sugar!

Unlike refined sugar, stevia contains nutrients and seems to increase people's energy. It has been used therapeutically to help alcoholics, diabetics, and

Lettuce Explain

Stevia is an herb used as a replacement for sugar by many and is even used by diabetics, although there is some controversy over its use. Stevia contains the following nutrients: phosphorus, magnesium, potassium, selenium, silicon, sodium, manganese, and small amounts of calcium, iron, and zinc.

those suffering from PMS, smoking withdrawal, stress, and hypoglycemia (low blood sugar). Its nutrients seem to help balance blood sugar levels rather than raising or lowering them; therefore, it is a favorite of both hypoglycemics and diabetics.

Because there has been a lot of controversy over the use of stevia as a sweetener, you might find that it, as well as cookbooks or books about its use, are hard to find. Its safety has been questioned based on the results of one rat study that showed (inconclusively) that it might interfere with the rats' reproductive cycle.

I suggest that before you decide on which sweetener you want to use, do some research on aspartame and then on stevia and come to your own conclusions. Keep in mind that some large corporations have a vested interest in the production of aspartame and other synthetic chemicals. Before you take the word of any study, find out who funded it.

Yes, Beer and Wine Are Vegetarian Foods

Finally, let's cover the issue of alcohol. We all know that an excess of alcohol (or almost any substance, for that matter) is detrimental to health. Abuse of alcohol kills brain cells, is hard on the liver and kidneys, and atrophies the muscles. We definitely do not want to abuse this substance.

Recent studies, however, have shown that a little alcohol in the diet not only might not be harmful, but also can be beneficial! Wine, for example, contains a substance called pyruvate, or pyruvic acid, that is found in apple skins, cheese, and grape skins. Some studies show that this substance may be beneficial to our circulatory system, structural system and may even help blood sugar utilization, although more conclusive studies are needed to be sure.

A little beer is known to be a mild depressant, which makes you feel relaxed. The same hops used in brewing beer are used as an herbal supplement because of their relaxing effects on the central nervous system. Beer also serves as a diuretic and can help flush the kidneys. So when it comes to alcohol, the secret is to use it in moderation, as in all things, and remember to enjoy life, be healthy, relax, and have fun!

The Least You Need to Know

➤ Beans are a fibrous, protein-rich food that can serve as the main course of a vegetarian meal.

➤ Grains are best in their whole state, slow cooked to retain nutritional value.

➤ Fruits are a cleansing food and should be eaten on an empty stomach.

➤ Nuts and seeds build the body and are best eaten as butters or chewed well to obtain full value.

➤ There is room for sweets and alcohol in a meatless diet.

Chapter 5

Supplements for the Vegetarian

In This Chapter

➤ Understand why some fats are essential

➤ Learn why you need B12

➤ Discover how to supplement safely with iron

➤ Learn the importance of herbs for health

➤ See how to use herbs in a variety of ways

It is difficult to obtain everything your body needs for optimum health on any modern diet, meatless or otherwise. Today, even those who eat the most healthful of foods still require some form of nutritional supplementation either on a regular basis or for additional aid during occasional health challenges. Everyone's specific nutritional requirements are different.

At the least we have some helpful boundaries to follow. You are no doubt familiar with the traditional Recommended Daily Allowances (RDA), which lists the average amounts of nutrients needed to prevent a deficiency. Soon you'll be seeing updates on food labels that will include Daily Reference Intake figures, which supply a little more detail. You also might start seeing something called tolerable upper intake levels (UL), which tell you the maximum amount of some nutrients you can safely take.

But still, at best, these are general guidelines for average people, for average health. Too bad we are not all average. Eating your best to get all the nutrients you need on a daily basis can require almost as much effort as a macrobiotic or vegan lifestyle requires! Fortunately you can get a little help through some forms of concentrated nutrition, also known as supplementation.

How much and what types of supplements you use will be as individual as you are. Please work with a guide trained in vegetarian nutrition, herbal supplementation, and holistic healthcare to come up with a game plan. Now let's take a look at meatless sources, for both food and supplements, that will let you get all of the nutrients you might need.

The Essential Fats

Everyone talks about cutting out fat from the diet these days, but what you might not realize is that there are dietary fats that are good for you. We know that at least two of them are essential to your health, and in fact that's what they're called: *essential fatty acids* (*EFAs*). Your body cannot produce them on its own, so they must be provided in the diet. The good news is that these fatty acids can be found in a variety of nuts, seeds, fruits, and vegetables, as well as in vegetarian supplements.

We really need to concern ourselves with getting only two of these fatty acids: alpha linolenic acid, an Omega 3 fatty acid, and linoleic acid, an Omega 6 fatty acid. When you supply both of these to your body, it can then synthesize the other "conditionally essential" fatty acids on its own. (Isn't the body amazing?) If either of these two EFAs is missing in the diet, their by-products may then become "conditionally essential" in the diet. Conditionally essential means that there are times when the body cannot make enough for your needs. Essential fatty acids provide the following general health benefits. They help ...

➤ Support the immune system.

➤ Balance body chemistry.

➤ Improve blood circulation and vascular dilation.

➤ Protect against heart disease.

➤ Balance hormones and eicosanoid (EPA) production.

➤ Regulate cholesterol levels.

➤ Regulate blood clotting, blood pressure, and heart rate.

Lettuce Explain

Essential fatty acids (EFAs) are fatty acids that are not manufactured by the body but are essential to its proper functioning. Essential fatty acids are the building blocks for hormones, cell membranes, and various chemical messengers.

The essential and conditionally essential fatty acids have been used therapeutically for overcoming some of these problems:

➤ Allergies

➤ Arthritis

➤ Asthma

➤ Cancer

➤ High blood pressure

➤ Hyperactivity

➤ Infertility

➤ Inflammation

- ➤ Eczema
- ➤ Glaucoma
- ➤ Hair health
- ➤ Headaches
- ➤ Heart disease
- ➤ Low infant IQ

- ➤ Lupus
- ➤ Menstrual difficulty
- ➤ Migraines
- ➤ Premenstrual syndrome
- ➤ Skin health

Veggie Soup for the Soul

Omega 3s and Omega 6s include groups of essential fatty acids with differing chemical makeup. If you supplement with essential fatty acids, you need to make sure you provide a balance between them. Not all supplements will tell you which is which, so here's the breakdown. The Omega 3 group contains alpha-linolenic acid (LNA) (essential), eicosapentaenoic acid (EPA), and docosahexaenoic acid (DHA). The Omega 6 group includes linolenic acid (essential), gamma-linolenic acid (GLA), and arachidonic acid. Just make sure you get some of each.

See? We do need fats after all! However, do be wary of one very bad fat known as "trans fat," seen on labels as "hydrogenated" or "partially hydrogenated" oils. These oils can be found in all deep-fried foods (heating oils to high temperatures causes this chemical change). Trans fats are not found in significant amounts in nature except in meat and dairy products. The body can't use them properly and they interfere with production of good fatty acids, cell membranes, and apparently even with brain development. Pregnant women should avoid trans fats—they are found in fried foods, commercial snacks (hydrogenated oils), and most margarines.

The following table shows how you, as a nonmeat-eater, can get the fatty acids you need, provided you don't have a problem with fish or egg sources.

Sprouts of Info

Monounsaturated fatty acids, or Omega 9 fatty acids, are also very important and are good for our skin and circulatory system, and even used to help prevent cancer. Good sources include olive oil, peanut oil, nuts, and avocados.

It is important to keep a balance between the Omega 3 and Omega 6 fatty acids, so if you are supplementing with Omega 3 fatty acids, be sure to balance them with supplements or foods containing Omega 6s. If you're not careful, taking only one type can lead to a depletion of the other! Here's a list of sources for each kind.

Essential Fatty Acid Sources for the Meatless

Sources	Rich In
Almonds and their oil	Omega 6s
Black current oil	Omega 6s
Borage oil	Omega 6s
Canola oil	Omega 3s and 6s
Cod liver oil	Omega 3s
Corn oil	Omega 6s
Dark fleshed fish	Omega 3s
Egg yolks	Omega 3s
Evening primrose oil	Omega 6s
Fish oil lipids	Omega 3s
Flax seed oil	Omega 3s
Peanuts and their oil	Omega 6s
Safflower oil	Omega 6s
Soybeans and their oil	Omega 3s and 6s
Sunflower seeds and their oil	Omega 6s
Walnuts and their oil	Omega 3s and 6s
Wheat germ oil	Omega 3s and 6s

B12 and Be a Vegetarian

Vitamin B12 is one of the B vitamins and is critical for the metabolism of every cell in our bodies, especially the bone marrow, GI tract, and nervous tissue. B12 is created in our intestinal systems but also must be supplied in the diet.

If we don't receive enough, we can eventually use up our body's supplies, which leads to health problems that can include headaches, bruising, depression, fatigue, anemia, and irritability. We can go several years without ingesting any B12 before symptoms of the deficiency show up.

B12 (cobalamin) is used therapeutically to reduce or reverse fatigue, nervous irritability, pernicious anemia, insomnia, stress, mental illness, multiple sclerosis, poor memory, neuritis, and many ailments of the nervous system.

Veggie Soup for the Soul

Lecithin (from soybeans), although often mistakenly thought of as an essential fatty acid, is manufactured in the body and is therefore not called "essential." It is essential (in the sense of being necessary), however, to the health of your nervous and circulatory systems. Lecithin is a well-known brain food and is used as a supplement along with extra fiber in the diet to help lower cholesterol. It even helps emulsify dietary fat.

B12 is produced by bacteria and is naturally found in animal products as well as some cooked sea vegetables. However, this doesn't necessarily mean that a deficiency is strictly a vegetarian problem. Most reported B12 deficiencies occur because of the digestive system's inability to absorb the vitamin or a lack of a carrier protein called "intrinsic factor." If you are unable to absorb B12, it can be taken by intra-muscular injection or through sublingual (under the tongue) supplementation.

An Added Attraction

It is true that the obvious sources for vitamin B12 are found in animal products, so if you are a lacto, ovo, or pesco vegetarian, you don't need to worry about getting B12 because you obtain it via the animal products you eat. However, there are some strictly vegetarian sources for this vitamin.

There are differing forms of vitamin B12 found in foods, and studies are now being conducted into whether the different forms of this vitamin compete with each other and actually lead to a B12 (cyanocobalamin) deficiency! Until we know more, stick to the form of B12 called *cyanocobalamin*.

The best way to be sure you are getting usable B12, at least until all the research is in, is to take a B12 supplement (2 mcg per day) and don't worry. You can also make sure that the processed vegetarian foods you buy, such as soy or rice milks, have been enriched with cyanocobalamin. Many health food manufacturers are beginning to do this, so vegetarians will have more variety available.

Sprouts of Info

Do you remember your dreams? Insomniacs and those with no dream recall are commonly deficient in vitamin B6 and/or zinc. Tell your dietician, herbal nutritionist, or doctor that you do not remember your dreams so they can help you get what you need. Remember, though, that too much zinc or B6 is *not* better than too little. Always follow the recommended dose.

Nature's Garden

If you are from the school that believes nature's garden provides everything you need to keep you healthy, you can take your chances with foods that have been found to have B12, but that have not proven necessarily to contain any *real* amounts of the cyanocobalamin forms of B12.

Lettuce Explain

Cyanocobalamin is the usable part of the B12 vitamin. Other forms of B12 are called analogs, and scientists believe that the analogs could interfere with the useful cyanocobalamin, leading to a deficiency.

These strictly vegetarian natural foods contain vitamin B12:

➤ Alfalfa—more in fresh than dried

➤ Rice polishings

➤ Legume sprouts such as mung beans and lentils

➤ Algae (usually sold in nutritional supplements such as spirulina and green drinks)

➤ Sea vegetables such as kelp, nori, and kombu

➤ Bee pollen

➤ Nutritional yeast

Bee pollen and nutritional yeast are naturally occurring sources of B12 for many vegetarians, although these are unacceptable sources for some vegans.

Ironing Out Your Mineral Needs

We all know that you need vitamins and minerals to stay alive. Vitamins nourish your body and keep you vital. However, vitamins cannot be utilized without minerals. Minerals are the activators that help the vitamins get to work where they need to be in the body. You cannot survive on one without the other.

Veggie Soup for the Soul

Homemade vegetable soup is an excellent source of minerals and vitamins. Season it with natural ingredients such as kelp (for a salty flavor), garlic powder, cayenne (for some heat), and onions. Use purified water and avoid unnatural seasonings, especially those containing MSG or hydrolyzed vegetable protein, which are excitotoxins. Excitotoxins are substances added to foods and beverages that can destroy brain neurons. For more information, check out *Excitotoxins: The Taste That Kills,* by neurosurgeon Russell L. Blaylock, M.D. This is an important read for anyone concerned about brain health.

How you choose to feed your body these necessary mineral elements can vary dramatically from person to person. Let me help you understand a few ways you can obtain these nutrients without meat. Let's start with iron.

Plant Blood

Iron is a blood element, meaning it is one of the main constituents of animal and human blood. Red meat, being flesh rich in red blood cells, is therefore high in iron content.

However, you can obtain iron by ingesting the blood of plants, otherwise known as chlorophyll. This is good news for vegetarians who are worried about not getting enough of this abundant mineral. An iron deficiency is not necessarily a concern with folks who eat a variety of vegetarian foods, but some people (especially pregnant women) who tend toward anemia, or others with a tendency toward a low blood count, will need to understand how to get supplemental iron in their diets.

The mineral iron is an element in our dirt, which is also full of all the other minerals and trace minerals you can think of, including calcium, copper, nickel, magnesium, and so on. In dirt, iron is in an inorganic form—they make nails with this type of iron. When a plant's roots absorb iron along with other nutrients in the soil and process it, it becomes iron made biochemically available to our body. Neat trick, huh?

Iron from Nature

Generally, products enriched with iron and most iron supplements are made from synthetics and other nonliving materials. It is difficult to get rid of iron once it's in the body, and extra iron can build up in the liver and tissues and cause irreversible damage. Iron also promotes the growth of infectious bacteria, so don't supplement indiscriminately! Iron supplements can also make you constipated.

Your body is better able to utilize natural forms of iron from food. This may be why plant sources of iron are not absorbed as easily as iron from meat—perhaps it is a natural protective mechanism to keep us from ingesting too much iron! Plant sources of iron are much safer to use, so vegetarians are generally safe from getting too much iron in their diets.

Sprouts of Info

Since vitamin C helps the body absorb iron, eating foods rich in vitamin C along with your meals helps to increase your iron absorption. So go ahead and add that slice of tomato to your veggie sandwich!

Some symptoms of an iron deficiency include:

➤ Anemia

➤ Headaches

➤ Bruising easily

➤ Depression

➤ Dizziness

➤ Constipation

➤ Breathing difficulty

➤ Heart palpitations

➤ Slow wound healing

➤ Heartburn

➤ Fatigue

Hopefully you don't have any of these symptoms, but if you do and are diagnosed with iron deficiency, see your natural health consultant and consider taking in some extra plant sources of iron, along with vitamin C to help you utilize it more effectively. See the following table to find some good vegetarian sources and herbal supplements for this mineral.

Herbs for All

Herbs are like wild vegetables. They are wonderful healing plants that can serve you both medicinally and nutritionally. The study of herbs certainly is vast, but there are some specific herbal supplements that might be of interest to the vegetarian.

We discussed in Chapter 1, "Why Eat Less Meat?" the use of herbal cleansing to rid your system of excess wastes, undigested proteins from meat consumption, toxins, and built-up mucus. You learned how a cleanse can give you a clean start, making your transition to a meatless diet easier. But beyond using herbs to cleanse before a change in your diet, you can also utilize them as nutritional supplements to round out your vegetarian meals.

Herbs are great because ...

➤ They are plants with nutritional value.

➤ They are a concentrated form of nutrition.

➤ They can be used as shortcuts to fill in nutritional gaps.

➤ They are whole foods.

➤ They are meatless.

I suggest to almost everyone that they work with an herbalist, nutritional consultant, or dietitian schooled in herbs, or some other holistically oriented health practitioner familiar with herbal nutrition. This person should be able to create a customized preventative medicine program for you geared to your particular needs.

Steer Clear

Never cleanse when pregnant, nursing, or in a severely ill and weakened condition. The elimination of too many toxins too quickly could be uncomfortable to a nursing baby and can be dangerous to a severely ill person or a pregnant mom. Use common sense, and work with a professional when considering a cleanse if you have any health concerns. If you can't do a cleanse, try "cleaning up your diet" instead—just eat more fresh fruit and veggies.

The Power of Nature

We all have our individual genetic strengths and weaknesses. If your family has a long history of heart conditions, for instance, there is a good chance you are predisposed to that problem. But the beauty of working with an herb specialist is that he or she can customize an herbal program for you that can help you avoid having these problems.

By starting now, nourishing your system, and keeping it clean, you might be able to avoid future troubles. Herbs can certainly help you recover from health problems, but it's even better to take your herbs for prevention and save a pound of cure.

Just to demonstrate to you the power of nature and your body's ability to heal and rebuild, I'd like to share with you a recent success story.

Health from the Heart

One of my clients had come to me several years ago with major heart problems among her concerns. I started her on an herb and supplement program geared toward nourishing and cleaning her entire circulatory system. She also remained on heart medications and had a host of other medical conditions. We knew her healing was going to be a long process, but we went to work nourishing her circulatory system and helping it to work better on its own.

She had been taking her supplements for approximately three years when she felt some tingling down her arm. Her doctor scheduled surgery immediately: She would

Sprouts of Info

For more reading on the specific uses of herbal remedies for common ailments, pick up a copy of my book *The Complete Idiot's Guide to Herbal Remedies* (Alpha Books, 1999), and keep sending me your success stories!

have either bypass surgery or possibly a simpler procedure called angioplasty, depending on what the surgeon found. In a bypass, a healthy piece of an artery is taken from another part of the body and used to build a new pathway for the blood to get to the heart.

After her initial surgery, the surgeon remarked that he couldn't believe what he had found. My client's body had actually *built its own bypass* around one of the clogged arteries, sparing her the bypass surgery and letting her have the simpler angioplasty! This miraculous feat demonstrates the remarkable power that the body has to heal itself if it has the nutrients it needs to do its job. Her body, given the right raw materials to build new tissues, had managed to save her from a dangerous surgery and possibly a fatal heart attack!

Eating right, exercise, stress reduction, and the right attitude are always part of being healthy. And because your requirements will be very different from the next person's, depending on your individual history and biochemistry, a good customized herbal and nutritional program is a valuable insurance policy to keep you from having health problems later. The good news is that it is never too late to get started!

Encapsulated Herbs

We all need minerals, vitamins, amino acids (proteins), and essential fatty acids. Plant life contains all of these things, and herbs contain them in a concentrated form.

You can get your herbs in tablets, loose in bulk, or in capsules, teas, liquids, concentrates, standardized extracts, and more. You'll have to decide what works best for you. Personally, I enjoy using encapsulated herbs for my concentrated nutritional supplements because this form is easier for me to take, travel with, and put in my purse when I'm out and about.

You can use herbal teas, too. Try some nice chamomile tea to relax with when you curl up to read one of my books before bed (notice the shameful subliminal advertising here?), or some peppermint tea to boost your mental energy or to calm an upset stomach. Herbs are versatile and can be not only nutritious and effective but delicious as well.

The Well-Rounded Vegetarian

Now that I've showed you why herbs make good nutritional sense, which ones might you consider as a vegetarian? Most vegetarians are pretty well nourished due to the variety of fresh foods they eat, but strict vegetarians especially can benefit from herbal supplementation, if only for a little extra nutrition to ensure their diets are well-rounded.

The following table gives you a list of the most common elements missing in the average American diet, along with herbal sources of B12 and iron, which tend to be a concern for those on strict vegetarian or vegan diets.

Common Elements Lacking in Most American Diets

Element	Herbal Source	Vegetarian Food Source	Things That Deplete This Element	Purpose
Calcium	Alfalfa, buchu, chamomile, dandelion, chickweed, horsetail, oatstraw, moringa, parsley	Cashews, seeds, carrots, carrot juice, broccoli, organic yogurt, sesame seeds, sprouts	Coffee, table salt, sugar, high animal protein diet, excessive phosphorus, oxalic acid, soda pop	Bones, structural system; teeth; joints; stomach acid; buffer bone and skin mending.
Silicon	Horsetail, alfalfa, dandelion, yucca, barley juice, cornsilk, skullcap, gotu kola, chlorophyll	Asparagus, leaf lettuce, cauliflower, apricots, apples, cooked whole rice, wild rice, barley, nuts, seeds	Fats, starches, sugar	Hair luster, and strength; more youthful looking skin; prevents cracking skin and nails.
Iodine	Kelp, dulse, black walnut, spirulina	Seaweed, sea fish (white fish with fins and scales), garlic, onions, eggplant, mushrooms, potatoes	Radiation from TV, x-rays, power lines, stimulants such as caffeine, ephedra	Feeds thyroid gland, which controls metabolism, weight, energy levels.
Sodium	Hydrangea, alfalfa, safflower, rosehips, peppermint, parsley, licorice, dandelion	Celery, cucumbers, strawberries, goat milk and whey, okra, parsley, whole sesame seeds, Swiss and Roquefort cheeses, raisins, red cabbage, black mission figs, watercress, goat's milk	Table salt, antacids, prescription diuretics (such as potassium)	Can prevent stomach disturbance or joint distress. Dissolves hard calcium build-up in the body. Adds flexibility.

continues

Common Elements Lacking in Most American Diets (continued)

Element	Herbal Source	Vegetarian Food Source	Things That Deplete This Element	Purpose
Potassium	Kelp, parsley, Irish moss, ginger, peach bark, licorice, horsetail, moringa, capsicum	Bananas, raisins, potato peel broth, parsley tea, bitter greens, almonds, whole grains	Red meat, coffee, alcohol, laxatives, diuretics, salt, sugar	Helps regulate water retention, muscle cramps, or spasms, muscular fatigue, hypertension, hardening of the arteries.

Additional Elements Helpful to Vegetarians

Element	Herbal Source	Vegetarian Food Source	Things That Deplete This Element	Purpose
Iron	Yellow dock, capsicum, butcher's broom, kelp, red beet root, red raspberry leaves, chickweed, nettle, mullein leaves, dong quai, moringa	Black cherries, blackberries, dried fruits, strawberry juice, dark leafy greens, spinach, black strap molasses	Food additives, coffee, black tea, excessive phosphorous, food preservatives	Necessary for hemoglobin production a remedy for anemia, improves protein assimilation, mental vitality, circulation, liver and kidney functions, promotes vitality
B12	Alfalfa, ginseng, bee pollen, comfrey, spirulina, dandelion	Sea vegetables, nutritional yeast, miso	Junk food	Essential for healthy gastrointestinal tract, formation of blood cells, supports the nervous system, healthy skin and mucus membrane

Gelatin-Free, Please

One easy way to take your herbs is in gelatin capsules, but gelatin is an animal product, as we mentioned before, made from boiled bones and hoofs. Many herbal companies are sensitive to the needs of vegans and vegetarians and offer herbs in pills or capsules made without the use of animal products.

If you can't find what you want in vegetarian form and if you have some extra time on your hands, you can purchase herbs in bulk and encapsulate them yourself! You can find products like VegiCaps, a Nature's Way product that contains no gelatin and is also kosher, in most places where health food and herbs are sold.

The Least You Need to Know

➤ Most people, even with generally healthy diets, need supplemental nutrition at some time to ensure optimal health.

➤ Iron and other minerals are found abundantly in plant life, and those requiring extra can supplement with herbs rich in plant iron and other minerals.

➤ B12 is most commonly found in animal products. It can be supplied in trace amounts in the vegan diet by alfalfa and other herbs, but to be safe, a vitamin supplement may be necessary.

➤ Herbs are good food and come in a variety of forms that will fit into anyone's lifestyle.

➤ Given all the nutrition and natural elements it needs, the body has an amazing ability to rebuild, repair, and restore itself.

Your dirt, Madam...

Chapter 6

Nourishment from the Plant Kingdom

In This Chapter

➤ Understand the benefits of eating your vegetables

➤ Find out about fruit

➤ Discover the role enzymes play in health

➤ Learn some simple biochemistry

➤ Find out how and why to change your diet with the seasons

Getting more vegetables and fruits in your diet has plenty of advantages. For instance, did you know that fruit is a cleanser for the body, while vegetables are the real body-builders? Did you know that you can get different effects from eating raw fruit than you can from dried fruit? Did you know that eating cucumbers can keep you cool or that fresh plant food contains life force energy? Yep, your food is alive and well, and in this chapter, I am going to show you how you can take the best advantage of your fruits and vegetables so that you can live well by eating them.

What the Vegetables Tell Me

In their book *The Secret Life of Plants,* authors Peter Tompkins and Christopher Bird brought it to the attention of the public that plants actually can and do communicate. Their experiments showed that plants have their own chemical reactions that can be detected by changing energy patterns. Scientists used specialized equipment to detect and record the changing energies of plants during various scenarios.

Sprouts of Info

The amazing book *The Secret Life of Plants* showed that plants understand and react to humans and human thought and intention. This book spurred a lot of people in the 1970s to talk to their houseplants to help them flourish. Today, it still makes great reading if you want to learn about the life force in your plant food.

Dramatically different patterns were found when listening to pleasant, soft music and when the plant was just about to be uprooted. They basically showed that all plants have communication skills and can respond to music and even human intent.

They found that tomatoes and other fresh produce, even after being picked, continue to transmit energy. The energy is detectable with special machines similar to lie detectors. The fruit or vegetable may emit energy right up until it is chopped or otherwise prepared for cooking. The energy detected just before the fruit or vegetable is chopped is a distinctive spike in energy followed immediately by a flat-line energy reading (nothing).

A Force of Nature

These experiments led many to the philosophical conclusion that a vegetable or fruit might be able to detect its demise, and therefore, to release its life force energy upon the moment of destruction or consumption. Some even believe that the energy enters the organism that ingests it! You might think this is pretty far out, but not when you consider that food actually does give us life!

These scientific experiments certainly lend a new dimension to the prayers many religions say before meals. For example, the Hindus, who are traditionally vegetarians, give thanks to their food before consuming it. Christian religions teach prayer before meals to thank God for their food, and Native Americans ask permission from the plant before harvesting it for their own needs.

Everything that is alive has a natural vibration resulting from its energy force. These vibrations can be measured in units called hertz frequency (Hz). Hertz frequencies osculate at differing levels and vary from one person to another, although there are ranges for health and illness. Your own hertz frequencies vary from one part of the day to another. There are ranges of frequencies that are used to detect possible malfunction in the body.

Some believe the hertz frequency is directly related to how much life force an organism has. For example:

➤ A healthy human vibrates at about 62 to 72 Hz, but a sick person, depending on how ill he or she is, can dip from 58 when struck with a minor illness to as low as 42 Hz with a major one.

➤ Degenerative conditions such as cancer are detected below 48 Hz.

➤ Illness cannot survive in frequencies above 60.

Veggie Soup for the Soul

Not only are humans affected by sound, so are plants and the crops that come from these plants. Here's an example: In the 1960s, an agricultural researcher at West Virginia University in Morgantown, Rabindar N. Singh, performed experiments in which flute, violin, and other harmonious music was played to various plants for half an hour daily. He concluded that harmonic sound waves positively affect the growth, flowering, fruiting, and seed yields of plants. Singh also used his music to increase a rice crop's yield to 25 to 60 percent higher than the regional average!

These levels of frequency are detected in other living things as well, including foods. For instance, a freshly picked piece of fruit grown on a healthy tree can have a hertz frequency reading of about 15 Hz or more, but a can of processed food registers zero on the Hz scale.

Dried herbs have a fairly high frequency; however, fresh herbs are even higher. Essential oils extracted from plants have the highest frequency. *Essential oils* are the naturally occurring oils in plant life. Because all plants have their own essential oils, which are the liquid essence of the plant, you will obtain some of their frequencies when you eat live plant food.

Lettuce Explain

Essential oils are naturally occurring oils extracted from plants. They are known to have the highest hertz frequencies, ranging from 52 to 320 Hz, which can run even higher than human frequency. Essential oils are also loaded with living enzymes and have been used for centuries to promote health and healing.

Food for Life

Even if all this is too out there for you, when we talk about enzymes later in this chapter, you'll see that plant food does contain life in the form of enzymes and why enzymes are so beneficial to our health. Could these enzymes be the key to life energy? Is your raw salad really giving you its life force energy? I believe it probably does, and many people who live on primarily raw-food diets, who have an abundance of energy, tell me the same.

This means that whole foods can not only give us roughage, vitamins, and minerals, but can also share their vitality! Once you know about enzymes, hertz frequencies,

73

Sprouts of Info

For a healthy view on eating, re-member the old proverb, "Eat to live, don't live to eat."

and energy, it is obvious that there are many things going on in life that you cannot see or touch but that can actually make a difference in the way you feel.

Since whole live foods do have a detectable vitality, just as your body does, then why not feed your body live, vitalizing foods fresh from nature? Doesn't it seem reasonable that your body will recognize fresh fruits and vegetables from nature as having vibration it can gather life force from? Prepared, chemical-laden, processed, preserved, and de-vitalized foods from cans and boxes do not provide the energy your body needs.

Eating for life is more than trying to get your vita-mins. Eating for life means consuming live foods be-cause eating is a form of energy exchange. Live foods have a positive charge. Dead foods have a negative or neutral charge, which force the body to create extra energy to process the dead food—to give it enough life, if you will—in order to process it through your system. If you choose to eat more live fresh foods in your diet, your reward will be more vitality.

Phytochemical Power

Phytochemicals are naturally occurring chemicals found in plants. New phytochemi-cals continue to be isolated and identified by scientists and are touted through differ-ent media as being healthful. We don't yet know exactly how many more of these phytochemicals will be found, but I bet that Mother Nature knows! Nature has had some practice in creating a mixture of phytochemicals in naturally grown fruits and vegetables, and she doesn't give up her secret recipe easily. So take it from your "Mother" and eat the veggies and fruits she serves!

We also know that phytochemicals like to work together to provide you the best ben-efit. In other words, even though beta-carotene is a photochemical that can be iso-lated from carrots, there are many other elements in that carrot that can help the beta-carotene be more efficient in your body. The bottom line is that whole foods promote a balance of phytochemicals, which is thought to be better for you than relying solely on a particular photochemical (as in a supplement pill) for your plant-based nutrition.

Vegetables are the builders of the body. They pack a powerful punch of vitamins, minerals, and, eaten raw, they contain enzymes. They supply roughage in the diet and give us sustainable strength.

Veggie Soup for the Soul

Before a test or other important event where you are expected to be alert and clear, avoid eating a big heavy meal full of starches and carbs. Fruit can give you a lift but may leave your blood sugar low shortly after you eat it. Your best bet is to eat fruit with a low water content, which is digested more slowly—a banana is a good example. Add a protein source for the brain, such as several raw almonds. This will help keep you focused on your performance, rather than overloaded with a heavy meal or anxious and sweaty from low blood sugar. Knock 'em dead!

In contrast, when you eat meat it can stay in the system for a much longer time than vegetables or fruit. Meat can ferment in the system, creating decay, foul gas, and improper absorption, and can lead to related health problems. Even if you are constipated, a rotting carrot in your system is going to have fewer toxic side effects than a rotting hamburger.

Imagine what happens in your garbage can at home. The smell of the decaying flesh shows up faster and will smell more foul than a decaying carrot. The same process goes on in your intestines when your digestion is slowed. Besides, the meat you purchase has been dead for a long time before it ever reaches your plate, whereas the raw carrot will be fresh by comparison.

Fantastic Fruit

Well, after that, you're probably ready for a change of pace. Let's switch from rotting meat to something much nicer—fruit! Why don't you have a piece now, and we'll go from there! What a beautiful versatile variety the fruits offer. Fruit is very special, and I'd like to share a few ways you can utilize the gifts they give. First we'll look at a list of why fruits are awesome, and then I'll explain the benefits in more detail.

Sprouts of Info

Take some advice from Harvey and Marilyn Diamond, a couple of the best nutritional gurus around and authors of the best-selling book *Fit for Life* (Warner Books, 1985). Here's what they say about fruit: "From the time you wake up in the morning until at least noon, consume nothing but fresh fruit and fruit juice."

Here's the list. Fruits ...

➤ Cleanse your system.

➤ Offer a source of pure water.

➤ Are loaded with life-enhancing enzymes.

➤ Offer a boost of energy and are low in calories.

➤ When dehydrated can be used to help you rehydrate.

With all these things fruits have to offer, you can't afford to go fruitless for long. So belly up to the fruit bowl, and let's get the lowdown on how to take advantage of your fruit intake. (While you're at it, peel me a grape or two, would you?)

Fast Food

Fruit can be eaten as a cleanser for the body. Ripened, fresh fruit is so alive and so easily digestible that it flushes through your system rather quickly. This is why it is advisable that you eat fresh fruit on an empty stomach. Fresh fruit contains a number of enzymes that cause it to ripen (and then rot) fairly quickly. Therefore, if you clog your system with foods that go through the body slowly, such as breads, pastas, cheese, and meats, and then eat fruit on top of it, the fruit will catch up with the other foods in the digestive tract, sit on top of them, and begin to rot! This can cause you digestive grief, such as gas, bloating, and belching.

Steer Clear

Fruit should not be mixed with other foods because this can hinder the digestive process and give you gas. For the most part you should eat only one type of fruit at any one sitting. Also, remember to eat fresh fruit on an empty stomach to avoid gas and indigestion.

You can visualize this scenario as being like an alpine slide—the kind where you get in a little car and whoosh down a winding tube-like slide. The slide is your digestive tract.

The slower people (meat, dairy, eggs) should go last because they are the cautious types and will be pulling vigorously on the brakes most of the way down. Then there are the wild-eyed dare-devils winding their way down the track as fast as they can, hair blowing wildly in the wind. They need to go first. If you make them come after the slow pokes, they are going to have to slow down, and you just know they're going to complain about it!

Bet that changes the way you look at a cantaloupe, doesn't it? So that's the idea. The fruit passes through your digestive system quickly and cleans things out. Eat it first, and it can do its job. Wait to eat other foods for at least a half-hour to let the fruit whoosh its way through your system.

Quenching Your Thirst

Those of you who hate to drink water (and I will be nagging you about that later, by the way) will be happy to know that fresh fruit is a good source of naturally distilled water and is one way you can boost your water intake.

When the fruit plant is producing a fruit, it gathers water from the earth, it naturally filters the water through its system, and by the time the water enters the fruit, you have distilled water! Neat, huh?! So next time you are thirsty and don't have any water available, bite into a fresh juicy peach to quench your thirst!

All Dried Up

Dried fruits are excellent snacks, but you need to be aware that because they are dried, they are concentrated foods. This means that you are still getting the same amount of calories from the whole fresh fruit, but you usually eat more than one dried fruit at a time. I suggest that if you are eating dried fruit for a snack, eat a piece at a time along with a large glass of water. Then wait at least 10 minutes to see if you are satisfied before eating another piece. That gives the water time to soak in and expand the dried fruit in your stomach. You might find that you have had enough and will spare yourself becoming uncomfortably full.

Dried fruit is an excellent way to put on healthy weight without the use of junk food. Some teenage boys who want to beef up quickly for school sports will turn to hogging out on junk foods. This can lead to health problems later on, not to mention aggravating a common teenage problem—acne— that sometimes gets worse from consuming fatty and sugary foods.

It is important to build a strong healthy body, especially during growing years, and natural foods were designed to do just that. Snacking on dried fruits and nuts is tasty, won't give you zits, and you can eat all you want between meals for added weight gain. Put a variety of dried chopped fruits and nuts in a bowl and leave it out to munch on whenever you're in the mood.

Steer Clear

Dried fruit can provide an opportunity for bugs to lay eggs. Here's a tip: Before consuming raisins, pour boiling water over them and strain. Then let them dry and re-package them in a baggie or other container. This process will kill any existing bug eggs and save you from possibly picking up uninvited guests.

Sprouts of Info

My favorite homemade trail mix for hiking and cross-country skiing (or anytime I need extra energy) includes raw walnut pieces, raisins, raw cashew chunks, semisweet chocolate chips, and shredded coconut. Try it, you'll like it!

If you're not working on putting on weight, and you don't have access to fresh fruit, you can soak dried fruit in cold distilled water overnight to help it regain some water content before you eat it. After you soak it, you'll find that you're satisfied with less than you would eat if the fruit were in its dried form.

Enzymes for Life

Enzymes are essential to life. They are present in all organic material. They are the catalysts that keep you alive, make things happen, and continue working in your body even for a while after you have died to break your flesh down and turn you back into "dust." They are inherent in fruit and vegetables and all living foods and animals. They are manufactured in your body to help with all your bodily functions.

Most important for our purposes, your body relies on the enzymes in whole raw foods to help you with the digestive process. Cooking your foods at high temperatures destroys the living enzymes. When you eat these now-dead foods, your pancreas, liver, and other organs must create more enzymes to break down the cooked foods you consume, creating more stress on these organs than they were designed to deal with.

The main benefit to eating raw or lightly steamed fresh foods is to receive these enzymes that are so vital to life. Enzymes are great at digesting, and because your body requires more energy to digest food than almost anything else you do, give it a break once in a while and go for some raw foods, rich in their own enzymes. The less your body has to work to digest and make enzymes, the more it can spend on other life processes, leaving you with more energy. This can mean a longer, more vibrant life for you.

What the Body Is Made Of

"Sugar and spice and everything nice, that's what little hypoglycemics are made of."

—Author undisclosed

Too much sugar or any one type of food in anyone's diet is unhealthful and can lead to health problems. That is the great thing about the vegetarian diet. There are so many foods to choose from. And all plant foods vary in their vitamin and mineral content, based on the type of mineral-rich soil a plant favors and where it grows. For instance, if you study herbology or botany, you become aware that certain plants favor certain soil conditions, and if left in the wild, these plants grow where the soil is favorable to them. Our farmers learn about which crops favor which type of soils and then use different chemicals, soils, and conditions to help their crops grow.

Veggie Soup for the Soul

Refined sugar is not only an empty calorie, it is stripped of all of its original nutrients, so in order to break it down and use it, your body has to raid its own stores to supply the missing vitamins and minerals (especially the B vitamins) needed to process it through your system. Therefore, sugar is not only void of nutrients in itself, it has the effect of leeching nutrients from your own system.

Your body is also made up of various minerals and vitamins, and you can think of your organs as favoring certain nutrients for health. When there is a dietary deficiency of any of these nutrients, the body picks up what it needs from your own organs. I think this is an important factor in keeping healthy with nutrition. By learning what your major organs are made up of, you will understand what type of nutrients you need to keep them healthy.

For instance, you might take kelp as a supplemental herb for problems with your thyroid, but did you know why it helps? Kelp is rich in iodine. The thyroid is an iodine organ. Therefore, feeding this organ what it needs keeps it healthy.

The following table lists some of the elements that comprise your body. You can consider your body as one big mineral and vitamin warehouse, made of the same items found in nature.

What the Body Is Made Of ...

Element	Major Organ	Plant Source (Examples)
Calcium	Bones, teeth	Sesame seeds
Iodine	Thyroid gland	Seaweed
Iron	Liver, blood, bone marrow	Black cherries
Lecithin	Semen, nervous system	Soybeans
Magnesium	Muscles (relaxer)	Wheat germ
Potassium	Muscles (heart)	Blackberries
Zinc	Eyes, prostate, thyroid, pancreas, liver, kidneys, skin, hair, nails	Pumpkin seeds

continues

What the Body Is Made Of ...   (continued)

Element	Major Organ	Plant Source (Examples)
Silicon	Skin, nails, hair, glands, nerves	Barley
Sodium	Joints, stomach lining	Celery
Phosphorus	Bones, brain, nerves	Almonds
Chlorine	Digestive tract	Pineapple
Fluorine	Teeth, bones	Brussels sprouts
Sulphur	Brain, nerves, bowel, liver	Cabbage

Eating Right for the Seasons

The vegetarian food pyramid generally accepted by the ADA (see Chapter 4, "A New Food Pyramid") is a great guideline for the average vegetarian to eating a wholesome diet. But in this chapter I'd also like to share with you another version of this pyramid that you can use as a guideline if you are not an active vegetarian or if you live in a hot climate. First let me tell you why.

Sprouts of Info

If you are not a strict vegetarian, goat's milk or dried goat's whey powder is a fantastic supplemental source of concentrated minerals such as calcium, iron, phosphorus, magnesium, zinc, selenium, chromium, molybdenum, chloride, sodium, and potassium. This nutty tasting powder can be made into a broth or tea, sprinkled on salads or chili, or added to smoothies for additional nutrition.

Beans and grains are heavier foods. By heavier I mean foods that provide protein and fiber, which make the body work harder to digest them. When we digest we are actually increasing the body functions, which generates energy in the form of heat. You're going to need tons of pasta and other grains and beans if you are living in Anchorage, Alaska, or Banff, Canada, but a person in southern Florida is not going to do well on this diet because of the internal heat generated by these foods.

The same is true if you are sedentary and fill yourself up with excess breads, pastas, beans, and cereal. You will work your way into blood sugar imbalances and will probably gain weight and have no energy. So, in general, we need to be careful about the carbohydrates from grains, pastas, and starches.

Let me provide some guidelines to help you rearrange the general vegetarian food pyramid to suit your needs more closely.

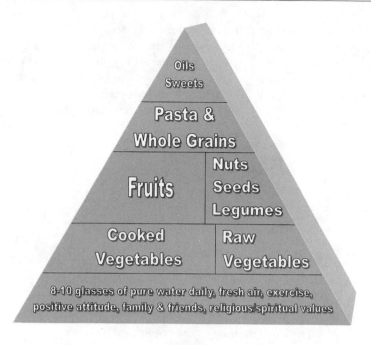

Veggie food pyramid for hot weather.

Here's what a diet might look like for a strict vegetarian in the summer or living in a hot climate, with moderate activity.

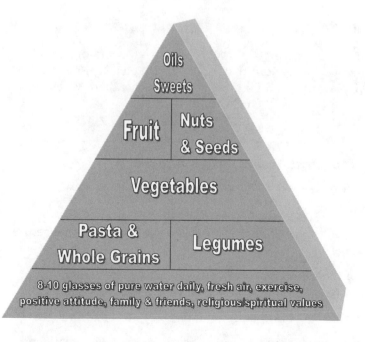

Veggie food pyramid for cold weather.

Here is a strict vegetarian diet to follow in the winter or in a cold climate, with moderate activity.

Vary your diet to suit your needs by increasing your grain-based foods, such as pasta, breads, and rice, when you increase your activity level. Most grains quickly turn to glucose in the body, and if you don't use up that extra sugar, it is going to be stored as fat eventually. So, if you have moderate to low activity levels, eating more vegetables than grains and beans will keep you more slender and help you to maintain your energy level. When you feel the need for protein, by all means, go for the beans!

Veggie Soup for the Soul

In hot weather, your body eliminates more water through the skin to keep you cool. When you sweat you lose minerals, such as sodium and potassium. Therefore, eating vegetables and fruits, which are all rich in minerals, helps keep your mineral balance intact, which aids in keeping you cooler. Fruits and vegetables also require less digestive work from your system and so enable your body to remain cooler during hot weather. That means eating a cucumber salad (cucumbers are high in potassium) in the summer actually *can* keep you cool as a cucumber!

If you really want to get into eating correctly, you'll also have to work on combining foods to feel your best, and we'll talk about that aspect in Chapter 22, "The Health Nut." Until then, eat well, play well, and I'll meet you in the next part, where we are going to focus on the health benefits of being a vegetarian.

The Least You Need to Know

➤ Fresh vegetables and fruits contain a detectable life force energy that may be transferred to its consumer.

➤ Fresh uncooked fruits and vegetables contain enzymes that aid in the digestive process and save energy.

➤ Your body is made of the same organic materials as plant life; therefore, you can supply these materials to your body through your vegetarian diet.

➤ Fruit acts as a cleanser for the body, and vegetables work to build strength.

➤ The vegetarian food pyramid should be varied according to your climate and your activity level.

Part 3
Veggin' Out for Your Health

We all want to be healthier, have more energy, feel good, and look our best, right? This section shows you how and why you can feel healthier, have more energy, feel good, and look your best by eliminating a lot of meat from your diet. You'll get the lowdown on how you digest, learn about the effects of meat eating on your health, and discover how to utilize a meatless diet to gain energy and lose weight. If you are going to include some animal products in your diet, I'll show you how to make the best choices for that as well.

Chapter 7

The Digestion Question

In This Chapter

➤ Understand how your digestive system works

➤ Compare your digestion to that of a *real* carnivore

➤ Take an inside look at the colon

➤ Learn how to avoid parasites

➤ Protect yourself from food-borne pathogens

Are you ready to digest something that may make you feel a whole lot better? Well here's a fact: Strict natural carnivores have dramatically different body systems than you do. You will soon be learning what those differences are and what they mean for your health. We'll discuss why eating less or no meat can save some of your digestive energy, keep you clear from parasitic infestation, and lower your chance of picking up a bacteria found primarily in meat. Eating contaminated meat can be dangerous—at the very least, it can sure ruin a vacation!

After I explain more about meat digestion and food safety, you can decide whether you were born to be wild ... or mild.

Chew on This

I understand that you are supposed to chew with your mouth closed, but after you've swallowed, take a look inside your mouth and check out those molars. They are well-developed for a reason. They were designed as grinding instruments. Our teeth are primarily made for chewing and grinding vegetation to get it ready for the rest of the digestion process.

If you want to live your best, you need to follow nature's laws. Nature is what it is, period. It cannot be fundamentally changed or manipulated, despite what science tries in vain to do. Nature will always win out in the end. Your body is part of nature. If you observe your human design, you will see how you are designed to live. The farther you live from nature's laws, the more out of balance you become.

When we look at our teeth versus those of, say, a lion, which is a strict meat-eater, we can notice some striking differences. First, humans do not have sharp fangs for ripping open tough animal hide and sharp claws that tear through prey (can you imagine ripping into a burger like a wild animal?), nor do humans have a jaw that is limited to an up and down movement.

Your jaw allows your teeth to move in a lateral motion as well as up and down. This motion enables you to grind your foods well before swallowing. The lion's jaw places its emphasis on the canine teeth and has relatively undeveloped molars. Lions are not designed to chew their food 29 times before swallowing like we are told to do.

Steer Clear

Chew properly and avoid gulping your food. Your molars are designed to help you chew thoroughly, and when you do, it helps the rest of your digestion by making the foods you eat more available to your system. Chewing properly and eating slowly can also help eliminate intestinal gas. Gas can be caused by air spaces trapped between big chunks of improperly masticated food.

Veggie Soup for the Soul

Can osteoporosis be detected in the mouth first? The teeth are tiny samplings of the condition of the rest of the bones in your body. If you are suddenly having dental problems but haven't changed your dental hygiene, it could be a clue that your body is over-acidic due to poor diet. Cavities could indicate poor calcium absorption and mineral imbalance. Work with your dentist and your nutritional guide to help you get the supplemental nutrition you need to counteract your problem. If you can get your teeth in shape by improving your nutrition, you can bet you are doing the rest of your bones good as well.

Generally speaking, most lions and other strict carnivores gulp down the flesh of their prey. This fact brings us to the next striking difference between a typical carnivorous animal and a typical human animal—the rest of the digestive system.

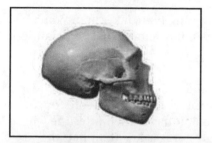

A human's skull contains well-developed molars and a jaw that moves laterally. These features are designed for grinding vegetation to make it suitable for digestion.

A carnivore's skull shows enlarged canine teeth and limited jaw movement.

The Truth Is Hard to Swallow

Digestion begins in the mouth, and you might as well start out right. Your body is designed to work best if you chew your food thoroughly, using your molars to grind down the food, allowing time for your saliva to mix completely with the food. Your saliva contains enzymes that begin the digestive process.

When you swallow, the food enters your stomach, where hydrochloric acid (HCl) and other digestive secretions surround the food as the stomach churns and continues the digesting process. After the food is sufficiently broken down in the stomach, it is called *chyme*. (A few hours after you eat dinner, this matter can be called dinner chyme. Just kidding.)

The chyme passes into the small intestine, which is approximately 20 feet long. It gets slowly pushed through the tube-like intestinal tract by wavelike movements called *peristalsis*. Fingerlike projections inside the small intestine are called *villi*. It is through these villi that you absorb most of your nutrients.

Lettuce Explain

Chyme is the term for food that has been broken down in the stomach. **Peristalsis** is the wavelike contraction of the intestines that moves partially digested food through the digestive tract. **Villi** are fingerlike projections in the small intestine that absorb nutrients.

The mostly digested food then passes into the large intestine, also known as the colon or lower bowel, where more minerals and vitamins are absorbed, along with excess water. The final material is then passed to the rectum, where it is eliminated from the body.

This entire process in a healthy functioning body takes approximately 12 to 18 hours. This is called transit time, which we will talk about in more detail soon.

No, I'm Not Lion

Now let's talk about the digestive system of a strict carnivore for comparison. Again, we'll use the example of the lion. The lion has a small intestine whose length equals only about three times his trunk length. This is less than half the size of a human's intestinal tract. When the lion eats his or her meat, it passes through this short digestive system, and the waste products from the meal are eliminated rather quickly. There is no time for the meat to sit and fester, as it does in the human system.

Remember that the length of a human's digestive process is about 12 to 18 hours. When meat enters the human digestive system, it is subject to a warm, moist environment for a long period of time. In this type of environment the meat begins to rot and decay. This decaying meat creates *free radicals* that can be released into the body.

Free radicals are unstable oxygen atoms created in everyone's body. We live with a certain number of them all the time. However, under certain conditions, excess free radicals are created. The conditions include exposure to toxins in the air, water, and diet, and also things like constipation and stress. When we have too many free radicals in our system, the damage they do increases and can cause cancer, premature aging, and other degenerative conditions.

Besides the damage that free radicals can do, when your body breaks down the complete proteins from meat, it naturally creates a tremendous amount of nitrogen by-products, such as ammonia and urea. It can cause a buildup of uric acid, and can be felt as sore, achy, stiff joints. When uric acid crystallizes, it forms glass-like splinters that can then cause sharp pains, arthritic problems, gout, and neuritis.

Lettuce Explain

Free radicals are unstable and destructive oxygen atoms created by the body's natural processes.

Sprouts of Info

Meat-eating creates uric acid in the body. Uric acid overload can lead to many health conditions. A carnivore's body produces uricase, which breaks down uric acid. Humans do not produce or have uricase.

The Raw Truth

Another major difference between lions and humans is that a lion eats his meat fresh and raw. Humans cook meat. Remember in Chapter 6, "Nourishment from the Plant Kingdom," when we talked about how raw food contains enzymes? Enzymes are present in all live foods and are critical to the digestive process.

Cooking food at temperatures above 130°F kills the enzyme life in the food. When enzymes are destroyed, it makes the food dead. This is a double whammy for meat. Not only is the animal killed, sometimes months before it winds up on your dinner table, but any possible live enzymes that could have been left in the meat are killed when you cook it!

Any time you eat foods that don't have their own enzymes, your pancreas must come up with extra. This puts wear and tear on it over time. Just like any machine, when a body part is overworked and forced to deal with fuels that weren't designed specifically for its best functioning, it will wear out faster. I do not advocate eating raw meat; please don't get me wrong. But the lion does eat raw meat with all its enzymes intact. The enzymes present in fresh meat help the lion's body digest it at a rapid rate (similar to when you eat fresh fruit), and the waste from the lion's meal is both digested and eliminated quickly.

So, not only is cooked meat hard to digest, your body has to come up with a lot of enzymes of its own to process it. This causes a drain of energy on the system, energy you could be using to help change the world, spend more time with friends or family, or start that new hobby you never seem to have the time for. When you supply your digestive system with live food with its enzymes intact, it works more efficiently and repays you with extra energy.

Veggie Soup for the Soul

Native Eskimos who live on the flesh and blubber of Arctic animals rarely cook their food, which means that their flesh foods still have their inherent enzymes. Interestingly enough, these folks generally enjoy exceptionally good health. Although they eat meat, there is no extra wear and tear on their body from producing the extra enzymes needed to digest cooked foods.

Is Your Stomach Acid Placid?

Along with bacterial enzymes in the gut, it takes a tremendous amount of hydrochloric acid (HCl) to digest beef and other animal flesh, and, unfortunately, the amount of naturally occurring HCl your stomach produces declines with age. Although you might have been able to handle meat digestion in your teens and early 20s, your body has less and less ability to handle it the older you get.

In contrast, the lion's stomach makes about 10 to 15 times the HCl that a human's stomach produces! Isn't nature revealing? Hydrochloric acid is critical for more than just digestion. It also sterilizes the foods that enter the stomach by a process that bursts apart matter, ensuring that any foreign debris, such as bacteria, parasites, or parasite eggs, are rendered harmless to the system.

Your stomach could actually be considered part of your immune system since it works to protect you in this way. But when you eat lots of meat, you put a great demand on this acid, which can leave you more vulnerable to parasites and other invading bacteria picked up through your food.

Just in case you thought you were only vulnerable to parasites in foreign countries, guess again. You don't have to travel or eat dirty foods to pick up parasites or unwanted bacteria. These critters live everywhere and are part of the ecosystem of the world. Use caution by cleaning fresh vegetables and fruits before you consume them. Make sure that foods are cooked to their proper temperature to destroy any bacteria that may have been growing on them.

A lack of HCl not only leaves you vulnerable to bacterial and parasitic infections, it is linked to a host of other ailments, including thin fingernails, indigestion, red blotches on the face (rosacea), cold extremities, and blood-sugar imbalances.

No matter how you look at it, meat is tough to digest. Our body can handle small amounts once in a while, but nature shows us that we are definitely not designed to eat it on a regular basis, and certainly not like we do in our meat-centered Western culture. Now let's continue on down the digestive tract to the colon to see how you as a vegetarian can take better care of yours.

Sprouts of Info

Granted, there are some parasites designed to withstand our stomach's acid. But many of those that we unwittingly ingest will be destroyed by the hydrochloric acid in your stomach.

Sprouts of Info

Vegetarians who eat many fresh foods require less HCl to break down their foods and therefore have fewer digestive complaints. However, any vegetarian who eats processed foods, dairy, or eggs might benefit from supplementation with food enzymes containing HCl. Consult with your natural health care provider to find out whether you are a good candidate for supplementing and to help you choose a quality supplement.

Veggie Soup for the Soul

Blood type Os tend to make plenty of HCl, more than other blood types, and this helps them digest many foods, especially protein. If you are type O you will probably not need to supplement with HCl. Vegetarians who incorporate some animal products in their diet might benefit greatly by adding an HCl supplement. If you are a strict vegetarian who eats plenty of raw fruits and veggies, you will probably not need an HCl supplement because your own HCl and enzyme reserves will last longer. However, after age 55, no matter what blood type you are, you might consider a food enzyme with HCl if you experience digestive distress or lethargy after eating.

The Colon: More Than Punctuation

The colon serves as the septic system for the body. It is involved in the final process of digestion. The colon is about five to six feet long. Its main function is to eliminate moisture and the final vitamins and minerals from the processed food it receives from the small intestines.

The colon is prone to becoming sluggish and constipated, especially when you eat starchy processed foods, meat, and other animal products. Constipation is a major cause of many ailments. Because meat is generally hard for the human body to digest, it can slow the entire process of digestion and elimination, creating a sluggish, constipated colon.

The body works as one system, and no one organ or area is completely separated from the others. One under- or overactive organ affects the overall health of the whole lot.

That's Toxic

Your circulatory system acts as a vehicle to transport and distribute oxygen and nutrients throughout your body. Because you do most of the absorption and breakdown of nutrients through the intestinal system, this is where the blood goes to get the nutrients from the foods you eat.

When the blood visits the intestinal system to pick up these nutrients, it receives not only nutrients but also the remnants of toxins created by festering undigested meat. It carries these toxins along with the nutrients and distributes them throughout the system. Therefore, when you are constipated, your whole body becomes polluted.

Lettuce Explain

Autointoxication is a condition caused by a constipated bowel in which bowel toxins are harbored and circulated throughout the rest of the body by the blood stream.

Lettuce Explain

Haustras are the bulbous pouches that make up the large intestine. They work by peristaltic action, moving food material back and forth inside the intestinal walls for final processing before elimination. **Diverticulitis** is the inflammation of pockets in the lining of the colon, causing severe abdominal pain often accompanied by fever and constipation.

When the body is constantly circulating toxins, it can create a condition known as *autointoxication.* Symptoms of autointoxication can include …

➤ Headaches.

➤ Achiness in joints and muscles.

➤ Bloating.

➤ Swelling.

➤ Pimples.

➤ Lethargy.

➤ General malaise.

➤ Intestinal gas (foul smelling).

➤ Halitosis (bad breath).

➤ Body odor.

➤ Excess mucus.

When a person reaches a state of autointoxication, he or she feels lousy. This is when people will often take an aspirin for the aches and pains, a water pill for the bloat, or maybe a pep pill for energy.

What you really need is to cleanse your colon by eliminating the meat for a while (if not entirely), doing an herbal colon cleanse (see Chapter 1, "Why Eat Less Meat?" for a good cleanse or ask your herbalist), and flushing your system with some fruit, vegetables, and fiber for a few weeks. You'll find you won't need all those medications.

Not Very Diverting

If your colon is weak in any area and is not functioning as well as it should, the *haustras,* which are tiny bulbous pouches that make up the large intestine, can stretch and form tiny pockets. These pockets can gather waste products and fester, harbor toxins, swell, and sometimes cause pain. This condition is called *diverticulitis.* If you have this condition you probably know it because you are likely to have had enough distress to send you to your doctor for a diagnosis.

If you are experiencing intestinal gas, it could be a clue that you have some bowel pockets. As matter decays in these areas, noxious gasses are released, and you know the rest. If all this isn't bad enough, these pockets are also a great place to harbor parasites.

Parasites: Hosting a Party

Parasites love to live in the intestinal system. They hang out in areas of the colon where purifying oxygen and an adequate fresh blood supply are limited due to hardened mucus and other waste materials that have become compacted in the intestinal walls. These putrefied wastes, left from years of meat-eating and processed foods, limit the ability of the body to cleanse itself.

Parasites can wreak havoc on the body and the health and can lead to such problems as ...

➤ Blood sugar imbalance.

➤ Insomnia.

➤ Teeth grinding.

➤ Diarrhea.

➤ Itching.

➤ Sugar cravings.

➤ Weight loss or weight gain.

➤ Bloating.

➤ Nightmares.

➤ Malnutrition.

➤ Irritability.

➤ Fatigue.

➤ Lowered immune system.

➤ Anemia.

Steer Clear

A parasitic infestation is often at the root of illnesses that cannot be properly diagnosed or symptoms that come in cycles. Parasitic infections might be incorrectly diagnosed as chronic fatigue, irritable bowel syndrome, allergies, nervousness, and dermatitis.

You might be surprised how easy it can be to pick up a parasite, even in developed countries. It has been estimated that at one time or another over 90 percent of Americans contract a parasite of some kind. As a colonic therapist and herbalist myself, I would have to agree with that observation.

So how do you prevent parasites besides eliminating meat? Let's talk about that next.

Improving Colon Transit Time

Your colon transit time is the entire time it takes to digest something, from the time you eat it until the time you eliminate it as waste. (Technically this includes much more than your colon, of course, but it's a catchy phrase, and many nutritionists and holistic health practitioners use it.) The time is around 12 to 18 hours for most healthy folks.

The longer waste materials stay in the colon, the more likely you are to become constipated. The colon absorbs water from the matter in the bowel, and if it sits too long, the fecal matter becomes dried and hard, making it very difficult to pass. Constipation leads to autointoxication and can be linked to more health ailments than I have room here to list, including the harboring of parasites.

Keep Moving

Here are some tips on preventing constipation besides eliminating animal products from your diet:

Sprouts of Info

Meat goes through your system more slowly than other foods, which slows your colon transit time and adds to the possibility of chronic constipation. Most pure vegetarians do not have troubles with digestion or constipation; however, lacto ovo vegetarians might because cheese and other dairy products and eggs all tend to be constipating.

➤ Exercise. Exercise stimulates the bowel to keep things moving.

➤ Drink plenty of pure water. Water helps flush toxins and wastes from your system.

➤ Get extra fiber in your diet. Fiber supplements include psyllium hulls and flax seeds. Fruits and vegetables, along with their skins, are a great source of natural fiber.

➤ Chew your foods well.

➤ Eat on a regular basis. The body likes to be in a routine.

➤ Reflexology, acupuncture, and acupressure are all good therapies to help you relieve constipation and keep your energies balanced.

➤ Do an occasional herbal cleanse to cleanse your digestive tract and bowel.

Sprouts of Info

It is estimated that 90 percent of all 24-hour flu bugs are actually cases of food poisoning from ingesting bacteria- or parasite-contaminated food. Most of these occur when eating outside the home.

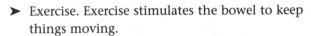

Food Safety Concerns

Now more than ever we seem to hear about food poisonings, food-borne illnesses, viruses, bacteria, flu epidemics, and so on. It's enough to turn almost anyone into a paranoid hypochondriac!

The truth is that you do need to watch out for some of these things and make sure you don't subject yourself to contaminated foods. A few simple precautions can help you avoid these problems. Let's take a look at some of the most common food-borne illnesses related to animal products, and then I'll give you some precautions you can take with all foods.

E. Coli: Not Just for Breakfast Anymore

E. coli 0157:H7 is a toxic acid-loving bacteria transmitted by contamination with feces. It is found in meat, cheeses, unpasteurized animal milk, raw fish, and other prepared foods.

Hamburger meat is among the most vulnerable to E. coli contamination. After the meat is contaminated by fecal matter, the grinding process spreads the contamination throughout the meat. If the hamburger is not cooked thoroughly at high temperatures, contamination can pass to the person who eats it, and severe illness can occur.

You Want Fries with That?

Some other forms of bacteria also cause food poisoning in meat and other animal products. These bacteria can cause severe intestinal distress and flu-like symptoms that include diarrhea, vomiting, painful stomach cramps, and fever. They can lead to serious illness and even death.

The following shows some common bacteria and parasites that can cause poisoning, the animals or animal products they seem to have an affinity for, and their symptoms.

Food-Borne Illness	Mode of Transmission	Symptoms
Norwalk virus	Shellfish, eggs	Nausea, vomiting, diarrhea, abdominal pain, headache, low-grade fever
Listeria	Meat, unpasteurized milk products	Nausea, vomiting, headaches, delirium, coma, collapse, shock, lesions on vital organs
Salmonella	Poultry, eggs, pork, cattle, and rodents	Headache, abdominal pain, diarrhea, nausea, vomiting, dehydration, fever, loss of appetite
E. coli	Beef, cheeses, unpasteurized milk, raw fish, and prepared foods contaminated with feces	Severe abdominal pain, nausea, vomiting, cramps, diarrhea, fever, kidney failure, central nervous system disease, seizures, coma, blood clots in the brain, death
Vibrio vulnificus	Improperly cooked or raw shellfish from contaminated waters	Fever, chills, nausea, vomiting, diarrhea, shock, abdominal pain, severe fatigue, skin or blood infections progressing to ulcers or sores

continued

continued

Food-Borne Illness	Mode of Transmission	Symptoms
Hepatitis A	Contaminated water, any food contaminated by infected food handlers, raw or undercooked shell-fish from contaminated waters	Abrupt fever, fatigue, loss of appetite, nausea, abdominal discomfort, jaundice, dark urine, joint aches
Dysentery	Contaminated water; prepared foods such as tuna fish salad, macaroni salad, and sliced turkey	Cramps, chills, fever (sometimes), diarrhea
Staphylococcal Food Poisoning	Ready-to-eat foods such as meats, poultry, and dairy products, especially if they have been subjected to varying temperatures	Vomiting, diarrhea, dehydration, nausea, cramps, lowered blood pressure and body temperature

What's a Vegetarian to Do?

Eating a vegetarian diet consisting of whole live foods limits your exposure to many of these food-borne illnesses. But just because we're vegetarians doesn't mean we're immune. A vegetarian isn't completely safe from food-borne toxins, and those who are not strict vegetarians, whether you eat fish, eggs, dairy, or meat occasionally, must know what else can be done to avoid problems. No matter what level of vegetarian you are now, please consider the following precautions:

Sprouts of Info

E. coli found in burgers that were slightly undercooked caused the famous fast-food food poisoning outbreak that caused illness and deaths in the United States in the 1980s.

➤ Wash your hands thoroughly before you eat.

➤ Do not accept food in a restaurant that is not served at its ideal temperature. For example, if it is meant to be served hot, send it back if it is lukewarm or cool. If it is supposed to be served chilled, do not eat it if it is warm. Bacteria grows rapidly in foods left at room temperature.

➤ If you are ordering meat, make sure it is cooked around all the edges and that it looks as if it were cooked thoroughly and properly.

➤ If you are taking an enzyme containing HCl or any HCl supplement, make sure to take it during or right after eating.

➤ Don't eat leftovers if they have been sitting in the car or anywhere but the refrigerator. It is also not wise to eat any leftovers after about 14 hours.

➤ Do not refreeze food items you have defrosted.

So what do I suggest? Pass on the meat, wash your hands, wash your vegetables, and take an HCl supplement when eating in questionable places. And most of all, enjoy yourself.

The Least You Need to Know

➤ Your body's digestive system is not designed to accommodate regular meat consumption.

➤ Consuming less meat reduces the demand for enzymes from your liver and pancreas to break down the cooked meat.

➤ Eating less meat can help you avoid the buildup of uric acid in your body, which can lead to gout and other health conditions.

➤ A meatless diet reduces the amount of HCl your body has to secrete, and the more HCl you have in reserve, the more your body can use to protect you from parasite infestation.

➤ Your chances of becoming ill from food-borne bacteria and parasites are lower if you abstain from flesh and animal products.

Chapter 8

Meatless for a Healthier Heart

In This Chapter

➤ Learn how meat consumption affects your heart

➤ Understand the effect meat-eating has on blood pressure

➤ Manage your cholesterol levels by going vegetarian

➤ Understand how to avoid heart disease

"I didn't claw my way up the food chain to eat vegetables!"

—Seen on a bumper sticker

As a human you are privileged to make your own choices to select what is best for you and your body. You can choose to break bad habits, recondition old patterns, and make new choices. You are using your freedom of choice when you read this book and learn how and why to eat a better, cleaner, more healthful diet without meat and animal products. You may also choose to question the advertising propaganda and conditioning you have been trained to believe for so long.

You probably have seen for yourself that meat consumption is not necessary for life or even health because of the growing number of thriving, healthy vegetarians among us. You should know by now that the vegetarian diet is simply a dietary choice made by informed individuals and that meat-eating is not a necessity.

Now that you know you are free and do not have to follow any childhood conditioning that says you were born to eat meat, please take your claws out of my back so that we can talk about how going vegetarian might save you from a heart attack!

Clawing Your Way Up the Food Chain

So you've climbed the food chain, but where has it gotten you? Face it, people are dropping dead from heart disease daily. You hear about strokes, heart attacks, high cholesterol levels, angina, arteriosclerosis, high blood pressure, and bypass surgery all the time. The good news is that although these diseases and treatments are abundant in our world, especially among North Americans, they are almost nonexistent among vegetarians.

Some of you might argue that eating a healthful vegetarian diet is too expensive, but how much are you spending on medications, hospitals, and doctor bills to take care of your mostly diet-related illness?

Sprouts of Info

Did you know that each year, non-vegetarian humans consume about 15 cows, 24 pigs, 12 sheep, 900 chickens, and 1,000 pounds of assorted fish and other poultry?

Another interesting fact about all this is that coronary heart diseases and some forms of cancer are at the top of the list when it comes to the leading causes of death. What is ironic about this is that both of these diseases can be either prevented or made worse by diet!

Recently I attended a convention in Philadelphia where Beverley Nicholson, a naturopathic doctor from Illinois, was speaking. Nicholson, a very vibrant woman herself, has a radio show and a private practice in Illinois where she specializes in colon cleansing, herbs, and nutritional counseling for health.

Nicholson instructed the audience to write down the word "death." She had us cross out the "d" and the "h" and look at what was left. Her point? People are eating themselves to death! Most of the people in Western countries consume an enormous amount of fat and too little fiber, and they are paying for it with diseases that lead to their disability and death.

To balance the impact of Nicholson's "lexigram," I made up my own: Write the word "health" and cross out the "Hs" and the "L." If you do this, you also come up with the word "eat." Once again, it looks as though you are going to have to make a choice: whether to eat yourself to death or eat yourself to health! Pretty cool, huh? Keep reading, and we'll work on the health part.

Circulating Rumors About Cholesterol

Let's start with how eating meat and animal products adds to or creates circulatory system problems. Most of these problems start with eating too much saturated fat. Saturated fat is found abundantly in all animal flesh and animal products. Too much dietary fat can lead to high cholesterol levels, which is what begins most types of diet-related heart problems.

If you are concerned about lowering your cholesterol level, consider becoming a pure vegetarian. Lacto ovo vegetarianism might be okay for some, but not when you are serious about getting your cholesterol to a healthy level.

That's because all animal products, including animal flesh, eggs, and dairy products, are high in fat. Fat is found not only in an animal's fat, but also in the muscle of animal tissue. Even if you trim the fat from your steak, you are still getting a concentrated amount of animal fat in the meat. This is true of all animals, from pigs to poultry to fish.

Take My Fat, Please

Beyond meat, egg yolks contain a high amount of concentrated fat. And milk is just as fatty and is even worse when it is processed into other concentrated hardened forms of fat such as ice cream, butter, and cheese. (More on dairy products and eggs when you get to Chapter 13, "High Ho the Dairy, Oh!")

When you eat animal products, your body takes the fat into your blood, resulting in a condition known as *lipemia,* which literally means fat in the blood. This slimy greasy fat then circulates throughout your system for hours (at least four hours) until the liver can process it.

It All Adds Up

Eating meat and other animal fats might seem okay once in a while, but most people eat meat or some animal product at every meal. Some people believe that eliminating red meat from their diets lowers their cholesterol or blood pressure. Although this can be somewhat effective, a lot depends on what type of foods replace the red meat.

Remember that animal products such as eggs and cheese are included in a lacto ovo vegetarian diet. Foods like milk chocolate, French toast, and other seemingly nonanimal products still contain hidden animal fat. The result is that the fat builds up in the body and can lead to disease.

Dear Diary

I sometimes have my clients write down everything they consume for two solid weeks. We then take a look at where they can clean up their diet. This also helps to pinpoint food allergies and possible nutritional deficiencies.

Lettuce Explain

Lipemia is a condition in which dietary fat is accumulated in the blood. This condition lasts for about four hours after you consume fat as the liver attempts to break it down and eliminate it from the body.

This food diary, although tedious to maintain, is a great self-awareness tool for helping folks see what they are eating. The diary also forces them to see how much they are eating. This practice alone often helps people get motivated to make necessary changes. Give it a try yourself for a week and see how much of an eye-opener it can be.

A Sensitive Subject

Although most of my clients come to me for health counseling and herbal programs, they do not usually wish to change their diet, at least not right off the bat, because they believe they eat pretty well already. Being respectful of the fact that eating habits are wrapped up in the psyche, changes in diet should be approached gently and progressively to allow for a permanent transition to the positive.

The clientele I see are a small sampling of people who seek complementary, alternative, holistic health counseling and guidance. Because I have clients in different pockets from all across the United States and some in Canada, England, and even Belgium, my clientele represent a fairly varied group and can serve as a good example of what a diet that is "generally healthful" means to most people.

Healthy Choices?

Most of my clients describe their diet in the following ways:

➤ Fairly good

➤ I eat low-fat foods

➤ I rarely (or don't) eat red meat

➤ I eat a lot of vegetables and fruit

When it comes down to evaluating their food diaries, I see that most of these diets are abundant in animal products, which can not only strip the body of calcium, but also load the body with fat!

Al's Inner Life

To illustrate, let's look at a day in the life of the digestive tract of a fairly typical guy we'll call Al. This example is taken from a person who considered his diet to be "fairly good." He refrains from red meat, but still has high cholesterol.

Let's see what Al's eating.

➤ **Breakfast:** Al gets up before a hard day at work, unusually hungry, cooks up scrambled eggs and toast with a little butter, and washes it down with some coffee with a little 2 percent milk added to it.

➤ **Lunch:** Lunch consists of a big fresh vegetable salad with a little shredded cheese and ranch salad dressing.

➤ **Dinner:** For dinner he has chicken and some green beans with a pat of butter and a glass of milk.

Al goes to bed happy knowing that he had no red meat that day and that he got his fresh vegetables to boot. This might have been okay for Al if he was just beginning on a cleaner diet or maintaining a generally good diet, but the point is that Al needs to get his cholesterol under control, and this day's food won't help.

Sprouts of Info

In order to make any positive changes in your health, healthy practices must be repeated over and over and consistently for some time (at least 30 days in a row) until they become a habit. Changes that are turned into habits generally stay with a person forever.

Al's Digestive System

This is what is happening inside Al's body:

The eggs, butter, and milk from Al's breakfast contained condensed animal fat (not to mention high protein, which causes calcium loss). After eating breakfast, this fat enters his blood and raises his blood fat level. Shortly thereafter, his liver begins to eliminate the excess fat. Before Al's liver has a chance to process the fat from breakfast, in comes the cheese and salad dressing from lunch, both containing high levels of condensed, greasy animal fat.

This fat continues to circulate as the liver attempts to catch up with the overload. By the time Al sits down to consume his chicken, which also contains concentrated animal fat, the fat in his blood looks about like the pat of butter he's about to add to his green beans—hardened, greasy, and white. Over time, this kind of animal product consumption leads to high cholesterol levels. High cholesterol is a warning that Al could be headed toward heart disease.

What can Al do besides cut out red meat and get his cholesterol under control? Al's a big guy, and we want to keep him satisfied, but we also want to severely restrict the amount of animal fat he takes in.

Al's New Diet

Let's take a look at some circulatory-system friendly food that Al could have eaten instead of the no-red-meat diet he has been following:

➤ **Breakfast:** Scrambled tofu with chopped green and red peppers, a slice of toast with a little strawberry jam, coffee with a splash of rice milk.

➤ **Lunch:** The same large fresh salad but hold the cheese; instead add extra garbanzo or kidney beans to beef up the protein intake and make the salad more filling. Hold the ranch dressing and use olive oil and vinegar or ripe avocado and lemon juice. He could even add a nondairy fruit smoothie if he's really hungry.

➤ **Dinner:** Tempeh and vegetable stir-fry (fried in tamari sauce instead of oil), served with steamed wild rice.

➤ **Snacks:** Fresh fruit, as always!

Veggie Soup for the Soul

Reports show that only one percent of what the average American is eating comes from whole-grain foods, even though there is overwhelming evidence showing that more whole grains in the diet lowers the incidence of heart disease and cancer. Surveys show that most Americans say they want more whole-grain foods in their diet, but they are confused about what whole grains are. We're here to help. See Chapter 4, "A New Food Pyramid," to learn how to prepare whole grains. For more on purchasing different grains, see Chapter 15, "Let's Talk Shop!"

This meatless dairyless day keeps the fat level in Al's body to the minimum, provides plenty of protein, vegetables, and whole grains, and is packed with vitamins, minerals, and natural calcium. To make this day's food therapeutic for Al, he could add a couple of cloves of garlic to his stir-fry. Garlic helps thin the blood and can help to reduce cholesterol levels.

The solution seems pretty easy because these replacement foods are quite satisfying and tasty. Sometimes it simply takes a little more awareness and creativity to get where you want to be. If Al continues to eat dairy, eggs, and other flesh foods, he will not be able to effectively lower his cholesterol level and maintain it without intervention, such as chelation therapy, cholesterol-lowering drugs, vitamin/herbal therapy, and so on. Although eating less red meat is better than eating a lot of it, it's not always enough to keep your cholesterol down.

Cholesterol and You

Now that you know how you can utilize the vegetarian diet to keep your cholesterol levels healthy, let's take a closer look at cholesterol's role in the body and find out why you want to pay attention to yours.

The fat that builds up in the blood after you eat a high-fat meal is like sludge. In order for your blood to keep circulating, it needs to move past this sludge. Meanwhile, the liver is working hard to break down the fat in your blood, but it can handle only so much at a time, so the fat builds up while it waits for the liver to work. But before the liver gets the chance at it, you go and eat more animal products, and it's traffic jam time!

The fat has no place to go and accumulates in the blood stream, which continues to be pushed through the veins by the constant pumping of the heart. The blood attempts to bypass the fatty sludge by forcing its way through the veins and arteries to complete its duty of supplying nutrients and oxygen to the body.

Eventually the blood fat begins to get shoved to the outside of the walls of your arteries. Factors such as stress, bouts of high blood pressure, and lack of nutrients can compromise the inside walls of your arteries as well, making them more susceptible to fatty build up. This condition is known as atherosclerosis.

Tone Up Those Arteries

Because atherosclerosis is the primary cause of cardiovascular disease, it is important not only to limit your animal fat intake, increase your exercise, and find a stress-relieving therapy, but also to feed the circulatory system with the nutrients it needs, such as antioxidants to protect your arteries from damage. When the arteries become damaged they are more vulnerable to scarring and more vulnerable to the buildup of fat that leads to atherosclerosis.

After the process of fat adhesion begins, it makes it easier for more fat globules to stick, too, as they pass by. The result? Hardening of the arteries due to fat/cholesterol adhering to the inside of the arterial walls.

If the level of fat in the blood remains high and you continue to eat animal products, your blood fat will continue to accumulate and form plaque, which clogs up the arteries. This plaque begins as fatty material, but the longer it remains stuck to

Steer Clear

Although good cholesterol, or low density lipoprotein (LDL), is not considered dangerous to the body, it does become harmful if it has been oxidized by exposure to free radicals such as chlorine. Chlorine is added to most tap water to kill water-borne bacteria. Drinking chlorinated water turns your good cholesterol against you. That's a good reason to drink only pure filtered water!

Sprouts of Info

Your circulatory system needs the B vitamins, vitamin E, vitamin C, CoQ$_{10}$, selenium, magnesium, calcium, potassium, and chromium to keep it healthy. Garlic and capsicum have also been shown to be helpful in maintaining circulatory system strength.

the arterial walls, the harder it becomes. It tends to calcify, and, over time, becomes a substance called arterial plaque.

These conditions build up over time and can lead to emergency situations. Usually one main artery clogs, notifying its owner of a major problem. For instance, if an artery that supplies blood to the brain clogs up with hardened fat, stopping the blood supply to the brain, the condition results in a stroke.

If an artery supplying blood to the heart clogs up, you will have a heart attack. People with high cholesterol are at a much greater risk for developing thrombosis, which is basically a blood clot which blocks the flow of blood through the vessel. If an artery to a limb clogs up, the limb will turn blue due to lack of oxygen. If not treated right away, this condition may force the limb to be amputated.

Sprouts of Info

Besides working with your diet to help lower your cholesterol and increase your circulatory system health, don't forget about giving your liver some extra support. Years and years of high fat intake take its toll on your liver. You should work with your holistic practitioner or herbalist to help you design a program to support your liver function.

Blood Is Your Lifeline

Remember, your blood supply is your life supply. Your entire circulatory system is the highway your blood uses to carry oxygen and nutrients to the organs and other parts of the body. When this transportation system is hindered due to "bad road conditions," the organs that rely on the delivery suffer.

It's largely the veins and arteries carrying blood back and forth that keep your heart alive and ticking. And the liver has an important role to play as well because it has the job of filtering these dense fats from your blood—kind of like a fat-globule colander.

Failing to clear the fat from the blood results in what is essentially a constipated circulatory system, with its host of related problems. Dr. John Christopher, well-known naturopath and founder of the School of Natural Healing, says there is only one disease—constipation. And constipation, in all its forms, is caused by a faulty diet.

Bypass the Meat Platter

The difference between plant fats and animal fats is dramatic. All animal fats are saturated, but plant fats are not nearly as dense. This allows the vegetarian to eat a large vegetarian meal and get the same grams of fat that a person eating a slice of cheese gets, without the associated health risks. The choice is yours: a nice big vegetarian meal or a small dense piece of cheese or animal flesh. If you are watching your fat intake, the vegetarian meal is clearly the better choice.

Certainly we need to thank the surgeons, cardiovascular specialists, and those incredibly skilled transplant teams who save so many lives with their skill in treating heart attacks, angina, and other heart and circulatory system conditions. But why not thank yourself in advance by bypassing the meat platter and saving yourself the need to meet one of these doctors as a patient! Wouldn't you much rather meet a cardiovascular specialist over a nice veggie burger at your favorite whole-foods restaurant?

Of course there are other factors that contribute to cardiovascular and coronary heart trouble, including genetic tendencies, but eliminating animal products can alleviate an incredible burden on your body. You might as well take charge of the areas that you can control, such as your diet and exercise, rather than adding to your risk factors.

The Kidneys and Blood Pressure

Because your kidneys play a role in regulating your blood pressure, it is important to know how meat and animal products affect them. In Chapter 7, "The Digestion Question," we discussed one reason why eating meat is hard on the kidneys: When your body breaks down animal protein, it creates uric acid and ammonia by-products, which the kidneys have to filter, making the kidneys work much harder than if they had to break down only plant protein.

Processed meats contain high levels of nitrates, preservatives, and other toxins, and the kidneys have to filter some of these toxins from the body as well. And all animal flesh, processed or not, contains high amounts of sodium. Sodium exists in the muscles of animal flesh, and when you eat the flesh, you get the sodium. When you take in an excess of sodium, the sodium attracts water. When you have too much sodium in your diet, you might notice bloating, swollen fingers, and bags under the eyes, and you may feel and look puffy. Although there is excess water being held by the body, the kidneys are unable to release it because the water is suspended in the blood by sodium. The excess sodium and water in the blood increase the volume of liquid inside the arteries, and the result is high blood pressure.

Please Don't Pass the Salt

But didn't we say back in Chapter 6, "Nourishment from the Plant Kingdom," that sodium is good for us and is found in the stomach lining and joints? Good point. Glad to see you remembered, but I also said that the sodium you need should come from plant life such as celery and strawberries. The sodium in animal flesh and animal products, table salt, and processed foods is inorganic and is too concentrated for your body to process easily.

An abundance of inorganic sodium in your diet depletes the amount of potassium in your body. Remember that your heart is a "potassium-loving organ." When there is an excess of sodium, the body can rob the heart muscle and other muscles in the body for the extra potassium it needs to balance the excess sodium.

Potassium helps keep the body flexible, and when you have a potassium deficiency, you also get hardening of tissues, such as hardening of the arteries, muscle cramps, and hardened skin and other organs. Symptoms of a deficiency include muscle weakness, paralysis, and confusion.

Balancing Those Deposits

How does all this relate to the kidneys? While all this fighting among minerals is going on, the kidneys continue to try to maintain your mineral balance. In order for your body to maintain its proper functioning, it constantly attempts to manage the correct balance of minerals and other nutrients in the right proportions. So chemical signals trigger the body's demands for sodium and water.

These signals cause the walls of your kidneys to become more or less permeable to these substances, which are reabsorbed accordingly from the urine, which again leads to overworked kidneys. On top of it all, you still have high blood pressure because you have too much sodium, and more than likely your arteries are clogged and hardened with plaque.

Now that you've taken a look inside your body and seen what all that meat and animal food can do to it, you can rest much easier eating your tofu, vegetables, fruits, nuts, seeds, beans, and grains and knowing that not only will your circulatory system thank you, but so will your liver, your kidneys, *and* your insurance company.

The Least You Need to Know

➤ Animal flesh and animal products are high in saturated fat and raise the blood fat level, which can lead to high cholesterol.

➤ Eating a diet high in meat and dairy dramatically increases the amount of sodium in the diet, which can cause high blood pressure.

➤ Cutting out only the red meat in your diet won't necessarily help to lower your cholesterol level as long as you still eat animal products like dairy, but a pure vegetarian diet can help lower and manage your cholesterol and high blood pressure.

➤ Eating right and taking care of yourself can go a long way toward preventing heart disease and increasing your overall health.

Chapter 9

In Sickness and in Health

In This Chapter

➤ Find out why vegetarians have a lower risk for cancer

➤ Look at the whole picture when working toward health

➤ Learn why limiting meat limits your exposure to toxins

➤ Discover which meats to choose if you choose to eat meat

➤ Understand the role attitude plays in your health

We all are willing to change our lifestyle to lower our cancer risk, as long as it is within reason, right? What if I told you that by choosing a vegetarian diet you were eliminating almost every major risk factor associated with contracting cancer? Would you do it? I hope so! This chapter shows why and how vegetarians are generally at lower risk for cancer than meat-eaters. It will also explain the other factors in life besides eating your vegetables that are important in achieving and maintaining health.

You'll learn that you don't have to be perfect, with a totally wholesome lifestyle and strict diet 100 percent of the time, to be healthy! Isn't that a relief? In case you are planning to eat meat occasionally, this chapter provides a list of your best choices when buying it so that you can avoid some of the negative side effects associated with animal flesh consumption. Keep reading for the benefits you can expect by going meatless and by making better choices when and if you do choose to eat meat occasionally.

Lowering Cancer Risks

Can eating less or no meat lower your cancer risk? Maybe. But first a little background. We talked in Chapter 7, "The Digestion Question," about free radicals, which are unstable atoms or groups of atoms with an unpaired electron. They are found naturally in everyone's body. I think of them as little Tasmanian devils on a rampage inside the body.

Free radicals can and will destroy or damage anything they come into contact with—that includes other cells, and even your genes! Excess free radicals are created by a host of things, but exposure to toxins or other stresses can increase their numbers. The damage they can do thereby increases and can cause health problems, including cancer. It is best to limit your exposure to these free radicals to help keep things in balance in the body.

Lettuce Explain

Antioxidants are free radical scavengers that fight off and destroy questionable or unstable cells that can be cancer-causing. Antioxidants are found naturally in fruits and vegetables, grains, and herbs, and can be taken in supplement form.

Antioxidants are compounds that are referred to as free radical scavengers. They can tame these free radicals, and are abundant in fresh fruits and vegetables. The main antioxidants that help fight off free radicals and the damage they do include vitamin C, vitamin E, vitamin K, vitamin A, vitamin D, beta-carotene, magnesium, chromium, selenium, and zinc.

Risky Business

Let's take a look at the high-risk factors associated with cancer. They include ...

➤ Smoking.

➤ A diet low in fiber.

➤ Constipation.

➤ High-fat diet.

➤ Obesity.

➤ Alcohol abuse.

➤ A diet low in antioxidants.

➤ Excessive exposure to chemicals.

The one factor that isn't directly food-related in this list is smoking, but one thing they all have in common is that they cause or allow lots of free radicals to be produced in the body. Cancer risks related to smoking are fairly obvious because each cigarette contains about 2,000 chemicals that go directly into your system when you inhale. But how and why do these other factors increase the risks? Let's take a look.

More Fiber, Less Fat

A diet low in fiber can lead to constipation, and in Chapter 7 we discussed the problems associated with a slow colon transit time. Meat in particular goes through the digestive system more slowly than vegetarian foods, and the putrefying meat and other processed food products left in the colon for long periods have time to release toxins and free radicals, which are believed to increase your cancer risk.

Fat intake and obesity are often related and are both factors in causing cancer and other illnesses. Excess dietary fat not burned as energy soon turns into stored fat in your tissues and arterial walls. Your body stores a lot of toxins in your fat cells, including pesticide residues; pollutants that you eat, breathe, and drink; and food colorings, preservatives, and many other chemicals used in foods and medicines.

If you choose to do a weight-loss program, consider incorporating an herbal cleanse before or during your weight loss. Extra antioxidants should be added to your diet as well. These protect you from any free radicals and toxins released during fat reduction.

Sprouts of Info

Your daily intake of dietary fat should not exceed 20 percent of your total calories for that day. In addition, getting at least 25 grams of dietary fiber in your diet daily can decrease your risk of colon and other cancers.

Take Your Toxins in Moderation

Although moderate alcohol consumption can be beneficial, heavy consumption has the opposite effect. Heavy consumption depletes the body of many vitamins and minerals, leading to malnutrition, and it leaves the body more susceptible to illnesses and degenerative conditions of the liver, pancreas, kidneys, and immune system.

Finally, exposure to toxic or otherwise unnatural chemicals increases your risk of cancer. These chemicals can come from foods, like the nitrates you find in processed meat (we'll discuss more about this later in the chapter), and from chemicals found all around you and even in the air you breathe.

Sprouts of Info

A vegetarian who chooses organic foods can limit his or her chemical intake much more effectively than a nonvegetarian because meats tend to have a lot of hidden additives.

Chemicals such as pesticides, car exhaust, industrial air pollution of all sorts, house cleaning products, cosmetics, radiation, industrial materials, and out-gassing from paints, dry cleaning, carpet, and construction materials can all increase your chances of getting cancer. They can also overburden the liver, which can then lead to other sensitivities and illnesses.

Unfortunately, it's almost impossible to avoid being exposed to chemicals on a daily basis, so it is a good idea to limit the chemicals you do have control over by making wise choices in the foods you eat. Choose naturally grown foods that are organically produced. I'll talk more about that in Chapter 15, "Let's Talk Shop!" when I get you ready to go shopping.

Vegetarians vs. Meat-Eaters

Now that you understand which choices increase your risks for cancer and other diseases, let's see why the vegetarian who eats for health could be at lower risk. (If you happen to be a vegetarian who lives on junk food, potato chips, chocolate, and soda pop, however, then all bets are off.) Generally, vegetarians …

➤ Eat a diet high in fiber. Fruit, vegetables, grains, and legumes contain more fiber than meat and other animal products.

➤ Are not constipated because their diet contains plenty of fiber, which keeps the colon clean.

➤ Have a fairly low-fat diet due to the low-fat content of most vegetarian foods.

➤ Are leaner than meat-eaters because vegetarians eat plenty of fiber and keep high-fat animal products to a minimum. Both of these factors are key to maintaining a weight.

➤ Are not heavy drinkers. Because many vegetarians are extremely health conscious, vegetarians who smoke and drink are not found in abundance.

➤ Get plenty of antioxidants by eating a diet rich in fruits and vegetables.

➤ Choose their fruits and vegetables wisely because these foods are the main course in most vegetarian meals. Many vegetarians choose organic foods over commercially grown crops to limit chemical exposure and to make a positive contribution toward the health of the environment.

All of these factors are in direct opposition to the high-risk factors associated with cancer. As a result, vegetarians are among those least likely to get cancer.

Get Enough Exercise

Limit your meat, increase your fresh organic fruits and vegetables, and there you have it, pure health, right? Don't we wish it were that easy! Total health is a bigger picture than simply limiting your meat consumption. I want to remind you of some of the other things you can do in your life to keep you feeling your best.

Exercise is important for your overall health and happiness. You don't necessarily have to join an athletic club, although it does give you an excuse to go work out, but you do need to do something active, even if only a little, every day for your well-being. Find something you like to do.

Walking is one of the best, easiest, and safest forms of exercise, but there are many creative and fun things to do. Try swimming, jogging, weight-resistance exercise, yoga, tai chi, chi kung, stretching, aerobics, dance, mini-tramp, jumping rope, isometrics, any type of sport, exercise balls, kick boxing, and even housework.

Exercise gets the blood pumping, helps you release stagnant toxins, burns calories, increases oxygen supply, stimulates lymphatic movement, which helps keep the immune system up, builds muscle tone, and helps you maintain your weight, bone density, and strength. It can also make you feel good simply because you are doing something positive for yourself.

Drink Lots of Clean Water

Drinking pure clean water is a very important element in total health. Not feeling thirsty doesn't necessarily mean you have met your requirement for water. Although eating foods with high water content tends to keep your thirst at bay, you still should drink your required eight glasses of water daily.

Steer Clear

Diuretics such as coffee or soda increase your need for water fourfold. This means that for every cup of coffee or alcohol you consume, you need to add four cups of water to your minimum daily intake to prevent dehydration.

Where does that eight-glass figure come from? It's an average. The general formula is to divide your body weight by half, and the total is the minimum ounces of water you need to drink every day. Other factors can increase this minimum, however, such as breast-feeding, hot weather, and increased activity level.

Here are some reasons water is important to health:

➤ The human body is made up of about 70 percent water.

➤ The body can lose three quarts of water per day; this water needs to be replenished.

➤ Drinking enough water daily reduces bloating.

➤ Water washes away waste and toxins from the system.

➤ Water aids assimilation, digestion, and elimination.

Now that you know why drinking water is important, let me tell you why it is important to drink the purest water you can find.

What's Swimming Around in There?

Most tap water is contaminated by some source. Here are some good reasons to filter your tap water:

➤ Chlorine is a chemical added to tap water. The good news is that it kills waterborne critters that can cause typhoid, cholera, and dysentery. However, a study published in the *American Journal of Public Health* a few years ago found that chlorinated drinking water is directly responsible for more than 4,200 cases of bladder cancer and 6,500 cases of rectal cancer every year.

➤ The Environmental Protection Agency has learned that chlorinated drinking water decreases good cholesterol (HDL) and increases bad cholesterol (LDL).

➤ Fluoride is added to most drinking water. There has been great controversy over it. Proponents say fluoride helps build strong bones and teeth. Opponents say that toxic levels of fluorine (the poisonous substance that fluoride is derived from) build up in the body and degenerate the immune system.

➤ Lead can be found in our tap water. Lead has been shown to harm the brain and other systems.

➤ Industrial and agricultural pollutants are now showing up in water supplies. Several years back you might remember the cryptosporidium bug that contaminated chlorine-treated tap water and caused thousands in Milwaukee to become ill. It leaked into the water supply from fecal matter at an upstream dairy farm.

Steer Clear

Don't always rely on chlorine-treated tap water to protect you from water-borne critters. Several bugs are resistant to chlorine, such as the one that causes Legionnaire's disease. Consider installing a filtering system for your water supply.

Clean It Up

Okay, now that I've totally grossed you out, let's talk about how to get clean water:

➤ Buy it. There is a wide assortment of bottled water available these days, and some places let you bring your own container. In some areas you can have water delivered right to your door. Be certain to read your water labels! Believe it or not, companies will bottle simple tap water and sell it as drinking water. Some even add fluoride! Look for pure water or pure spring water, no additives, and if you can find reverse osmosis water that's even better.

➤ At the minimum get a carbon filter for your tap. Carbon removes the chlorine and pesticides and some heavy metals such as lead.

➤ Buy distilled water or make it at home with a home distiller. Distillation involves vaporizing water by boiling it. The steam leaves most bacteria and other pollutants behind. It is then condensed and cooled back to a liquid. However, the water is also de-mineralized by this process, so I suggest distilled water to my clients who are cleansing, but not over the long term.

➤ Sometimes tap water is your only choice, like when you are in a restaurant. Adding a drop of pure essential oil of lemon helps purify it. When you see nitrates floating on the surface (looking like a transparent oil slick), use a straw to drink the purer water from the bottom.

➤ I personally believe that reverse osmosis water is the purest and best tasting. The water is filtered through a pressure vessel with extremely fine membranes that keep out chlorine, fluoride, lead, bacteria, and pollutants.

Don't forget that water is necessary for your health, and you must continue to drink plenty of it. However, you should be aware of tap water contaminants and get purified water whenever possible. Fortunately there are now plenty of options available.

Don't Forget to Breathe

Fresh air is just as important to our health as clean water and good foods. If you are a city dweller, it is not always easy to get clean air. Fortunately your nose and bronchial tubes work constantly to filter particles and toxins from the air that you breathe.

If you work indoors, get outside at least once during the day to take a few deep breaths through your nose, then exhale through your mouth. You will be taking life-giving oxygen into your blood and feel refreshed and rejuvenated. For some great deep breathing exercises, read *The Complete Idiot's Guide to Tai Chi and QiGong* (Alpha Books, 1998) or *The Complete Idiot's Guide to Meditation* (Alpha Books, 1999).

Try to find an area that is not on a busy street. If you are lucky enough to have a spot with some nice fresh air hanging around, go there for your oxygen intake. This daily ritual can be a refreshing part of your health maintenance. You can even give yourself an "air break" like smokers take smoke breaks. A few minutes of centering yourself and taking in some fresh air can be good for the body, mind, and soul!

Adding plants to your environment can help create your own fresh air. If you are in an office, why not put some fresh plants around your work area? The plants breathe carbon dioxide, filter the air, and provide fresh oxygen.

Sprouts of Info

Air filters are a great way to limit dust and pollutants in your home and give many people relief from allergies. Another more temporary solution is to purchase an essential oil diffuser for diffusing fresh pure oils, such as lime or lemon, into the air. These oils can refresh a room quickly and help to limit particles and floating toxins from the air you breathe.

Get a Little Sunshine

Because of the increase in skin cancer, our sun is getting a bad rap these days. I have even seen sunshine listed as a cancer risk factor by some cancer research groups. However, as a holistic practitioner, I refuse to put sunshine on my cancer-causing list. I believe a little sunshine is necessary for everyone seeking a balanced holistic lifestyle.

Obviously anything in excess is not good for you—not even an enormous amount of broccoli! Sunshine is essential to our life. And for many who suffer from seasonal affective disorder (SAD), it is an essential ingredient for happiness. Here are some of the positive effects of sunshine's healing rays:

➤ Sunshine on your skin works with your skin's oils and creates vitamin D. Without vitamin D you could not utilize calcium.

➤ Sunshine helps the body break down bilirubin, or bile. Babies who are born jaundiced are given sunlamp or sunshine therapy to help their bodies break down the excess bile that causes it.

➤ A little sunshine works to stimulate the immune system.

➤ It serves as a disinfectant by killing off some bad bacteria.

➤ A little sunshine on the skin keeps it healthy and helps you maintain a resistance to sunburn when you have to be out for long periods of time.

➤ A few minutes of daylight exposure (without sunglasses) can keep eyes healthy. (Of course, never look directly at the sun.)

➤ Sunshine stimulates the pineal gland in your brain, suppressing the amount of melatonin in your system. Melatonin helps regulate sleep patterns, and its presence makes you sleepy. This explains why some people have a hard time getting up before the sun rises—their melatonin has not yet been switched off by the sun. This is also a key element for those with SAD.

Steer Clear

Filtering out the sun's rays all the time makes the eyes become more and more sensitive to light. I always recommend wearing sunglasses and a sunscreen when outdoors, but consider taking off your glasses for a few minutes every now and then and taking a look around (never at the sun, of course). Your eyes will thank you.

If you have a hard time waking up in the morning, consider keeping your bedroom shades open at night. When the sun comes up, it will wake you peacefully.

The bottom line is don't be afraid of the sun! Take precautions and use the sun in moderation, as with all things. You need about 15 minutes of sunshine every week to make all the vitamin D your body needs. If you want to use a tanning bed to get your dosage of sun, go ahead. Just make sure you wear protective eye coverings.

Consider using full spectrum lighting in your home or office, especially if you tend to get depressed during darker months. Wear your sunscreen when you are out in the sun for long periods, but get out there and see the light of day when you can—it's good for you!

Veggie Soup for the Soul

If you need to get up before daylight, consider a clock that simulates the rising sun by progressively turning up special lighting before you are due to wake up. These lights are designed so they reach their peak at your desired wake-up time, allowing the light to stimulate melatonin suppression in your brain. These clocks, full-spectrum light bulbs, air and water filters, and other products can be purchased through a company called Harmony. You can get a catalog by calling 1-800-869-3446 or visiting its Web site at www.gaiam.com.

Keep a Positive Attitude

All the vegetables, clean water, fresh air, and exercise in the world will not do you a lick of good if you have a miserable attitude. Well, I guess they could make you a healthier miserable person, but your attitude and the way you go about living your life are fundamental to living a good life. If you live resentfully as a vegetarian, you will still be vulnerable to diseases. A bad attitude on the outside is a message that you have negative inner feelings about yourself on the inside.

These destructive thoughts, no matter how you came up with them originally, need to be dealt with so that you can lead a positive, healthy, harmonious life. If there is a lesson you have not learned or refuse to deal with, your body will often manifest unresolved issues as a health condition. You can change your diet, but you have to change your mind to completely overcome and avoid re-creating any disease state.

Toxic Thoughts

Did you know that your thoughts are like records that play in your head and that if they are negative, they can be erased and re-recorded with more positive messages? There are many counselors and self-help experts who can help you change your self-talk and create new recordings. And remember that whatever the mind believes, it manifests in your body as reality.

Negative self-talk is actually a physical toxin. This toxin not only poisons the mind, but your entire body. Toxic thoughts create emotions, and emotions are chemical reactions that take place in your body. These reactions create hormonal by-products that your liver has to filter. If you think about how anger or frustration make you feel, just imagine what they're doing to your poor liver!

Let It Out

The best advice is to continue to work on yourself, foster healthy relationships, and keep an attitude of gratitude for all the good things you do have going for you. Temper your emotions appropriately when in company, but when alone, don't suppress them. This can be as unhealthy as suppressing a cold. When you're sad, cry. When you're angry, yell at the moon. And when you're happy and you know it, clap your hands!

Keep Things in Balance

I stress balance as being the key to all things. Keeping a balance in your life is essential, but of course everyone's idea of balance is different, depending on each person's physical, mental, and emotional needs. For some, exercising five times a week, eating a generally wholesome diet, getting adequate clean air and water, and having a good attitude is balanced.

Others can match that, take the weekends off, have a few beers, sit on the couch and watch TV, and eat a cheese pizza all by themselves and still have balance! What matters is what you do most of the time. This is what shapes your reality, your health, and your entire life.

Just as your spouse or family or friends can forgive you for being a jerk once in a while, your body can forgive you for overeating, drinking too much, or not getting enough exercise in a particular week. Your body is truly an amazing machine that does the best it can with what it has to work with. If you generally fill your life with positive habits, a few bad habits once in a while are going to make little difference in your overall life and health.

The only exception to this might be if you are working on a serious health issue. With a serious or life-threatening illness, you sometimes cannot afford to go off your therapeutic routine until you are strong enough to make occasional exceptions. But overall the body bounces back to the shape it is given most of the time.

Dissecting the Additives in Processed Meats

Now let's talk a little more about toxins and how to avoid them. Specifically let's talk about processed meats. Processed meats include most lunchmeats, like bologna, lunchmeat spreadables, canned meats, and individually packaged, cured, smoked, or otherwise processed meat.

Nitrites are used to cure meat, and processed meats contain them in high levels. According to the American Cancer Society, salt-cured, smoked, and nitrite-cured foods have been linked to esophageal and stomach cancer. (Makes you want to sing, "My bologna has a first name, it's t-o-x-i-n," doesn't it?)

In addition to nitrates, animal products increase your intake of toxins because of the pesticides and fertilizers found in animal feed. The animals are fed chemical-laden foods, and these chemicals build up in their bodies, just like they do in yours. When you eat animal flesh or animal products, you eat these toxins. So, if you really are what you eat, remember that you're also what *they* eat.

The good news is that you are going vegetarian or limiting your consumption of animal flesh. At least I hope I have given you some significant health reasons to go veggie and stay that way. Eating less meat and fewer animal products can significantly lower your intake of the chemicals that increase your risk of cancer.

Toxins and You

If you are already a vegetarian, go ahead and skip this section. But there are a lot of people out there, like my average clients, for example, who aren't totally vegetarian but who want to cut back on their meat consumption and make sure what they do eat is as safe as possible.

Since we know that there are nitrites and other toxins in processed meats that are linked to cancer and that a high-fat, low-fiber diet can increase your risks as well, what's a part-time carnivore to do? I'd like to offer some ideas that will allow you to eat meat occasionally and still keep your risks low.

➤ First of all, seek out organic meat. Yes, there is such a thing. You can find it at most health food stores or request it from your grocer. Organically raised animals have not been fed on pesticide-laden feed. The animals were probably free-ranging and fed naturally on seeds, grass, and other natural food. They are also probably free of antibiotics.

➤ Choose lean meats. This is good in two ways. You lower your fat intake and reduce the toxins you take in since the fat is where most of the toxins are stored.

➤ Avoid processed meats, such as luncheon meats, and instead use organic chicken or turkey breast to make sandwiches.

➤ Choose hormone-free meats. It is hard enough to keep your own hormones in balance without adding hormone residues from animal products. Hormones are injected into farm animals to force their growth and fatten them up more quickly so they bring a higher

Steer Clear

Generally, animals that are free range are not kept in the deplorable conditions that most farm animals are raised in. When in these filthy conditions, animals are subject to a host of diseases, so farmers regularly inject them with antibiotics. When you eat the flesh and products of these animals, you also get some of the antibiotics.

price in the fastest possible time period. You will pay more for meat without hormones, but your health is worth it. (If you eat beef, look for the label "BGH free." BGH stands for Bovine Growth Hormone.)

No Ham, No Foul

One more problem with meat is the by-products that come along with it. Hot dogs, for instance, contain those yummy nitrites, and the FDA even allows a certain amount of animal hair and other unmentionables, such as rat droppings, to be included in the product. If that isn't enough to stop you cold porky, remember that the intestines are a part of the body that processes waste, and they're precisely what is used as a casing for some sausages and hot dogs. This idea is not too appetizing to many people.

Sprouts of Info

Vegetarians who used to like the taste of hot dogs are happy to learn that there is a totally vegetarian replacement made from tofu. These dogs taste just like the real thing without the unmentionables found in flesh-based hot dogs.

Some people think they're better off when they go from pork and red meat to chicken and other poultry. Sorry—poultry is at high risk for contamination with the dangerous bacteria salmonella because chickens and other fowl are fed mass amounts of antibiotics. These antibiotics also kill off the beneficial bacteria that help fight off toxic bacteria. Poultry and eggs therefore become a breeding ground for bad bacteria.

So if you decide to eat meat, remember to do so in moderation and to choose the best organic products you can find. And don't forget to get out after dinner for a nice long walk. Take some deep breaths, and smile at the neighbors. You'll all feel better for it.

The Least You Need to Know

➤ Vegetarians generally have a lower risk for cancer because their diet and lifestyle let them avoid many high-risk factors.

➤ Drink plenty of water daily, but be sure to filter your tap water to eliminate possible contamination.

➤ A balance of sunshine, a wholesome vegetarian diet, exercise, clean water, fresh air, and a positive attitude all are integral to total health and wellness.

➤ Vegetarians lower their toxic chemical intake by avoiding meat.

➤ If you do choose to eat meat occasionally, choose organic, hormone- and antibiotic-free meats to avoid taking in more toxins than necessary.

Chapter 10

Lose Weight, Feel Great

In This Chapter

➤ Find out why not *all* vegetarians are thin

➤ Learn how to get and manage a healthy weight

➤ Understand weight management philosophy

➤ Find your particular body shape

➤ Learn to balance all the factors associated with weight loss

---

"I consider a balanced diet to be a large cookie in each hand."

—Author unknown

Not all vegetarians are lean, and not all meat-eaters are overweight. Everyone has his or her own makeup and body shape, metabolism, and eating habits. But vegetarians who follow a healthful balanced vegetarian diet, eat whole foods, and work a little with food combining, are likely to be slender, as are most occasional meat-eaters who balance their diet and eat mostly vegetarian foods.

If you are ready to slim down and tone up, your new vegetarian diet can help get you there. I'll tell you why and how in this chapter. I'll also help you implement your new diet and give some tips to help you stick to it long enough for it to become your habitual way of eating and living. On top of that, I'll share my philosophy—one that makes it all so simple that you won't want to NOT do it! Promises, promises, you say? Well, you'll have to read on to find out for sure now won't you?

You Are What You Eat

Feeling sheepish about eating that lamb chop now that you know what it's going to do inside your circulatory system? (Baaaad joke, but sometimes I just can't help myself.) Or maybe you skipped all the background material to get straight to what's really important—losing weight! In any case, let's review some of the background information that applies here so you'll understand what's going on when the pounds start to melt away!

In Chapter 6, "Nourishment from the Plant Kingdom," we saw how your body takes the nutrients from foods to create new cells and rebuild tissues, and that the organs and tissues themselves are made of the very nutrients you feed them. For example, your heart is a potassium organ. It is made up largely of potassium and requires foods rich in potassium for its health. Your bones are made largely of calcium and require foods rich in calcium to feed them. Your thyroid is an iodine organ and needs iodine from sea plants, such as kelp, to feed it. And so on.

The point is that the foods you feed your body are what it uses to rebuild your body—you really are what you eat!

Sprouts of Info

By allowing your body to use nutrients more efficiently it will naturally level at an ideal weight that suits you. See Chapter 1, "Why Eat Less Meat?" and look for my suggested colon cleanse, or ask your herbalist or natural health practitioner to help you design one specifically for you.

Extra Energy for Exercise

We also saw in Chapter 6 that the nutrients in plant foods are more easily available to the body than animal products. Not only do plant foods require less digestive energy than is required for digesting animal products, but raw fruits and vegetables and slow-cooked whole grains contain live enzymes, which go directly to your body's cells for nourishment.

If you save digestive energy by eating the majority of your plant foods fresh and raw, your body's metabolism can be spent on keeping you feeling more active. Feeling more active means you have the energy to exercise, which is always an important part of weight management.

Better Absorption Means Smaller Appetite

Then in Chapter 7, "The Digestion Question," you learned that it's not just what you eat that matters, but what your body has the capacity to *absorb* and use to build and rebuild itself and burn for fuel. Absorption can be inhibited by toxins and mucus and debris left in the colon. And debris in the colon and digestive tract tends to accumulate with the consumption of meat and animal products.

If you haven't already started an herbal cleansing to give yourself a clean start on your new vegetarian diet, you might want to do one now, especially if you need or want to lose a few pounds. See Chapter 1, and look for my suggested colon cleanse or ask your herbalist or natural health practitioner to help you design one.

Why is this so important? A good cleansing allows your body to use nutrients more efficiently. This helps it naturally level off at an ideal weight that best suits you. Now let's talk about more reasons why a vegetarian diet helps to keep you trim.

Fat Cow Disease?

In Chapter 8, "Meatless for a Healthier Heart," we saw that not just animal flesh but all animal products, like cheese and eggs, contain a high amount of saturated fat. Saturated fat makes your blood fat, which can lead to heart disease.

But what I was saving up to mention in this chapter is that not only can the fat in your blood adhere to the inner lining of your arteries, but the excess fat that the liver cannot process is stored as body fat and adds to the plumpness of your own fat cells! That is why animal fat makes you fat.

Hold the Water

In Chapter 8 I also talked about meat and animal products containing a high amount of sodium. Excess sodium consumption makes you retain water. Water retention tends to make you look and feel puffy and bloated. This makes you feel or look fat by causing puffy eyes, a full face, bloated abdomen, swollen ankles, and swollen fingers.

Eat More, Weigh Less

Remember our friend Al from Chapter 8? Al was the big guy, a hard worker, who had high cholesterol. We managed to get Al to replace his semi-vegetarian diet with a pure vegetarian diet, which lowered his fat intake level dramatically.

As a bonus, by switching to vegetarian fare, Al was able to eat larger quantities of food that satisfied his appetite, but because they were all vegetarian foods, his calorie intake was significantly reduced. Therefore, Al not only dropped his cholesterol level, he also lost excess weight.

Meat, dairy, and eggs are all concentrated foods, especially compared to fruits and vegetables. They contain heavy concentrations of sodium, protein, calories, and fat. Unless you are a super athlete, your body won't be able to burn off these dense foods adequately. This means that the excess is naturally stored in your body, and the bottom line is more unwanted weight.

Diet Downfalls

Most diets that include meat and other animal products and that actually seem to work are effective because of either of the following factors:

Steer Clear

Sixty to 80 percent of your foods should include foods with a high water content, like fruits and vegetables. Also try to eat only one concentrated food at any meal. A concentrated food is one with little or no water content, including bread, most starches, cheese, and meat products. If you eat this way, you will lose weight naturally.

➤ They utilize proper food combining. By eating only one type of food, for example, all protein, or eliminating one type of food, such as starches, you effectively improve your food combining by default. Food combining will automatically help you lose weight because it improves your digestive and absorption ability. (But if you don't understand the fundamentals of food combining, then you will gain back the weight once you complete the diet.) Food combining is described in detail in Chapter 22, "The Health Nut."

➤ They restrict quantity. (This usually leads to feelings of deprivation and can lead to bingeing after the diet, which of course causes you to put the weight back on.) Anyone can lose weight by cutting back on the quantity of foods he or she eats—it's called starvation.

Most people will eventually go off a restrictive diet and gorge on food only to gain back all the lost weight they struggled so hard to lose!

Veggie Soup for the Soul

Most restrictive diets work by simply cutting out one or more of the major food categories (starch, sugar, fat). These types of diets might help you drop weight quickly and get an initial start on your weight loss, but permanent weight loss is achieved and then maintained by eating a variety of whole fresh vegetarian foods.

You have two choices for weight loss. As a meat-eater or a lacto ovo vegetarian, you can choose to continue to eat meat and dairy, but you will have to eat less often and in smaller quantities than you would being a stricter vegetarian. And you will have to exercise more (to work off the excess fat and calories in your meat and dairy foods).

The second option is for you if you really love to eat (most of us do!). You can choose a mostly vegetarian diet and eat plenty of food! When you eliminate the dairy and meat, your diet automatically lightens up in calories and fat. The more whole, fresh foods you eat, the faster your body will settle at its ideal weight for you.

The choice is yours, although I suggest the latter because for those who love to eat, the vegetarian diet can bring a positive and permanent change in body weight.

Lean, Mean, Primitive Machine

You need to understand a little more about how your body was created to understand why it even has the capacity to get fat. Let's talk a little about natural evolution, and then we'll take a walk back in history to understand why the body does some of the things it does.

This next statement is a biological fact and is not meant as an insult. I'm sorry to have to tell you that the way your body works has not caught up with technology. The human body still works just like it worked for your great, great, great grandma.

The brain sends the same impulses, and the digestive and eliminative systems continue their same old ways. Our hearts beat like our ancestors' did, and so on. Our DNA contains memories that are passed down from generation to generation. These genetic codes, if they change at all, take hundreds of years to show even the smallest changes—a process we call evolution.

Because we are generally a compassionate world, empowered humans do not stand by and watch while others suffer, nor can doctors deny life to those they have the skills to help. Because of these and other factors, the natural course of human evolution is intercepted by human technology. Because of this, DNA is kept in the gene pool that is not necessarily stronger or heartier.

Who's Swimming in the Gene Pool?

For example, those who have a genetically weak organ can have a transplant that can extend their life at least long enough to have a family of their own, therefore passing on their genetic tendency to their offspring. Nature's processes are also changed when those who are naturally infertile are artificially inseminated and have several children at one time.

Now physically weak or naturally infertile people who can afford medical intervention can pay to survive and propagate their genetic material. Of course, left alone, nature would have allowed the person with the weak organ to die and left the infertile to stay infertile, and these traits would eventually be eliminated from the gene pool.

125

The moral implications linked to these scenarios are deeply controversial and can raise emotional arguments in any crowd. But we need to understand that humans can adapt naturally over time when left on their own. It is impossible for humans to evolve naturally while using scientific intervention.

What the heck does all this have to do with weight loss? The bottom line is that our bodies are the same bodies, good or bad (and sometimes worse), than they were when our species was hunting and gathering foods directly from nature. Your brain actually still recognizes good, old-fashioned, whole foods as nourishment for your body. It understands what to do when you pick a ripe peach from the tree and eat it. It doesn't necessarily understand what to do with foods that don't have a trace of nature in them.

Some of the body's reactions to these odd things we eat can make us fat, and I'll tell you why soon. For now, understand that when your body is fed what it needs (assuming your digestive system is clean), it can utilize it. When your system is regulated because of proper absorption and a diet of whole fresh foods, you will crave only the amount of food (fuel) that you burn for that day. Therefore what you eat will be utilized instead of stored as fat.

Hunting for a Meal Deal

Now that we hunt and gather at the grocery store, picking out the brightest packages filled with processed denatured foods, it doesn't mean that your body has changed its nature or its primitive basic need for real whole foods from nature.

What has changed is what, how, and when we eat. There are all kinds of extra things in our modern diets that we call "food." We now deal with more than 2,000 chemicals, such as additives, preservatives, food colorings, flavorings, and flavor enhancers, not to mention the chemicals that are sprayed on crops and fed and injected into farm animals! Our processed foods are denatured and then re-injected with so-called nutrients that have been produced from coal tar derivatives.

We are not necessarily evolving by adapting to these chemicals. Instead we are getting ill, becoming obese, creating cancer and heart disease, and becoming undernourished even though we are overfed. We then take medications and have surgeries to "correct" these problems, when a change in our diets could help reverse and change these problems permanently.

A natural cure would be in line with natural evolution. Then we would pass on genetically stronger material to our offspring, and they would be more adaptable, and so on. Instead we get liposuction and tummy tucks and continue to eat an unnatural diet. As it is now, the weaknesses we inherit from the "sins of our forefathers" are harder for us to deal with than they would have been if our forefathers straightened out their diets. Our weaknesses will get worse as we hand them down the genetic line through our offspring.

The bottom line is to take control of your health now, not only for yourself but for your offspring. Do what you can naturally to feed your body the things that keep it and make it strong, and you will enjoy not only your ideal weight, but you and your genetic line will have a greater shot at health!

Feast or Famine?

Another thing you need to understand when attempting weight loss is that your body is primitive in that it genetically still "remembers" times of famine. This is exactly why you cannot starve yourself by severely restricting your calories and achieve permanent weight. Let me explain more thoroughly.

Steer Clear

Food manufacturers use specific colors and packaging on products to stimulate your brain to purchase them. Being aware of this stimulation helps keep you in control. Just because a package is green, which is generally associated with "health foods," doesn't mean it is good for you. When purchasing processed foods, always read your labels. If there are more ingredients on the list that you don't recognize than ones that you do, consider a whole food instead.

In the past, primitive peoples didn't get to run to a grocery store. They had to forage and round up what was needed and what they could find. Sometimes they would have to go long periods without food. Primitive people's bodies learned how to store food energy for long periods.

Your body has kept this amazing ability to store reserves of food. Unfortunately, it isn't very discriminating. It can also hold onto toxins, fat, waste products of all kinds, mucus, chemicals, excess water, and so on.

This fact is key in understanding why dieting and severely limiting calories for periods of time does not work for long-term weight loss. When the body detects that famine is setting in, it slows down your *metabolism*. When your metabolism slows, you naturally burn fewer calories, your energy levels decrease, and your body holds on to your foods for longer periods. You can think of it as your body rationing out the fat because it believes famine has set in, and it wants to make every calorie last as long as possible. Your body actually believes you are starving, and it is trying to help you survive.

Lettuce Explain

Metabolism refers to the ongoing interrelated chemical activities in your body that process and provide the energy and nutrients to sustain life. Your metabolism is controlled by glandular activities in your thyroid, adrenals, and pituitary glands and can be slowed or increased depending on how your glands perceive the needs of your body. A slow metabolism can be linked to weight gain.

Sprouts of Info

Remember that your body is not your enemy. It wants what is best for you and does what it can to keep you alive. Your body works hard to keep you going despite the abuse and neglect it withstands. A little body awareness can help anyone become thinner and healthier just by paying attention to what it is trying to tell you.

Stuck on the Plateau

So, although you might initially lose weight by severely restricting your calories, your body slows down and plateaus rather quickly. When you restrict your caloric intake, you do something unnatural because you make an effort to hold back from eating. You eventually go back to eating the amount you are comfortable with. No one can live with restrictions forever—it is just too tense a way to live.

The bad news is that while you were restricting your calories, your body got ready for a famine. Now every time you eat, your body quickly grabs all the calories and hoards them for later! Suddenly you are back to the weight you were. And once you can no longer live with the restrictions and go back to consuming the amount of food you did before, you quickly get even heavier because your body is waiting for the next famine.

Reverse Training

You have effectively trained your body to *lower* the amount of calories you are able to survive on effectively. Therefore, if you go back to the amount of food you used to eat, there is a good chance you will gain weight consistently.

So how are we going to change this vicious cycle? The good news is that you can retrain your metabolism by allowing yourself to eat as many wholesome fresh vegetarian foods as you want on a consistent basis. By eating primarily vegetarian fare, you naturally keep your quantity of food up but your calories—along with fat and other elements you don't need—at a moderate level.

My Body, My Strife

By incorporating the philosophies in this chapter, you'll soon be enjoying your life as a slender vegetarian. But first let's talk about body awareness and how to spot your body type. We all can't look like Cindy Crawford or Kevin Costner, but we can look our best by being healthy and fit. Most people agree that a healthy body is the most attractive.

Let's figure out your general body shape. There are a few different varieties. Understanding yours will help you see what your ideal body would look like if you were at your healthiest weight.

➤ If you have a thyroid body shape, you tend to be tall, thin, and very slender all the way up and down. This is the typical model body we see in designer clothing at fashion shows. At your thinnest, you can appear too thin; at your healthiest, you can look like a supermodel.

➤ A gonadal body shape is like a pear, with an emphasis on shapely hips and buttocks. Even at your thinnest, you will have curves on the hips, thighs, and derriere, which is considered one of the most attractive (and common) feminine shapes.

➤ An adrenal shape holds the weight on top and all around the trunk area. Women with this shape tend to have large busts, small bottoms, and usually broad shoulders. Linda Carter, the model and actress who played Wonder Woman on TV, exemplifies this shape. Men with this shape have strong upper bodies and spindly legs.

➤ The pituitary type tends to be petite and slender, with a large head and big attractive smiles. They usually are young looking and gain weight evenly around the whole body. Martin Short, Michael J. Fox, and Farrah Fawcett are examples.

You are born with a basic body shape, and no matter how little meat you eat, you won't be able to change that. You can, however, work with it and accentuate your best features.

Fake Foods

Nothing shows me more clearly how conditioned a person has become to the manipulation of advertising and the media than when I see someone who sincerely desires to lose weight pass up snacking on a banana and a handful of raw nuts because of the perceived fat content. This same person, however, reaches for a denatured highly refined and processed, but fat- and sugar-free chocolate cookie!

This does you no good! In fact, that cookie is a paste to your internal system. And guess what? The flour products and other chemicals it contains are going to turn to sugar in your system anyway, and the unused sugar is going to turn directly into fat!

Steer Clear

Although a strict diet of animal products makes you fat, wrecks havoc on your circulatory system, overloads your system with acid which causes calcium loss, throws your mineral balance out of whack, and makes you constipated, excessive carbohydrates can make you just as fat as eating a strict diet of animal products! The difference is how the body metabolizes these items.

The fats and sugars from the banana and nuts are whole foods, in correct balance with nature, and your body can use them as fuel. The fake food merely tricks the body into feeling full. You will just feel hungrier later because your body hasn't gotten what it needs and will prompt you to eat again.

Watch the Pastabilities

Let's talk a little about refined carbohydrates and weight loss. Refined carbohydrates include pasta, rolls, bread, muffins, cookies, pancakes, cakes, pies, and other flour-based products. Eating excessive amounts of them makes your insulin shoot up, causes blood sugar problems, creates mucus in your intestines which inhibits your nutrient absorption, and makes you fat.

Those who tout high-protein diets are right about the carbohydrates and starches causing obesity. On the other hand, those who blame weight problems on meat and animal products are also right. No wonder everyone is out there trying diet after diet and still winding up fat!

The true lasting answer lies in the middle. I just love the middle ground, and that's where plant foods are found. Whole foods are the median, the balance if you will. You cannot eat a well-rounded, plant-based, whole-foods diet and become obese. I really don't believe it's possible.

The weight loss food pyramid.

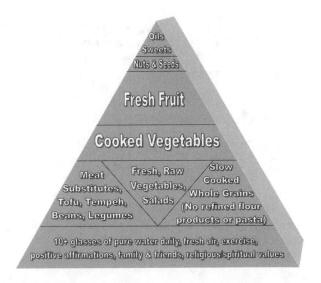

Make sure your food pyramid looks mostly like this one if you are trying to lose weight. All you need to do is leave out animal products and replace pastas and refined bread products with whole grains. If you get hungry, fill up on beans, fatty fruits such as avocados, fruit that goes through your system more slowly like bananas, and a handful or two of cashews!

If you happen to be an athlete and are getting ready for an event, loading up on carbohydrates like pasta and other refined flour products should be not only okay, but great for you. Because these carbohydrates turn into sugar, you are going to get a lot of energy from them—energy you'll need to keep going! As long as you use up this sugar energy, your body won't have time to store it as fat. The bottom line on the pasta is this: active, yes; couch potato, no.

Feeling Porky? Forgetaboutit!

Letting yourself lose weight is another key to losing weight. Anything that is forced creates a tension. Just like a rubber band, tension always snaps it back to its original shape. If you are striving and working hard to lose weight, you may achieve it. But—and you knew there was a "but" coming, didn't you?— what happens when you reach your goal and your "tension" snaps back or worse, breaks?

If it snaps back, you go directly back to your old habits and wind up with the same body (or fatter) than you had before you started creating your tension. If it breaks, you could be left with associated health problems caused by your over-the-top attempt at weight loss. The middle ground, nature's way, is the way you were meant to live.

Your body wants to be healthy for you. It doesn't want to be fat, working to filter out all the abuse you give it.

Accentuate the Positive

You can work to make your body shape its best by not trying to change its basic shape, but by working with it. This is how I believe you will get permanent results. All you need to do is fill your life with the positive things we've talked about in this book. You can begin adding these things slowly or all at once—it doesn't matter. Do what makes you feel the most comfortable, and you won't create tension.

You know that exercise is important in health and weight management, so add it to your life if you haven't already. Begin by taking a walk every day. Is that easy enough? If not, start by doing 10 sit-ups every day. And try the food replacements listed in the following table.

Sprouts of Info

You have two hands for feeding yourself, which is perfect because your stomach can accommodate only about two handfuls of food at a time. If you eat more, it can inhibit your digestion, like an overstuffed clothes washer inhibits how clean the clothes get. When you eat, see if your meal would fit in two hands. If not, you're probably overeating!

Steer Clear

Mentally or physically forcing yourself to fit an ideal image that is not possible works against you by creating tension in your life. Tension must always be released or illness results.

Instead of trying to give up the things you know are bad for you, keep adding good things until one day you find that there is no room for the bad. At some point, something has to go. I'm betting it will be your old eating habits, and your excess weight along with them.

Fill Yourself Up with the Good Stuff Replacements

The Good Stuff	Replaces
Water	Soda
Fruit	Candy
Vegetables	Dairy products
Tofu	Meat
Rice, soy, or nut milk	Cow's milk
Egg replacer	Chicken eggs
Whole grain	Refined flour products
Rye crackers	Flour-based crackers and bread
Exercise	Inactivity
Positive affirmations	Negative self-talk and excuses
Bulk kelp and/or capsicum	Table salt
Stevia, honey, molasses	Sugar
Eating lots of high water-content foods	Starving yourself
Whole foods	Refined carbohydrates (pasta, flour products)

Here's how it works. Let's say you add a gallon of water to your diet every day. You have to drink so much water to get that gallon down that you find that you have no room or thirst left to drink your usual afternoon soda.

Then add two pieces of fruit every day. You know you have to eat fruit on an empty stomach and alone, so you eat a piece as soon as you get up. This means you skip the cereal under your banana, and you just don't have room for that Pop Tart. You want to get your next piece of fruit in before dinner while your stomach is empty, and darn—that just killed your appetite for a candy bar!

To create a new good habit, choose one thing and do it consistently every day for at least 30 days. Once that one's a habit, choose another good thing to do the next month.

Building Good Habits

Do you see how it works? Of course you can do this with not only diet, but with exercise, positive thoughts, good relationships, and so on. As you continue to fill your life with all the good things, you have no room for the bad! You would have to create tension just to shove down that piece of cake, really!

Remember that I promised you an idiot-proof philosophy on how to lose and maintain a healthy weight? Did you miss it? If so, I'm going to sum up here, and then at the end of the chapter I'll give you 10 simple, practical things you can do to get and stay trim as a vegetarian. Here are the things to keep in mind when you want to lose weight:

➤ Don't fight to be thin. Let yourself become thin by making better food choices.

➤ Fill up your life with positive healthful choices that will eventually crowd out the not-so-healthy ones.

➤ Understand that you are what you eat and eat that way.

➤ Eat all the veggie foods you want and avoid the processed foods. The more whole foods you eat, the happier you'll be, and you'll be able to keep your metabolism burning!

➤ Get familiar with your body type and envision yourself at your best.

➤ Always choose whole foods over processed foods, even if the natural food seems to contain more calories or fat.

A Commitment to Yourself

And finally, all good things worth working for require commitment. Commitment gets and keeps you at your desired weight. With a strong desire, you can commit yourself to almost anything and get there! If you can conjure up enough desire to want to lose weight and feel good, you can certainly be the weight you want to be and live in the body that you want to live in.

Use that desire to start yourself on the right track. Then, after you get to where you want to be by using my replacement method, your life will be so filled with positive things and foods, there won't be any room left for the bad things. You won't be able to gain weight unless you try! And that's a subject for a more advanced book on the psychology of weight loss.

Here's a handy-dandy reference list to use when you are working on "letting yourself be thin."

The Ten Keys to Weight Loss as a Vegetarian

1. Make 60 to 80 percent of your foods high-water content foods, like fresh fruits and vegetables.

2. Eat only one concentrated food at any meal. Concentrated foods include most starches (bread, pasta, potatoes) and foods that do not contain much water. All animal products and most proteins (beans, tofu, nuts, seeds) are considered concentrated foods.

3. Avoid refined carbohydrates such as breads and crackers.

4. Eat only two handfuls of food at a sitting and stop eating at least four hours before bedtime.

5. Exercise.

6. Drink plenty of clean water. Divide your body weight in half to figure out how many ounces you should get daily and add more when you're losing weight or cleansing.

7. Don't force or rush yourself to lose weight! Let yourself be thin by adding more and more good foods and good things to your life. Let yourself evolve over time naturally.

8. Understand your body type and work with it.

9. Don't starve yourself. You'll just mess up your metabolism.

10. Good self-talk is just as important as healthy habits. Wake up each morning and ask yourself, "What positive things am I going to do today to achieve my goals?"

The Least You Need to Know

➤ Effective weight management must be a balance of wholesome foods, exercise, adequate water intake, and a positive attitude.

➤ Everyone has a basic fundamental shape that cannot be changed, but a fit body of any type is an attractive body.

➤ It is most effective to make lasting or permanent changes in your body by allowing yourself to evolve by slowly incorporating good things into your life, which wind up crowding out the things that are bad for you.

➤ Vegetarians must avoid loading up on refined carbohydrates such as flour-based products and pastas, which can turn easily to fat in a sedentary person. Instead, fill up on fruits and vegetables to maintain perfect weight.

Chapter 11

The Beauty of Being Vegetarian

In This Chapter

➤ Discover what being a vegetarian can do for your skin

➤ Understand why it is best to build muscle with plant protein

➤ Learn why vegetarians smell good

➤ See why a plant-based diet helps your mood

Can being a vegetarian make you beautiful? Well, if nothing else, it can certainly make you healthier. So far you've learned that meat and animal products can lead to heart disease and cancer, obesity, constipation, and lethargy. This doesn't sound like the profile of a beautiful person, does it?

The good news is that you've also learned that a diet consisting of mainly plant foods gives you energy, can help keep you at your ideal weight, and can provide lots of nutrition to help maintain health. Let us discuss why and how all of these things can make you look and feel even more beautiful.

You Have the Skin of a Vegetarian

Whether or not beauty is only skin deep, the skin is still your largest organ and needs proper care. Although you probably take your skin for granted, it is a living, breathing part of you that serves to protect your insides from invaders and deserves to be taken seriously. Besides, the health of your skin reflects how it looks, which affects your appearance.

Let's talk a little bit more about the functioning of the skin so you get an idea of how and why it does some of the things it does. Your skin, first and foremost, is a protective organ that holds the body together. Your bones, ligaments, and all the rest are nicely gift-wrapped in flesh that makes up about 12 percent of your body weight. The human body is like a hermetically sealed living container. When the skin is punctured in any way, the body is at risk for infection because of its exposure to the outside elements.

Veggie Soup for the Soul

Some spas offer sea salt exfoliation treatments, and you can also do this at home. Here's a favorite: Mix some olive oil, Epsom salts, and, if you like, a few drops of your favorite essential oil in a bowl. Step into an empty bathtub. Take a handful of the salts and, beginning at your ankles, rub the salt mixture into your skin using a circular motion. Work your way up to your neck. You can finish off by soaking in the tub, or simply rinse off in the shower. Your skin will be left soft and glowing.

In Chapter 1, "Why Eat Less Meat?" I told you that you have new skin on the palms of your hands every 24 to 48 hours. That's pretty quick work. The skin is one of the fastest organs to recuperate because of its importance in protecting your insides.

Let's take a look at what happens when you accidentally cut yourself.

➤ Blood flows to the site to flush out any foreign debris.

➤ Your immune system cells rush to the area to fight off foreign invaders, such as bacteria, that could cause infection.

➤ Your body puts out a call for nutrients, such as calcium and zinc, to provide the skin cells with the raw materials they need to repair the damage.

All that for a little paper cut! Your body is amazing, isn't it?

Feed Me, Heal Me

The skin heals quickly, but it requires nutrients to repair the damage. Under normal conditions the skin needs a daily supply of sodium, silicon, zinc, and many other nutrients to maintain its health and integrity. When damaged, it needs extra calcium and zinc, along with antioxidants such as vitamin C, bioflavonoids, beta-carotene, and vitamin E with selenium.

The antioxidants help to inhibit free radical damage that occurs anytime you are injured or have trauma to the body. Vegetables and fruits are excellent sources of antioxidant vitamins. Green leafy vegetables, nuts, and seeds provide plenty of calcium as well. Herbs such as plantain, horsetail, and oatstraw are all rich in nutrients that feed the skin and can be used to help facilitate skin healing and maintenance.

Vegetarians Get Bioflavonoids

In addition to the fuels the skin needs for repairing itself quickly, your skin, as a living organ, needs its own nourishment. This leads us to another area where being vegetarian can benefit the appearance of your skin.

First of all, plant foods like fruits and vegetables contain phytochemicals called *bioflavonoids,* which give the plant's skin strength and integrity. In your body, bioflavonoids have many purposes, including nourishing and strengthening the cellular walls of the tiny blood capillaries found throughout your body. These fragile blood vessels need bioflavonoids to help keep them from breaking or leaking blood.

Lettuce Explain

Bioflavonoids are phytochemicals found mainly in the rinds of citrus fruits and in the edible skins of most other fruits, such as grapes and apples. They play a role in strengthening the capillaries and serve as antioxidants.

Broken blood capillaries, also called spider veins, look like tiny red or purplish colored splotches on your skin. They can be anywhere, but many people find them on their legs, nose, and cheeks. Delicate skin and areas where skin is exposed to the elements are more vulnerable to broken capillaries.

By eating lots of fresh fruits and vegetables with the skins, you will certainly get plenty of bioflavonoids, which can help you avoid weakened blood vessels. Weakened blood vessels can cause you to bruise easily and can produce unsightly broken blood vessels that make your skin appear blotchy.

The extracts of grape seeds and maritime pine bark have been found to contain high concentrations of bioflavonoids, known commercially as pycnogenol (proanthocyanidins). Therapeutic doses of this supplement have been used to help restore blood vessel integrity, which can eliminate the problem of bruising easily, can slow down or stop broken blood vessels, and can even help repair eyesight and some forms of hearing impairment. Ask your herbalist or vitamin specialist for their recommendation on this supplement.

Skinny Dripping

Your skin also is an eliminative organ and is sometimes thought of as your third kidney because it eliminates a waste product known as perspiration to advertisers and sweat to the rest of us. Sweat is made up of the same constituents as your urine, that is, mainly urea, which is a digestive by-product of protein.

137

Animal flesh and most animal products contain very concentrated protein. When the body is forced to break down excessive amounts of protein on a daily basis, the urea tends to build up in the system. Your kidneys work hard to process, filter, and eliminate this waste as urine, and your skin picks up the excess that the kidneys can't handle and eliminates it through the skin's pores.

When the skin is not able to eliminate the excess urea, the waste tends to clog up your skin, causing it to look dull and flaky. If urea continues to be held back from proper elimination, it tends to settle back into your tissues, and cause or at least aggravate an overly acidic body condition. And you remember what acidity does to you from Chapter 5, "Supplements for the Vegetarian," don't you? It causes your body to leech its own calcium away from your bones, weakening your overall structural system.

Eating a diet high in plant foods won't overload your kidneys or your skin with all this urea, and you won't have to worry about creating all that excess acid and losing calcium because of your diet.

Veggie Soup for the Soul

The skin's breathing capability is hindered somewhat when covered by clothing. This is especially true for those of us in colder climates who have little skin exposure during winter months. I don't advocate walking around naked in public, mind you, but just so you know, wearing clothing does tend to keep skin less active.

Don't Forget to Brush Your Skin

Whether you have just started to incorporate a plant-based diet into your life or have been a vegetarian for a while, your skin could still be clogged from years of eating too much protein. Here's a tip to give your skin a jump-start to health. Dry skin brushing is one of the simplest, easiest, most inexpensive things you can do to benefit your skin, whether you eat meat or not!

Dry skin brushing can be done by almost everyone to rejuvenate the skin and benefit circulation. You can purchase a skin brush at most health food stores. The brush bristles need to be made from natural vegetable fiber, not plastic or other synthetic materials because these could damage your skin. Most dry skin brushes have a long wooden handle so you can brush your back.

Every day before you bathe, use your skin brush and brush your skin in small circular motions, starting with your feet and working up toward your heart. Avoid brushing your face with this brush. If you choose to skin-brush your face be sure to seek a soft-bristled, dry-skin brush specifically designed for your face.

A Quick Brush Up

Brushing your body should take about two to five minutes. At first your skin might be sensitive to the brush, and you will have to be gentle. After a few weeks of brushing, you will find you can tolerate more vigorous brushing. Some of my clients tell me that now that they are in the habit of brushing before their shower, they don't really feel clean unless they brush first!

To see how effective this dry-skin brushing habit can be, stand on a dark piece of material while you brush. When you are done, take a look at the pile of white flakes you created on the material. These white flakes are uric acid buildup that you've effectively removed from your skin's surface. Brushing while in the shower is not as effective because wet skin brushing tends to pull and stretch the skin. Brushing before you shower is best.

Sprouts of Info

By the time a person is 70 years old, he or she has eliminated about 40 pounds of dead skin!

Glowing Good Health

Besides taking a uric acid load off your kidneys, skin brushing stimulates circulation to the skin. More blood flow brings more nourishment, and when skin is better nourished it becomes healthier. Skin brushing also has the effect of stirring up your oil glands, which are just under your skin. The oil glands help turn sunshine into vitamin D, which is needed to help your body break down and utilize calcium.

After a few weeks of daily skin brushing, you will probably find that you won't need skin lotions anymore. Your skin's oil glands will be activated, your layers of dead tissues will be exfoliated, blood supply to the skin will be increased, and your skin will look glowing and beautiful. Now you'll not only save money on your grocery bill from not purchasing meat, but you'll also save a bundle on skin lotions and have glowing skin to boot.

Greasy Kid Stuff

I mentioned that your skin contains oil glands. These glands help to lubricate your skin to keep it young, glowing, and supple looking. But if you have too much fat and oil in your system due to meat and dairy consumption, these extra fats can cause a greasy complexion that can easily break out with pimples.

139

The extra fat from a meat-based diet can clog your system with sludgy, oily substances and might contribute to overactive oil glands, which cause acne. By eating a vegetarian diet you are going to have lots of variety and less than half the amount of greasy oils that you get from eating meat and cheese. Overall, the vegetarian diet helps keep your skin from being too oily, so there's another reason a plant-based diet can help you have better-looking skin!

Eliminate the Negative

Because your skin is an organ of elimination, it is always on call to help take up the slack from your other elimination channels, which include the bowels, the respiratory system, and the urinary system. So, for example, we saw how too much animal protein in the system produces extra uric acid, which causes the kidneys to work hard. Whatever the kidneys can't handle gets thrown off via the skin.

Excess fat from animal products forces the liver to filter out the excess cholesterol it produces to attempt to keep the blood clean. The skin is a reflection of the condition of the blood. If the blood is toxic due to an overburdened liver or constipated intestinal track, the skin reflects these toxins through rashes, boils, dullness, acne, pimples, and other skin conditions. The blood continues to carry toxins until they can be eliminated via an elimination channel or until the toxins settle in to a weakened body organ.

Toxic Traffic Jam

Overall, meat and animal products can clog up your eliminatory channels. Because the skin serves as the closest eliminatory channel to the blood vessels, when the colon or other organs are clogged up, waste products build up in the blood stream and your body uses the skin to throw off these excess toxins.

Fruits, vegetables, and grains provide plenty of fiber and help to keep your digestive system and eliminatory channels moving along. Therefore, a vegetarian diet doesn't lead to constipation or a clogged system, which can lead to skin eruptions and autointoxication (a toxic condition caused by the buildup of wastes).

Hot Dog You Have Nice Buns!

So now you have clean, vibrant, fresh-looking skin because of your vegetarian diet and daily skin brushing. Beautiful! But you want more. You want to begin working out and sculpting your muscles to a more desirable shape. As a vegetarian you'll be glad to know that there are several body-builders, some of them world champions, who have been or still are vegetarians and vegans.

You've learned that a vegetarian diet can help keep you slender because it contains fewer calories and fat than a meat-based diet. It also helps regulate metabolism and helps the body to release its own excess fat stores. Lean is okay, but now you are thinking about getting buff. Okay, okay, let's talk about building a muscular body on plant food.

Toning Those Muscles

In Chapter 2, "Smokin' the Meatless Myths," I talked about how plant foods provide all the protein your body needs to build and repair muscle, so you know you've got the raw material you need. Next, the best way to get toned and build large muscles is through proper weight training.

Weight training creates a demand on your muscles. With properly controlled lifting, your muscles strain under the pressure. Then, as they recover and repair, extra muscle tissue is built where the muscle was strained to compensate. With a body building program, the amount of weight you lift is gradually increased and your muscles respond by becoming bigger and stronger to deal with the heavier weight.

Extra muscle building requires protein (amino acids) to build new and repair damaged muscle tissue. What does this mean to the vegetarian working on building his or her body? You might want to increase your intake of protein-rich foods, such as soy, when you are weight training seriously. Extra calcium to balance the increase in protein is also a good idea.

When you weight train, your best bet is to eat right after you finish a workout. Remember, most of the protein-rich foods, although they are vegetarian foods, still go through your digestive system more slowly because they take a little longer to process. If you eat a lot of protein just before a workout, you might find yourself feeling a little tired or generally bogged down since much of your energy is concentrating on digestion. But don't try to work out when you are hungry. Listen to your body. It will tell you when you need food.

Workout Fuel

A few carbohydrates just before a workout help many athletes feel good throughout their training. A few examples include a bagel, a cup of cereal with rice milk, a banana and a handful of raisins, and a strawberry soymilk smoothie.

The body begins to repair itself immediately after you are done with your workout, so it can be helpful to replenish your stores of proteins as soon as possible. Some protein-rich vegetarian foods include hummus spread and sprouts wrapped in a wheat tortilla, a banana and a handful of cashews, a peanut butter and jelly bagel, a bean taco and guacamole tostada, and a falafel ball sandwich in pita with tomato sauce.

Remember that it is very easy to get too much protein in your diet. If you work out regularly to maintain health at the gym, your protein requirements are just about the same as a fairly inactive person. (See Chapter 2 for a list of protein requirements.) If you are a serious athlete, your need for protein might be double that of the average person. Talk to your trainer, who should be knowledgeable in this area.

B.O. No Mo

I remember when one of my clients came into my office incensed with what had just taken place at her gym. Apparently, after a vigorous aerobics class, everyone began their floor exercises. A man in the class stretching nearby leaned toward her and quietly said, "You know, you could really eliminate that body odor if you gave up eating red meat." My client was taken aback and of course appalled. But it did make her wonder why her body odor was so terrible, especially after a workout.

Let's talk about how meat can contribute to body odor. I've said it before and I'll say it again, meat and animal products are generally constipating. Constipation leads to a toxic blood stream. The blood uses the skin as an elimination channel, and when the blood is toxic, these toxins can get released through the pores of your skin. And they don't smell like roses.

Lettuce Explain

Halitosis is bad breath and can be caused by constipation. Constipation can be caused by eating animal flesh and dairy products.

Hey, Meat Breath!

Another way meat eating can add to body odor is in the form of bad breath. A toxic, constipated body continues to circulate toxins until it finds an open elimination channel. Bowel toxins that are not eliminated and that continue to circulate through the body can wind up going to the lungs for elimination, creating *halitosis*—the nice term for bad breath.

Colon cleansing has cleared up many bad cases of bad breath. And it is not usually a problem for vegetarians who eat plenty of vegetables, fruits, and grains because these foods are not commonly associated with clogging the bowel. If your colon is clean and you still have bad breath, see your dentist for possible dental problems. Bad breath can also stem from an acidic sour stomach, which can usually be corrected with diet and supplements.

Burning Toxic Fat

Another reason for bad breath in meat-eaters is that most meat contains concentrated toxins in the fat found in the tissues of an animal. When you eat the flesh, you get the toxin-laden fat, and your body has to process these chemicals. When you work out strenuously you burn fat, which releases the toxins that have been stored in your own fat. The result can be malodorous sweat.

And finally, remember earlier when I said that one of the elimination channels is the respiratory system? The lungs and sinuses are part of that system. The respiratory system gets rid of gaseous wastes. It also eliminates waste products that your body surrounds in mucus (phlegm). Mucus is laden with toxic materials and can be odorous as well.

Veggie Soup for the Soul

Liquid chlorophyll can be a great addition to your drinking water if you have halitosis or body odor. Chlorophyll, which is the green stuff in plants, is a natural deodorizer for your body. It detoxifies the blood and helps your body process toxins in the blood stream and bowel. Parsley is another good detoxifier. Try a fresh sprig of parsley after a meal to freshen your breath. Parsley is sometimes used with garlic to mask the garlic odor. It is also a great cleanser for the kidneys, and when you clean your eliminatory channels, you smell better overall.

Beauty and the Beef

I have two final words on going meatless for beauty reasons: energy and prostaglandins.

Prostaglandins are hormone-like substances found in the oils in meat and animal products. As humans, we make our own prostaglandins, which play a role in regulating our hormone levels and reproductive cycles, among many other functions. Sometimes an imbalance of prostaglandins throws off your own hormone levels, and in women, this can create a phenomenon known as premenstrual syndrome.

Symptoms of PMS can be exacerbated by eating meat and animal products because of the high fat content. An imbalance of hormones can cause water retention, inflammation, and swelling, which can all make you feel miserable. A vegetarian diet can help balance hormones by reducing or eliminating the problem with excess dietary fat.

Lettuce Explain

Prostaglandins are hormone-like substances that are made by fatty acids and have functions that include controlling smooth muscle contractions and regulating body temperature and inflammatory responses. They also play a role in controlling blood pressure, blood clotting, and water retention. Their balance is important in preventing PMS.

143

If you are a lacto vegetarian who suffers with PMS, consider limiting your intake of all cheese and dairy products for 1 week to 10 days before your period. By cutting your fat intake your hormones might have a chance to balance themselves, and you will be spared some discomfort.

We know that beauty is in the eye of the beholder, but when you are bogged down, lacking energy, and feeling sluggish, you probably aren't feeling vibrant enough to let your inner beauty shine through. By eating life-giving vegetables, fruits, grains, nuts, and seeds, you can help yourself gain back your energy and allow your inner beauty to shine! As a vegetarian who lives on a wholesome diet, you will feel lighter and more vibrant, and you won't have to worry about smelling bad or having constipation-related skin blemishes. You'll naturally be leaner and bright-eyed and will suffer less from PMS. There's no doubt about it—all those things add up to help you be your most beautiful self.

The Least You Need to Know

➤ The skins of fruits and vegetables contain bioflavonoids, which give strength to the tiny blood capillaries, which can help prevent broken blood vessels.

➤ Dry skin brushing is a great way to help your skin eliminate uric acid, regain suppleness, and gain new vitality.

➤ Heavy weight lifters and serious athletes may need almost double the vegetable protein of the average person who works out regularly.

➤ Vegetarians rarely suffer from body odor because their plant-based diets are not constipating and are not filled with toxic fats that can smell when released through perspiration.

➤ A vegetarian diet can help you overcome PMS because it eliminates the excess hormones found in a meat-based diet that can add to or create moodiness and other PMS symptoms.

Chapter 12

Fishing for Health

In This Chapter

➤ See why some people choose a pescatarian diet, and discover what that means

➤ Learn to choose fish wisely to avoid food poisoning

➤ Discover some of the health risks associated with seafood

➤ Learn about the benefits of plants from the sea

This chapter is divided into two sections. The first has information for the pesco, or fish-eating, vegetarian, and the last half provides ammunition for those who want a reason not to eat fish. If you are a pescatarian or thinking about being one, you will probably like the first section better.

You will find some tips on what to look for in purchasing and cooking your fish and shellfish. These tips will help you to avoid getting ill from the many hazards that accompany eating sea creatures. The second half covers the cons associated with fish consumption. Read the whole thing and decide for yourself.

The Benefits of Seafood

Let's start by discussing fish; later we'll get into shellfish. Fish are commonly divided into two categories: those that have both fins and scales, and those that don't. Fish with fins and scales are the ones most commonly eaten, partly because of various cultural preferences and partly because of the health benefits associated with them. Most freshwater fish are in the fins-and-scales category. The saltwater fin-and-scale species tend to be the deep-water fish that live farther away from the polluted shores. Fish with both fins and scales (white-meat fish) include the following:

➤ Anchovies	➤ Herring	➤ Smelt
➤ Bass	➤ Plaice	➤ Trout
➤ Cod	➤ Pollack	➤ Tuna
➤ Haddock	➤ Salmon	➤ Whitefish
➤ Halibut	➤ Sardines	➤ Whiting

Examples of seafood without both fins and scales, which are not highly recommended for consumption, include:

Sprouts of Info

The Bible is very specific about which types of seafood to eat and which to avoid. Deuteronomy 14:10 states, "And whatsoever hath not fins and scales ye may not eat; it is unclean unto you." And from Deuteronomy 14:9: "These ye shall eat of all that are in the waters: all that have fins and scales shall ye eat."

➤ Dogfish

➤ Eel

➤ Shark

➤ Shellfish (including shrimp, oysters, clams, scallops, lobster, crawfish)

➤ Sturgeon

➤ Swordfish

➤ Catfish

Fishing for Health

Many people eat fish simply for its taste appeal, but others associate fish consumption with better health. Some nutritionists and other health advisors have touted the benefits of eating more fish and less red meat because fish generally contain less fat than land-dwelling animals. It's also easier for your body to digest and provides dietary protein.

Fish and seafood in general contain less calories than land animals. On top of that, the flesh of fish contains natural oils, especially the Omega 3s, that have been shown to be beneficial to your circulatory system, nervous system, skin, hair, nails, and immune system.

A Lighter Choice

Fish is a lighter choice overall for those phasing out red meat and other animal products from their diet. Generally, fish is served with a grain or vegetable and makes a light meal. A typical dinner that includes fish, a salad, and a green vegetable is a good example of proper food combining, which aids your digestion and can keep your weight in balance (see Chapter 22, "The Health Nut," for more on food combining).

This lightness is especially true when you compare it to a typical meat meal of a steak and baked potato or a cheeseburger with French fries and a milkshake. If you eat fish that has been battered and deep-fried in oil, however, the fat and grease far outweigh any health benefits associated with fish consumption. A deep-fried fish sandwich can contain more fat and calories than a double cheeseburger!

Overall, if you are a pescatarian who eats mostly fish from the white-meat category and avoids eating deep-fried fish, you still have an advantage over the typical meat-eater because you will eliminate many of the animal fats from your diet and you won't take up as much digestive energy as you would on a land-animal diet. In general, seafood is also a rich source of iodine, which nourishes your thyroid gland. The thyroid regulates your metabolism and energy levels.

Safe Fishing

If you are going to keep fish in your diet, you'll need to know how best to shop for it and to cook it to avoid the food-borne hazards associated with seafood consumption. We'll discuss that yummy subject right after I show you what to look for when purchasing fish.

When selecting fish, test for ...

➤ **Smell.** If the fish smells fishy, it has probably begun to decay and should not be purchased.

➤ **Appearance.** If a fish appears dull, lacks sheen and color, or has loose scales, pass it up.

➤ **Feel.** A fresh fish should seem as if it is fresh out of the water. Its flesh should spring back when you push on it, its eyes should be clear, not cloudy, and its scales should be smooth and firm with everything intact.

Steer Clear

If you are a fisherperson and want to catch and consume your own fish, you might want to check with your local health department to ensure that the waters you are fishing are safe for harvest. Some areas are contaminated and not posted.

If the fish you are considering for purchase does not have all the freshest features, don't buy it. Don't risk illness. If you want more details, finish (or at least troll) the rest of this chapter for more info; otherwise, take my word for it.

Here are some safety tips on preparing fish at home:

➤ Make sure raw fish dishes, such as sushi, has been frozen solid for at least 60 hours and then thawed.

➤ When defrosting seafood, keep it cold. Do not allow seafood to defrost at room temperature. Keep it in the refrigerator or put it in the sink under cold water until thawed.

➤ Cook fish thoroughly and properly. Avoid microwaving fish because microwaves don't usually cook foods evenly. Fish is properly cooked when the thickest part of the meat becomes opaque and it flakes easily with a fork.

➤ Prepare cooked and raw foods separately. Don't share cutting boards or knives, for example. Sanitize your food workspace after it has been exposed to raw food.

Finally, now that you know all the precautions when purchasing and preparing fish at home, make sure you shop and eat at reputable markets and restaurants where you know the strictest precautions are taken. If you aren't sure, order the vegetarian meal instead!

Catch and Release: The Cons of Fish

You probably are aware of the cons involved with some kinds of fish, such as being surrounded by great white sharks while swimming out in the middle of the ocean! But that's not the type of hazard we'll discuss here. Instead, we'll stick with your dietary choices and their consequences.

I want you to have the health information you need about fish and also to be aware of some of the ethical concerns vegetarians have that compels them to exclude fish from their diets. Then you can decide if these reasons are convincing enough for you, too.

Drowning Some Worms

Let's first address why you need to be so careful with fish. In a nutshell, the precautions you should take when choosing, fishing for, and preparing fish have to do with avoiding poisoning by the bacteria and toxins that are prevalent in fish and other seafood, and with avoiding parasites, especially in raw fish.

Proper storing, freezing, thawing, and cooking of fish usually kill most of the parasites and bacteria, such as tapeworm, anisakine larvae, and flukes. However, even fish cooked thoroughly in a microwave has been found to contain live worms. It is believed that worms can survive cooking because microwaves do not cook food evenly.

Even some types of food processing fail to kill parasites. Live larvae have been reported in pickled herring sold in supermarkets (yuck)! Parasites can also be transmitted easily through the consumption of dried, salted, or raw fish.

The *Anisakis simplex* is a worm that measures about a half-inch long and is found mostly in the stomachs of seals but can also be transmitted to humans via sushi. Its symptoms mimic symptoms of stomach cancer or appendicitis and can lead to a false diagnosis of these conditions.

Just a Fluke

Liver and lung flukes, as well as tapeworm and the eustrongylids worm, are very prevalent in the Orient, where raw fish is a big part of the diet. These infections are becoming more prevalent in the Western world as sushi becomes more popular.

Unfortunately, there are at least two toxins that are not affected even when you cook fish properly. *Scombroid poisoning* can occur if you eat fish that hasn't been properly refrigerated and has begun to decay. After the scombroid toxin has had the opportunity to form in the muscle of an improperly chilled fish, it cannot be eliminated, even when the fish is properly cooked. Scombroid poisoning is most commonly linked to mahi mahi, tuna, bluefish, swordfish, mackerel, and bonito.

Steer Clear

Although you can get parasites from processed or cooked fish, if you eat raw fish, such as sushi and sashimi, you dramatically increase your chances of parasitic infection.

Toxic Pond Scum

Ciguatera is another toxin found in fish that cannot be eliminated via proper handling or cooking. It is caused by eating fish contaminated with the ciguatoxin. This toxin is produced by microscopic organisms that grow on the surface of marine algae. The poison gets into reef fish when they feed on the algae, and then the toxin accumulates in the fish that eat them.

It is most commonly found in red snapper and barracuda. Other fish reported to carry it are mullet, gray snapper, solider fish, goatfish, blue snapper, and Moray eel. Those most at risk for ciguatera poisoning are people who consume the eyes, guts, eggs, liver, or brains of fish, where the toxin seems to concentrate.

Lettuce Explain

Scombroid poisoning occurs from eating fish that has not been completely or properly refrigerated and that has had the chance to begin decomposing. **Ciguatera** poisoning occurs mostly in reef–dwelling fish from tropical and subtropical climates, and the toxin *is* spread up the food chain.

This poisoning causes cramps, vomiting, diarrhea, burning sensations in the mouth and throat, and numbness, and it can affect the nervous system, heart, and respiratory system. Symptoms can last for weeks in some people.

A Few Words for Flipper

If health concerns aren't enough to send you flying from the sushi bar, you need to know about some of the ethical concerns many vegetarians have about how commercial fishing affects our seas and other animals of the water.

Many people began to change their minds about eating tuna when the media revealed that tuna fishermen were sacrificing hundreds of thousands of dolphins annually for the sake of harvesting it. Humans generally have a soft spot for dolphins, which are intelligent, warm-blooded mammals who have historically maintained a benign and often playful relationship with humans.

Dolphins' favorite food happens to be tuna fish, and the two species are often found in the same areas. When fishermen cast their nets into the seas, dolphins can get tangled in them. Because dolphins are mammals and breathe air, many struggling dolphins are drowned in their struggle to free themselves.

This was enough to make pescatarians, vegetarians, and meat-eaters of all sorts eliminate tuna from their diets. In addition, those who wanted to continue to consume tuna guilt-free created enough demand that some responsible companies began offering tuna in cans labeled "Dolphin-Safe." Look for this on your labels and if you can't find it, call the manufacturer and ask them why not!

Another animal that is needlessly killed as a by-product of fishing is the sea turtle. Sea turtles wind up killed in mass numbers when shrimpers cast their funnel-like shrimping nets. The gentle sea turtles are tangled up in the nets and die. Sea turtles are becoming an endangered species.

Another reason many vegetarians object to eating seafood and fish is the environmental impact that fishing takes on other animals and the environment. Even ecologically conscious fisherpersons who do not directly pollute the water by throwing their personal trash overboard occasionally snag their fishing line, causing them to leave behind hooks, lines, sinkers, and lead weights.

Fishing lines and hooks can and do get tangled around the legs, wings, beaks, and necks of sea life, such as birds, seals, otters, turtles, and the animals that prey on these animals. Lead weights add to the heavy metal contamination of the waters, and currently the MTBE additives found in gasoline from boats are destroying marine life at an alarming rate.

Bacteria That Won't Float Your Boat

The earth's water supplies, from the oceans to the rivers and streams, are continually being contaminated. Contamination comes indirectly and directly from industrial waste products, human waste and sewage, oil spills, acid rain, and runoff from agriculture, city streets, mining operations, and landfills.

Sometimes bodies of water harbor such a high bacteria count that designated swimming beaches are barricaded off and shut down because they are deemed unfit for humans to swim in. What about getting your food from these waters? If it's no good for you to be in, why should it be good enough for you to eat from?

Heavy Metal

Beyond the living food-borne hazards like parasites and bacteria, we also have another factor to deal with when eating fish—the mercury and other toxic heavy metals found in the bodies of fish. Here's a sampling:

➤ Chemical fertilizers

➤ Chemical pesticides such as DDT

➤ Heavy metals such as lead and mercury

➤ Industrial by-products and chemicals such as dioxin and Polycholorinated Biphenyls (PCBs)

All these chemicals are known carcinogens.

The problem with eating fish is that fish are higher up the food chain than many organisms in the waters. Heavy metals build up in the food chain. When a fish eats contaminated plant materials and other contaminated fish and organisms, its body absorbs the toxins, and on up the food chain it goes. By the time you eat the fish you are getting toxins from a number of sources, all in a highly concentrated form!

Toxins tend to hang around for a long time. Although PCBs were banned in 1972, for instance, they can still be found in measurable amounts in the bodies of fish today.

Mercury is a highly toxic material that causes mental disturbance through damage to the nervous system. It is sometimes found in high concentrations in fish where the water has been contaminated with industrial waste via leakage. Mercury can cause birth defects and damage kidney and liver functions.

Mercury is used in film processing and is found in factory smoke and other industrial output. If you are worried about keeping mercury out of your diet, eliminate fish and all animal products. Land

Sprouts of Info

The State of New York closed off some areas of the Hudson River to commercial and recreational fishing due to high concentrations of PCBs that had been dumped into the water by an electric company. Although the dumping was discontinued in 1977, fisherpeople can no longer fish for trout or striped bass in these areas.

Steer Clear

If you are trying to avoid toxic metals in your diet, you are on the right track by going vegetarian. Many of the fish that are harvested are ground up into animal feed for farm animals. Even if you don't eat fish, you might still be getting its toxins indirectly through animals that you would never dream were eating fish, such as cows, pigs, and chickens.

Sprouts of Info

If you suspect any type of poisoning from the food you've eaten, call your local poison control center immediately. Also, keeping a bottle of activated charcoal in your medicine cabinet can be a lifesaver. Activated charcoal absorbs poisons and can help to pull toxins out of your system before they can become fatal.

animals are often fed fish from toxic waters that have been ground and added to animal feed, which continues the toxic build-up through the food chain.

The Tumor Rumor

Another reason to avoid consuming fish is the high incidence of tumors found in them. A healthy body cannot harbor tumors, but with the amount of pollution the fish have to live in these days, they are now vulnerable to more and more illnesses. Why consume anything less than vibrant and healthy foods, especially if you are what you eat, and you're eating to live?

Hey, Aqua Farmer!

One way to avoid all these polluted water toxins and still eat fish is to purchase your fish from aquatic farms. These farms raise fish in controlled environments that are not subject to the toxic pollution that occurs in natural bodies of water. You also avoid the ethical problems associated with deep-water harvesting.

But you're not out of the water yet. Although seafood from aqua farmers is a better choice overall, you are still subject to other toxins that fish farmers incorporate into these environments, including the addition of antibiotics and fungicides to the water to control aquatic weed growth.

When it comes to limiting the amount of toxins you ingest, your best bet is eating organic foods only. If you must eat fish, get them from an aquatic farm source.

Feeding on the Bottom

Some people refer to shellfish and other bottom-feeding marine life as nature's undertakers. They earn this name due to the fact that most shellfish, including shrimp, scallops, lobsters, clams, oysters, and muscles, feed on toxic waste and are found to grow best in areas that are contaminated with human sewage.

Our environment certainly benefits from these types of critters because they help clean up contaminates, viruses, and other bacteria from our waters. I've never seen any evidence that shows that we need to consume these bottom feeders in order to remain healthy. But you certainly might be in danger of contaminating yourself with viruses and toxins if you consume the critters that feed on them!

For example, clams that are subjected to contaminated water are found to have a 60 percent higher concentration of contaminants than their surrounding environment.

Typhoid fever and hepatitis outbreaks have been associated with consumption of raw oysters and clams, not to mention the bacteria and other larvae found on the outside of these creatures.

Here's just a partial list of toxins linked to shellfish that you don't have to worry about when you are a vegetarian:

➤ *Vibrio vulnificus.* A bacterium that causes severe illness and is fatal in 50 percent of its victims. Contamination can occur in shellfish or fish.

➤ **Cholera.** Caused by the organism vibrio cholerae. The infection can be fatal and can be contracted by ingesting seafood.

➤ *Listeria monocytogenes.* Bacteria found in raw shrimp and other seafood. Contamination occurs when these foods are eaten raw or partially cooked. Flu-like symptoms occur in most cases; these symptoms can turn fatal in those with weakened immunity.

➤ **Norwalk virus.** A virus that mainly attacks the intestinal system, causing diarrhea and vomiting lasting from 12 to 60 hours. Contamination has been linked to clams and other shellfish, especially when eaten raw.

➤ **Hepatitis A.** An infection causing inflammation of the liver due to fecal contamination. Infections can occur through eating shellfish that are harvested in waters where there is a high coliform count.

➤ **Paralytic shellfish poisoning.** Caused by ingesting shellfish containing microscopic organisms called dinoflagellates. This poison is resistant to cooking and causes numbness in the mouth, abdominal cramps, flu-like symptoms, and at worst paralysis and death.

Veggie Soup for the Soul

When you use a sponge to wipe up your dirty kitchen counter, would you squeeze the water from that sponge into a bowl and drink it? Of course you wouldn't. But this is in effect what humans are doing when they consume creatures that feed on elements unfit for humans, such as shrimp that thrive in waters contaminated with human waste. These bottom feeders are known as nature's undertakers. They serve as catalysts for the decomposition of organic matter, just like the maggots that thrive on rotting food and bacteria. For your health, try to consume foods that don't feed on wastes.

Sprouts of Info

You can purchase kelp in bulk and use it to replace your salt shaker. Kelp is rich in sea salt and is a good source of iodine. Use it to give a salty flavor to your foods.

Vegetables from the Sea

Okay, now that you are thoroughly grossed out about fish consumption, don't forget there are some good things you can get from the sea that can give you nourishment without the toxic side effects. That's right, it's vegetarian seafood, such as sea salt, kelp, dulse, Irish moss, and other edible algae and vegetables.

Remember, though, to be just as careful about where you get your marine vegetables as you would be with your fish. If, for example, you are taking kelp or dulse therapeutically to support your thyroid gland, make sure you are getting your herbs from a manufacturer you trust. A reputable manufacturer can assure you it harvest its kelp from nontoxic waters and helps you limit your toxic intake and increase your health. Plant foods, as well as fish and other marine creatures, tend to soak up the toxins from their environment.

The Least You Need to Know

➤ Fish contains a rich source of Omega 3 oils known to be nourishing to the body.

➤ When properly chosen and prepared, white-meat fish can be a healthy alternative to red meat.

➤ Fish and other seafood serve as a breeding ground for parasites.

➤ Toxins in seafood are concentrated as you go higher up the food chain, and many of these toxins are not eliminated even when the seafood has been properly cooked.

➤ Improperly grown, handled, and prepared fish and seafood are a common source of food-borne illness, food poisonings, and parasitic infections, and they can even cause death.

Chapter 13

High Ho the Dairy, Oh!

In This Chapter

➤ Learn about the health risks connected to eating eggs

➤ Discover why drinking milk doesn't actually make strong bones

➤ Find out how dairy products can lead to poor health

➤ Learn why dairy can make you fat

➤ See what substitutes you can use for dairy and eggs

This is the last chapter in Part 3, "Veggin' Out for Your Health," and the last chapter where we'll look at the health concerns connected with consuming animal products. Hopefully by now you've learned that plant proteins are superior to animal proteins, that vegetables, grains, fruits, legumes, nuts, and seeds are very nutritious, and that you can survive quite comfortably on those alone. This chapter lets you in on the health risks associated with eggs and dairy.

As a past ice cream lover myself, this information was hard for me to swallow (Ben and Jerry *were* my friends!). If you are going to eat dairy and eggs no matter what, you might spare yourself the information contained herein. If you want some information to help you decide whether to limit or eliminate eggs and dairy, read on.

Because I hate to leave you with egg on your face but nothing in your frying pan, I'll also give you a list of egg and dairy substitutes you can use to help you make a simple transition from egg to eggless and from dairy to nondairy. I do suggest that you enjoy your favorite decadent milkshake before reading this chapter because I'm not sure you'll have the desire for one again. Just remember, after your system is cleansed of animal products and you are on a wholesome vegetarian diet, you'll probably lose your taste for eggs and dairy products anyway. And you'll look and feel great! So what are you waiting for?

Too Chicken to Eat Eggs?

You might be too chicken to eat eggs when you realize that the shells of eggs are a breeding ground for *salmonella* bacteria, which causes many violent episodes of food poisoning every year. The eggshells get contaminated with this bacteria in many ways, including contact with chicken feces. Although most people discard the eggshells, contamination occurs if any part of the egg comes in contact with the shell when the egg is broken open.

Steer Clear

Raw eggs and their shells carry salmonella, which causes acute illness. Did you ever accidentally drop an eggshell into the cake batter after you cracked it? Even if the yolk wasn't carrying the bacteria, you probably contaminated the batter with the eggshell. Don't let your kids lick the bowl or spoon when making foods that include raw eggs.

Even if you are careful when handling raw eggs and their shells, you still might not be protected from salmonella poisoning. Researchers have discovered a new evolved strain of the salmonella bacteria that is found in the egg yolk itself.

The problem with salmonella is compounded when the carcasses of dead chickens carrying the bacteria are ground up and added to chicken feed. This bacteria is continually circulating inside and outside of the chickens and their eggs.

Which Came First, the Salmonella or the Egg?

Salmonella is effectively killed by thoroughly cooking eggs or chicken. Unfortunately the poisoning does not always come from the eggs themselves. (This brings up another rhetorical question, which to cook first, the chicken or the egg?) The most prominent problems occur when food handlers touch a contaminated eggshell and pass it on to other food.

Contamination is also transferred via cutting boards where eggshells or chicken flesh have been. And of course you can get salmonella poisoning by eating egg containing products that are not cooked thoroughly enough to kill the bacteria. Mayonnaise and potato salad are frequent trouble spots.

Getting a Rise Without Eggs

Okay, so you don't want to use eggs anymore. How can you make your cake rise? Here are some simple substitutes to use in place of eggs for cooking:

➤ Ener-G Egg Replacer. This product is a powdered mix and can be found where health foods are sold. One box is the equivalent to about 120 eggs and therefore lasts a long time. Furthermore you don't need to worry about it spoiling like eggs would!

➤ A half of a smashed ripened banana can be used in cooking to give stickiness to your baked goods.

➤ One teaspoon of soy flour mixed well with 1 tablespoon of water can substitute for one egg in baking.

➤ If you like eggs for breakfast, try tofu scrambler, a dry mix you add to tofu to make it similar to scrambled eggs. Add some chopped peppers and onions and fry it up. Yummy.

Lettuce Explain

Salmonella is a bacteria commonly found in and on eggs and in and on poultry products, such as chicken. Three types exist. The two common strains of salmonella cause the food poisoning called salmonella gastroenteritis, which creates acute symptoms such as diarrhea, cramps, fever, and vomiting, and can be fatal for immunosuppressed individuals. A third type of salmonella is responsible for typhoid fever.

Got Milk? Got Osteoporosis?

Canadians and Americans eat more dairy products than any other country and also have the highest incidence of osteoporosis. Could there be a link to these two facts? Milk contains a great deal of protein in the form of casein. Casein, as we discussed in Chapter 3, "Defining Meatless," is a group of proteins derived from milk and dairy products. Eighty percent of the protein in milk is made up of casein, and it is the chief ingredient in cheese. It is a remarkably sticky substance that is also used as an adhesive for wood bonding!

Animal products provide too much protein in the diet, and milk and other dairy products have the same effect as meat as far as protein goes. Remember that protein cannot be stored in the body, and the kidneys must filter the excess. Too much protein in the diet is directly related to calcium loss, and according to Michael Klaper, M.D., three to four hours after you drink a glass of milk, you will urinate calcium from your body. That's something to think about, especially if you are relying on your daily intake of dairy products to prevent bone loss.

Sprouts of Info

Calcium feeds the bones when it is made available to the body through a proper balance of minerals. Protein contains high amounts of sulfur, which promotes calcium loss in the body. You need to take in about 16 mg of calcium for each gram of protein you consume. This balance occurs naturally in most green vegetables.

In addition, you know that your body requires a great deal of HCl to break down and digest animal protein. You put more demand on your body's glands to produce HCl when you consume animal products because of this excess protein. Did you ever use milk therapeutically to calm an overly acidic stomach? If you have you know from experience that milk is a very alkaline substance and actually has the capability to neutralize your stomach acid.

A Viscous Cycle

Are you seeing the cycle? Here's the scenario: For lunch you eat a grilled cheese sandwich and wash it down with a glass of milk. Among other things you have just ingested a lot of dense protein (cheese) that began the stimulation of HCl in your gut. Then you drink the milk (more dense protein), which enters the stomach and neutralizes the acid, forcing the stomach to work harder to produce and release more acid. This situation is made even worse if you drink milk throughout a meal, which constantly suppresses your digestive acid.

Just like any machine, your body acts mechanically (in addition to being influenced by your mind, of course). When you do physical things that over-stimulate any part of your body by forcing it to work harder than it was designed for, you wear it out more rapidly. A worn-out digestive system can lead to digestive problems. Digestive system problems are commonly found to be a root cause of other ailments, such as malabsorption, allergies, arthritis, asthma, Candida, and obesity.

Veggie Soup for the Soul

Mother's milk is the perfect food—for the species it was designed for. For instance, the high amount of protein and fat found in cow's milk is great for a rapidly growing 64-pound newborn calf designed to grow to a full 1,500 pounds in adulthood within 24 months. Human milk is the only milk designed to be the perfect food for a 5- to 10-pound human baby who takes 18 to 21 years to grow into a 100- to 250-pound adult. Nature had figured this out for us long before the dairy farmers told you differently—cow's milk is for baby cows.

Milk vs. Veggies

If the dairy industry wants to advertise the health benefits of milk, it should steer away from making the point that cow's milk nourishes human bones. Let's look at some examples of how the ratios of calcium to other elements in milk compare to the ratios in a green vegetable. You'll see that although calcium and protein are abundant in milk, the balance of the other factors contained in milk, the ones that make calcium *usable* to your body, are way out of balance. Take a look:

➤ A glass of whole cow's milk contains:

291 mg calcium

34 mg magnesium

228 mg phosphorus

370 mg potassium

8.0 mg protein

➤ A cup of raw broccoli contains:

42 mg of calcium

22 mg magnesium

58 mg phosphorus

286 mg potassium

2.6 mg protein

Sprouts of Info

Lightly steaming your green vegetables begins the breakdown of their cell walls and brings out the calcium, making it easier for you to absorb. Steam broccoli just until it turns bright green, but no longer. Further cooking results in nutrient loss.

Keeping in Balance

To keep your body functioning correctly, you need a balance of minerals. Balance is naturally maintained in natural foods and becomes lopsided when we eat foods that nature didn't intend us to eat or that are overly processed by humans. Too much or too little of any element in the body leads to health concerns. Too much of one type of mineral might inhibit how you utilize calcium and can even cause calcium loss. A lack of another vitamin or mineral can make calcium ineffective to your body.

The message is clear: Health cannot be maintained by dosing yourself with one mineral or another (unless of course there is a deficiency). Health is maintained by getting a balance of foods, which naturally occurs when you eat natural plant foods, but not with processed foods or animal products. Foods that are naturally balanced help keep your body more balanced.

Minerals for Your Bones

Following is a list of some of the major minerals essential for bone health. You've probably seen the new DRIs (Daily Reference Intakes) on labels for certain minerals and vitamins. The DRIs are taking the place of the old Recommended Daily Allowances because the DRIs take into account age groups and specific categories.

The new recommended intakes come from the Institute of Medicine and the Food and Drug Administration, two big organizations that set the guidelines for the suggested daily intake of nutrients. We are using them here to compare the recommended ratios to each other. We'll use milk and a green vegetable to compare numbers.

Let's take a look at the recommended intakes. For every 1,000 mg of calcium daily you should also be getting about ...

➤ 350 mg of magnesium.

➤ 1,000 mg of phosphorus.

➤ 2,500 mg of potassium.

➤ For every 1 gram of protein eaten, you should be getting 16 times the amount of calcium in milligrams.

Keep in mind these numbers are general averages and are for either male or female adults over age 30. Everyone's needs vary depending on age, activity levels, sex, and diet.

Veggie Soup for the Soul

Of what ilk is your milk? Goat's milk is the closest in composition to human milk, and therefore is better accepted, digested, and utilized by the human body. Goat's milk has been successfully substituted for mother's milk for infants who, for whatever reasons, are not breastfed or who have an allergy to soy formulas.

Good to the Last Drop

Just in case you were wondering which foods contain lots of calcium, here's a condensed vegetarian list:

➤ Nuts and seeds, especially sesame seeds and walnuts

➤ All greens

➤ All unrefined cereal grains

➤ Sea vegetables such as kelp and dulse

➤ Carrots

➤ Beans

To sum up the dairy and bone health issue, don't rely on it to be your source of calcium. Instead, consider taking a calcium or other multimineral supplement from a plant source. If you are a strict vegetarian, you'll get plenty of calcium along with the other minerals you need in a balanced ratio through your plant-based diet. You might also consider an herbal supplement to make sure you get the recommended 1,000 to 1,200 mg daily.

Growing Hair in All the Wrong Places? No Whey!

If salmonella poisoning and osteoporosis aren't enough to motivate you to cut back or eliminate dairy and eggs, then you'll be happy to learn about another health concern over these foods.

The meat and dairy industry is a business—a business that might not be too interested in your health, although the ad campaigns might lead you to believe otherwise. The bottom line in big business is profits. Profits are made in the dairy industry by selling volume. Volume in the animal industry means more weight. And what is the best way to increase weight? Again, by manipulating nature.

Sprouts of Info

Research has found that there are an average of about 600 million somatic cells (pus cells) in each quart of cow's milk. To help clean up this problem, the Dairy Industry is getting on the herb kick, and has found that feeding garlic, a natural antibiotic, to cows reduces the pus count dramatically. Now there's a natural solution!

Hormones are messengers that constantly send signals through your body to regulate your sex drive, digestion, moods, sleep, reproductive cycles, growth, and maturity. Their balance is also involved with your weight. Hormones are such a deep subject that we cannot afford the space here to go into them in detail. However, just as the minerals in your body need to be in the right ratios for your body to utilize them properly, hormones also need balance. In fact, the hormone equilibrium is much more delicate and therefore more easily thrown out of whack than minerals and vitamins (as some victims of PMS will certainly attest!).

Good for Agribusiness

Here's the bottom line on hormones and why agribusiness benefits from their use:

➤ Cows are given hormones to manipulate their natural hormone balance to create more milk.

➤ Pigs are given hormones to induce rapid growth and to produce fatter pigs, which are sold for slaughter by weight, not by how much healthy lean meat they have.

➤ Poultry such as chickens, turkeys, ducks, and other birds sold for slaughter or used for the production of eggs are given hormones to make them fatter and heavier and to make them produce more eggs.

You might want to consider that the human female's pituitary gland creates hormones that circulate throughout her body to control the production of breast milk. The same holds true for other animals that produce milk, including cows. These hormones are found not only in their milk, but in muscle tissue as well.

Steer Clear

Cow's milk contains hormones that are secreted by the pituitary gland of the cow. These hormones are not necessarily destroyed through the pasteurization and homogenization process that milk is put through before it reaches your table.

Hormones Everywhere

Excess hormones can be found in not only the muscles and fat of animal flesh, but in eggs, milk, cheese, yogurt, sour cream, ice cream—all milk-based products. How do these animal hormones affect our own hormones?

If you have ever taken any type of hormone, including steroids, estrogen replacement, birth control pills, or cortisone shots, you know that it takes only an infinitesimal amount to create a dramatic change in your body, not to mention your emotions.

You can imagine how even a small amount of residual hormones ingested through dairy products and eggs could make a dramatic difference in your health and moods. An imbalance of hormones in your body can …

➤ Create accelerated maturity in young children or adolescents.

➤ Aggravate or increase sexual maturity in adolescence.

➤ Cause excessive hair growth.

➤ Cause abnormal or excessive facial whiskers or hair in both sexes.

➤ Add to feelings of depression.

➤ Make you feel aggressive.

➤ Cause you to feel overly emotional.

With our already stressful world, why would we want to add to the discomfort by feeding ourselves excess hormones that can cause us to feel things that don't serve us?

Antibiotics for Breakfast

Antibiotics found in eggs and dairy products are another concern for individuals who consume them. Just like hormones and bacteria, the medicines given to farm animals can be found in their eggs and milk.

The problem with ingesting too many antibiotics, directly or indirectly, is that antibiotics are indiscriminate. They have the effect of changing your body's flora and bacterial balance because they kill off good and bad bacteria at the same time. (Boy there is a lot of balancing going on in your body isn't there!?)

You need a certain amount of good bacteria, such as acidophilus and bifidophilis, both on your skin and inside your body. These good bacteria serve to keep the bad bacteria in control by eating up toxins and feeding off the waste products that naturally occur in your system. Without the proper bacteria in and on your body, your immune system is disarmed. One of your body's first lines of defense against foreign invaders is bacteria.

Taking antibiotics, whether indirectly through the food chain or directly via antibiotic medications, lowers your resistance to bacterial bugs, such as salmonella, which is widely found in animal products, eggs, poultry, and meat. This could make you more susceptible to bacterial food poisoning.

Let's say you have just finished your antibiotic prescription, then you eat a cheese omelet that happens to contain a tiny amount of active salmonella bacteria. After you eat the infected food, the salmonella finds no resistance in your small intestines because of your previous antibiotic use. Where there was once a nice population invader-fighting bacteria, salmonella now has the opportunity to populate your intestines freely and rapidly. This means you will become violently ill for 7 to 10 days—and you will probably be treated with more antibiotics.

Steer Clear

Antibiotics found in animal products add to the problem of recurring illness because they inevitably do not kill all bacteria. The survivors then mutate and become resistant to the antibiotics that were once used to control them.

Sprouts of Info

Consider substituting a tofu scramble, hash browns, and a soy sausage patty for a big egg and dairy breakfast to avoid excess antibiotics in your diet. An egg omelet with cheese, toast with butter, and a glass of milk can overload your system with antibiotics, protein, fat, sodium, and animal hormones!

Cow to Buck the System

Now remember, as if we didn't have enough to complain about already, dairy products and eggs contain a concentrated amount of other unhealthful stuff, like fat and sodium, even without all the chemical additives.

Not only does dairy contain high amounts of the fats that contribute to obesity and heart disease, it also contains excessive sodium, rating second only to the sodium content in animal flesh. Excess sodium in the diet is known to raise the blood pressure in sensitive individuals.

Furthermore, most dairy products are subjected to a process called pasteurization. Pasteurization kills bacteria that can cause disease, such as some strains of salmonella that can cause typhoid fever. That's the good news. The bad news is that pasteurization also kills the good bacteria that we need in our bodies to keep these bad bacteria at bay. To make matters worse, the pasteurization process subjects milk to high temperatures, which kills the natural enzymes necessary to health and digestion.

Lettuce Explain

Listeria monocytogenes is a bacteria that can be found in and on dairy products, poultry, and eggs. Listeria poisoning is termed listeriosis, and symptoms include headache, nausea, fever, and vomiting and can be potentially deadly to those with a weak immune system, including the elderly, those with immune system diseases, and young children.

Passing on the Cheese

The cold, moist environment that many cheeses and other dairy products are kept in is, unfortunately, an ideal breeding ground for the bacteria *Listeria monocytogenes,* and soft cheese is an excellent carrier for the food-borne illness it causes, called listeria. This bacteria has even been linked to milk and ice cream that was contaminated after pasteurization.

Speaking of cheese, here's another thing to be aware of. Unless specifically labeled, most cheese contains an ingredient called rennet. Rennet is usually derived from the stomach lining of calves, cows, or sheep and is used to coagulate cheese products. Many lacto vegetarians seek rennetless cheese. It's a bit softer usually, but worth bypassing the gut ingredient. Alta Dena makes a rennetless cheese. Check your labels.

Eating Dairy and Eggs Safely

To sum up I guess you can see that dairy and eggs have their bad side. Still, daily consumption of eggs and dairy is common among Americans and Canadians and throughout Europe. This can lead to digestive disturbances, allergies, constipation, hormone imbalance, immune system dysfunction due to ingesting antibiotics found in these products, bacterial and parasitic infections and/or poisoning, calcium loss, obesity, high blood pressure, and heart disease.

So what can you do, especially if you don't want to be a strict vegetarian? Here are some tips to make your life easier and more healthful if you choose to continue eating dairy and eggs:

Sprouts of Info

Excess fat in the diet is linked to a host of health problems. The top three sources of fat in the North American diet, in order of their fat content, are meat, egg yolks, and milk.

➤ Take the American Dietetic Association's suggestions for consumption of these items. Limit your intake of eggs to three to four yolks per week. Try to use low or nonfat dairy products.

➤ When choosing cheese, eggs, yogurt, and other dairy products, purchase those produced by hormone-free, pesticide-free, organically fed, free-ranging animals. Read the labels. If the product label does not clearly say otherwise, you can count on it containing at least trace amounts of pesticides, hormones, and antibiotics.

➤ Avoid getting food poisoning by taking all the precautions for proper food handling, cooking, and preparing your dairy and egg products. Avoid eating raw eggs.

➤ Choose rennetless and/or raw cheese products.

Those of you who have ethical concerns about dairy and egg production can skip ahead to Chapter 27 for more info on that aspect of the ovo lacto equation. Consider the options and make your best choices. Then, in the next section of the book, get ready to launch your new diet—and a new you!

The Least You Need to Know

➤ Dairy products and eggs are breeding grounds for bacteria that can cause food poisoning, such as salmonella and listeriosis.

➤ Green vegetables provide a much better ratio of calcium to protein and other minerals than milk products, making plant-based calcium easier for your body to utilize.

➤ Traces of hormones and antibiotics can be found in dairy products and eggs, which can lead to hormonal imbalances and immune system difficulties of your own.

➤ Eliminating dairy and egg products from your diet will help you naturally eliminate excess dietary fat, protein, and sodium, which have all been linked to health problems.

Part 4

Starting Your Meatless Lifestyle

At this point you should now be convinced that switching to a mainly vegetarian diet is good for you. Hopefully you have learned that you will not only be satisfied by your new way of eating, but that you'll probably feel better, avoid diet-related ailments, diseases, and the many food-borne illnesses associated with animal products. You will even be more likely to lose a few unwanted pounds.

Now that you are informed, this next section gets you started incorporating your new change into your home life. We'll walk through making a game plan, going shopping, and cooking at home. You'll even get some ideas for some of my most excellent vegetarian-based meals. Yum! Let's get started.

The First Bite: Where's the Beef?

Well, I hope by now you've decided you're ready to give meatless a try. Maybe you're still feeling a little cautious. In either case this is the chapter that shows you how to get started. Parts of this chapter are abstract; I share ideas and give you thoughts to ponder to help you find yourself in the garden of sprouting vegetarianism. Changing your diet to meatless is going to be like anything else you do—you have to do it *your* way. But we'll have some fun discussing some different ways to approach it.

For those who desire a concrete, systematic way of making the transition to meatless, we'll make a plan and walk through it together. Then I'll sum it up in a reference table at the end, so you will have a handy place to go for support. I'll also provide some ideas about making your new diet more fun, not only for you, but for those around you. Let's take a look at how we are going to make this all work.

One Bite at a Time

How do you eat a 2,000 pound falafel ball? One bite at a time, of course! And for many people, including you perhaps, this is the best way to approach any big change in your life. Going slowly helps to make any change permanent.

When I first made up my mind to become a vegetarian, I gave up red meat immediately. This seemed to be the most logical choice at the time and was my first step toward total vegetarianism. Although it was only a start, it had a huge impact on me, causing me to shift the way I ate dramatically.

Sprouts of Info

You can make more of a psychological impact if you make your elimination of animal flesh a memorable celebration. This celebration will make your choice seem more significant, and really, to you, going meatless *is* significant because it can mean a longer, healthier life.

I was used to eating hamburgers at any possible moment (my mantra was, "I will gladly pay you Tuesday, for a hamburger today"), so what was I to do now? Here's where we shift our attention to you. What would make the biggest impact on your diet if you eliminated it? Do you eat a lot of red meat? What about chicken, fish, cheese, lamb, or eggs?

It wouldn't, for instance, make too much difference to most people if they decided to put their foot down and give up rhino nuggets. Think about what you eat most of the time. If you draw a blank, you need to get more in touch with your diet. I suggest you keep a food diary for a while to see what keeps coming up (or should I say, going down?) in your daily food intake.

When you can pinpoint a certain animal product as being a big part of your diet, you should choose to eliminate that one first.

Celebrate for Impact!

Many people have given up a certain food after they contracted food poisoning from it. The strong reactions to feeling ill linked to a food are great for motivation, but you can choose to make your impetus more positive. You don't have to wait to get poisoned! Instead, make a positive emotional impact on yourself by doing something outrageous with the commencement of your new diet.

Here are some examples. Please take note that this list is not meant to offend you or any religious beliefs you have, but just to give you a laugh and some wild ideas to work from. (I'll never tell you which ones *I* tried!)

Some ideas to celebrate ending the consumption of a certain animal:

➤ Start a fund for farm animal abuse specifically for the animal that you discontinue eating.

➤ Post cute, fluffy, doe-eyed close-up photos of the baby animal on your refrigerator and circle it with the "no" symbol.

➤ Do a little dancing ritual around a statue of the animal while singing "Old MacDonald had a farm, E.I.E.I.O.," giving special attention to the sounds of the animal you are giving up eating (example, *with a quack, quack here, and a quack, quack there, here a quack, there a quack* …). Please keep the shades drawn while you perform this one.

➤ The next time you get invited to a costume party or Halloween rolls around, dress up as your animal.

➤ Give a lecture, write an article or a book, or build a Web site dedicated to the qualities of the animal and its purpose (besides serving as food) on this earth.

➤ Research your religion's stance on diet. Find out the official stance on this particular animal. (Sometimes people learn things they didn't realize before!) Then skip to Chapter 25, "A Higher Purpose." There we'll talk more about religion and ethics.

➤ Invent a new food that tastes just like the animal you are giving up. (Maybe you could be a little creative here and try *not* to make it taste just like chicken, though.)

Veggie Soup for the Soul

To tell the truth, in order for me to train my brain not to think that hamburgers looked good, I had to force myself to visualize what the hamburger really was: ground up muscle flesh of an animal. I had to remember all the grotesque things I had read on the way meat is produced and the filthy conditions that exist in the meat-processing plants. If that will help you, use it. You can skip to Chapter 27, "The Joy of Being Humane," for some more ammunition many have found convincing.

Okay, that should get you started. But seriously, you do need to think about why you want to go on this new diet and choose your changes carefully. You want to make it last. From what you've read in this book so far, maybe you're making this change for your health and for the people who care about you, so you can continue to run, play, walk, talk, and thrive until your time comes.

You owe it to the folks who love you to be as healthy as you can. But if that's not enough motivation for you, you'll find out later in this book how your choice to give up meat affects all sorts of other things in the world. And that's something to feel good about, too!

Meatless Tuesdays

Still some skeptics out there? All right, let's try an easier approach. Instead of choosing one animal to eliminate at a time, why not work on choosing a day of the week where you eat no animal flesh at all? Tuesday's a good day. Let's say that every Tuesday you have a straight vegetarian meal for breakfast, lunch, dinner, and even snacks. Make it fun. Tuesday is your day to experiment with this new way of eating.

Look forward to it. Start planning on Monday night. Imagine all the animal fat oozing from your veins in excitement. You'll be giving your digestive system, your heart, veins, kidneys, and liver all a big break for a whole day! Do this every week until it is so fun that you'll want to do it on Wednesday. Wow, this is getting really exciting!

Or you can try a variation of the two approaches. If you're a slow starter you could choose an animal you eat daily, pork for example, and eliminate all pork products from your diet one day a week. Work your way up from there: once per week for a week or two, then twice a week, and so on, until you hear Porky Pig stuttering in the back of your mind, "That's all, folks."

Whichever way you choose, setting up a plan to make a shift to the next level of your diet will help enormously. In other words, if you choose to go vegetarian once a week, do that for two weeks, then move up to twice a week for two weeks, and so on. Set a target date when you are going to be a pure vegetarian (or the vegetarian type of your choice). Mark that date on your calendar, and that will be your day to proclaim yourself vegetarian!

Veggie Soup for the Soul

Be prepared! After you reach your goal, you will immediately be flooded with letters of admiration from your vegetarian brothers and sisters around the world commending you on your accomplishment. Cows will look at you differently and birds will flutter around your head with utter excitement and joy. (Just kidding, but you might feel that way in your heart!)

Behavioral psychologists tell us that it takes a consistent amount of time (about 12 weeks) of doing something repeatedly until it becomes habitual. We want to try to make meatless a habit for you so that it becomes easy to continue. Humans are creatures of habit, so why not make some new meatless ones?

Twelve Weeks to Meat-Free

Twelve weeks to make this a habit? Piece of cake! Here are two tables that will help walk you through a 12-week transitional period and make it easy to switch to a new meatless diet.

Of course the meals and types of food I'm sharing here are just suggestions. They are mostly hearty meals with plenty of meat replacements, just so you won't feel deprived. Someday you'll probably look back at this chart and think, "Ugh, how could anybody eat all that food in one day!" But as a meat-eater, your body is used to working hard digesting heavy protein and fats all the time, and it will take your body a while to adjust.

Sprouts of Info

When transitioning from daily meat-based to a plant-based diet, you might need to eat more than usual in order to be satisfied enough not to miss meat.

If you find the suggested meals in the table don't fill you up, don't hesitate to go back for seconds. Most vegetarian meals contain much less fat than you would get in meals containing meat, so chow down! If you want to use the examples and follow the meal suggestions exactly, you are free to do that as well. Either way, take it at your own pace and enjoy your transition!

Choose one of the following plans, and then, if you're ready, skip to the appropriate table to get started:

❏ I would like to transition into a vegetarian diet one day per week. Show me how to do it. (Skip to the Twelve-Step Program for Meat Addicts table for your game plan.)

❏ I want to start by eliminating one main animal product at a time. (Skip to the Meat-Free Transition Diet, Per Animal table for your game plan.)

❏ I want to do it all at once and eliminate all animal products right away. (Skip to Chapter 22, "The Health Nut," to refine your diet and make it even more healthful!)

The Twelve-Step Program for Meat Addicts

Week	Day	Breakfast	Food Suggestions for ... Lunch	Dinner	Optional Snack
1 to 2	Mondays	Fruit and soy yogurt smoothie	Hummus and veggie pita wrap and chips	Lentil loaf, mashed potatoes, and green vegetable	Fruit
3 to 4	Add Tuesdays	Tofu scrambler and hash browns	Veggie chili and cornbread	Indian dinner*	Celery sticks with nut butter
5 to 6	Add Wednesdays	Breakfast burrito (leftover tofu scrambler wrapped in wheat tortilla)	Baked potato covered with salsa and vanilla soy yogurt	Mediterranean meal*	Carrot sticks with spinach and artichoke dip
7 to 8	Add Thursdays	Bowl of oatmeal with raisins and rice milk	Large Greek-style salad	Spaghetti squash and falafel balls	Wild rice sticks
9 to 10	Add Fridays	Carrot juice and a handful of raw cashews	Veggie soup, fresh spring salad, and wild rice sticks	Vegetarian lasagna	Popcorn sprinkled with yeast flakes and tamari
11 to 12	Add Saturdays	Tofu French toast with Boca sausage patties	Baked sweet potato and corn chowder	Veggie pizza	Dried fruit and nuts
Full time vegetarian	Add Sundays	Potato veggie scrambler covered with melted soy cheese	Black bean burger with guacamole dressing and French fries	Mexican style dinner*	Smoothie

See Chapter 17, "Meatless Meals," for more details on these meals.

The Meat-Free Transition Diet, Per Animal

Week	Meat or Product to Eliminate	Replacements
1 to 2	Red meat	Vegetarian burgers, Fried tempeh falafel balls, tofu balls, textured vegetable proteins, lentil loaf, tempeh sloppy joes (tofu can be made in many ways to resemble and taste like beef).
3 to 4	Pork	Tofu pups, veggie sausage patties, fake bacon cubed, marinated, breaded, and fried tofu, fake pepperoni products (it's amazing), fake baco-bits.
5 to 6	Poultry (turkey, chicken, duck, etc.)	Stir fry with tofu strips, tofu cordon blue (really!). The good news about tofu is that it can be made to taste like anything, and the chicken taste isn't hard to copy. Use vegetable bullion cubes to replace chicken stock.
7 to 8	Fish and seafood	Veggie sushi. Tofu can be made to taste and look just like fish and seafood. Seaweed for the iodine you may crave.
9 to 10	Eggs	Tofu scrambler, egg replacer, soy mayonnaise
11 to 12	Dairy	Soy milk, rice milk, nut milks, soy cheese, rennetless cheese, ghee, tofu everything from ice cream to yogurt, sour cream, soy-based margarine, nutritional yeast flakes in place of butter on popcorn and other foods. Plus, all the vegetables, fruits, grains, nuts, seeds, nut butters, breads, pasta, cereal, crackers, chips, fruit juices, vegetable juices, herbal teas, vegetarian soups, chili, sandwiches, stir fry, and other wholesome foods you want!

The Replacement Diet

The replacement diet can be used holistically to make your entire diet better and more healthful. You can start out utilizing replacement foods for meat and animal products and then move on to substituting better foods for other unhealthful foods such as sodas and other sugary foods, salt, and processed foods.

Meat replacement foods can look, taste, and smell so much like the real thing that long-time vegetarians won't even eat them! They make delicious replacements for the real thing and can be a welcome substitute, especially if you are just starting on a vegetarian diet.

Now that you've chosen your path—once a week, cold turkey, or one animal at a time—let's talk about what types of foods you might choose during your transition and how to sneak some meat replacements into the food of your unsuspecting roommate or other household members.

Veggie Soup for the Soul

Beginning your transition to a meatless diet is not the time to start worrying about losing weight. It is best if you can simply get used to the way you feel without meat while you transition to your new diet. The weight loss, if you need it, will come soon enough, although you might notice that you will begin to lose excess water weight right away. This can initially be due to a decrease in sodium, which is found in excess in animal products.

Fake and Bake

You'll sometimes find that you wind up liking the meat replacement food better than the meat. In other cases you won't be able to tell the difference between them. If you're planning to trick your family into going vegetarian on the days that you want to eat veggie, it's best not to serve up a lentil loaf and try passing it off as a meatloaf. They will surely be on to you right away.

Here are some more subtle suggestions for slipping in a fake-and-bake once in a while:

➤ Textured vegetable protein in chili in place of ground beef

➤ Boca sausage patties in place of pork sausage patties

➤ Rice or soy milk on cereal

➤ Tamari-marinated tofu cubes, breaded with seasoned breadcrumbs and fried, added to stir fry in place of chicken (you can say it's your special chicken recipe)

Take a look at the photo of this big plate of tofu scrambler and hash browns and see whether you can tell that there are no meat or eggs anywhere on the plate.

Sometimes tricking your family doesn't go over big, and you will end up with a grouchy family who resent being suckered, and no one wants that. If you're not into subterfuge, try presenting your new food choice as a fun thing that everyone can be involved in.

Sprouts of Info

Trying to avoid flour products such as bread and refined crackers? Try Ryvita or Wasa crackers, found at most health food stores. They contain whole grains such as sesame seeds, rye, and wheat germ, and only a bit of salt. They are hearty tasting, low in fat, and high in fiber, and make a great substitute for bread.

This meal is completely vegan, but it looks hearty enough to be a mountain man's breakfast!

You can start by giving your family this book and getting them to choose some meatless meals to try. Or try a meal that is completely different from what your family normally eats, like an Indian feast or a Mediterranean spread. Don't even attempt to make the foods you prepare meat-like. You might be surprised at how quickly everyone adopts the new foods as favorites!

Here's a photo of a wonderfully delicious Mediterranean meal my husband fixed for us not long ago. It contains a little feta cheese, which the strict vegetarian or vegan can leave out, but otherwise is deliciously vegetarian.

Vegetarian Mediterranean meal. For times when meat substitutes just won't do, try something new by preparing a vegetarian meal that stands out!

This Is Getting Cheesy

It is easy for many people to eliminate meat from the diet, at least occasionally, but the problem often is that they give up the beef and increase the cheese. This is no better than the meat because cheese is itself a concentrated animal product with its own list of pitfalls.

Now don't worry, I'm not going to take your cheese away just yet, but I want you to know that jumping off the meat wagon doesn't mean you have to jump into the cheese vat! Throughout this section I will fill up your mind with many different options for meat replacements. You can then fill your cabinets with these items, and you won't need to fall into the trap of replacing one evil for the other. You'll find that you have more variety in your diet than you ever had as a meat-eater.

Sprouts of Info

Sometimes when you want something to taste like meat and it doesn't, you end up feeling cheated. To avoid this, make it a point to vary your new vegetarian menus with items that don't even resemble meat. This can get you used to the idea of not having to base your entire diet around meat products.

Educating Your Taste Buds

I recommend a slow, deliberate transition to your new diet not only because of its lasting effect, but because you also need time to retrain your taste buds. The good news is that most of our tastes are acquired and therefore can be changed.

Maybe you remember from science class that our tongues have different areas on them for tasting salty, sweet, and bitter flavors. Your taste buds are designed to protect you and send signals to the brain about what you are eating. These signals tell the body what to prepare for.

Steer Clear

Some folks who go meatless are unaware of all the options available to them and fall into a trap of replacing cheese for meat. Eating too much cheese has its own drawbacks. Read on for tips on what else to eat besides cheese.

Most poisons, for instance, are extremely bitter, and when tasted cause you to spit the substance out immediately. The system breaks down, though, because we can train our taste buds to accept new and different things by simply eating or tasting something over and over. Eventually, your taste buds recognize the new substance as "tasty."

An Acquired Taste

Anyone who has smoked realizes this. Think of that first nasty puff you took from a cigarette—choke! But it was cool, so you kept it up until you acquired a taste, not only for that first cigarette, but also different types of tobaccos; hence, you acquired a taste for your favorite brand! The same goes for alcohol. Most people tasting alcohol for the first time gag, but people continue to drink until the taste is acquired, and some even train their taste buds to become connoisseurs! The same process goes on for foods.

Adults who were raised as vegetarians say, when asked why they don't eat meat, that they've never had the desire to eat flesh. It's that simple. You too will lose your desire for meat and animal products over time, as long as you go meatless long enough to let the remnants of all those meat residues leave your body. Again, I can't stress enough how a good herbal cleanse can help facilitate your transition. Visit your herbalist or nutritionist or flip back to Chapter 1, "Why Eat Less Meat?" where you'll find the herbal recipe for a popular colon cleanse.

Sprouts of Info

It is thought that most babies are born vegetarians. Babies don't have acquired tastes. If allowed to grab at their foods of choice, they will almost always choose whole foods over cooked foods, processed foods, or meat. I have never seen a baby try to gnaw on a live animal—at least not to eat it!

Evolving Into a Better You

Now that you know how you can change your tastes, why not begin by choosing a substitute for an animal product, like soy milk for instance. When I first tasted soy milk, I thought I'd never like it. After a while, though, I began to enjoy it. My tastes evolved further, and now I drink rice milk because I find it much lighter and more appealing than soy.

Veggie Soup for the Soul

Even if you weren't consciously trying to be a full-time vegetarian, your body tends to get used to your new diet rather quickly, which can cause you to become ill after eating a heavy meat-based meal. I have never met a vegetarian yet who has gone without meat for six months and then for some reason or another chosen to eat red meat without his or her body reacting violently for several hours and sometimes days after. The good news is that the illness from the "meat bomb," as I call it, is usually dramatic enough to keep you from ever going back to meat again, although I don't recommended trying it.

Sprouts of Info

Tofu is definitely a food that takes a little adjusting to. Raw tofu isn't itself anything special, but it can be made into incredible dishes. Think of tofu as clay, and you are the sculptor. It can be transformed into anything you want. Try it in stir-fry or mixed with oregano and crumbled on pizza.

You have to start somewhere. When switching to soy or other nondairy milks, I suggest you try them first by using them in place of cow's milk in cooking and on cereal. You'll get used to the new nutty flavor, and you'll eventually develop a taste for it. In addition, you'll find that not only do you like soy milk, but you'll lose your taste for cow's milk.

You keep doing this, and your body begins to change and adjust. Really, your body actually likes these new healthful things. So on with your clean diet you go and your body evolves—but this evolution is upward, not downward, like it would be if you were acquiring a taste for new cheeses and chocolates! Soon you lose your desire for heavier foods and eventually find that you cannot tolerate meat or even the smell of cooking meat. Isn't that amazing?

In general, your body adjusts as best it can to the type of diet you feed it, so why not feed it the best diet you can? The goal here is not only to get you started on leaving out the meat, but to help you learn to feed yourself good wholesome foods in place of meat to promote nourishment, strength, and health. To help you get there, the next chapter provides a shopping list and walks you down the health food store aisles. So grab your grocery list, and let's talk shop!

The Least You Need to Know

➤ Celebrating each stage of your transitional diet can make a psychological impact that will keep you committed to your new changes.

➤ Creating a plan to transition to a plant-based diet slowly helps to make the change permanent.

➤ There are many tasty meat, egg, and dairy substitutes available that can make your initial transition to meatless easier.

➤ Some meat substitutes are so meat-like that your nonvegetarian housemate might not know the difference if you were to slip it in occasionally.

➤ Tastes are acquired and changed over time. You can retrain your taste buds and your body to enjoy vegetarian foods, and you will eventually lose your desire for meat.

Chapter 15

Let's Talk Shop!

In This Chapter

➤ Learn about vegetarian foods you can stock up on

➤ Plan your shopping list

➤ Take a guided tour through the health food store

➤ Learn why and how to choose produce wisely

➤ Discover some interesting grains

So now your mind is full of new ideas, but your cupboards are bare! You need to go shopping. As a vegetarian in transition the shopping experience may be a whole new event for you. That's what this chapter is for. I'll help you plan a shopping list for the staple vegetarian foods you can stock up on.

We'll talk about some foods you might want to try but aren't familiar with, such as tofu and tempeh. I've even included some photographs so you'll recognize them. I'll also give you the lay of the land in the health food store so you won't be looking in the canned food aisles for that package of tofu. After reading this chapter, you will be able to go to the market at least *looking* like a pro!

Before You Go to Market

Before you go to the market you need to think about how far you want to take your new diet. Are you going for it all at once or just weekly for now? Are you going to be a pesco vegetarian, a lacto vegetarian, an ovo vegetarian, or a strict vegetarian? These things, of course, will help shape your shopping list.

Yes, I said shopping list. Whether you're on a budget or not, it's always good to make a list. It can help you spend less and make smarter choices, and can ensure that you get everything you need—or at least that you don't go home without the two things you needed the most. The list is especially helpful now that you're going vegetarian because you are adding some unfamiliar foods to your cart, and maybe you don't even know what tofu or tempeh look like. I'll help you with that later. For now, let's take a look at what you're going to need.

Planning for the Future

On your first trip to the store as a vegetarian, you might want to stock up on some of the basic staple foods. Having staples on hand will enable you to whip up fantastic vegetarian meals in a flash.

Veggie Soup for the Soul

If you keep staple goods in your pantry or freezer, all you'll need to purchase every week are a few fresh vegetables, and you'll have everything you need to make countless veggie meals. Grains and mixes store for long periods in glass jars. Tofu, tempeh, soy hot dogs, and most meat substitutes can be frozen until preparation time.

Here's a list of foods that store either in your freezer or in your pantry and will help you turn your kitchen into a place where meatless gourmet meals are never-ending (or at least you can fill up those barren cupboards). Some good choices for vegetarian staple foods that store well include …

➤ **Bulk foods** (if your store doesn't have a bulk section, most of these foods can be found prepackaged): Raw nuts (cashews, almonds, or pistachios), grains (rice, couscous, quinoa, barley, bulgur, oats, whole-wheat berries), granola, nutritional yeast flakes, textured vegetable protein, seeds, beans, hummus mix, tabouli mix, spices, and sesame sticks

➤ **Prepackaged and dried goods:** Cereals, Nature's Burger, tofu scrambler mix, de-hydrated mashed potatoes, dehydrated soups, tofu burger mix, couscous mix, polenta mix, egg replacer mix, vegetable bullion

➤ **Frozen foods or items you can freeze for later:** Tofu, tempeh, bean burritos, French fries, frozen vegetables, shredded soy cheese, Garden burgers, vegetarian sausage patties, vegetarian bacon, tofu hot dogs

➤ **Canned goods:** Vegetarian refried beans, water chestnuts, diced chilies, veggie soup (Health Valley makes excellent organic vegetarian soups), veggie broths, tomato sauces or paste, veggie chili, artichoke hearts, bamboo shoots

➤ **Other:** Pita pockets, whole wheat tortillas, blue corn tortillas (all can be frozen), Ryvita crackers, nut butters (keep a long time if kept cool), soy milk or rice milk (purchase small individual boxes—they keep a long time unopened), stevia, frozen carrot juice or other frozen juices, olive oil

➤ **Produce that keeps a while:** Hard squashes such as spaghetti squash, acorn squash, onions, garlic, and potatoes

You should also consider which meals you want to prepare for the week in order to determine other ingredients you'll need.

Shop Hopping

Now you need to know where you're going to go shopping. Here are some places that carry the vegetarian items on your list:

➤ **Health food stores.** Find one in your telephone book.

➤ **Cooperatives.** Usually referred to as co-ops. These stores were started to meet the demand for hard-to-find health foods. Most offer just about everything you will need as a vegetarian. Most co-ops are open to the public for shopping, but if you become a member, you'll probably receive a discount.

➤ **Chain stores.** Many large grocery store chains now have entire sections dedicated to health foods and health-related books and products. These stores are like a mini health food store within a large store.

Sprouts of Info

Bring along your own paper or cloth shopping bags when shopping at a health food store. It is better for the environment to reuse bags, and most stores give credit for it. Always store a few bags in your vehicle to be sure you have them.

➤ **Regular grocery stores.** Local grocery stores are now carrying more and more health food items, so if you are in an area where you cannot find what you need, ask your local grocer to help you.

➤ **Import or ethnic shops.** Look in your Yellow Pages for Indian, Asian, Mediterranean, or other specialty food stores where many vegetarian foods can be found.

Next let's talk about some of these vegetarian foods, what they are exactly, and where to find them.

Introducing Meat Substitutes

Is it going to be Garden burgers, black bean burgers, tempeh sloppy Joes, Nature Burgers, or tofu burgers tonight? My, how many choices you have as a vegetarian! These tasty processed meat substitutes are a tempting alternative to your typical hamburger and are loads better for you.

Meat substitutes are big business, and therefore you'll find plenty of different types. Some are strictly vegetarian, and others contain eggs or cheese; just because it says meatless on the package doesn't mean its vegan, so be sure to read the labels on any processed foods you purchase. Although whole foods are always the best choice, it can be difficult to avoid *all* processed foods, even in the most healthful of diets. Not everyone can maintain a whole-food diet, nor is it completely necessary for health, but reading labels is a good idea when taking more responsibility for your diet and is especially useful when changing the way you eat.

The practice of reading labels when making a new food choice helps raise your awareness of exactly what you are eating and can help you avoid unnecessary chemical additives such as MSG, food dyes, and coloring, which are unnatural substances to the body.

Let's look at what some of these foods used as meat substitutes really are.

Tofu ... Gezunheidt!

Did you ever wonder what the curd was that Little Miss Muffet, who sat on her tuffet in the nursery rhyme, was eating? It was probably a tofu dish! Tofu is a curd made from soybeans.

Tofu is white, resembles cheese, and usually comes in blocks or tubs. Tofu is a favorite of many vegetarians because it makes a great meat substitute and soaks in the flavor of anything you cook it with. Its natural taste is fairly plain, and that's exactly what makes it so versatile.

Tofu comes in different varieties, from soft-textured to extra firm. Tofu labeled soft is usually used to make things like tofu cheesecake, dips, and spreads, and tofu labeled firm or hard can be cut in pieces and used in stir-fry or other dishes in place of meat. There are now some different textures available, such as extra firm, firm, soft, extra soft, and silken. (Silken tofu has a texture similar to the white of a hard-boiled egg.) Recipes will usually specify which to use, and from there you'll have to experiment to find the ones that appeal to you most.

This vegetarian favorite is usually found in the refrigerated produce section, often where the organic produce is displayed, or in the dairy section next to the cheeses. Silken tofu does not require refrigeration before it is opened and may be found on the shelves along with other Asian foods.

You can also purchase tofu and freeze it for later use. Freezing tofu makes it more porous and gives it a gritty texture that makes it even more meat-like. After you unpack it, unused portions can be covered with fresh water in a container and stored in the refrigerator. Change the water daily. Tofu keeps for several days this way.

Tofu is high in protein, low in calories, cholesterol-free, and contains calcium and iron. Some tofu is certified kosher.

Tempting Tempeh

Tempeh is a conglomerate mix of whole fermented soybeans, sometimes mixed with some other grains such as millet or rice, and made into cutlet-shaped patties. Its use dates back more than 2,000 years in its native Indonesia. Tempeh has a pale brown color and a bumpy-looking texture that I can only describe as resembling alligator skin. It is found either with the frozen foods or in the dairy section with other foods like tofu and cheeses.

Sprouts of Info

Make sure to squeeze the excess water from the tofu before you cook it, especially if it has been frozen first. The effect is like squeezing out the excess water in a sponge. Tofu is porous, so it soaks in the juices and spices you cook it in, and squeezing the excess water from it makes it a bit more receptive to your flavorings.

Tempeh is usually found in shrink-wrapped plastic packages or in reusable plastic zippered bags. It has a somewhat nutty flavor. Tempeh is hearty and is used to replace meat and to make vegetarian dishes more filling. Tempeh contains no cholesterol, almost no fat, and is high in protein and fiber.

Tofu (the white cube) and tempeh (the darker of the two) are both derived from soybeans and can be used as meat substitutes. They are a versatile vegetarian food and can be found in most stores where health foods or imported specialty foods are sold.

Textured Vegetable Protein (TVP)

Textured vegetable protein, or TVP, is another interesting meat substitute made from soya flour. It can be found in bulk or prepackaged and has a tough, chewy texture much like beef steak. It is grayish-brown and is sold either in small chunks or shredded and flavored to taste like meat. This product is used to add a meat-like texture to vegetarian foods such as bean burritos and chili, and can add to the nutritional content in meals.

Steer Clear

Some textured vegetable protein (TVP) is high in fat content, so read your labels. TVP made from de-fatted soy flour is low in fat.

Making You Falafel

Falafel (pronounced *fa-LOFF-ul*) is a mix of spices and ground dehydrated garbanzo beans. It is a popular Mediterranean food. You prepare falafel by mixing it with water and deep frying it. It can be used to make falafel balls to replace meatballs or as patties in place of hamburger patties. It is a delicious choice for use in salads and sandwiches.

You can sometimes find falafel mix in the bulk section of health food stores, but it also comes prepackaged, usually in a box. I have found boxes of falafel mix, tofu burger mix, Nature's Burger mix, and Perfect Burger mix near the spices section in grocery stores, but in health food stores they are usually on the shelves along with other dry goods.

Falafel is hard to describe and can't be compared to any meat I've ever tasted, but it is delicious in itself. It has a distinctive flavor that is somewhat nutty and a bit like sweet corn.

In this same genre is dehydrated hummus, which is also made from ground garbanzo beans, and can be used as a dip or to make sandwiches. While you're in this aisle, look for dehydrated tabouli, which is a mixture of grain and parsley and can be used as a side dish.

A Closer Look at Produce

These days not all vegetables are created equal. As a vegetarian you will want to become more familiar with your produce and choose it more carefully. After all, vegetables and fruit will be the focus of your new diet, so you want to get everything you can from these foods.

Remember, food production is a business, and making food more profitable doesn't necessarily mean that it is better for your health. If you are what you eat, then you should know what you are eating. One food question we are hearing a lot about lately is genetic engineering, and you will probably run across references to GMOs, or genetically modified organisms.

What does genetically engineering or altering foods mean? It means that scientists have changed what occurs naturally in a plant by manipulating or cross-breeding its DNA. For instance, most commercially grown tomatoes are now genetically altered to remain firmer, so fewer are lost by crushing during shipping. Sometimes plants are spliced with genes from completely different organisms, including bacteria, fish, and insects—combinations that could not happen naturally.

A Question of Genetics

Many crops are altered to resist strong herbicides and pests. About half of the United State's soybean crops are genetically engineered, as well as about one third of the corn. The FDA assures us that these foods are safe for consumption, but there is much debate. If you do want to avoid them, pay attention to the labels, especially on foods that contain soy. If the company does not use genetically altered food in its products, it says so on the label.

Some food companies have shown their concern over genetically altered foods and have promised to stop using them in their products. Baby food makers Heinz and Gerber will discontinue using genetically modified soybeans, and Japan, one of the world's largest tofu makers, is phasing out purchasing genetically altered soybeans. Some beer makers have cut out the use of genetically altered corn in brewing their beer.

Steer Clear

Some years ago genetic DNA from a Brazil nut was crossed with soybeans. Since nut allergies are common, some feared that unsuspecting consumers could have allergic reactions when eating these genetically manipulated soy products. This brings up more issues about labeling our "natural foods."

Commercially Grown vs. Organic

Most people already understand that going organic is better for the environment. It keeps toxic pesticides from getting into our waters, air, and soil, and, of course, choosing organic foods helps limit your personal exposure to pesticides.

Toxins are everywhere. They can be found in the air you breathe, on and in foods, and in your drinking and bathing water. Because there is no way to completely eliminate exposure to chemicals throughout your life, why not control what you can by choosing foods that are free from pesticides?

Testing individual food items for "safe" levels of pesticides does not take into account how many pesticides you've eaten in a day or over a lifetime. Pesticides and other chemicals add up over time and can leave residues in your body tissues. The information on pesticides and organically grown produce is so vast that we could go on forever, but you should be aware that limiting the amount of toxins you knowingly expose yourself to daily is a good commonsense safeguard.

187

Sprouts of Info

For an interesting look at exactly how many chemicals you are getting in your food and what effects these pesticides and chemicals can have, visit *All You Can Eat* at www.foodnews.org. It has an interactive questionnaire that lets you check off what you've eaten in a day. The results show a breakdown of the chemicals you've consumed.

My advice is to work on your health preventatively and actively. Believe me, it is much easier to maintain your health than it is to reclaim it. Choosing organically grown foods when possible is an easy preventative step you can take.

Hybrid Just for You

I talked about the importance of seeds and legumes in Chapter 4, "A New Food Pyramid." The seeds of fruits and vegetables are the glandular system of the plant and therefore can serve to nourish your own glandular system. However, many foods you find these days are hybrids.

If I have my choice, I choose foods that are as whole and natural as possible. When choosing watermelon, I choose the watermelon with seeds versus seedless. However, I believe that balance is the real key. Just make sure you get a variety of foods and learn to incorporate whole, fresh, natural foods as a prominent part of your diet, and you should be in good shape.

Vaccinated Vegetables?

How would you like to be vaccinated against the Norwalk virus when you eat a banana? Some researchers in the United States have been experimenting with adding bacterium to fresh produce that reacts with the plant's own structure to create different types of vaccines in the fruit itself. The purpose is to create edible vaccinations that consumers can ingest in their uncooked foods. If this is done, you will need to give serious consideration to whether you want to consume these foods.

The average consumer needs to become more educated on the effect of vaccines, the research on the aftereffects of vaccines, and the related risks versus benefits of inoculations in general. This should prove to be a very interesting and controversial subject. For now let's stick to foods. Just keep in mind that foods from nature are the perfect foods. Read the signs and labels, even on fresh produce.

Ripe for the Pickin'?

Try to get your fruits vine-ripened when possible. Most commercially grown produce is picked green, and much of it, oranges, for example, is then gassed and dyed to the color that appeals to the consumer. When you eat unripened fruit, such as a green orange, its acids are not yet fit for consumption and can stir up your own body acids, creating discomfort. You also miss out on nutritious phytochemicals that can be created only by nature through vine ripening.

Take some of your food lessons from nature. Notice that animals do not eat fruits or vegetables from your garden until they are ripe. (They think you are growing it for them, you know!) Their instincts tell them when foods are ready for consumption.

Humans have altered not only their taste buds over time, but, through the use of chemically laden foods, have deadened the natural instincts related to food and eating. As you turn more and more toward whole foods, your taste buds and eating instincts will come back to life, and you'll learn to enjoy obeying them. You'll even come to understand how well these natural instincts serve you!

Bulking Up on Grains

Grains are found in bulk in most health food stores. If you think grains end with wheat, oats, and barley, think again. You'll find a wide variety, probably even some you never knew existed.

Sprouts of Info

Most bananas are picked and sold green. Here's a tip from my produce expert. Apples emit a natural gas that serves as a catalyst to ripen other fruits. If you purchase a bunch of green bananas, put them next to an apple or two (an enclosed sack speeds up the process). If you want your bananas to slow down, keep them away from the apples!

Veggie Soup for the Soul

When buying in bulk make sure you ask for cooking instructions if they aren't provided (sometimes you'll need to copy them off the bin yourself). Or pick up a copy of *The Moosewood Restaurant Cooks at Home* (Simon & Schuster, 1994) for details about how to turn many different grains into delicious easy-to-prepare meals.

I'll introduce you to a few of the less common grains here so that you will know what I mean when I encourage you to incorporate a variety of grains into your diet. Have fun experimenting!

➤ **Quinoa** (pronounced *KEEN-wah*) is getting more recognition. It provides a hefty supply of protein, minerals, and vitamins. Quinoa has a mild, nutty flavor and is somewhat crunchy when prepared. It can be used in place of rice or added to stews and casseroles.

➤ **Rice** comes in many varieties besides plain white, including basmati, brown basmati, jasmine, wild rice, long grain, short grain, and brown rice. Brown rice is generally the heartier rice, where basmati and jasmine are more buttery and sweet tasting. Wild rice has its own unique flavor. Always choose rice with hulls over polished rice.

➤ **Barley** is rich in nutrients that feed the brain. It can be purchased in bulk and slow cooked to eat as a cereal (see Chapter 4 for cooking instructions), or added to soups and casseroles.

➤ **Couscous** is actually a pasta derived from durum semolina wheat but is usually found near the grains in the bulk section. This tiny, yellowish, granule-shaped pasta is a staple in African dishes and is very versatile. It can be seasoned with your favorite vegetable broth and spices, or you can add garlic, chopped vegetables, some pine nuts, and a dab of olive oil to spruce it up.

Couscous can be served as a side dish, or try it in place of rice in stir-fry or with other saucy toppings. I like to add it to a pita pocket and top it off with sprouts for a couscous sandwich. Make sure to flavor it, though, because couscous alone is bland.

Shopping on a Pared-Down Budget

Some people think it is terribly expensive to be a vegetarian. The reality is that shopping for a vegetarian is much more economical than it is for a meat-eater! Actually, the healthier you eat, the lower your food bills get—for many reasons.

Veggie Soup for the Soul

Some people argue that being a vegetarian is way too expensive. Other folks say the same about supplements such as herbs and vitamins. My reply is that you have to pay at some point. Either pay for your nutrition or pay for your hospital bills. The choice is yours, but most people agree that paying for wholesome delicious foods that will keep you healthier longer is more appealing than paying for medications and surgeries related to a poor diet.

First, most of us have unclean digestive tracts that are clogged with debris and mucus from processed foods. This keeps the body from absorbing properly, which leaves you hungry. This means that people are eating much more than they need, and much of the food is wasted. After your system has been washed—after a cleansing and detoxification program followed by a clean vegetarian diet—you will notice that the amount of food you desire decreases dramatically.

Second, if you are eating more vegetables and grains, and few or no animal products, you are eating whole foods. Whole foods are grown, harvested, and then brought to your store, often from local sources. These foods do not require extra handling, chemicals, preparation, labeling, and packaging, which all add their own costs.

More for Your Money

Try this experiment sometime: Fill up a shopping basket with fresh fruits and vegetables and bulk grains such as rice and millet. Fill up another basket with processed foods such as breads, cheeses, prepared dips and butters, prepared juices, boxed cereals, boxed mixes, and so forth. If the whole foods basket rings up more expensive than the basket of processed foods, I'll pay for your vegetables!

Here's an extra-economical savings tip—purchase a juicer. A Vita-Mix or a Champion juicer makes an excellent choice because they are all-in-one type machines that can whip out smoothies, nut butters, soups, and vegetable and fruit juices. Although a good juicer is spendy up front, over time you will be repaid a hundred fold.

Finally, to shop economically, shop wisely. Although some health food and co-op stores do carry nonfood items such as batteries and aluminum foil, these items are usually carried as a courtesy to you, and the courtesy comes at a higher price than at a large grocery store. So look at your list before you go shopping and divide it into two sections, one for nonfood items such as sandwich bags, aluminum foil, and batteries, and another for your food. Then choose the best stores for each.

Sprouts of Info

Compare the price of a bag of organic juicing carrots to an equivalent amount of juiced prepackaged carrot juice. The difference alone is a good start toward paying for your juicer.

Sprouts of Info

I'll share with you a shopping tip from a great nutrition teacher I had who told us to shop only along the outside walls of the grocery store. That's where you will find the fresh produce and whole foods. Most everything in between is processed, dead, denatured food. It changed the way I look at grocery stores forever!

Budget Tips for the Complete Vegetarian

Just to put all this information in one place for you, here's a handy-dandy list of budget tips for the frugal vegetarian.

➤ **Buy in bulk.** It saves packaging and labeling costs.

➤ **Eat more whole foods and fewer processed foods.** Whole foods naturally cost less than prepared processed packaged foods, which require more handling.

➤ **Don't buy nonfood items at health food stores.** Items such as aluminum foil and sandwich bags are generally more expensive in health food stores than at regular grocery stores. This can run your food bill up in a hurry and make you think (erroneously) that health foods are more expensive.

➤ **Work with your holistic practitioner to help you choose and implement a colon and digestive system cleanse** that will help you absorb better and eat less.

➤ **Purchase a juicer** and make your own juices, nut butters, and soups. These items can be made all at once on your day off and frozen for use later. This saves not only money, but time!

➤ **Avoid prepared foods except for certain occasions.** Deli items and prepared foods can be delicious and convenient, but they cost more.

Before you spend money for a prepared food, consider whether you could make it yourself almost as easily. If so, you can save a bundle. Consider buying tabouli in bulk, for example, versus pre-made or boxed. All you need to do to bring dehydrated tabouli to life is add water. Besides, dried tabouli keeps much longer than prepared tabouli from the deli.

A Guided Tour Through the Health Food Store

Now that you've got some ideas about what you're going to buy, and which stores you're going to visit to find it, you still need to know where in the store you are going to find each of these items, right?

I've put together a little table to help you locate the foods in the aisles of your local food store. When you get home from shopping, head for the next chapter, where we'll talk about cooking up some of the interesting new foods you've bought. For now, happy shopping, and I'll meet you in the kitchen later!

Vegetarian Staples and Where You Can Find Them

Frozen Foods	Bulk Bins	Prepackaged and Dry Goods	Produce Section
Prepared meat substitutes such as frozen bean burritos, tempeh, Garden burgers, vegetarian sausage patties and bacon, Natural Touch, Lentil Rice Loaf, frozen vegetables, French fries, tofu hot dogs	Grains, dry mixes, some spices, nuts, seeds, cereals, snacks like banana chips and sesame sticks, nutritional yeast flakes, granola, beans, flours, carob flour (in place of chocolate), dried fruit	Nonbulk items such as grains, cereal, spices, hummus, falafel, tofu scrambler mix, tabouli, dehydrated refried beans, dehydrated soups, dehydrated mashed potatoes, egg replacer	Produce, tofu, seitan, frozen carrot juice

Reading this chapter will help you get oriented before you find yourself looking for tofu in all the wrong places!

The Least You Need to Know

➤ Avoid having to shop a lot by stocking up on vegetarian staples such as bulk grains and frozen meat substitutes.

➤ Chain and local grocery stores and ethnic food stores, as well as health food stores and co-ops, are all good sources of vegetarian foods.

➤ Try some of the many meat replacements, like tofu and tempeh, to round out your vegetarian diet.

➤ Purchase the majority of your produce in as close to a natural state as possible, including vine-ripened, pesticide-free, nongenetically altered, nonvaccinated, and nonhybrids.

➤ Keep variety in your diet by experimenting with different grains.

➤ Eating vegetarian can be very economical. Save money by investing in a juicer and prepare foods and juices at home that you can freeze for later use. You can also save money by buying in bulk and eating more whole foods.

Chapter 16

Cooking at Home

In This Chapter

➤ Learn to make smoothies for any occasion

➤ Find out how to have a vegetarian barbecue

➤ Serve holiday meals your whole family will enjoy

➤ Discover some easy vegetarian snacks

➤ Equip your vegetarian kitchen

This chapter is a smorgasbord of ideas for making vegetarian meals and snacks a hit in your home. From your kitchen to your dining room to your outdoor barbecue, you need to know what to do with all the new foods you've discovered, and how to make a smooth transition to a plant-based diet.

Now that your refrigerator is full of new things, let's start off with some easy ideas on what to do with it all. We'll start with making smoothies because you can make almost everyone happy (including yourself) by serving delicious and nutritious smoothies for breakfast.

From there we'll fill up your snack bowls with veggie snacks and take a look at what to cook at a barbecue and on holidays. Then I'll share some interesting gadgets you might want in your new vegetarian kitchen to make food preparation easier.

Making a Smoothie Transition

Smoothies, a shake-like drink, have become very popular, and not just among vegetarians. Smoothies can serve as a full meal, a dessert, a pre- or post-workout nutritional boost, or just as a refreshing snack. The smoothie's cold, fresh creaminess is what makes it so appealing, and smoothie recipes are as varied as the people who make them! You can have totally vegan smoothies, lacto smoothies, even lacto ovo smoothies, all depending on what you like.

Juice bars, health food stores, and many health clubs are preparing smoothies to order on the spot. Many health food stores sell different varieties pre-made. Look for them in a refrigerated area, usually near the produce or dairy sections.

The basic ingredients needed to make a smoothie are a blender, some ice or another liquid base, like yogurt or juice, and a main ingredient, which is usually fresh or frozen fruits. Use the following list to get ideas about creating your own smoothies at home. If you have a few of these ingredients at all times, your smoothie recipes can be endless.

Sprouts of Info

When your bananas get too ripe to eat fresh, peel them, put them in a freezer bag, and store them in the freezer. When you are ready to make a smoothie, add a frozen banana. The blended frozen banana not only adds flavor, it also makes the smoothie creamy and cold.

Smooth Starts

Any of the following ingredients can serve as your base ingredient(s) for a smoothie:

➤ Yogurt (soy yogurt for strict vegetarians or organic yogurt for lacto vegetarians)

➤ Soy milk

➤ Rice milk

➤ Almond milk

➤ Fruit juice of any kind

➤ Tofu (preferably soft)

➤ Cold filtered water and ice

Fruitful Additions

Any fresh or frozen fruit can be used to make your smoothie. I've listed a few here that you might enjoy, along with some nutritional tidbits:

➤ Strawberries (good source of sodium; used to nourish joints and stomach lining; rich in vitamin C)

➤ Pineapple (high in enzymes, which aid digestion)

➤ Bananas (good source of potassium; helps replenish muscles after a workout; slower to digest and therefore makes it a good fruit for those with a tendency toward blood sugar imbalance)

➤ Mango (an excellent source of enzymes)

➤ Papaya (used by some people around the world to expel parasites; also serves as a wonderful digestive aid)

➤ Blueberries (have properties that strengthen blood capillaries; have been used therapeutically for eyesight improvement)

➤ Pear (helps purge the gallbladder of excess bile)

➤ Coconut (rich source of fatty acids)

In addition to fruits, consider keeping the following on hand to make all sorts of yummy recipes. A pinch of these ingredients can add heartiness or a complementary flavor to your base ingredients:

➤ *Carob* powder (Carob is a natural ingredient used as a chocolate substitute. It looks like chocolate and has a similar taste, but doesn't contain caffeine. It is somewhat bitter if a little sweetener is not added.)

➤ Your favorite raw nuts, such as cashews, almonds, or walnuts

➤ Vanilla extract

➤ Nut butters

➤ Cinnamon

If fruit alone isn't enough to sweeten your smoothie, consider the following:

➤ Honey

➤ Stevia

➤ Black strap molasses

➤ Maple syrup

➤ Grape juice

Lettuce Explain

Carob, also called locust bean, is a tree prized for its bittersweet, leathery beans. The tree is native to the Mediterranean area and other warm climates. Carob is frequently used as a chocolate substitute.

Smoothies are to cold food what soups are to hot. In other words, you can throw almost any ingredient into a smoothie after you have your basic "stock" ingredients in there. Smoothies are best made in a blender but can be made in a versatile juicer if you have one.

A Nutrient Boost

Smoothies are an excellent way to drink your supplements. For those people who have trouble swallowing pills, a smoothie makes a delicious liquid carrier for these ingredients.

Here are some nutritional items that many folks add to their smoothies for their therapeutic benefits:

➤ **Flax seeds** used as a bulk laxative. They are a good source of essential fatty acids that nourish the brain and circulatory system. Some folks use flax to help lower high cholesterol levels.

➤ **Psyllium hulls** are an excellent source of fiber. Fiber is necessary in the diet to keep the colon clean and lowers the chances of colon cancer and other diseases.

➤ **Aloe vera juice** is a mucilaginous-type laxative used for those who cannot tolerate rough fiber such as psyllium. Aloe is rich in vitamins and other nutrients and is used for soothing irritated tissues, bowel cleansing, eliminating wrinkles, and boosting the immune system.

➤ **Chlorophyll liquid** is the blood of plants and can be used to thin the blood slightly, deodorize the body, protect you from pollutants, provide iron to help with anemia, and is a body cleanser and builder.

➤ **Protein powder** is used by some super athletes who need extra protein before and after workouts. Adding protein powder to a smoothie is a delicious way to get it.

➤ **Dehydrated goat whey** is not for strict vegetarians, but it is one of the richest sources of natural sodium, choline (a substance that may improve brain function), and other nutrients. Goat whey has been used to promote joint health and can serve as a mineral supplement.

What to Slap on the Barbee

Ahh, summer. The fresh outdoors, children playing, sun shining, and the smell of fresh tofu dogs frying on the grill. Huh?

Typically you don't think of barbecues as a vegetarian event, but you don't have to get rid of that barbecue grill just yet! I'll give you several ideas for foods that are just as delicious (if not better) grilled on an open flame outdoors than cooked on your stove inside.

Here are some delicious ways to cook vegetarian foods outdoors and the best ways to prepare them. Consider using foil on the grill if it is also used to cook meat, to avoid getting animal grease on your veggie food.

➤ Tofu kabobs are made by cutting tofu into cubes, marinating them in tamari sauce, and dipping them in a seasoned breadcrumb mixture. Add cubed green and red peppers, zucchini, and onions. Alternate tofu and veggies onto skewers. You can cook them directly on the barbecue and turn them frequently, or you can cook them in aluminum foil.

➤ Veggie or bean burgers of all types can be substituted for hamburgers and cooked on the grill in place of meat burgers.

➤ Chop vegetables such as zucchini, onion, yellow squash, and red peppers. Place in aluminum foil. Add spices and a pat of butter if you like. Place on the grill and remove when vegetables are slightly crunchy.

➤ Corn on the cob can be cooked wrapped in aluminum foil and thrown on the grill. Or you can simply soak the corn in water for 20 minutes or so, leaving the husks intact, then place directly on the grill. Make sure to turn it a few times to ensure even cooking.

➤ Tofu hot dogs (referred to commercially as Soy or Tofu Pups, or Not Dogs) can be cooked directly on the grill.

Here are some more healthful eating tips for the outdoor feast:

➤ If you are a strict vegetarian, make your own coleslaw with soy-based dressings. Most coleslaw is made with dairy products.

➤ Most baked beans are made with lard or bacon, but lard is not a required ingredient when making baked beans. Skip the beans or bring your own.

➤ Bring along your own sprouted whole-wheat buns, but be sure to bring enough for everyone!

➤ Bring a bag of alfalfa sprouts or organic leaf lettuce and tomatoes to top your veggie burger. Most toppings offered at parties include head lettuce and nonorganic vegetables. Head lettuce is typically void of most nutrients and high in pesticide residues.

Sprouts of Info

If you've been invited to a barbecue, don't expect your host to have something vegetarian for you to eat. Take along something you can substitute for hamburgers or hot dogs, or you might wind up eating potato chips all afternoon.

Steer Clear

Stay away from baked beans unless you've made them yourself. Most baked beans, commercially prepared or not, have a glob of lard (hardened animal fat) floating in them. To be safe, make your own vegetarian version or seek out canned beans that are labeled vegetarian.

199

Veggie Soup for the Soul

Because vegetarian dishes are more wholesome and tend to be interesting, enticing, and delicious, meat-eaters will also find them desirable. In my experience most meat-eaters will hog up vegetarian side dishes and high-quality breads quickly. For instance, I've brought sprouted whole-wheat buns for veggie burgers to a barbecue, and when I went to prepare my veggie burger I found there were none left! However, there were still plenty of bleached white flour buns. Keep this in mind, and either bring your own personal serving or enough to feed everyone.

Holidays and Special Events

You might be personally happy and satisfied with your vegetarian-based dishes, snacks, and barbecue foods, but holidays are a time usually spent with family and friends. More than likely you will be in the minority with your vegetarian choice.

Holiday time is full of joy, but it also seems to be a time when families feud and emotions run high. Knowing this, you should discuss having a vegetarian holiday dinner with your guests long before the scheduled event. Give your guests the option of bringing their own meat dishes. Old habits die hard, and many people will cling to the idea of eating meat harder than they cling to anything else.

Although you have good intent, by springing a meatless meal on meat eating guests, you could unwittingly create a great deal of resentment or angry outbursts from family members. It is best to allow everyone a meat option and then to do your best to provide a variety of vegetarian foods that will delight your guests and help them see that they didn't even need to bring meat.

If you have a difficult family and sense resentment when notifying them that you will not be baking a turkey or ham for the holiday event, consider passing up having the holiday meal at your home for that year. Give family members some time to warm up to the idea (10, maybe 12 years?). And when you attend

Sprouts of Info

Say no to turkey with a vegetarian holiday meal. Soy-based Tofurky, Unturkey, and Tofu Turkey roasts are delicious and kind alternatives to the real thing. For more information on having a vegetarian holiday, call 1-888-VEG-FOOD.

as a guest for holiday dinners at their homes, just make sure to bring a few vegetarian dishes to share. Eventually you might be able to enjoy having a vegetarian holiday meal at your home with grateful dinner guests who have learned to enjoy a meatless meal.

What Do We Eat for Thanksgiving?

Here's a phenomenon long-time vegetarians are all too familiar with, and if you put all you've learned here to use, you'll hear it, too. Invariably, shortly before each upcoming holiday, someone will say something to the effect, "My gosh, you're a vegetarian? What on *earth* do you eat for Thanksgiving?" Their question should strike you as interesting year after year, and maybe make you pause, because not only will you remember the time when you would have asked a vegetarian the same question, it will be a chance to reflect on how far you've shifted your own thinking about food.

You will have gone from thinking of your meals as needing to be centered around flesh to the expanded perception that your diet is now chock full of a daily variety of earthly delights that you might never have discovered had you never chosen to go veg. And as far as Thanksgiving goes, just think of all those grateful turkeys!

Alternative Classics

You would think by the way some meat-eaters talk that the only thing they have for a holiday meal is the turkey or the ham. But there are plenty of other delicious and mostly vegetarian foods traditionally served at a holiday meal, like mashed potatoes, cranberries, sweet potatoes, and pumpkin pie!

So what do you have on a holiday that traditionally centers on meat? You have two options:

➤ Leave out the ham or turkey completely and spice up your vegetarian dishes. Here's a list of some of the vegetarian things found on our holiday dinner tables: salad, cornbread, muffins, rolls, soup, cooked vegetables, broccoli casserole, three-bean salad, cranberries, red grapes, sweet potatoes made with maple syrup, raisins, and walnuts, and stuffing with celery and water chestnuts. If you can't fill up with a mixture of these foods, you have a second option …

➤ Use a meat substitute to replace your main meat, such as tofu turkey or imitation ham. Ask your health food store or specialty store what you might use as a roast beef substitute. I have never met anyone who felt the need for a meat substitute with all the other wonderful foods to fill up on!

Veggie Soup for the Soul

My husband's family and I share a Thanksgiving tradition each year that includes a five-course purely vegan meal that we all swear is our best meal of the year! The food is prepared by Real Food Daily, a pure vegan restaurant located in Santa Monica, California, that uses not an ounce of animal flesh, oil, or refined sugar in any of its dishes. Our vegan Thanksgiving meal includes a green salad and dressing, soup, tofu turkey, collard greens, sweet potatoes, stuffing, cranberries, and pumpkin pie with tofu whipped cream. Besides the catering business, this place is usually jam-packed with customers!

Snack Attack

Now you've got a plan for the holidays, but what about those in-between munchies? Well, good news! Most snacks are vegetarian in nature anyway, even if you are a meat-eater. Of course, many processed snacks tend to be bad for you in other ways. Here are some healthful ideas that can satisfy a snack attack:

Sprouts of Info

Many vegetarian snacks can be packaged for car trips, camping, hiking, or picnics.

➤ Smoothies

➤ Raw nuts

➤ Fruit, fresh or dried

➤ Rice cakes with jelly

➤ Granola, dry or with rice milk

➤ Carob-flavored soy milk (individually packaged)

➤ Soy yogurt

➤ Popcorn sprinkled with tamari and nutritional yeast flakes

➤ Muffins

➤ Veggies, pre-washed and chopped, such as carrots, celery, green pepper, broccoli, and cauliflower

If you want to get fancy, spiff up your raw veggies with a dip. Try hummus, black beans, or spinach and artichoke dip. And remember to keep prepared veggies in the refrigerator ready to eat. You'll be more likely to reach for them if you don't have to haul out the cutting board.

The Sophisticated Vegetable

There are only so many ways to dress a turkey, so to speak, but as a vegetarian cook you get to experiment with a whole new variety of foods. After you get past not having a meat main course or even a meat substitute you can enjoy a whole new range of dishes. You'll no longer see vegetables or salads as a garnish or a side dish, but as a delicious part of the main course.

You'll get to mix tastes with a variety of textures. And instead of trying to force your vegetarian meat substitutes to look, taste, and smell like meat, you'll soon be putting your energy into tasting new things and enjoying the tastes of all types of plant foods.

Going Gourmet

If you're into using food strictly for gaining or maintaining health and don't pay much attention to food beyond making sure it's fresh and clean, you will probably eat plenty of whole raw foods as the staple of your diet. Because of this others might consider your diet plain, but I say that as long as you're healthy and happy, who cares?

Steer Clear

When you are fighting an illness your diet should be as plain and close to nature as possible. This saves energy for healing that would otherwise be needed for digestion.

Face it, for most of us food is part of our entertainment and social life, and there's nothing wrong with that. You "break bread" with friends, you share a nice romantic dinner with a lover, and you celebrate accomplishments by going out to dinner. Most holidays are celebrated with a large meal. The use of food as something to be enjoyed, shared, and celebrated is truly ingrained in all cultures.

So if food is a celebration, why not think gourmet vegetarian once in a while and make your meals really interesting? While a meatless burger and French fries count as a vegetarian meal, why not celebrate with your favorite vegetarian ethnic dish? Turn your typical vegetarian bean and rice–based Mexican feast into gourmet enchiladas with blue corn tortillas, goat cheese (or tofu cheese), pine nuts, and special cilantro cream sauce?

Sprouts of Info

Seitan is a brown, slick-textured, high-protein, low-fat form of wheat gluten found in health food stores, generally near the tofu. It is made from whole-wheat flour and is used in sandwiches, stir-fry, and as a meat substitute.

When you get the hang of it, you will see that making interesting vegetarian dishes can open up a whole new world to you, not only in your kitchen, but in your mind. You might even discover that although you struggled to bake a turkey correctly and had a hard time poaching an egg, vegetable-based foods are much more versatile and easier to put together. You might discover that you make a very good vegetarian cook. (See the next chapter to get all sorts of ideas for meatless gourmet meals.)

Eating for Texture

When first changing your diet in any way, you might notice that you sometimes eat more for texture than for taste. Do you eat chips at every meal or only with soft foods? Do you crave the creaminess of a milkshake or abhor the fuzz on a peach? Even when I was a meat-eater, I didn't care how much anyone touted the delicious taste of raw oysters or clams, there was no way that I would eat such a cold, slimy, wet creature. Not without some serious gagging anyway!

The same goes for slimy tofu or overcooked spinach—yuck! I am definitely a person who eats for texture, and you might find that you are too, once you think about it. For those who are kinetically sensitive like me, check out the following table for some tips to help you satisfy your meaty texture craving with your veggie meals.

Eating for Texture	Vegetarian Suggestions
When you're craving crunchy (fried chicken, country fried steak texture)	Crispy fried falafel balls, thinly sliced tofu that's been battered, seasoned, breaded, and fried until crispy
When you're craving creamy (like ice cream or creamy cheese)	Yogurt or soy-based smoothies blended with a frozen banana, melted soy cheese, vegetarian lasagna, tofu cheesecake
When you're craving tough/chewy (steak or red meat texture)	TVP added to burritos, chili, and casseroles, frozen and thawed extra firm tofu, seasoned and sautéed
If you crave slippery	Silken tofu, extra soft tofu, seitan

This Gadget's for You

If you are going to become a vegetarian gourmet, or even just a plain old, everyday, vegetarian cook, there are a few appliances essential to your kitchen. A well-equipped kitchen for the vegetarian might include the following:

➤ Wok to whip up stir-fry

➤ Cutting board designated for produce only

➤ Sprouter to make your own alfalfa or other bean sprouts

➤ Bamboo steamer to steam vegetables lightly

➤ Strainer to drain pastas and rinse fruits

➤ Juicer to make your own vegetable and fruit juices

➤ Blender for making smoothies and sauces

➤ Food processor to make applesauce, veggie dips, and spreads and to quickly and easily slice, shred, or dice veggies

➤ Vegetable brush for cleaning vegetables and fruits

➤ Vegetable cleaner to remove outer wax, pesticides, and dirt

➤ Rice cooker to perfectly cook rice and other grains

➤ Thermos or slow cooker to slow cook grains to keep them alive

➤ Crock pot for making soups and chili

➤ Clear jars to store all your bulk items, nuts, mixes, etc.

➤ Salad bowl (for what else?)

➤ Waterless cookware for cooking without the use of water (it can be expensive, but it keeps the nutrients in the foods intact)

➤ Skewers for making vegetable kabobs for barbecues

➤ Reverse osmosis water filtering system

If you don't already have these items in your kitchen, add them to your birthday wish list. They make preparing vegetarian and whole food meals easier and more nutritious, and are especially helpful for anyone who wants to make his or her kitchen a safe and friendly place for preparing wholesome foods.

Steer Clear

If you share a kitchen with a meat-eater, make sure to keep separate cutting boards. One should be used only for produce and the other only for animal products. This helps avoid contaminating the vegetables with bacteria spread by raw meat and eggs and is especially important when eating produce raw or steamed.

Sprouts of Info

A Vita-Mix is an all-in-one blender that does the job of 10 kitchen appliances. It makes whole juices without eliminating the pulp and has at least 40 other functions. Call Vita-Mix at 1-800-848-2649. Nature's Sunshine Products offers a nice selection of waterless cookware and a highly rated reverse osmosis water unit, Nature's Spring. Call NSP at 1-800-223-8225.

The Least You Need to Know

➤ Smoothies can be made from a variety of ingredients and can serve as a meal, a snack, or as a way to get your supplemental nutrition.

➤ Meat substitutes such as tofu hot dogs, meatless burgers, and tofu kabobs are an excellent way to have a vegetarian barbecue.

➤ Holiday meals naturally offer a variety of foods that are meatless. When hosting a vegetarian holiday meal, be sure to let your guests know about the meatless menu well in advance to avoid resentment. Offer to let people bring their own meat if they wish.

➤ Food texture is important to many people, but you don't need meat for texture. Vegetarian foods can be prepared in various ways to satisfy your different texture cravings.

➤ Vegetarian cooks can benefit by having some special kitchen equipment, including a blender, a juicer, a steamer, and a wok to prepare fresh, wholesome vegetarian snacks and meals more easily and economically.

Chapter 17

Meatless Meals

In This Chapter

➤ Find out how to make traditional American meals meatless

➤ Learn what to do when the menu calls for meat

➤ Discover the vegetarian benefits of ethnic foods

➤ Enjoy spicy meals that are tastefully meatless

This is not a chapter of recipes but rather a collection of many types of meals from all over the world that can be made to fit any vegetarian menu. First I'll share some ideas for making traditional meat-centered American meals into filling vegetarian substitutes. Then we'll move on to look at the rest of the globe.

You'll find some ideas for interesting meals that might be foreign to you but that are typical fare in their home countries. Many of these dishes are themselves vegetarian. For the rest I'll show you how to turn meals from Italy, India, the Mediterranean, Mexico, China, and Japan into wonderful, tasty, vegetarian dishes with flair! *Bon appétite!*

American as Tofu Pie?

Are you a steak and potatoes man or woman? Or maybe you're cooking for one. How are we going to satisfy that type of hunger? Well believe it or not there are some meatless meals that can pack the same hefty punch as a big plate of red meat. Let me give you a few ideas for changing meat-and-potato-lovers into happy eaters of meatless meals. I'll help you do this without frightening anyone off with foods that might be considered "foo-foo" to some red-meat types.

For certain we don't want you to offend anyone's meat-loving sensibilities with a prissy plateful of neatly arranged vegetarian puffed pastries glazed with a tender honey sauce. No, sometimes you need to prepare meals that could be pulled off in a truck stop, and puffed pastries just won't do.

What do you do instead? Let's list a few typical American dishes, and I'll suggest some meatless replacements for each. These meals are not necessarily centered around proper food combining, nor are they considered the best, lightest, or purest vegetarian meals. They are, however, great meals for those making the transition to less meat, and they are certainly less fatty and more healthful overall than their meat-centered counterparts.

These meals are also great for those times when you are hungry and have a craving for the meals that grandma used to make. When you want to sit down to a family-style American meal, vegetarian style, here's where you can come for help.

Traditional American Meal	Vegetarian Alternative
Meatloaf and mashed potatoes	Tofu meatless loaf or Natural Touch Lentil Rice Loaf with mashed potatoes and a green salad.
Steak and baked potato	Grilled tofu cutlets with your baked potato. You can fry, grill, or barbecue tofu and flavor and color it with your favorite steak sauce. See Chapter 16, "Cooking at Home," for ideas to give your tofu more texture.
Hamburger and French fries	Any of the following vegetarian burgers: Boca burgers, tofu burgers, various grain burgers made from dry mixes, tempeh burgers, Garden burger. You can still have your French fries.
Chicken pot pie	Tofu pot pie (most folks won't believe the tofu isn't chicken!).
Beef stew	Tofu or TVP and vegetable stew. Hint: Freeze and then thaw tofu to give it tougher texture.
Reuben sandwich and sauerkraut	Fried tempeh or seitan strips served open-faced on toasted rye bread, topped with sauerkraut and served with a side of hot mustard.

Once you get used to using the various meat substitutes (see Chapter 15, "Let's Talk Shop!" for a list) you'll be able to come up with good substitutions for all your favorite meaty meals. But there's more to life than American food. Let's take a trip to the sunny Mediterranean and visit a high-heeled, boot-shaped country called Italy.

Now That's Italian

The thought of Italian food conjures up the intoxicating smells of oregano, provolone cheese, simmering tomato sauces, and hints of wafting garlic, along with the haunting strains of accordion music playing in the background. How romantic our image of Italian foods! And how delicious!

The good news is for the lacto ovo vegetarians because you can still eat most Italian foods as they are. Just think of all the yummy, cheesy (and fattening) possibilities:

➤ Fettuccini Alfredo

➤ Cheese pizza with vegetarian toppings

➤ Cheese ravioli

➤ Vegetarian lasagna

➤ Spaghetti with marinara sauce

➤ Vegetarian manicotti

Steer Clear

Most pastas are made with egg so if you don't eat eggs, choose eggless pastas. Spinach and other vegetable pastas made without eggs can be found in most stores.

What do you get if you are dairy- and egg-free or even a vegan? There's still plenty to choose from right off the menu, such as these favorites:

➤ Eggless angel hair pasta tossed with garlic, olive oil, and roasted pine nuts

➤ Eggless spaghetti noodles with meatless sauce

➤ Eggless pasta salad

➤ Pasta Primavera (made with eggless noodles)

Or you can replace the cheeses in some the popular Italian dishes with the following:

➤ Shredded soy cheeses for mozzarella

➤ Crumbled soft tofu for ricotta cheese

➤ Soy-based Alfredo sauce

You can make things more interesting for everyone by considering these additions:

For ...	Try Adding or Substituting ...
Spaghetti with meatless sauce	Tofu balls or falafel balls
Plain cheese or strict vegetarian lasagna	Eggplant parmesan or five-vegetable lasagna
Marinara sauce	Pesto sauce
Meatless marinara	Add TVP
Any spaghetti or pasta dish	Add veggies, pine nuts, or chopped tofu cubes to the sauce while heating

Lettuce Explain

Pyruvate is a naturally occurring substance in the human body that is also found in apples, red wine, and cheeses. It is an antioxidant and is being studied for its use in weight loss, diabetes control, endurance, and heart health.

If you drink alcohol, red wine goes great with most Italian dishes. And you'll be happy to know that there is a naturally occurring substance in wine and cheese, *pyruvate*, that may help make red wine good for your health! In the book *The Pyruvate Phenomenon: The Facts, the Benefits, the Unanswered Questions*, author David Prokop reports that researches have studied the effects of supplementing with pyruvate and have found that it may benefit humans by acting as an antioxidant and that it can be useful in weight loss, diabetes control, endurance, and heart health.

However, science also shows that pyruvate causes lactic acid to build up in the muscles. Obviously, more research needs to be done on this substance before supplementing with it. But since it is found naturally in grape skins (and therefore wine), in the meantime, enjoy your glass and as the Italians say, *salute!*

Meatless Mexican Fiesta

Most Americans are fond of Mexican food—or at least the Americanized version of it known as Tex-Mex. To make Mexican dishes vegetarian is quite simple because the staples that make up Mexican food include beans, corn, tomatoes (salsa), cilantro, peppers, onions, rice, and cheese.

These meals are fine as is for lacto vegetarians, and vegans or strict vegetarians can choose either to replace the dairy items with the following list of substitutes or just eliminate them completely:

➤ Veggie burritos topped with melted cheese, salsa, and sour cream, with a side of Spanish brown rice and vegetarian refried beans

➤ Enchilada combo (one cheese and onion; one cheese, spinach, and water chestnut; one cheese) and sautéed mixed veggies covered with red enchilada sauce, served with Spanish brown rice and side of black beans

➤ Bean and bulgur tacos with diced tomatoes, onion, shredded lettuce, shredded cheese, avocado, and dollop of plain or vanilla yogurt or sour cream

➤ Guacamole tostadas, beans, and rice

➤ Taco salad, hold the beef, and add three types of beans, cheese, shredded lettuce, onion, corn, salsa, and jalapeños and top with sour cream, guacamole, and black olives; serve in a large taco shell

➤ As an appetizer or as a meal, consider making nachos with the same ingredients used in the taco salad

➤ Bowl of vegetarian chili with added TVP for the meat-like texture of your liking, served with a wedge of green pepper cornbread

Replacement items for strict vegetarians:

➤ Soy cheese

➤ Tofu cheese

➤ Soy-based sour cream

➤ Guacamole instead of sour cream

Replacement items for lacto vegetarians watching their fat intake:

➤ Low-fat, partly skim milk cheeses

➤ Plain or vanilla low-fat yogurt in place of sour cream (try the vanilla mixed with salsa—yum)

Tasty Indian Foods

India is a land of colorful textiles and spicy foods. Indian dishes are often mostly vegetarian fare and include foods such as basmati rice, peas, carrots, lentils, cauliflower, spinach, eggplant, tomatoes, potatoes, a variety of spices, and a popular spice mixture known as *curry*.

Curry is a pungent mixture containing up to 20 spices and herbs. Curry originated in India and is used to flavor many Asian foods. A chief ingredient is turmeric. Other ingredients can include sesame seeds, cloves, cardamom, fennel, nutmeg, red pepper, black pepper, coriander, saffron, and pimento. Curry is generally found in powder form, but it also comes in pastes and liquids.

If you decide to make Indian food in your home, you will surely tempt your family and friends with the mouth-watering aromas that will fill your kitchen. And unlike foods like popcorn or coffee, which smell better than they taste, Indian dishes taste even better than they smell. In fact my husband decided he could give up meat altogether after I introduced him to what is now our favorite Indian restaurant in New York. I remember him waving his fork over a plateful of food, enthusiastically exclaiming, "If I can eat like this everyday, why in the world would I eat meat?"

Let me introduce you to some ingredients you'll need to prepare and season your homemade Indian dishes. You should be able to find all of these ingredients at Indian specialty shops, health food stores, or gourmet food stores:

Steer Clear

If you aren't making your own refried beans from scratch, be sure to read the labels on the cans of beans you purchase. Canned refried beans typically contain lard (animal fat). To avoid the lard, look for cans that are clearly labeled vegetarian. You can also purchase dried refried bean flakes, which are whipped up in a flash simply by adding water.

Lettuce Explain

Curry is a pungent seasoning mixture, containing up to 20 spices and herbs, that is used to flavor many Indian and Asian foods. A chief ingredient is turmeric, which gives curry its distinctive yellow color.

➤ **Garam masala.** A mixture of spices, predominately ground cumin, ground coriander, and ginger.

➤ **Curry powder.** A mixture of spices, usually yellow or gold in color.

➤ **Asafetida** or **hing.** Can be used as substitute for onions and garlic.

➤ **Ghee.** A substitute for cooking oil, ghee is basically purified butter essence. Butter is slow cooked and most of the fat solids are removed, leaving a golden liquid—ghee. It does not smoke or burn at high temperatures and can be used for deep-frying.

➤ **Filo.** Thin sheets of pastry, usually found refrigerated.

Here are some items on an Indian dinner menu that you might not be familiar with:

➤ **Dahl.** A soupy mixture usually with a bean (lentil or mung) base, which might also include chopped vegetables. It can be eaten alone or served over rice.

➤ **Kofta balls.** A deep-fried, meatlike ball, usually made from a mixture of garbanzo bean flour, cauliflower, cabbage, and spices.

➤ **Chutney.** A chunky vegetable- or fruit-based relish.

➤ **Paneer** (or **panir**). Cheese cubes.

➤ **Samosas.** A fried pastry stuffed with cauliflower and peas.

➤ **Aloo samosas.** A fried pastry stuffed with potatoes and peas.

➤ **Naan.** Similar to flat bread, usually warmed.

➤ **Pakoras.** Various vegetables dipped in a chick-pea batter and deep-fried.

➤ **Subjis.** Cooked vegetables served with cheese.

Now that you can see how many choices you have when choosing Indian foods, *curry* up and cook—I'm getting hungry!

It's Greek to Me

Mediterranean and Middle Eastern fare share some ingredients with Indian fare, such as eggplant, garbanzo bean-based foods, and filo pastry, but Middle Eastern food includes items like feta cheese, cucumbers, raw tomatoes, and olives. Just like anywhere else, Mediterranean foods vary with the region. Overall these foods have a cool aromatic flavor due to the use of seasonings like mint, parsley, and cilantro.

Mediterranean and Middle Eastern meals share a similarity with other countries' cuisines in that there are often several dishes at one meal rather than one main dish, creating a variety of tastes and interest. After you experiment with these foods, mix and match them to create a meal of your favorites.

Let's introduce you to some choices here:

Sprouts of Info

By preparing meals from other countries that do not focus on meat, you will gradually change your engrained beliefs about how meals are defined.

➤ **Baba ghanouj.** Blended eggplant, usually flavored with lots of garlic. Served chilled, sometimes with a little olive oil added, and often scooped up with pita bread.

➤ **Falafel.** Made from spices and garbanzo bean flour, shaped into balls and deep-fried until crunchy. They are often stuffed into pita pockets with salad fixings and tahini or hummus spread to make a delicious sandwich. They are also great added to a Greek salad.

➤ **Tabouli.** Mostly served as a side salad but can be added to any or all of the foods mentioned. Tabouli is a mix of bulgur, grain, parsley, and mint. It tastes cool, light, and refreshing.

➤ **Stuffed grape leaves.** Grape leaves are usually stuffed with basmati rice and spices such as parsley. They are best chilled.

➤ **Greek salad.** A combination of red onion, feta cheese, cucumber, tomatoes, and olives. The dressing is usually olive oil and vinegar with oregano. A traditional Greek salad does not include lettuce, but the American version does.

➤ **Spanakopita.** A filo pastry filled with layers of cooked spinach, egg, feta cheese, and spices. You can make your own vegan version of this yummy entrée by leaving out the egg and feta and replacing them with tofu-based substitutes. Beware if you are in a restaurant—this food is typically not suitable for a strict vegetarian.

➤ **Pita bread or flat bread.** Pita bread is made without egg, but always check your labels when purchasing pre-made pita or flat breads. Use these breads cut into wedges for dipping into baba ghannouj or hummus. They can be used to make sandwich wraps as well.

➤ **Hummus.** Ground garbanzo beans made into a smooth paste. It can be served plain or with spices such as garlic or capsicum for a change of flavor. Hummus is versatile. It can be eaten as a dip or sandwich spread, a burrito filling, or a condiment in a falafel sandwich.

➤ **Sesame tahini.** A creamy seed-butter made from sesame seeds. You will probably purchase this product pre-made. It comes in a jar and is similar to nut butters. Use it to add flavor and creaminess to your sandwiches and as a salad dressing or condiment in any of these dishes.

Veggie Soup for the Soul

If you are cutting back on your consumption of refined carbohydrates like bread, try my favorite lettuce burrito. I clean a large leaf of Romaine lettuce and spoon on some hummus along the inside edge down the length of the leaf. I then add a handful of sprouts and sometimes a few diced tomatoes, fold it up lengthwise, and chow down!

It's an Asian Art

The Japanese diet has traditionally centered on vegetables, rice, and some fish. Researchers used to think that it was genetics that kept Japanese people at low risk for heart disease, cancer, and obesity, which are prevalent in the Western world. However, it was found that when Japanese people change their diets from traditional to more Westernized fare, they begin to develop the same diet-related ailments as the people of the West.

The Orient has had a great influence on the diets of Westerners. The foods from countries such as Japan, Korea, China, Vietnam, and Taiwan all share similar staples: rice, vegetables, and soy—perfect foods for the vegetarian.

You should have no trouble finding all sorts of foods from the Orient to fill your plate or your stomach. You can make delicious stir-fry with or without tofu or tempeh. Then there's steamed or fried rice, noodle soups, vegetable soups, and vegetable spring rolls. Tempura batter can be used to cover tofu or vegetables for deep-frying.

The main things you'll need to whip out some interesting stir-fry are cooking oils. Personally I like the taste of sesame oil, but you can try others, such as garlic oil or ginger oil. You can use a vegetable oil as a carrier oil and then add a tiny amount of the flavored oils to season your stir-fry.

Lettuce Explain

Tamari is a less-salty version of soy sauce. It is a dark, salty liquid made from fermented soybeans and used as a flavoring agent, especially in oriental foods.

You will also need some soy sauce or tamari. *Tamari* is a low-sodium version of soy sauce made from fermented soy beans. For more bite, try spicy mustard, found in powder form with other spices. If you like hot foods, it makes an excellent dip for a veggie spring roll and can be used therapeutically to help clear out stuffed sinuses. Seaweeds, pickled plums, and picked radishes are some other vegetarian favorites.

Around the World in Seven Days

Let's sum up with a meal menu for each day of the week taken from a different country. Even if you're not so worldly yourself, you'll surely have well-traveled taste buds by the end of the week!

A Week of Vegetarian Meals from Around the World

Day of the Week	Country	Dinner and Dessert (If There's Room!)
Monday	All American	Walnut tofu loaf, mashed potatoes, brown gravy, corn on the cob, vegan brownies
Tuesday	Italian	Organic bitter spring mix salad with oil and vinegar dressing, breaded zucchini sticks, veggie calzone, peach sherbet
Wednesday	Indian	Aloo samosas, mung dal, basmati rice with cashews and raisins, tomato chutney, palak paneer, garlic naan, bengali kheer (rice pudding made with rice, almond, or soy milk)
Thursday	Middle Eastern	Appetizer plate including baba ghanouj, hummus, falafel balls, stuffed grape leaves, freshly sliced ripe organic tomatoes and cucumbers, warmed pita triangles, baklava
Friday	Mexican	Vegetable burrito, bulgur taco, spinach enchilada with Spanish-style brown rice, side of refried vegetarian beans, sopapilla with honey
Saturday	Chinese	Hot and spicy tofu and vegetable stir-fry fried in sesame oil, served over eggless spinach pasta, fortune cookie
Sunday	African	Chunky vegetable stew served over couscous, key lime pie

You can find recipes for many of the foods we've talked about in a favorite vegetarian cookbook of mine, *The Higher Taste: A Guide to Gourmet Vegetarian Cooking and a Karma-Free Diet,* published by Bhaktivedanta Book Trust. See Appendix B, "Vegetarian Cookbooks," for this and other wonderful cookbooks to make your vegetarian meals into globe-trotting feasts.

The Least You Need to Know

➤ Almost any meat-centered meal can be turned vegetarian without compromising taste or heartiness, either by using meat substitutes or adding other ingredients to the dish to make it more satisfying.

➤ Lacto vegetarians can eat many Mexican and Italian dishes as they are, and strict vegetarians can substitute tofu or soy cheeses for the cheese and choose eggless noodles.

➤ Indian, Middle Eastern, and Asian foods are often naturally meat-free and are a good choice for a vegetarian meal.

➤ Preparing meals from countries that do not focus their meals on meat lets you shift your own ideas about what you think a meal should be.

➤ Try a meal from a different part of the world to turn your taste buds international.

Part 5

Lifestyles of the Rich and Meatless

Now that your head and shopping list are full of this new vegetarian fare, you know where to shop, and you are getting comfortable experimenting with vegetarian foods at home, you know what this means, don't you? You are now officially a closet vegetarian!

This next chapter helps you come out of the closet with your new diet and lifestyle and share the good news with friends and co-workers. I'll give you tips on how to help others around you feel more comfortable about your choices, and I'll also help you figure out how to work your new diet into real-life situations like dining out, eating on the road and at business luncheons, dating, and traveling.

Then we will take your diet a step further and help you elevate your diet to be even more healthy. I'll help you to get the information you need to correctly nourish yourself while pregnant, show you how to raise a healthy vegetarian child or pet, and even how to make vegetarianism a business. So this is your opportunity to come out and experience life on the streets without meat!

Chapter 18

Mr. Meat-Free Goes to Work

In This Chapter

➤ Discover some of the challenges that accompany the change to vegetarianism

➤ Find out how to handle teasing and downright antagonism

➤ Learn classy ways to deal with eating vegetarian on the job

➤ Find out how to be a good guest at a meaty meal

"Don't despise empiric truth. Lots of things work in practice for which the laboratory has never found proof."

—Martin H. Fischer (1879–1962), German-born U.S. physician and author, in *Fischerisms*

This chapter will help you come out of your kitchen and step into the world as a vegetarian. You will get some tips on how to handle yourself in a classy vegetarian way when politely declining meat, and learn what to do when the majority of the group votes on a steak house for lunch. I'll even show you how you can get your boss to order something for you to eat during catered business luncheons.

Although it might seem unnecessary to read about how to live as a vegetarian outside of your own environment, when you take your new diet out there and realize how deeply others are entrenched in their meat-eating ways, you might be glad for the interesting and even face-saving tips I offer!

A Poke in the Tofu Ribs

Going without red meat is pretty well accepted nowadays. This is probably due to all the media attention that highlights studies about heart disease and other medical problems related to meat consumption. This means that vegetarian ideas aren't quite as alien to most people as they were a few decades ago. But giving up red meat isn't nearly as big a change as becoming a total vegetarian.

Steer Clear

Remember that vegetarianism might be right for you, but it's not for everyone. Don't be surprised if you are insulted or attacked for your beliefs just because you don't fit the norm in some areas. Although attitudes are rapidly changing in many places, it never hurts to make it clear that you are not trying to challenge anyone's beliefs.

Of course levels of acceptance vary radically depending on where you live. The townspeople in a cattle town probably won't embrace you with enthusiasm for giving up red meat. In striking contrast, however, you will find plenty of social support living as a vegan in a place like Venice, California, or other liberal social environments.

Although you might be excited about your new diet and want to share its benefits with everyone, not everyone is going to want to hear it, and some will outright challenge or insult you for doing what you think is best for you.

Sometimes your vegetarian diet will cause others to think you are radical, a troublemaker. Some egomaniacs might even believe that because you abstain from meat while they are eating meat, you are trying to appear better than them somehow. For some it will trigger hidden, guilty feelings they have about not doing something to better themselves. Not at all your intention of course, but it happens.

What Are You, Some Kind of Nut Burger?

As long as you stay humble about your choices and respect others' choices you should be fine. But it won't hurt to prepare for some things you might come across when you take your vegetarian diet out in public. For instance, when I first became a vegetarian, I was confronted with some very antagonistic remarks. Here's a sampling:

➤ Come on, one piece won't hurt you!

➤ I won't tell anybody if you have just a little with me!

➤ You're wearing leather shoes, why won't you eat a burger?

➤ You're going to be sick if you don't eat meat.

➤ I understand that you won't eat most meat, but you'll love *my* meatloaf.

➤ Come on, try just a bite; it's so good that I bet you'll change your mind about being a vegetarian!

➤ Vegetables are alive, too. Where do you draw the line?

➤ What are you, some kind of religious guru or something?

What is this, Satan's temptation hour? Even if you are silent and humble about refraining from animal products, when others find out about it, know that anyone who is the least bit insecure about his or her own diet will scrutinize everything you eat!

Doing anything beyond what is considered ordinary, like becoming a vegetarian, means you will stand out. Being different draws attention, whether you want it or not. Being a vegetarian in public involves a certain amount of risk—risk of being criticized, challenged, or mocked. Your best bet is to be secure in your reasons for making your choice, step up to the plate to take a stand for yourself, and realize that anyone who criticizes you vehemently is only in it to "win," not to learn, and to let them be. Those who want to learn will continue asking questions, and maybe you can give them some information that will help them go vegetarian or at the least to think about the consequences of their diet.

Sprouts of Info

After you have finished this book and have learned the reasons to be vegetarian, why not come up with a short spiel for yourself to use when you are asked why you are a vegetarian? Be concise and passionate and keep it personal. People admire passion and conviction, and your answer could make more of an impact than you realize.

Let Me Explain

Once in a while you can avoid antagonism by explaining your reasons for being vegetarian. For instance, most of the taunts you are going to get are from folks who are uneducated or misinformed. Instead of getting frustrated or ignoring these remarks why not offer a little education to fill them in?

First, though, you'll have to feel out the tone of the person you are talking to. Consider this when being asked about vegetarianism:

➤ Is the inquirer asking you in sincerity? If so respond with courtesy and give him or her an honest answer that educates.

➤ Are they asking you to show off or make you mad? If so walk away. Or you can try a little sarcasm or humor yourself, depending on the situation.

There is no better way to diffuse a tense situation than with a little humor. This is a much classier way to handle a bully than to flat out fight over your idea of the right way to eat. Not only will you save face, you'll also educate by making a point. If nothing else you will demonstrate that vegetarians have a good sense of humor!

There will be times when you just won't want to be bothered. Maybe you're tired, or you know the person challenging you will never stop no matter how good a response you come up with (you know the type). In these situations I often feel that a little white lie is justified if it will cut an unwelcome conversation short. I'll give you some harmless examples that will help you get past your antagonist with relative ease.

Of course there is always the truth, which is my favorite policy. Or you can simply say you really don't want to get in to that subject right now, or that your choices are very personal to you and you'd rather not discuss them. You don't have to justify yourself to anyone, and it isn't your duty to defend the cause every time you are challenged, at least not if you don't want to.

Veggie Soup for the Soul

If someone persists in trying to get you to eat meat, he or she is being disrespectful and trying to bully you. After you have given a polite no to an offer of meat, anyone who continues to push it has a control problem. Consider hanging out with folks who show you respect instead. Those who respect your choices are telling you by their actions that they believe you are an intelligent, level-headed person who is mature enough to make your own decisions.

Some Snappy Comebacks

For those occasions when you are feeling a little more wordy, I've put together some sample responses you can use, depending on your inquirer and your mood.

Let's take a look at the same questions we saw earlier, this time with some suggested replies. Feel free to modify them to suit your personality and reasons for going vegetarian. If I have not included the truth, you'll have to make that up yourself!

➤ Come on, one piece won't hurt you!

Did you know that the average piece of red meat can linger in the bowel for years? I'm still working on digesting the meat I ate seven years ago.

No thanks, it gives me really bad gas, and I have a date tonight.

➤ I won't tell anybody if you eat some with me!

I didn't choose this diet for anyone but myself, but thanks for trying to protect me anyway.

Don't you realize it's National Meat Out Day today? Even if I was a meat-eater, I would have to abstain today just on principle.

➤ You're wearing leather shoes, why won't you eat a burger?

The animal was not killed for my shoes, it was killed for your burger. By wearing these shoes I'm contributing to the reduce, reuse, and recycle principle.

Oh, are shoes made from meat?

Actually, they are 100 percent synthetic materials. I have them custom-made and imported from Bangladesh, and they really do look like leather don't they?

These shoes are actually symbolic of a new religious cult I joined. Let me run and fetch a brochure on our mission ... (as you're walking away mumble something about accepting donations to make sure the person won't be around when you get back).

Steer Clear

Vegetarians generally don't appreciate conflict, so be careful with sarcastic responses. If you choose to use them, be sure to have your facts straight if you are challenged further. Use humor to diffuse the situation and try to keep emotion out of the picture in any debate.

➤ You're going to be sick if you don't eat meat.

Statistically, cultures that do not have a meat-centered diet are healthier. I thank you for your concern over my health, but I have researched how to be a healthy vegetarian, and so far I have never felt better.

Actually it was because I was sick that my doctor told me I shouldn't eat meat in the first place.

➤ I understand that you won't eat most meat, but you'll love *my* meatloaf.

If there was one thing that would change my mind about being a vegetarian, it would be your meatloaf; however, I changed my diet based on my (health, ethics, compassion for animals, concern for the environment, political convictions, religion). Abstaining from your meatloaf is a true test of my ideals, which I hope earns your respect.

I bet you say that to *all* the vegetarians!

I'll pass on the meatloaf, but I've grown quite fond of your potatoes. May I have some more?

➤ Come on, try just a bite, it's so good that I bet you'll change your mind.

I have risen above the temptations of my taste buds for something I feel strongly about. No taste is more important than my principles!

Sprouts of Info

Professional chefs or not, some people attach their self-esteem to their cooking. Use caution in your response to these folks because you don't want to hurt someone's feelings by rejecting their "famous" meat dish. My advice is to rave about a vegetable or other item the person makes to offset the rejection they might feel when you decline their nonvegetarian item.

Is that how you make all your important decisions?

Meat just repulses me. I think I was born with a meat-free enzyme or something.

➤ Vegetables are alive, too. Where do you draw the line?

I draw the line at eating anything with a face.

➤ What are you, some kind of liberal religious guru or something?

No, I am just utilizing my God-given right to make educated choices about what I eat. My personal choices aren't meant to make you uncomfortable—quite the opposite; they are meant to help me feel better.

Yes, I'm on the first level of guru mastership, how did you know?

I'm not a vegetarian! Where did you get that idea?

Table Manners for the Meatless

Making your new choice in diet is just that, a choice. It doesn't have to be catered to by others, although that's nice sometimes, but you also don't have to be wimpy about requesting meat-free food.

Your best bet as a vegetarian is to be assertive, but not aggressive. And don't be too passive, or you'll go home hungry. Take this quiz and see how well you'll do in public:

Table Manners for the Meatless

1. At a dinner banquet you are served the wrong meal, consisting of a heaping pile of rare beef. You …

   a. Loudly proclaim, "Oh GROSS!" and proceed to make gagging noises until your server (or someone else at your table) takes the plate away from you.

   b. Politely remind the server that you requested a vegetarian plate and nibble on a roll while you wait for it.

   c. Refuse to eat at all.

2. At a catered dinner engagement you are served a meat platter. You …

   a. Tell the server, "I don't eat dead animals," and force him or her to bring you something else.

   b. Ask politely if the server can bring you a plate with everything but the meat instead, and if not, make do with the vegetables on the plate.

   c. Gently and meekly pick the few vegetables farthest away from the meat to eat, while squinting your eyes and making pained facial expressions. When you are done eating your measly amount, sigh heavily, push your plate forward, and frown.

3. Your dinner guest orders a meat dish and offers you a bite. You …

   a. Whip out a brochure on the dangers of meat eating and request that he follow along while you begin a dissertation on how many resources were used to create his meal, how long meat stays in the colon, and how many parasites and bacteria are found in each square inch of beef.

   b. Enthusiastically refuse, continue to enjoy your own meal, and offer your guest a taste of *your* delicious vegetarian meal.

   c. Take the bite, then turn your head and spit it into a napkin.

4. When asked on a dinner date you …

   a. Expect your date to remember you are a vegetarian. If he takes you to an inappropriate place anyway, you call him a meathead and stomp out of the restaurant.

   b. Speak up ahead of time and let your date know that you would like to choose the restaurant since not all restaurants are vegetarian-friendly.

   c. Don't mention anything ahead of time, and when you wind up at a place that is not vegetarian-friendly, sulk.

5. Your host at a dinner party is serving her "famous fried chicken" and asks whether you prefer legs or breasts. You respond …

   a. I am appalled that you would even serve something that you can call by its body part! I will have no parts of any animal on my plate!

   b. I'm a vegetarian, so I'm going to fill up on all the rest of this wonderful food, for which you should be just as famous as you are for your chicken.

   c. Whatever you want to serve me is fine.

Scoring:

   A answers are aggressive and hostile reactions to situations. If you answered A to any of the questions, you've got an attitude! Consider the alternative assertive choices, which are the B answers. Although it might be noble to be a vegetarian, it is a mostly free world, and antagonizing people won't help your digestion any.

B answers are the most assertive answers and the most appropriate way not only to help yourself get what you need, but not to offend others.

C answers are too passive. Choosing these answers shows that you feel embarrassed about your diet. I suggest that you read up on reasons for being a vegetarian to help yourself become more passionate about your beliefs. You will feel more confident in asserting yourself, and you'll live more happily for it.

Veggie Soup for the Soul

Although you might want to help meat-eaters turn to vegetarianism by pointing out that their filet mignon in reality is the flesh of a dead animal, presenting this information at a dinner party is highly inappropriate and will reflect poorly on your table manners. The gross-out effect might work temporarily, but later on, most people will remember *you* as the cause of their discomfort, not the meat they ate. My best advice is to explain vegetarianism to those who are interested, but never around a dinner table where meat is being served.

Sprouts of Info

The best cure for passivity is flaming passion. Become involved and convicted with your vegetarian diet, and it will help you be more assertive (not aggressive) in getting your needs met.

Handling Business Luncheons

At work you can probably either pack your own lunch and snacks for the day or choose the restaurant where you go for lunch. This gives you plenty of flexibility for getting vegetarian foods during your workday. However, sometimes you will have to deal with business luncheons or catered business meetings that require you to eat what the caterer brings.

Let me give a couple of quick examples from a lacto vegetarian computer consultant who worked for a large corporation at its headquarters in upstate New York, where the local fare is famous for its meat-centered meals. I thought the way he handled these situations was interesting, and you can learn from them, too. After that I'll give you some more specific tips for eating on the job.

Let's Not Do Lunch

My friend, let's call him Tyson, attended a catered lunch meeting where the entire buffet consisted of beef on a weck (a kind of roll), a traditional dish in Buffalo, New York. The meal consisted of a rock salted hard roll, shaved beef in gravy, and potato chips and cola. (I wonder what the statistics are for high blood pressure in Buffalo?) Anyway, there was obviously nothing that Tyson could eat except maybe the chips, which didn't do much for him.

Tyson decided to sit quietly at the conference room table and eat nothing. Many people soon asked why he wasn't eating. He replied, "I'm a vegetarian. There is nothing here for me to eat." To which most responded with a solid "hmm" or "huh!"

The best part, however, was when his boss came over to inquire why he wasn't eating. He told her the truth, and she replied, "I didn't know. We'll keep that in mind for next time." Because of that incident, there was always at least one vegetarian item at each catered meeting, and everyone seemed to enjoy the vegetarian foods as well.

Another situation occurred when Tyson was at an offsite executive-level business meeting at a hotel where the meal choice was pre-made sandwiches of ham or turkey. Along with this meal came a pasta salad with ham, a bag of potato chips, and a cookie.

When Tyson took a look at this meal, he got up and ordered a vegetarian pizza. This made the point that a vegetarian selection should be included at any catered event and that vegetarians can enjoy foods that look, smell, and taste good, too. In fact, most of the attendees were asking Tyson for a slice of his onion, pineapple, and jalapeño pizza!

Veggie Soup for the Soul

Interestingly enough, Tyson's request for a vegetarian meal on that one occasion helped get at least one vegetarian option at every catered lunch from then on. Within the two years that Tyson worked for the large company, vegetarian items increased to half of the menu choices at catered lunches! Requests for the vegetarian items skyrocketed once people were introduced to these new foods. The trend caught on and even though Tyson wasn't personally thanked, he was able to eat well at all his meetings from then on, even in a place known for chicken wings and hoagies!

Catering to Vegetarian Tastes

Here are some bottom-line tips for being a vegetarian at a catered business lunch. I've separated them into two categories, one if you are at a catered meeting and you didn't have an advance food choice, and another where you know about it ahead of time. Here are some things you can do to survive and to make future meetings more veg-friendly.

When you get caught in a meeting that is catered, and you didn't have the heads up to make a request:

➤ If there is nothing for you to eat, besides maybe some potato chips, draw attention to the fact that you cannot eat what is being served at the meeting simply by sitting quietly and abstaining from eating *anything*. When asked about this, quietly tell others your situation and make a suggestion for future meetings. Most people care about making others comfortable and will be happy to help you by making a change for the next meeting.

➤ Rush the buffet! Tyson suggests this one. He says this is the bottom line for vegetarians in any buffet situation. There are two reasons for doing this. First, you can scope out everything available. If there is nothing for you to eat, you still have time to run to a local restaurant or office cafeteria to get something else or to order something like a vegetarian pizza. Secondly, by getting your food first, you have less chance of the vegetarian items being mixed up with or contaminated by the meat items, which often occurs in most self-serve buffets.

Sprouts of Info

Collect packets of mustard everywhere you go. Save them up and keep a few in your desk drawer for those occasions when you are served a dry lettuce and cheese sandwich at a business meeting. If nothing else, you can at least spice it up. Mustard also makes a great dip for pretzels.

➤ If there is a buffet with at least a few items that you can eat, such as salad and rolls, make a meal of it. Take a roll and stuff every vegetable they have into it as a sandwich. Use salad dressing as a condiment and pile up the carrot sticks, salad, and potato chips on the side. Make it colorful and enticing, and I'll bet a few meat eaters in the group will copy your idea and make their own salad sandwiches!

When you know ahead of time about a catered lunch meeting …

➤ Talk to the person who does the ordering for the lunches to make your vegetarian request.

➤ Request that catered meals be served buffet-style versus pre-made. If sandwiches are pre-made, make a request for yours to include vegetables only, hold the mayo. It might be a good idea to bring some of your own condiments to make your sandwich more interesting—keep packets of mustard handy for these occasions.

➤ If the meals are going to be catered buffets, request that the meat items be separated from the cheese and vegetable items to avoid cross contamination. (If you've ever eaten a piece of lettuce that had been sitting under a piece of bologna, as a vegetarian, you'll know what I mean about contamination.)

The bottom line is that you can get through a business lunch without starving to death, but you might have to use your creativity. Think of it as an opportunity to showcase your wonderful problem-solving skills! And remember to stay professional. Don't sulk if you hate the food, and don't even think about telling your boss what's really in her bologna sandwich!

Veggie Soup for the Soul

When requesting vegetarian items at a buffet luncheon you'll have to make suggestions. Most lunches are served with some type of salad or other items that don't depend on meat. Here are a few examples:

➤ Pasta salad, hold the ham

➤ Green tossed salad, hold the egg, dressings on the side

➤ Beans or bean salad, hold the bacon

When You're Invited to a Roast Beef Dinner

When you are on your own time, things are a little easier. If you are invited to dinner at someone's house you probably know the hosts, so you can let them know ahead of time about your vegetarian diet. Offer some suggestions, because they honestly might not know what to cook for you.

To make it easy on your hosts (who usually aim to please their guests), have them make their traditional foods and leave the meat (and dairy, if need be) on the side. They might have to make spaghetti with a side of meatballs rather than beef stew, but most people won't mind going this far out of their way for you. If you know the person well enough, you can even send them a recipe for one of your favorite vegetarian dishes.

If this doesn't seem appropriate, offer to bring a dish. You might want to bring two, however, since most meat-eaters just love these new vegetarian dishes. You never know who'll wind up going vegetarian because of your famous broccoli casserole!

If you've been invited as a guest of a guest, then you probably won't have much choice in the matter. In these cases, I suggest you make the best of the dinner. Try to serve yourself if you can and fill your plate with all the vegetarian fare you can find. If you're lucky, you'll get salad, bread, and a few side vegetables that will fill you up, and no one will ever notice.

Sometimes, upon discovering that you are a vegetarian, your host will apologize and run to the kitchen proclaiming, "Oh I didn't know. I'm sure I can make you something …." You can settle the matter by saying something like, "You know, this plate full of food sitting right in front of me is *exactly* the type of meal I eat at home as a vegetarian. Thank you."

The Least You Need to Know

➤ Not everyone is going to be receptive to your diet changes, and some will even be antagonistic. Your best response is to be clear and logical, keeping your reply light.

➤ It is better to be assertive rather than passive or aggressive when stating your vegetarian needs. It makes everyone more comfortable, including you.

➤ In business situations, plan ahead if possible when you know you are to attend a catered meeting to make sure there is a vegetarian option. Be the first in line at the buffet table, which gives you the most options for a compromise.

➤ When you are invited to someone's home for dinner, tell them in advance about your diet if you can. If not, there is bound to be something on the table you can eat. The most important thing is to be a gracious guest.

➤ Remember that vegetarianism is not for everyone. Make the best of the situations you find yourself in and don't criticize others for their choices.

Chapter 19

Dining Out Vegetarian Style

In This Chapter

➤ Learn how to find vegetarian fast food

➤ Discover what to order at a steak house

➤ Learn to avoid hidden animal ingredients

➤ Find out what to expect at different types of restaurants

If you live in a large metropolitan area your restaurant choices as a vegetarian are going to be abundant. If you don't you might need a little help figuring out where to go or what to do when you're stuck in a restaurant with no vegetarian entrees. This chapter serves as your vegetarian survival guide for any type of restaurant dining.

Here we'll look at many interesting possibilities, from fast foods to salad bars, and take a tour through different types of restaurant to see what you can expect. I'll list some vegetarian ethnic foods to try and help you recognize the hidden animal ingredients in places you'd never expect anyone to put meat.

Meatless Fast Foods

As demand grows for more healthful organic and vegetarian fare there are more and more vegetarian choices in fast-food places. In fact I've heard of one new U.S.-based chain called Healthy Bites Grill, which is supposed to be the first-ever restaurant chain serving healthful organic food in a fast-food format! Look for these restaurants to come to densely populated business communities first, and hopefully they will expand to more rural areas and across the world!

Until then, some other choices for fast food include stopping in at a local grocery store that has a soup or salad bar. With cash in hand you can run in, get your salad, zip through the express checkout line, and be out the door in less than ten minutes! And by now you should be familiar with your local health food store, so if you are lucky enough to have one with a deli, you know where to go for lunch.

Sprouts of Info

Fast foods should be eaten only occasionally, if at all, because the calories add up! But if you must, go to the fast-food places that can accommodate you best. Chains in Europe and in major metropolitan cities tend to offer more vegetarian menu choices, such as falafel sandwiches and tofu and veggie pitas. And chains everywhere are starting to offer salads.

Another good fast lunch can be found at your local bagel shop. Many of the bagel chains now serve lunch, making sandwiches with bagels. You'll find plenty of vegetarian choices, and they usually have good soups available.

Burgers Without the Burger

If you've got a hankering for some junk food or are secretly adding to your collection of fast-food-restaurant kid's toys, here are some tips on what to order at some of the major fast-food burger restaurants.

Burger King will understand what you mean if you ask for a "Veggie Whopper" (hold the meat), and lacto vegetarians can get it with cheese. There really is no such thing as a true veggie burger at Burger King (at least not yet). What you will get is a bun with lettuce, tomato, onions, ketchup, pickles, mayo (unless you have them hold it), and cheese if requested. If nothing else, you will cut down on your fat intake by eliminating the meat from this "burger."

McDonald's in the United States knows what to do if you ask for a Big Mac with no meat. This is the same as the Veggie Burger at Burger King, meaning that there is no substitute for the patty, just the absence of meat (again, tell them whether you want mayo or cheese). McDonald's in other countries usually has actual meatless patties that are quite delicious.

Wendy's hamburgers can also be ordered without meat, but Wendy's restaurants also have some things for vegetarians that the other burger joints don't, namely baked potatoes and a salad bar.

Jack In The Box offers many food items that can be made to accommodate you, such as Teriyaki bowls, salads, pita sandwiches, and other items.

Fast Meatless Alternatives

Here's a quick look at your veggie options at some other popular fast-food restaurants. Arby's offers baked potatoes and garden salads. Taco Bell offers veggie wraps.

Pizza Hut has mini cheese pizzas—call ahead, and they'll be ready to pick up in less than 10 minutes. Salad bars can also be found in most Pizza Huts.

Any fast-food restaurants offering subs can accommodate you with a vegetarian sub and usually a salad as well. See how easy this is getting?

Restaurants at Your Service?

If you have a little more time on your hands and want a sit-down, lunch, you can fill up on foods from any restaurant offering buffet-style dining. (Try to keep it to your two handfuls maximum here, eh?!) This even includes many chain steak houses, where you can skip the steak and fill up on the rest of the foods offered at the buffet. You will usually find a surprising selection of salad fixings, veggie salads, vegetables, soups, fruits, breads, pastas, and rice. Many of these places offer baked potatoes and sometimes taco salad fixings, too.

Sit-down, family-style, chain restaurants usually have at least one vegetarian item on the menu these days, but if they don't, don't count on them being able to make something special for you. Most items are pre-made in mass quantities where it would be impossible to remove the meat from the sauce, and so on. When choosing this type of restaurant you'll have to be more willing to make do.

Creative Dining a la Chain

Here are some tips on how to be creative at family-style or other meat-oriented chains when there are no vegetarian choices to your liking:

➤ Scan the entire menu for a la carte items, garnishes, or side dishes that are okay for you to eat, such as beans, avocado, various vegetables, and rice or potatoes. Other possibilities might be meatless appetizers or pastas with meatless sauces. Come up with your own combination of these items.

➤ Read the description of the sandwiches and meat items and check out the rest of the ingredients. Many dishes can be made without the meat. Consider the grilled chicken sandwich with grilled peppers, onions, tomato, and avocado, served with a veggie pasta side salad—hold the chicken, and you have yourself a satisfying meatless meal.

If you decide to piece together several side dishes or appetizers to make a vegetarian meal, you will almost certainly get all of these sides in separate little dishes. Be sure to ask your server ahead of time to bring you a big plate so that you can transfer your vegetarian items to it. It is a nuisance to accommodate five or six individual tiny plates at once. Be sure to ask ahead of time so you can quickly empty your dishes onto your plate and hand the server back the dishes that will clutter your table.

Good in a Pinch

It can be hard to find vegetarian fare in rural areas. I remember being in the boonies in northern Montana and having to survive on iceberg lettuce salads and grilled cheese sandwiches for a few days!

When you find places that offer nothing that is not deep fried in lard or boiled in chicken stock, it can wear on your vegetarian soul, so always plan ahead if possible. If you can't, here are some worst-case-scenario survival foods:

➤ Peanut butter and jelly sandwich

➤ Grilled cheese sandwich (if you're a lacto vegetarian)

➤ Pasta with plain tomato sauce or olive oil and parsley

➤ Bread and whatever raw veggies they have available—make your own sandwich

➤ Oatmeal or other breakfast foods that might still be available later in the day

➤ Baked potatoes can make a meal topped with raw vegetables, salsa, beans, or guacamole

Fine Dining

Finer restaurants are usually much more willing and able to help accommodate your requests than the family-style chains. The classier restaurants usually make meals per request, not en mass, so they have more flexibility in their output. Even so, it's not wise to show up expecting the chef to fulfill your requests.

It is best to call ahead and find out whether the chef can make you something vegetarian or vegan. Be specific about which ingredients you do not eat. I've been to places where the chef thought that vegetarians eat fish, for example. You are the expert on your diet, so help others accommodate you by being clear about your needs.

When making your food requests, be prepared to let them know what you need all at once—there is nothing more irritating to others than when you string a person along by requesting a meal and subtracting one ingredient at a time. Be clear and up front right away, make sure the person you ask takes notes, and you will save everyone a lot of extra time and hassles. Let me illustrate:

Scenario One: The Direct, Concise Approach

Customer to hostess: Do you know if your chef can accommodate a strict vegetarian?

Hostess: Yes, I believe he can.

Customer: Okay, would you please take a note of my request and find out if he can accommodate someone who does not eat any animal products whatsoever, including fish, all meats, poultry, eggs, chicken stock, and fish sauces and no dairy at all—that means butter, too?

Hostess: Okay, I'll get that to him and let you know.

Avoid presenting your question this way:

> **Scenario Two: The Roundabout, Scattered Approach**
>
> Customer to hostess: Does your chef accommodate vegetarians?
>
> Hostess: Yes, I believe he does.
>
> Customer: What kind of vegetarians?
>
> Hostess: What do you mean?
>
> Customer: Can he make something without cheese?
>
> Hostess: I think so.
>
> Customer: How about eggs?
>
> Hostess: I can ask.
>
> Customer: Okay, I also don't eat anything with fish sauces or chicken stock …
>
> Hostess: Okay, I will ask him.
>
> Customer: Oh, and don't forget to ask about butter, too …

Finding Meat in All the Wrong Places

Even when items are labeled vegetarian on the menu, you still need to find out what a particular establishment thinks "vegetarian" means. No meat, probably, but how about dairy? Eggs? Fish? You will often find that meatless items contain cheese or egg. Although some vegetable soups do not contain pieces of meat, such as tomato bisque or vegetable soup, the base is often chicken stock or beef bullion.

Sorry, but it's just the way restaurants work, so you'll have to plan ahead and watch your step until you find some favorite restaurants with reliable veggie foods on the menu. To help you narrow it down, here's a list of some items where you would never expect to find meat.

Sprouts of Info

It's best to call a restaurant to find out if vegetarian items are on the menu or if the chef is willing to accommodate you. Sometimes the folks who answer the phone won't be able to give you a good answer because most people aren't familiar with vegetarianism. Ask them to fax you a copy of the menu so you can decipher it for yourself.

Hidden Animal Ingredients in Restaurant Foods

Food	Often Contains
Vegetable soup	Chicken, pork, or beef stock
Baked beans	Ham
Bean soup	Bacon
Biscuits	Lard
Broccoli soup	Pork, cheese
Caesar salad	Anchovies and anchovies in the dressing
Chili	Ground beef (unless it says vegetarian chili)
Cooked greens	Salt pork (more prevalent in the southern United States)
Flour tortillas	Lard
French onion soup	Beef stock
Fried rice	Eggs
Greek salad	Anchovies, feta cheese
Green beans	Bacon
Green chili (used as a sauce in many Mexican dishes)	Pork
Marinara sauce	Beef
Pasta salad	Ham
Pie crust	Lard
Potato salad	Eggs, sometimes bacon
Potato soup	Bacon
Refried beans	Lard
Sautéed vegetables	Simmered in chicken stock (not always, but ask)
Spinach salad	Bacon, eggs
Steamed rice	Chicken stock
Stir-fry	Oyster sauce
Tossed or dinner salads	Eggs, bacon bits

For a free 16-page fact sheet listing over 200 animal ingredients that are used in food preparation or other items, along with their vegetarian alternatives, contact People for the Ethical Treatment of Animals (PETA) at 757-622-PETA. Or go to its Web site at www.peta-online.org/ and download a copy for yourself.

Something's Fishy!

Here's another quick story that some of my colleagues will laugh at if they read it, remembering my facial expression when I ordered a broccoli and rice dish at a popular

Thai restaurant in Denver. I took a giant bite of a delicious-looking piece of bright green broccoli. At once my mouth was filled with the saltiest, most repulsive (to me), fishy-tasting juice I could have dreamed of. It was completely unexpected and all I could do was turn away and spit it into the napkin, run to the bathroom, and wash my mouth out with tap water while my colleagues laughed uncontrollably. I can't tell you how horrible that experience was for me, so I'm recounting it here to spare you the same. The taste took at least three days (no kidding) to leave my mouth. I might as well have bitten into an uncooked fish. Be warned, if you go to a Thai restaurant, unless you are choosing the pesco vegetarian diet, watch out for the fish sauce!

Love That Lard

Some foods contain meat or other animal ingredients even though they are usually made at home without them. Common examples are biscuits and pie crusts made with lard. Another surprising lard-harboring food is cake, which might have frosting made with the fatty stuff. And don't forget that your favorite breakfast items, like French toast and pancakes, aren't going to be vegan when you eat out, even though your server might tell you they are vegetarian.

Let me share an experience so you can grasp how widely the food service industry, even when you would think they would know better, interprets vegetarian food. I recently attended an aromatherapy workshop held at a hotel where lunch was included in the price of the class. Being the seasoned vegetarian that I am, I called the company sponsoring the class ahead of time to ask whether a choice of lunches was to be offered, and if so, to request a vegetarian meal. The school assured me that they had already arranged with the hotel to serve a strictly vegetarian lunch for everyone.

I was delighted until lunch was served. The hotel's version of a vegetarian lunch included green beans. But mine had a big slab of bacon in them! I quickly and quietly notified the server that we were supposed to receive vegetarian meals. She left and came back with the reply, "These are the vegetarian meals. The bacon is just thrown in there to give it flavor!" I am constantly amazed how people interpret vegetarianism.

Steer Clear

In Thai and other Oriental restaurants, please watch out for the fish sauce, which is commonly poured over steamed vegetables or rice but is not necessarily listed on the menu.

Sprouts of Info

When traveling look for vegetarian restaurants in the Yellow Pages. If you can't find any there, consider ethnic restaurants, which usually have several vegetarian items on the menu.

Worldly Menus

In Chapter 17, "Meatless Meals," we looked at some good ethnic vegetarian choices. If you like dining out and are lucky enough to have some of these ethnic restaurants in your area, you'll know what to look for, and you can even discover new vegetarian items from these restaurants to prepare for yourself at home. Here I'll recap some of the ethnic fare we discussed so you'll know what foods to try. Strict vegetarians can hold the cheese on any of these items.

Vegetarian Selections from Around the World

Italian

Antipastos
Any pasta with meatless marinara sauce
Bread sticks or other bread dipped in olive oil and oregano
Foccacia
Minestrone soup (find out whether it contains beef)
Mixed green salads
Pasta dishes tossed with vegetables and meatless sauces or olive oil and herbs
Pasta primavera
Vegetarian lasagna

Mexican

Bean and jalapeño nachos
Chili rellenos (hot pepper stuffed with cheese and deep-fried)
Chips and salsa
Guacamole tostadas
Lard-free bean burritos, tostadas, or chalupas
Soft veggie tacos
Spinach enchiladas
Vegetarian fajitas

Indian

Chutney
Cucumber and yogurt salad
Dahl (or dal)
Naan, chapatti, roti, or pappadum (Indian breads)
Navratan korma
Palak paneer
Rice

Indian

Samosas (vegetable)

Vegetable curries

Greek or Middle Eastern

Baba ghannouj

Dolamads (rice stuffed grape leaves)

Falafel

Greek salad

Hummus

Pita bread

Spanokopita (spinach and cheese pie, might contain eggs)

Spinach salad

Tabouli salad

Vegetarian cabbage rolls

Ethiopian

Green salads

Injera (spongy bread used to scoop up foods)

Many lentil- and vegetable-based dishes, usually served family-style

Chinese

Vegetable or miso soup

Vegetarian spring rolls

Steamed rice

Veggie stir-fries

Tofu cooked in various ways

Seitan cooked in various ways

Ethnic restaurants can be a wonderful source of vegetarian foods. Some even cater to a vegetarian clientele. It's worth seeking out a good Indian restaurant, for example, because even if it is not completely vegetarian, many have vegetarian buffets, where you can experiment and not worry about finding meat in a sauce. Call the restaurant to find out.

I hope you find that eating out as a vegetarian can be a pleasant and tasteful experience where you can utilize your creativity to keep yourself satisfied.

Sprouts of Info

On Chinese menus tofu is often referred to as bean curd.

239

And who knows, maybe something you suggest to the chef will become your "special dish," and even a part of the permanent menu!

The Least You Need to Know

➤ Most fast-food restaurants can offer something without meat, and some health-oriented fast-food restaurants are beginning to spring up.

➤ Vegetarians can find plenty of things to eat at buffet-style restaurants, even if the restaurant is a steak house.

➤ To save yourself unexpected grief when dining out, call ahead or ask your server about ingredients up front to ensure your needs can be accommodated.

➤ Hidden animal ingredients are often found in vegetable-based foods, including soups, sauces, rice, and beans, and eggs, cheese, or fish are often added to salad. Always ask before you order.

➤ Visit a variety of ethnic restaurants for some excellent vegetarian selections. *Bon appétite!*

Chapter 20

The Traveling Vegetarian

In This Chapter

➤ Learn to plan ahead to get what you need when traveling

➤ Find out how to say "vegetarian" in different languages

➤ Discover what to expect when traveling by cruise ship, bus, or train.

➤ Get some great tips for eating healthier on a car trip

This chapter provides some preliminary things to think about while planning your business or vacation trips as a vegetarian. It also has some tips that can make the eating part of your travels more pleasant. By understanding the options you have as a traveling vegetarian and how to get what you need, you will at least know what to expect. This could save you from having to listen to your stomach disappointedly growling at you during a long vegetarian-meal-free airplane flight!

I'll also give you the heads up on some situations where getting wholesome vegetarian food is almost impossible. If you use my planning tips on these occasions, you'll at least have something to tide you over. Although there is no guarantee your trip will be spectacular, at least your stomach will be satisfied. Now get out your suitcase, and let's travel like worldly vegetarians!

Savvy Vegetarian Travel Advisor

Probably the most important component in getting your vegetarian needs met while traveling is proper planning. When you travel, you don't always have access to a kitchen, and certainly not your *own* kitchen. You will be at the mercy of unknown restaurants, train dining cars (or, more often, train cart food, if you're lucky), room service, vending machines, and airline foods.

When you are on a road trip, whether in your car or via bus, you'll be at the mercy of bus station cafés, designated pit stops at less-than-desirable greasy spoons, and truck stops. This just means you'll have to do a little planning.

Here are some things to think about before traveling as a vegetarian:

➤ Consider what type of transportation you'll be taking: plane, train, car, bus, cruise ship, or a combination.

➤ Will you have the use of a vehicle when you get where you're going?

➤ How long will you be gone?

➤ Will you be staying at a condo or another place with a kitchen when you get there?

➤ Will your destination be rural (far from restaurants), city (walking access to what you might need), foreign country (won't know what to expect).

The rest of the chapter addresses why you should be asking yourself these questions. But first, a few more important guidelines.

How You Say ... Vegetarian?

One essential element in making sure you get what you need is proper communication with those in charge of ordering your meals for you. Remember that it is important to be concise, up front, and clear with your server at a restaurant when requesting or inquiring about a vegetarian meal.

If you're in a place where you don't speak the language, being clear will be a little more difficult now won't it? The good news is that I've been in and lived in different countries and managed to get vegetarian meals just about everywhere. I learned from the locals how to say "no meat" or "vegetarian" in different languages, and I've included a little list.

Translating "Vegetarian" to Other Languages

Language	"Vegetarian"	"No Meat"
Arabic	bela lahem	bela lahem
French	végétarien	pas de viande
German	vegetarier	kein Fleisch
Hindi	shakahari'	shakahari'
Italian	vegetariano	nessuna carne
Polish	wegetarianin *or* jarosz	dieta beztluszczowa
Russian	vegetarianskii	Ya ne yem myaso! (I don't eat meat!)

Language	Vegetarian	No Meat
Spanish	vegetariano	nenhuma carne
Swedish	vegetarisk	aucune viande

You can see that the word "vegetarian" is quite similar in most languages, so that's a help, but try to memorize the words in the appropriate language to be sure to get your meal with no meat. If you're afraid of forgetting, write it down.

Anything You Say, Dear

Just as you can't expect the world to bow to your needs at restaurants or grocery stores at home, you'll have to figure out how to get what you need when you're on the road, in spite of a generally pervasive meat-ethic. This chapter will help you understand where you can and can't expect to get your needs met.

I'll also let you know the places where you will most likely be out of luck on a veggie meal—or at least a *healthful* meatless meal. For those times you'll be happy you've heeded my next piece of advice:

No matter how well you think you have everything planned out, *always have a backup plan!* And you're in luck! I'll give you one to use that you can vary for different situations and types of travel. So keep reading—I think I heard the conductor yelling, "All aboard!"

Steer Clear

Because flight attendants use seat numbers to deliver special meals, if you happen to switch seats with someone in another aisle, be sure to notify the flight attendant that you have a special meal coming and that you have changed seats.

Frequent Flying

As a vegetarian you are in luck in the sky because most airlines can accommodate vegetarian palates. All you need to do is request a vegetarian meal when purchasing your tickets. On airlines that are still offering in-flight meals, your request will go into the system, and you'll be served your special meal on your flight.

Even if you've forgotten to request a vegetarian meal when you purchased your tickets, you can call up to 24 hours before your flight, and the airline can usually come through with a special meal for you.

Another fun thing to know if you didn't already is that many of the airlines offer not only a vegetarian meal, but a variety of vegetarian choices for the selective traveler. These meals are available in all classes, although obviously first-class meals are first class, whereas coach meals can be less than desirable. If nothing else, at least you can get the vegetarian version of either!

Your Choices Have Wings

I remember sitting next to a gentleman during an in-flight lunch in coach. He was served the regular meal (a roast beef sandwich, potato chips, and a bite-size candy bar), and my husband and I were served a whole-wheat pita sandwich overflowing with shredded carrots, lettuce, avocado, sprouts, and several other veggies, along with baked potato chips, a veggie pasta side salad, and a juice spritzer.

The man took one look at our meals, handed his tray back to the flight attendant and said, "I'd like what they got!" When the flight attendant explained that you have to order special meals in advance, he frowned and begrudgingly continued eating his roast beef. (How much do you want to bet that the next flight he went on, he called ahead for a vegetarian meal?)

Dining the Friendly Skies

Don't be left out! Remember to call ahead but be precise. If you are not a strict vegetarian or vegan, you might not mind a cheese pizza once in a while, so ask your airline what they have available and order what you like.

Here's a list of some of the major airlines and their vegetarian choices (they have other meal options, but I've listed only the vegetarian ones):

➤ **Canadian.** Asian vegetarian, lacto ovo vegetarian, pesco vegetarian (seafood), fruit plate, vegan, and Hindu vegetarian.

➤ **Continental.** Strict vegetarian, lacto ovo vegetarian, Asian vegetarian, Hindu (theirs is most likely vegetarian, but make sure when you call).

➤ **Delta.** Fruit plate, vegetarian, lacto ovo vegetarian, Asian (Hindu), and pure vegetarian. (You only need to give them 12 hours advance notice.)

➤ **Northwest.** Specialty meals come in four choices: low calorie, low fat, low cholesterol, or low sodium (the same attributes of most vegetarian meals). These meals are not necessarily vegetarian, so inquire when you order.

➤ **Southwest.** It offers no in-flight meals (nuts are served on all flights).

➤ **Swissair.** Claims to be the first airline to serve naturally grown foods. It offers strict Asian vegetarian (Indian style), Hindu vegetarian, kosher fish or a vegetarian variant, Western vegetarian (no meat or dairy), Western lacto ovo vegetarian.

➤ **United.** Lacto ovo vegetarian (which are actually strict vegan meals; however, those in first or business class can have some dairy appetizers or desserts if they choose), Asian vegetarian (includes egg-free pastas, tofu, nonmeat/dairy gravy).

➤ **USAir.** Fruit plate, lacto ovo vegetarian, nondairy vegetarian, Asian vegetarian. (Some of these meals only require a six-hour heads up!)

➤ **TWA.** Offers a strict vegan meal.

If you purchased your airline tickets a long time in advance, be sure to call the airline a day or two before your trip to confirm that your meal request is in.

A Bad Travel Day

Did you ever hear about the straw that broke the camel's back? How about the ham sandwich that broke the vegetarian traveler's spirit? Imagine this scenario. You are on a business trip, traveling alone. You are going more than half-way across the country so you planned on a full day of travel anyway, but because of weather, your flight has been delayed.

You are on the waiting list for first class and because availability is looking good, you're confident you'll be able to have a decent meal on the plane. So you wait, and you continue to wait. Then the weather clears, and you get on board. Then you wait for two hours on the plane because of mechanical difficulties. By this time you are starving!

Your captain announces that passengers must deplane and you'll be scheduled on another flight leaving in less than 10 minutes. Of course the gate is all the way at the other end of the terminal. You notice how empty your stomach is on the frantic rush to the gate. You manage to get the last seat available on the flight, and guess what? It's coach, *and* you got the middle seat!

The Plane Ride from You Know Where

Shortly after takeoff, the man next to you begins clipping his nails, and with each click of the nail clippers tiny fingernail shards flip through the air and onto your dark blue slacks. The woman to your left wants to know your name, what you do, where you're from, where you're going, and what book you're reading. She then regales you with the details of her sister-in-law's recent operations.

Sprouts of Info

A good bet any time you are planning to travel for a good portion of the day is to bring along some snacks. You never know when you could get stuck on a runway for hours. You can make mini emergency ration packs to fit in a briefcase or purse.

There is a young boy sitting directly behind you with a mother who won't discipline him. The boy constantly kicks your seat. You finally give the mother a dirty look, which adds to your irritation because instead of stopping the boy from kicking your seat, the mother now begins a plead with the boy every time he kicks, and it goes something like this:

Boy: [Thud thud thud]

Mother: "Don't do that, *okay?*"

Three minutes later, boy: [Thud thud thud … thud]

Mother in a higher pitched whine: "Don't *do* that, *okaaay??*"

You thinking: I'm gonna take that foot and ….

Airline attendant to the rescue: "Excuse me, would you like some lunch?"

Oh boy, lunch! You've been starved for hours, and although you won't get your first-class meal, at least you can … what's this? A ham sandwich on a white hoagie roll with a packet of mayonnaise?

This is the part where you begin weeping uncontrollably into your ham sandwich. That is, unless you have a backup plan! And you will, because I'm going to outline one for you in a minute. Cheer up, it's only make-believe. Like I said, there are good and bad days traveling, but we might as well do all we can to increase your odds.

Murphy to the Rescue

When should you have a backup plan? I figure the time that you don't have one is the time you'll need one. This is a function of Murphy's Law. To overcome this all-too-familiar phenomenon, all you need to do is create a small bag that you can carry with you easily on your travels. We'll call it your *Murphy bag*.

Your Murphy bag should be some sort of easy-to-carry container that travels easily and fits in your carry-on baggage, like a small backpack, an insulated canvass lunch box, or whatever suits your style. Customize your bag any way you like.

A Murphy bag is good not only for the vegetarian, but also for people with diabetes or hypoglycemia who need to eat frequently. Here are some suggestions for things to include in your Murphy bag:

➤ Popcorn

➤ Vegetables, cleaned and cut into strips, such as carrots, celery, and green or red peppers (cucumbers don't travel well)

➤ Ryvita crackers

➤ Peanut butter or other nut butters in a small plastic tub

➤ Hummus or baba gannouja spreads

➤ Bottled water—small individual bottles

➤ Pretzels

➤ Sesame seed sticks

➤ Mustard packets

➤ Soy milk in individual boxes

➤ Cereal in small boxes

➤ Sliced cheese

➤ Pita pockets

➤ Apple or pear slices

➤ Dehydrated cup of soup, chowder, mashed potatoes, or chili

➤ Banana chips

➤ Raw nuts

➤ Protein bars

➤ Yogurt-covered nuts or raisins

➤ Moist towelettes

➤ Napkins

➤ Plastic silverware set

Lettuce Explain

A **Murphy bag** is a bag of emergency rations that you can use while traveling to supplement your meals or serve as a backup when you're stuck without food. Make your own Murphy bag to suit your specific travel needs.

Sprouts of Info

If you aren't hungry, save the little bags of pretzels, nuts, or fruit you receive on your flight to add to your Murphy bag.

I realize we can't all be the Martha Stewart of meal travel planning, and this is true especially if you are heading back home from your trip and your Murphy bag is depleted. That's when you want to look for free food or grab some prepackaged snacks along the way to stash away. For instance, most hotels offer a bowl of fruit at the check-in desk. When leaving the hotel to catch your flight, grab a piece.

Or when you stop to put gas in your rental car before you get to the airport, choose a convenience store gas station and grab a bagel and a small bottle of water or juice. This is a time-saver, and it can be an appetite-saver if your day goes awry.

Cruisin' for the Vegetarian

On cruise ships you will definitely have to inquire about the kinds of food available on-board beforehand. There are many types of cruise ships now. Some are inexpensive, some expensive, some family-oriented, some for adults. Cruise ships often have themes, such as holistic health cruises, sports fans' cruises, singles' cruises, jazz lovers' cruises, and so on. I haven't yet found a vegetarian cruise, but I don't doubt you could find one with a more thorough investigation!

Veggie Soup for the Soul

These days cruise ships cater more and more to the health-conscious. Some even have separate healthy menus, and many of the items are meatless. Most cruise ships offer a good variety, and just like in land-bound restaurants, the chefs in the nicer restaurants on-board are usually able to create something to order for you.

Your best bet is to make sure that the cruise ship has more than one restaurant that offers vegetarian meals. You don't want to wind up on a boat for two weeks eating the same meal every day. Ask questions and check out the specifics. If the cruise line offers at least one buffet a day it's a good bet since buffets usually offer a good variety.

The same goes for all inclusive resorts. Check with your travel agent to find out how many restaurants are available, what types of restaurants they are, and what vegetarian fare they have.

Another thing to think about is purified water. Make sure the cruise ship offers bottled water for sale so you don't get stuck drinking from the tap.

Room Service: Room for Improvement

Hotels are another place where planning ahead can save you time and give you a chance to change your reservation if you don't like what the hotel offers. For starters, do your homework and find out whether the hotel shuttle can take you to where you need to go, if you'll need a car or taxi service, or if the hotel can accommodate all your needs.

What does this have to do with being vegetarian? I'll tell you. I often attend seminars and classes in various hotels across the country, and I stay in the hotel where the classes are held and usually do not rent a car. However, I've learned that hotels can sometimes be miles away from anything else, and therefore you are stuck with either the hotel's food choices or a big bill hiring a taxi every day!

What I try to do now if I'm not planning to rent a car is to call ahead and find out where the hotel is located and how many restaurants are located within the hotel or within walking distance from it. Have the person you speak with be clear that the adjacent restaurants are actually five minutes *walking* distance, not a five-minute *drive!* If you are still unsure, have them fax you the hotel restaurant's menu. Then you can decide whether you can live with the foods offered for the number of days you'll be there. If not, make sure to budget taxi money or car rental.

Your Murphy bag can come in handy again here, at least on the first day you arrive and for snacks during seminars. When you've arrived late but hungry you can get hot water from your hotel and add it to your cups of dehydrated soup, chowder, or chili. Add a few slices of soy cheese to some rye crackers, and you have a warm meal.

All this advance work might seem like a time-consuming hassle at first, but before long it will become a part of your normal routine.

Road Trips: Avoiding Road Kill

In some ways it's a lot easier to get decent vegetarian food on road trips because you will have a car, which means you have more freedom to drive to a health food store and get what you need. However, interstate travel can still leave you hungry for good food, so it's always a good idea to take foods to eat at the rest stops. Most of the food you'll find close to the interstate consists of fast foods, truck stops, and greasy spoons, which are not always a Mecca for vegetarians.

Traveling by bus is even worse, since the busses seem to stop only in the greasiest of spoons and coffee houses. Be sure to take your Murphy bag with you on bus trips. Don't forget the moist towelettes either!

Here are some things to add to your Murphy bag when you are traveling by car. Because there's more space, you can spread out a little. Use a large cooler to keep larger amounts of food cool. Fill it up with your favorite sandwich items and plenty of fresh-cut veggies and fruit slices. Add some chilled bottles of juice or soy milk, and you're ready to roll.

> ➤ **Large cooler.** To store all your refrigerated food items. Bring your cooler in to your hotel room when you arrive. Don't let it sit in a hot car.
> ➤ **Straws.** To put in bottled juices and other beverages when you can't properly clean the container.
> ➤ **Plastic utensils.** For preparing sandwiches and for eating.
> ➤ **Aluminum foil.** To wrap sandwiches and leftovers.
> ➤ **Zippered baggies.** To hold the rest of your tomato or avocado once you slice it.
> ➤ **Bottle opener.** To open bottles of natural soda.
> ➤ **Paper plates.** To put your veggie sandwiches on or to use as a cutting board. Can also serve as a clean barrier between your food and a dusty picnic table.
> ➤ **Gallon jug of pure water.** You don't want to run out of pure water, and it can come in handy for rinsing the fresh fruits you purchase along the way.

Sprouts of Info

Consider adding a heating coil that can boil a cup of water to your Murphy bag. It can come in handy for late-night soups or early morning tea.

With all these items you can make yourself sandwiches and even whip out a salad for a great roadside picnic. Plan to hit a supermarket along the way once in a while to get more fresh produce.

Steer Clear

If you're hungry, don't wait for the train ride to find vegetarian cuisine (or much of any good food). The trains I've been on throughout Europe and Asia all seemed to have either no food or food I wouldn't want to eat, meat-eater or not!

All Aboard!

When traveling by train, you'll need to have some backup food with you, unless you are on a long trip and there's a dining car. Even then, since the food on dining cars tends to be expensive and is only available at certain times, extra food and water can still come in handy. Treat your train trip as you would traveling by plane or to a hotel. Find out what is available. And don't forget to buy some bottled water before you board! Trains often don't have any drinkable water.

Here's some good news for vegetarian train travelers in the United States. Amtrak now offers vegan and vegetarian Nile Spice soups on-board. Also, during quick trips, Amtrak offers raw carrot sticks, almonds, peanuts, fruit yogurt, granola bars, fruit juices, and herbal teas for snack foods. Vegetarian choices in the dining cars on longer trips include fettuccini with your choice of tomato-basil, primavera, or Alfredo sauce. Wherever you go and however you get there, the bottom line is this: The less control you'll have over a situation, like traveling without your own vehicle or to destinations where you don't have many food choices, the more carefully you should plan your Murphy bag! Bon voyage!

The Least You Need to Know

➤ When you are traveling, it is always a good idea to have a backup plan. Pack a Murphy bag (named after Murphy's famous law) with some emergency rations to snack on until you can get a good meal.

➤ Most airlines offer a vegetarian meal, but be sure to order ahead of time and to call again 24 hours before your flight to confirm it.

➤ Learning how to say "no meat" in the native language can come in handy.

➤ Always call ahead to check on restaurant and food options, whether you're flying, cruising, or staying at a hotel.

➤ Stock a cooler with fresh foods to take with you on road trips. Roadside picnics beat fast food and truck stops every time.

Chapter 21

The Meatless Family

In This Chapter

➤ Learn how to live with a meat-eater

➤ See how to have a great vegetarian pregnancy

➤ Discover how to raise healthy vegetarian children

➤ Learn about vegetarianism for your pets

Now you've traveled the world as a vegetarian and are getting ready to settle down with a family of your own. Ideally you see yourself with a vegetarian spouse, kids, and maybe even pets, right? Good, because that's what this chapter teaches you how to achieve.

Here you'll get some pointers on how to handle dating a nonvegetarian (especially when your ideal is to have a vegetarian spouse!). You get helpful tips on being a vegetarian through a pregnancy, and it will ease your fears about raising healthy kids as vegetarians. And finally, you'll learn what to feed your carnivorous pet without feeling like a hypocrite.

Date Night at the Steak House

So you're sitting there holding your fork over a plateful of salad, gazing at this man who could be "The One." You daydream as he talks to you, half listening, half thinking that he wears his hair just the way you like it, his clothes are just what you would have picked for him, and he seems to have just the right mix of humor, security, confidence, independence, healthy appearance, optimism, and interests.

Ahh, you sigh, and suddenly he forks up a big bloody hunk of beef. Blinded by love, you didn't notice before how unattractive his chowing down his steak was or how fast he was wolfing down his food. You wonder, "If this is my dream man, will he be healthy enough to live out our golden years together?"

I think that is a fair question to ask yourself! Since you now know the health benefits of going meatless, you will have some legitimate concerns about marrying a meat-eater. (Well that is if your intentions are pure!) What to do? Dump him right now? No! Meat eating has nothing to do with character, and his character is what you will be marrying, not his diet.

Beef Steak? "No Flank You"

The goal is definitely not to control anyone, nor should this list serve to add to your if-I-marry-him-I-can-change-him fantasy. But you can use it to assess your potential spouse's general eating habits and attitudes about health. This goes in the mix along with everything else. If you want to have a healthy, long-lasting mate who will help you raise healthy children, your mate's diet or attitude about food will matter. Warning: This list should be considered *only* after you feel this person's character meets or exceeds your standards.

So keep dating, and if he or she has good character, and you really think the two of you have potential, just observe his or her eating habits for a while and consider your options. Remember that vegetarianism shouldn't be the goal; the goal should be a healthy diet for your mate. You want to spend a long life together without watching the person you love eat deep-fried pork chops every night and wondering when the first heart attack will strike.

I have to admit that living with a vegetarian spouse is wonderful (although he's a pesco vegetarian, he doesn't bring fish into the home), and it sure makes things easy for shopping and food preparation. Plus I know my husband is healthier because of his diet. He'll be around to listen to my incessant talk about holistic health for years to come!

Rating Your Potential Mate

Okay, now let's see how your potential mate rates in the eating department.

➤ Does (s)he have a healthy attitude about food and eating, and about exercise and fitness in general? If so, you're probably in luck, because the health-conscious individual will be interested in what you have to say about the health benefits of a meatless diet.

➤ Does (s)he seem to like a variety of foods? Another good sign. If you will do the cooking at home and he or she enjoys a variety of foods, you will be able to satisfy your beloved's taste buds and never miss the meat.

➤ Does the person seem to be open to new things, ideas, traveling, and adventure? Again, another good sign you have a future meatless eater in your sights. Vegetarians tend to be people who are willing to take risks and try new things.

➤ Does (s)he seem to be a staunch meat-and-potatoes man or woman? This might be more of a challenge than a pure vegetarian will be ready to deal with; however, if everything else checks out, don't let a little meat and potatoes stop you. Help your mate with some food combining, covered in Chapter 22, "The Health Nut." At least you'll have a healthier meat-eater to marry.

Remember, you were once in the dark and had no idea about what a wonderful diet vegetarianism could be. After you found out and began this lifestyle, you couldn't see yourself going back to meat. But this might not be the case with your future spouse. Feel your intended out a bit to get a sense of his or her concern about health, and ask if he or she ever even thought about vegetarianism, or at least eating less meat.

You might be surprised that your love is open and interested, but simply doesn't know anything about the topic (perhaps like you several chapters ago). Decide what you can and can't live with, remember that the path toward vegetarianism can evolve slowly depending on the person, and remember that once you, too, were probably a meat-eater.

What I'm saying is don't throw the meat-eater out with the table scraps!

Your Meat–Eating Spouse

Okay, you've married the steak-and-potatoes man or woman (because of his or her good character, of course) or you're already married to a meat eater who tells you that you are going to have to "go it alone" if you insist upon vegetarianism. How do you handle this? Go for it! Don't worry, once your spouse sees the delicious meals you make he will probably become more of a vegetarian than he planned. There are just a few things you'll want to do to keep peace in the kitchen.

Keep meat and dairy products separate in all ways. Your spouse will need to respect your feelings about meat, and you will both have to designate places and kitchen appliances that will and will not be used for meat preparation. This is going to be more important to you than your spouse, so you'll need to stress how important it is.

His and Hers Refrigerators?

For instance, no meat-eater I know will complain if my broccoli touches his steak in the refrigerator, but goodness gracious, watch out if someone's bloody steak juice leaks in to the vegetarian's broccoli! It's a big difference.

You'll need to express this to your spouse and simply designate certain containers, parts of the refrigerator, and other items for meat. Once your mate understands that things that might come naturally to him are offensive to you, he will learn to be conscientious, and you can live harmoniously together—even in the kitchen.

Not in My Pan You Don't!

Designate separate pans, utensils, and cutting boards for cooking meat and vegetables. This not only helps to lessen the chance of cross-contamination while preparing meals, but helps to avoid disagreements in general.

For instance, if you go to chop some veggies and find all of the knives in the dishwasher are covered with meat remnants, you are going to be perturbed. If you have a designated knife for veggies, you'll always have something clean at hand.

You should also consider an agreement with your mate that he or she washes all the pots, pans, and dishes that contain meat. You should not have to clean up after a meat-eater. But of course, you need to do whatever works best in your family.

Meat-Free and Pregnancy

Let's say you've just discovered you're pregnant. First of all, congratulations! Now, what do you need to know to help meet your new nutritional needs? Well, almost everything that you've learned thus far will still apply. However, your needs for certain nutrients will go up, and I'll give you the rundown.

You might be nauseous, and I'll provide some vegetarian ideas to help you through. Other than that, you can continue your vegetarian diet as a pregnant and nursing mom with robust health and be able to get everything you need to build a healthy baby!

Steer Clear

Don't let others scare you about staying healthy as a pregnant vegan or vegetarian because, the truth is, what's good for you is good for building a baby. You'll simply need more of the same good stuff.

Getting Your Nutrients

As long as you aren't a "junk food" vegetarian, you should have no problems getting all the nourishment you need for pregnancy. Just follow some simple guidelines, like getting the extra calories you need and making sure you're getting extras of some nutrients, which are listed in a bit.

Besides that, work with a trusted midwife, doctor, or both to help monitor your progress and help with all the other aspects of pregnancy and delivery. You might also want to work with an herbalist. In any case, check with the practitioner you use for planning your pregnancy to ensure that taking an herbal supplement or any type of supplement is okay for you during gestation and breast feeding. Always get your herbs from a reputable source.

Extra Nutrients for Pregnancy

Nutrient	Amount	Why It's Important	Food Sources	Herbal Sources
Iron	30 mg	Keeps mother's blood count up, helps avoid pregnancy-related anemia	Black cherries, dark greens, black strap molasses	Liquid chlorophyll, spirulina, red raspberry leaves
Calcium	1,200 mg	Builds skeletal system for baby, prevents calcium loss from mom	Tofu, barley, kale, collard greens, carrots and carrot juice, sesame seeds, dairy	Alfalfa, parsley
Protein	60 g	Aids baby's development	Nuts, seeds, vegetables, beans, dairy, whole wheat, tofu	Spirulina, blue green algae
Folic Acid (B9)	Trace amounts (0.8 mg)	Essential for nervous system, formation of RNA and DNA cells, production of hydrochloric acid, absorption of B12, formation of red blood cells	Green leafy vegetables, fresh mushrooms, wheat germ, soybeans	Kelp, parsley, spirulina
Vitamin D (calcify-erol)	40 IU (same as nonpregnant women)	Helps the body utilize calcium	Spinach, dairy, egg yolks, fortified cereals	Alfalfa
B12	Trace amounts (2.2 mcg)	Essential in fat and protein metabolism, blood cell formation, bone marrow, gastrointestinal tract, and nervous system	Fortified cereals, most meat substitutes, most milk substitutes, nutritional yeast flakes, dairy	Alfalfa, bee pollen, spirulina

continues

Extra Nutrients for Pregnancy   (continued)

Nutrient	Amount	Why It's Important	Food Sources	Herbal Sources
Caloric intake for the day	300 extra calories daily	After about the third month of pregnancy baby needs extra nourishment to grow	Starchy snacks, thick soups with grains and beans, thick smoothies with added nuts, cereals, bean burritos	Spirulina, blue green algae
Water	Extra! (More than half of your body weight in ounces)	Water helps keep your body flushed, and can help allev-iate constipation	Drink purified filtered water	
Fiber	Extra!	Helps prevent constipation and hemorrhoids, as well as helps prevent toxemia	Raw vegetables and fruits	Psyllium hulls

Dealing with Morning Sickness

Nausea and morning sickness are common among pregnant women, and although ginger root helps many, it doesn't work for everyone. Here are a variety of foods to help with your upset stomach. Choose the one that appeals to your stomach most at the time.

Sprouts of Info

Ginger tea or red raspberry tea are excellent tonics for pregnant women that help control nausea and morning sickness.

➤ Smoothie

➤ Bagel with nut butter

➤ Warm bowl of oatmeal, grits, or slow cooked wheat kernels, millet, or barley

➤ Cold cereal with soy or rice milk

➤ Ryvita crackers

➤ Bean burrito

Pregnant women should always avoid over-the-counter medications unless they've talked to their doctor about taking them. But there are a few safe herbs that a mom can take to relieve her morning sickness. Ginger or red raspberry leaves are both excellent for this problem, and are safe in pregnancy. You can take them as a tea, in pill form, or even as a liquid tonic. Red raspberry is rich in iron and may help strengthen the uterus and reduce nausea, and ginger is clinically proven to reduce nausea. If one or the other doesn't help, try both together. And remember, al-ways buy your herbs from a reputable source.

Raising a Vegetarian Child

Breast milk is the best food to give your baby. It helps his or her digestive and intestinal systems to develop properly, it is invaluable for the immune system, and some studies even show that students who were breastfed as babies do better on tests than those who were not.

This indicates that breastfed children might have an intellectual advantage. Other studies show that breastfed babies are less likely to have problems with allergies later on in life and that they are more likely to maintain an ideal weight. Of course, the experience can build a strong bond between mother and child that can last a lifetime.

Breast milk contains foods that have already been digested by the mother, whose gastric juices have done the job for both mom and baby. Mother's milk is also a sterile food.

However, breastfeeding is not for everyone. Some babies are adopted, some moms have medical problems that prevent them from nursing, and some just plain choose not to breastfeed for personal reasons. What can you do instead?

Here are some alternatives to breast milk:

➤ Certified raw goat milk is chemically the closest to human milk, and babies can survive on fresh goat milk from a healthy goat. The milk needs to be diluted with some pure water.

➤ Soy-based infant formulas are available. Some brands include Soyalac, Prosobee, and Isomil. (These contain no animal products and are suitable for vegans.)

➤ Many infant formulas are based on cow's milk but are altered to make the formula more digestible.

Weaning the Baby

Most experts agree that a child should be breast-fed for a minimum of six months, and longer periods (even as long as two years) have been suggested if it is comfortable for the mother. This allows the baby's digestive system to develop fully.

After you wean your baby you can begin feeding him or her fruit or vegetable juice and then move on to strained vegetables and fruits. Try not to mix fruits and vegetables. Introduce one new food at a time. This will help you see whether your child is having discomfort with any individual new food.

Consider feeding your baby organic foods. There are many companies now making organic baby

Steer Clear

Do *not* feed your baby regular rice or soy milk—they are not suitable for an infant. You need formulas specifically made for infants. Your midwife or doctor should be familiar with the use of goat's milk and other milk alternatives. Consult with your practitioners about which they believe would be the most suitable choice.

Lettuce Explain

The **eye teeth** are also referred to as the canines. The **stomach teeth** are the molars.

food without sugar and artificial flavors. Many moms use food processors to puree their own baby food.

Nature's sign that your baby is ready for solid food is when their *eye* and *stomach teeth* come in. This indicates that their stomach's digestive juices are flowing and that they will be able to begin chewing and digesting a variety of starches and proteins.

Tofu-Touting Toddlers

After your toddlers' stomach and eye teeth are in and they are devouring solid foods it is easy to have them eat what you eat. Just cut up a portion of your foods into tiny bite-sized pieces and let them feed themselves. Allow picky kids a variety so they can choose what they like. As long as it is wholesome food, their bodies will lead them to what they need.

A couple of things to keep in mind for feeding growing kids:

➤ Toddlers need more calorie-dense foods for their growing bodies and less fiber. Bulky foods such as salads and raw plant foods can fill up a child's tiny stomach before meeting all of his or her caloric needs. Make sure to have available denser foods such as bananas, avocados, and nut and seed butters.

➤ A good food pyramid for the toddler (from the top down) includes the following: 1 teaspoon of vegetable oil, 3 small- to medium-size fruits, 1 cup of raw veggies and ½ cup cooked (equivalent to the recommended two servings of daily vegetables), 1 cup of rice milk or soy milk, 1 tablespoon of nut butter or nuts and 1 cup of cooked beans, 1 cup of cooked grains or pasta, 1 to 2 cups of cereal, 1 to 2 slices of whole-grain bread.

Seems like an awful lot for a tiny stomach, doesn't it? Let me give you a sample menu to help you visualize what all this food would look like:

➤ **First thing in the morning:** a banana

➤ **Breakfast:** 1 cup of slow-cooked grains with raisins and a cup of rice milk

➤ **Snack:** apple and carrot pieces

➤ **Lunch:** 1 small baked potato topped with sprouts and olive oil

➤ **Snack:** whole grain toast with nut butter on it

➤ **Dinner:** 1 cup of veggie chili

See, it's actually pretty easy. You shouldn't have to calculate anything. Feed them what you have, but make sure they get more dense foods and less bulky foods and avoid feeding them sugary snacks.

Veggie Soup for the Soul

Vegetarian moms tend to have breast milk that has substantially fewer environmental toxins due to eating clean organic foods. Remember, toxins are stored in fatty tissue, which includes the breasts. These toxins can be passed to a baby when breastfeeding. That's just another good reason to avoid processed foods, eat organic, drink clean water, and lead a more vegan lifestyle!

I Was a Teenage Vegetarian

Teens do very well on a vegetarian diet as long as they avoid the junk foods. A vegetarian diet helps keep the hormones steady and reduces constipation and acne troubles, and can help keep them at their ideal weight.

It can also serve them as a healthy way to be "cool," since being different for most high school kids means being hip. Vegetarians can stand out and even start a new trend in a school. They can use their diet to stand up for something.

If you forbid meat eating to your children, they could rebel and experiment with animal products away from home. You might even find them hanging out at the local fast-food joint! But if you have raised them as vegetarians and have fed them mostly wholesome foods for a decade or more, they are likely not to want to try meat. Furthermore, your beliefs about meat eating will be instilled in them from an early age and will help them be committed even in the face of peer pressure.

Or you may be reading this book because you have a teenager who just announced that he or she has decided to become a vegetarian. You probably not only want to support him or her but you would like to ease your mind about how healthy his or her new diet can be.

Either way, here is the lowdown on the needs of a vegetarian teenager:

Steer Clear

Aspects of the vegetarian lifestyle are mostly only good, healthy, and positive. However, anyone can be a sickly, overweight, toxic vegetarian if he or she chooses junk foods as his or her staples. Vegetarianism should be used as a term to describe health consciousness, not just an absence of meat.

➤ If your child is going vegetarian and you aren't, consider talking to your child about visiting a registered nutritional consultant or dietician who specializes in vegetarian nutrition to help him or her be more informed about his or her diet. Teens often are more willing to take advice from an authority other than a parent. If the teen sees that the practitioner is there to help him or her be healthy and feel good, he or she will be more likely to heed the advice. Discuss this option with your teen.

➤ Make sure your child is getting enough calories. Dense foods are better when the body is growing. A growing child needs a little extra protein, calcium, iron, vitamin B12, and vitamin D to grow properly.

Sprouts of Info

Chinese women, who develop later, also seem to have less breast cancer than those who begin menarche earlier. If you are worried about your child's physical maturity, be patient. Realize that your children's peers may be developing unnaturally early because of a chemical- and fat-laden diet. Always seek your pediatrician's advice if you are concerned.

➤ Expect a slower onset of puberty and give him or her until age 21 to reach growth maturity. Animal products contain naturally occurring hormones and can speed a child into menstruation and puberty earlier than purely vegan kids. Many holistic practitioners believe this is the more natural way to develop anyway. Who needs periods and wildly fluctuating hormones when trying to learn algebra?

➤ Make sure that the teenager has a variety of foods available. If you are a parent who is not a vegetarian, follow the guidelines in this book for cooking, shopping, and packing veggie snacks when you travel. If you already are a vegetarian, continue to set a good example for your child in your eating habits and dining choices.

➤ Help your teen choose the right foods while at school or buy foods to pack for a lunch that will be the envy of all his or her schoolmates!

Your Pet as a Vegetarian

So now everyone knows you, your spouse, and your kids are vegetarians. You have Sally over for tea and while you proclaim the benefits of your lifestyle, you remember you have to feed Fluffy. You go the cabinet, pull out a big can of dog food, and scrape a load into Fluffy's dish.

Your guest is a little confused. Why do you continue to feed your dear pet a diet of ground-up, poor-quality meat when you wouldn't feed it to the rest of your human family? Makes you think, doesn't it? Our pets now are suffering from all sorts of diseases and disorders that are not heard of in wild animals. This can be largely attributed to the diets we feed them.

Because our companion animals are near and dear to our hearts, we want what's best for them too. Why not save on diet-related vet bills later down the line and improve your pet's health today? Is a vegetarian diet really what's best? Let's explore that question a little bit.

Obviously you won't have to worry if your pet is a natural vegetarian, as are many birds, fish, horses, and rodents. And although it's a noble idea, I don't think that feeding your frog tiny tofu crickets is feasible, so we're just going to pass over the insect-eating pets for now. Here we'll talk about our most common meat-eating friends, cats and dogs.

Steer Clear

Dogs and cats do not have well-developed molars for grinding vegetation. If you put raw veggies in your dog's or cat's food, you should grate or process them first, to make them more digestible.

Miceless Meals for Kitty

In Chapter 7, "The Digestion Question," we contrasted your digestive system with a lion's to show that the lion's body is much better equipped than the human's to handle meat. Kitty cats are just mini-lions, and their bodies are designed to eat meat with no side effects. Remember, though, that most supermarket pet foods contain farm animal remains considered unfit for human consumption. These animal parts often come from diseased or dying animals. If you do purchase meat-based cat food, make sure it is of the highest quality.

If you just can't bring yourself to purchase ground-up animal parts, there are ways to avoid purchasing meat for your cats and still keep them healthy. Vegan and vegetarian dog and cat food can be found through the following companies:

➤ Evolution Healthy Pet Food, Bloomington, Minnesota, 1-800-524-9697; 612-858-8329; or 612-228-0467

➤ Harbingers of a New Age, Troy, Montana, 406-295-4944

➤ Natural Life Pet Products, Inc., Frontenac, Kansas, 1-800-367-2391

➤ Nature's Recipe Corona, California, 1-800-843-4008

➤ Heinz Pet Products, Newport, Kentucky, 1-800-237-3856 or 606-655-5700

➤ Pet Guard, Orange Park, Florida, 1-800-874-3221

➤ Boss Bars, Patagonia, Arizona, 1-888-207-9114

If you're more of an online shopper, check out my list of online pet food companies that offer vegetarian choices in Appendix C, "Web Sites for the Meatless." Make sure that the food you order for your cats (who are strict carnivores by nature) includes supplemental taurine and preformed vitamin A. These nutrients can be made synthetically and fed to your cat via a supplement or in enriched cat food.

Sprouts of Info

The makers of Beano offer an anti-gas supplement for pets called Curtail. Another product is Vegepet, created by James Peden, author of *Vegetarian Cats and Dogs*. His books and supplements are available through Harbinger's of a New Age. The book is suggested reading for anyone who wants to keep a pet healthy on a vegetarian diet.

If your cat is allowed outdoors, she might be getting these nutrients when she eats rodents or birds, but do try to tame the hunting (after all, you are a vegetarian!). Cats that are kept indoors have longer, healthier lives, and your neighbors will appreciate the fact that your cat isn't hunting the songbirds they're feeding!

Can Rover Go Veg?

Dogs are omnivores, meaning they are capable of surviving on meat and vegetation, and with the choices of vegetarian pet foods available nowadays, you should be able to give them everything they need. A dog's digestive system can be rather sensitive, so change its diet slowly. Start by mixing a little of the new food with the old, and gradually increase the amount of new food over a month or so. This helps their body adjust to the new diet without too much digestive discomfort.

A dog's health can be jeopardized if it receives too little protein, vitamin D, and calcium. Dogs also need the amino acids L-carnitine and taurine, which are not generally added to commercial dog foods and can be insufficient in homemade dog food as well. Be sure to properly supplement a pure veggie dog.

Dogs are omnivores, meaning that they can survive on a varied diet. Oscar here loves fruit and vegetables!

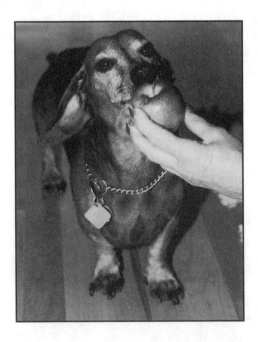

Another thing to watch out for is that Rover's gas can be way more than just a noxious bomb that disturbs your environment for 10 minutes. Gas in all creatures is a sign of poor digestion.

If you have a completely indoor animal that is not able to get nutrients from nature occasionally by eating grass (or the occasional houseplant) to aid digestion, you should take special notice if your pet has gas. A little chlorophyll added to a dog's water could help with the smell and aid digestion. Pets who eat commercial food can also benefit from supplementing with food enzymes. These are usually available through the companies that sell veggie pet foods.

The Least You Need to Know

➤ When considering Mr. or Ms. Right, take into account their general attitude about food and diet to determine whether you can live happily with them as a nonvegetarian or whether they might be open to a meatless diet.

➤ If you are married to a meat-eater, negotiate some kitchen guidelines to avoid cross-contamination, as well as unnecessary arguments and irritations.

➤ Vegetarians and vegans can get everything they need for a healthy pregnancy and subsequent breastfeeding. Just be sure to increase your caloric intake by eating denser foods.

➤ Nursing is the best way to feed your infant and is suggested for at least the first six months of the child's life. Beyond that, raising a child as a vegan or vegetarian can give him or her health benefits for years to come.

➤ Cats and dogs can be fed fortified vegetarian or vegan dog or cat foods without problems, although there are also more humane meat-based foods available from some health-conscious pet-food makers.

Chapter 22

The Health Nut

In This Chapter

➤ Learn the benefits of whole foods

➤ Discover the basics of proper food combining

➤ Meet some diet–based healing systems

➤ Understand what juicing and proper fasting can do for you

This is the chapter that takes your meatless diet to a holistically healthful new level if you choose. You'll learn about the use of whole foods, the principles of proper food combining, and how to help your body cleanse through undereating. You'll learn the definition of the mucus-less diet and understand how to use periodic fasting properly. You'll learn about the nutritional benefits of juicing fresh fruits and vegetables. Finally, we will look at the blood-type diet and see how it can work for vegetarians.

If you are not ready to take your diet and eating habits this far, skip this chapter for now. After you've been comfortable with your vegetarian diet for a while and are ready for more health, remember this chapter is here, waiting for you to take advantage of all of its wisdom.

The Importance of Whole Foods

When I mentioned the importance of eating whole foods in a cleansing class I once taught, I saw a teenage boy's eyes light up. I stopped to question him, thinking that he knew what I meant about whole foods. He commented that he was excited because he could now tell his family that he should have the *whole* pizza next time they

Lettuce Explain

Whole foods are foods that are unprocessed. They are eaten as they were created by nature in their unaltered state and include raw fruits and vegetables and grains that have been slow cooked to bring them to life.

ordered one because whole foods are good for you! That's not what I meant, although it was a good try.

Whole foods are unadulterated foods in their natural state. Anything that you can pick from a tree or a vine or pull from the ground is a whole food. Anything that has not been altered to change its fundamental properties and that has its own enzymes intact is a whole food, so this category also includes slow cooked whole grains.

The benefit of whole foods is that they contain all the right ingredients in the proportions nature intended. The body is nourished more easily with foods that are still in their natural state. You also get the added benefit of consuming everything the food has to offer, which makes it (and therefore you) complete.

Synthetic Health?

Currently many processed foods are enriched with synthetically produced chemicals. In other words, food manufacturers take a whole food, or a part of it, like wheat, for example, bleach it, cook it at high temperatures (killing the enzymes and destroying nutrients), and grind it down to a fine powder (eliminating the fiber). By the time it is made into flour, especially white flour, the nutritional value is almost gone. So what do they do? They enrich the flour with synthetically made vitamins and minerals.

How do they know exactly what to put back into the product? We have not isolated every phytochemical in every food, nor is it guaranteed that we ever will. There may be substances inherent in whole foods that researchers have not discovered. When possible, try to get your nourishment from whole foods, just to make sure you're getting what nature intended.

I believe whole foods are better because they contain all the components needed to help your body process the food correctly. Science has showed us that isolating some substances at the expense of others can cause various side effects. This is another reason to get your nutrients from herbs versus vitamin pills, which are isolated compounds of a whole plant or food.

Sweet and Low

Refined sugar is an excellent example of this concept. Let's say we eat a fresh stalk of sugar cane from a Hawaiian garden. The stalk of the sugar cane contains a lot of nutrients, enzymes, and vitamins, including the B vitamins, not to mention fiber, which helps slow down absorption, making it easier for the body to handle the sugar.

However, when that same sugar cane is refined, subjected to high heat, and strained through charcoal or bones, all of its nutrients and enzymes are stripped away. Refined sugar is so lacking in nutrients that it actually robs your own body of B vitamins, enzymes, and other nutrients just so your body can process it. When the sugar cane was still a whole food, these nutrients were intact, and there was no need to rob your body for them.

Whole in Spirit

I believe that foods that are less than whole not only weaken the body, but also the mind and spirit. This can apply to things beyond food. For instance, if you are an intelligent, capable, generally happy individual with a connection to your spiritual side, you are going to seek a partner who resonates on that same level with you, right?

Let's pretend that you, a balanced, whole individual, choose a partner totally lacking in some aspect (as an analogy for a processed food). Let's say that although this person appears on the outside to be whole (like a processed food might), inside he or she lacks self-awareness, emotional stability, and positive thinking, and rigidly refuses to grow or use his or her talents to make his or her life better.

How did this person get this way? Who knows what "processing" they've been through—maybe it was due to past traumas they've experienced or their refusal to deal with these past issues and other behaviors they choose to engage in that keeps them from being "whole."

How would you feel being with this person? Wouldn't you attempt to put your extra optimism into your conversations? Wouldn't you be working harder to please them by offering your abundance, influence, help, money, assistance, and encouragement? When we do this, we do everything the way the less-than-whole person wants it, so we ourselves become less than whole too. We want anyone we love to be whole, don't we? Don't fool yourself into thinking you wouldn't drain yourself giving yourself to this person. In contrast, when you choose a partner who is whole like yourself, the two of you can bounce along equally in life, adding more fun during good times and strengthening each other through bad times. It is uplifting to be with a whole person. But first, you must become whole yourself.

Just as it is an uplift to be whole and share your life with a whole person, it is the same uplift for your body to receive whole foods. Incomplete foods force your body to put out a lot of effort without receiving anything in return—reciprocity. A whole food nourishes your body, just as a whole person as a partner can nourish your mind, heart, and soul.

Proper Food Combining

Food combining can greatly improve your digestion. It can increase your energy level, aid in weight management, and improve your overall

Sprouts of Info

A favorite, must-read classic on food combining and proper eating habits is Harvey and Marilyn Diamond's top seller *Fit for Life* (Warner Books, Inc., 1985).

health. The basic premise of food combining is that starches require a certain mixture of stomach acid and enzymes for their breakdown and proper utilization. Proteins require a different set.

If proteins and starchy foods are eaten together in the same meal, the requirements on the body oppose each other and therefore can effectively stop or severely restrict proper digestion. Many have discovered that following some basic food combining guidelines has improved their digestion and aided in weight loss.

Even a vegetarian can stand to benefit by a few tips on proper food combining, so if you want to get more benefit from your vegetarian diet, keep these basics in mind:

Lettuce Explain

Concentrated foods are those with a low water content and include most starchy and heavy protein foods, such as animal products, baked potatoes, grains, nuts, and seeds. In food combining, you should only eat one concentrated food at each meal.

➤ Eat fruit on an empty stomach.

➤ Eat only one type of fruit at any one sitting.

➤ Do not mix starches, such as grains, with proteins (exception: beans and rice).

Food combining divides foods into two categories: *concentrated foods* and water-containing foods. If you can imagine squeezing a food and not getting any water (juice) from it, it goes in the concentrated food category. Concentrated foods include most starches, grains, and all animal products. You should eat only one concentrated food at a time in each meal.

Take a look at the food-combining chart and the list of foods in the different categories, and try some practice combinations to see how it works out.

Food combining flow chart.

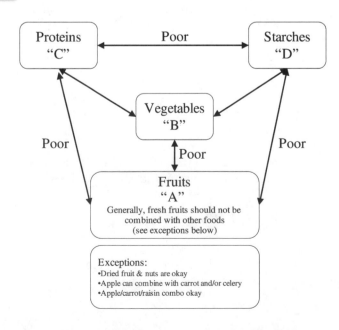

Food Combining Categories

Fruits "A"	Veggies "B"	Proteins "C"	Starches "D"
Apples	Artichokes	Eggs	Potatoes
Apricots	Asparagus	Nuts	Corn
Bananas	Beets	Seeds	Acorn squash
Blackberries	Broccoli	Tempeh	Butternut squash
Blueberries	Cabbage	Beans	Bread
Cherries	Carrots	All cheeses, soy, or dairy	Rice
Citrus fruits	Cauliflower	Tofu	Slow cooked whole grains
Grapes	Celery	All yogurt, soy or otherwise	All bread products, bagels, muffins, crackers, cookies, pastries, breads
Melons (cantaloupe, watermelon)	Cucumber	All animal flesh	
Nectarines	Green beans	Butter	
Peaches	Leafy greens	Sour cream	
Pears	Onion	All dairy	
Pineapple	Parsley		
Plums	Spinach		
Raspberries	Yellow squash		
Strawberries	Spaghetti squash		

Take a look at some examples of food combining.

➤ **Wrong:** Meatless burger on a bun with side salad

  Right: Meatless burger *without* bun, side salad

➤ **Wrong:** Green salad with cucumbers, sprouts, kidney beans and croutons

  Right: Green salad with cucumbers, sprouts, kidney beans or croutons

➤ **Wrong:** Baked potato topped with veggie chili (beans are concentrated food and so is the baked potato)

  Right: Baked potato topped with salsa and sprouts

➤ **Wrong:** Veggie pizza with soy cheese

  Right: Veggie pizza with pesto sauce, garlic oil, and tomatoes, but without cheese

Obviously, food combining can be a complicated matter at times. But once you get the hang of it, you will feel the difference in the way your body responds after you eat. For starters, try eating all water-content foods at one meal, such as a fresh salad made with only vegetables and no proteins (like cheese, eggs, beans, or pasta). At the next meal, eat all proteins (like a cup of chili with soy cheese) with nothing else. See how you feel when you eat only vegetables or only beans or only fruit. Experiment a little and notice the differences and keep learning. Two good books to help you out are *Fit for Life,* by Marilyn and Harvey Diamond (Warner Books, Inc., 1985), and *The Transfiguration Diet,* by the Littlegreen, Inc., Think Tank (a health and nutrition research team). It can be ordered through Christopher Enterprises: 1-800-453-1406.

The Cleansing Power of Diet

Professor Arnold Ehret was a well-known nutritionist in the late 1800s and early 1900s who recommended diet and long fasts to help the body rid itself of disease and restore health. His works, published in the book *The Mucusless Diet Healing System* (Ehret Literature Publishing Co., 1953), influenced and still influences many natural health practitioners, naturopaths, nutritional consultants, and holistic healers who use diet to help others get well.

The mucusless diet consists primarily of a combination of whole foods and a program of fasting. Ehret believed that eating too much and eating foods that are denatured creates mucus in the body, which leads to disease. He writes of his own dramatic *healing crisis* brought on by the mucusless diet and long periods (weeks) of fasting.

We'll talk about fasting at the end of this chapter, and I'll walk you through how to do a simple, safe fast if you are in fairly good shape. But first let's talk more about how your new positive changes can bring you to a healing crises, and what a healing crises is.

Lettuce Explain

A **healing crisis** is a positive, natural, detoxification process that the body performs when given the opportunity to release toxins. Symptoms are similar to cold or flu and vary for each individual, but usually involve the body's elimination channels.

Healing Crisis to the Rescue?

The healing crisis is basically your body's opportunity to eliminate excess toxins it has been harboring. It can be brought on through positive dietary changes or fasting, the elimination of toxins or the addition of herbs, colon cleansing, whole foods, pure water, or fasting and other natural therapies that help the body detoxify. The healing crisis varies for everyone, depending on where your toxic areas are and the state of your health. You can have several mini healing crises lasting for hours or a few days, depending on your particular constitution. Others can have healing crises that last for weeks, although the symptoms seem to change daily.

When mucus is loosened from internal organs and tissues, it is freed for discharge and is eliminated from the body via the lungs, urinary tract, vagina, bowel, and skin. There are many ways to help your body accelerate through a cleansing healing crisis.

It is important that you help your body through this process rather than suppress the symptoms. Because mucus is sticky, it tends to cause constipation if not helped along through the body. Herbal therapies can be particularly helpful for cleansing, as herbs can help dissolve mucus and speed up its elimination. Suppressing this elimination process leads to the toxins being trapped in the body and settling back into the tissues.

When we talk about fasting at the end of this chapter, we will go into more detail about what you might expect and how to help your body get through a crisis. Here I just want to let you know that making any positive changes in your diet can speed up your body's ability to eliminate toxins in all forms. The goal is actually to get to and then work through a healing crisis, which is basically an indication that your body is cleansing.

Sprouts of Info

Eliminating foods from your diet that tend to create mucus (i.e., anything that causes you to clear your throat within 20 to 60 minutes after ingestion, like milk) lets your body eliminate excess mucus stored in your tissues. This is to be expected, not feared or suppressed.

Cleansing Emotions

The healing crisis may have more than a physical effect—it can involve the emotions as well. Many people will experience an emotional crisis immediately following or preceding the physical healing crisis. The emotional healing crisis might include a short period of intense depression, anxiety, jitteriness, itching, irritability, feeling overwhelmed, and a vague feeling of expectation. It can also involve the emergence all at once of past traumas you have experienced.

It is best during these times to take time to cry, grieve, ask for the support of a loved one (not to fix you, just to hold you or stand by you), to beat up a pillow, or do whatever it takes to safely release these emotions. After you release and process them, you will be free from them.

Just as with physical toxins, if you suppress your emotional healing crises, it will lurk inside, to emerge later in a more severe form when you are at your weakest or feeling most vulnerable.

Vegetarians and the Blood-Type Diet

By now many of you might have heard the raves about Dr. Peter J. D'Adamo's book *Eat Right for Your Type* (Putnam, 1996). If not, let me give you a quick update. D'Adamo presents a theory, based on his research in blood analysis, that certain foods are more suited for people of different blood types.

If you eat the foods that are incompatible with your blood type, it can cause or aggrevate such things as allergies, weight problems, and a whole host of ailments. He also believes that the addition of compatible foods to your diet increases your health.

Because many of my clients and readers ask me what I think about the blood-type diet, I thought I'd include some of my own opinions and suggestions. Overall, my opinion of the blood-type diet research is that it is very interesting, and its application obviously helps many people. I have three general guidelines I share when clients ask me what I think.

1. **Eat foods that are as close to nature as possible, and you shouldn't suffer from a host of ailments.** Just switching from mostly processed foods to more natural foods can eliminate many nagging ailments. When the body is cleansed and is being fed nature's foods, it readjusts itself positively to the new changes.

2. **Transition slowly.** Most people have a hard enough time switching from processed foods to more whole foods. It seems that the more complicated a diet, the less likely it is that a person can follow it for long. I find that it discourages folks if, after I suggest that they include more whole natural foods in their diet, I then hand them a list of whole foods, such as carrots, apples, and pears, that they need to avoid based on their blood type. Remember, the blood-type diet is a theory. It's up to you to decide whether you would like to experiment with it.

   If you have already been a vegetarian for a while and you are going to make the transition from vegetarian to healthier vegetarian, I suggest step two for you would be to begin a whole foods diet and then to begin working on proper food combining. Once your diet is based on whole foods and proper food combining, if you want to take it a step further, then eliminating incompatible blood-type foods might serve as another good refinement for your health.

   Going at this pace allows your body and mind to adapt to the higher level of health you will begin to feel. It also allows for healing crises along the way. You will be more likely to be able to stick with your better eating habits than if you were to try doing everything at once.

3. **Read the whole list for possible daily culprits.** If you find Dr. D'Adamo's research compelling enough to try it right away, then I still suggest you look at the list of foods that should be *avoided* for your blood type. If you find that there are things on the list that you eat practically every day, you might want to eliminate that food for a few weeks to see how you respond.

Sprouts of Info

I think a diet should evolve over time (unless, of course, there is a serious threatening illness at hand). We all have our own pace, and I suggest you stick to yours. In other words, if you are just now giving up meat, you might want to skip this section until you are ready to refine your diet later.

If you feel better, continue to avoid the food. If you experience no difference, continue removing incompatible foods from your diet (starting with those you eat the most often) for a period of weeks to see how you do. If you still notice no positive changes, it's up to you to decide if the blood-type diet is working for you.

Too many people are motivated initially by good information and tend to jump head-long into complicated régimes. Although they might feel better, the enormous amount of adding, avoiding, and calculating eventually wears on people. Sooner or later they fall off the new diet and return to poor habits and poor health.

Because the goal of this book is to help your body, diet, and life evolve over time, I suggest you make your dietary transitions slowly to ensure that the positive changes become a permanent part of your life.

Veggie Soup for the Soul

Blood type A's, according to Dr. D'Adamo, are the natural vegetarians. They tend to make less HCl, which is necessary for breaking down heavy animal proteins, so they naturally do better on a pure vegetarian diet. Type O's are the natural meat-eaters, and tend to make extra stomach acid to help break down animal proteins. If you are a type O, you might be better off as a lacto ovo vegetarian. Type B's are the most flexible. The AB types seem to be sensitive to a variety of foods and take on characteristics of both A's and B's.

Juicing for Added Nutrition

Juicing fresh fruits and vegetables is a healthy and effective way to get more nutrition from less food. Juicing your fruits and vegetables breaks down much of the fiber and bulk, so you can get the same amount of vitamins and minerals from a glass of carrot juice, for example, as you could by eating a dozen or so raw carrots.

Here's how juicing can be used to improve your diet:

➤ Juicing can be added to your diet to fill up nutritional gaps.

➤ You can utilize juice fasting for body detoxification.

➤ Juicing fresh, ripe, organic, whole fruits and vegetables can be used therapeutically to help the body overcome ailments, just as other forms of concentrated nutrition like herbs and supplements are used.

By juicing, I don't mean buying the canned or bottled fruit or vegetable juices you find at the store. Most of these juices are from concentrates, have other ingredients in them, and contain high amounts of sugar, which overrides the nutritional benefits of the juice itself.

Juicing for health involves the purchase of a quality juicer (see Chapter 15, "Let's Talk Shop!" for hints on juicers) and then purchasing or growing your own produce to be juiced. By drinking your own fruit and vegetable juices you receive enzymes, distilled water from the fruit or vegetable, vitamins and minerals, cell salts, and other phytochemicals.

If you decide to try juicing, remember to follow proper food combining tips when creating juice. Don't combine incompatible foods, such as fruits and vegetables, in the same drink. In general, it is better to keep things simple and stick to a single fruit or vegetable at a time. Remember, you are juicing to aid your health, not add to or create digestive problems.

Tips on getting the most benefit from your juices:

➤ Always use fresh raw (uncooked or unprocessed) produce and buy organic whenever possible.

➤ Drink the juice on an empty stomach and do not eat anything with the juice—treat it as a meal or snack.

➤ Chew your juices before swallowing so that your saliva mixes with the juice and can aid your digestion. Gulping your juice can be a shock to the pancreas and can contribute to a temporary blood sugar imbalance.

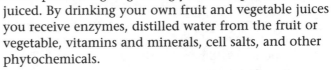

Sprouts of Info

Carrots can be juiced and drunk alone, but can also be used as a "base" juice to which you can add other, stronger-tasting vegetable juices. Most health food stores carry (or can order) "juicing carrots," which you can buy in large quantities to save money. Always clean your produce before juicing.

Steer Clear

Fiber is still an important part of any diet, so don't just juice your vegetables and fruits and forget to eat whole foods. Include juiced vegetables and fruits as a healthful addition to your overall diet.

Fasting Responsibly

Periodically refraining from food or simply undereating occasionally are excellent ways to give your entire digestive system a break. Undereating can benefit you by giving your digestive organs a rest while still keeping the alimentary canal moving. To undereat, simply skip dinner a few nights a week or eat about three-fourths the amount you normally would at each meal. You will probably notice that you sleep better and digest better, and most people will lose a few extra pounds if needed.

Fasting gives all of your digestive organs a break but needs to be done properly to get good results. Long fasts always should be supervised, especially if you are in ill health. Sometimes a person is too weak to fast, and abstaining from food can weaken them further. If you are in a weakened condition you will need to build up your body with proper nutrition first before the body is able to release toxic materials.

Also, if you have been eating a poor diet for many years—the average American diet—your body can have a tremendous amount of toxins stored up. It is imperative that you not take fasting lightly because the cleansing that begins when fasting can create an accelerated cleansing and detoxification which, *if not handled properly,* can clog up your elimination channels and cause obstructions, and could even cause death.

Sprouts of Info

Choose a day to prepare juices in quantity. Fill small plastic drinking bottles about three-fourths with juice (this leaves room for expansion). Label the containers and store in the freezer immediately. You can do the same with smoothies. Allow to defrost in the refrigerator. Defrosting usually takes about 24 to 48 hours.

You need to plan and study before taking on any type of serious therapeutic fast so you know what to expect. You should seek out an experienced guide to help you facilitate or monitor you through your fasting so that you do not inadvertently harm yourself.

Now that I've given you an idea of how serious a long fast can be, remember that occasional short fasting is something that just about anyone in fairly good shape can do, and I'll give you some guidelines for doing it safely.

Toxic Waste

Going from cupcakes and cola to total abstinence from food could do you more harm than good. It is best to transition to a whole food diet, then on to proper food combining, and then to periodic fasting. This ensures that your body is cleaner and that there is less toxic sludge to cause you harm when it is released.

And don't worry, you'll still have plenty of toxins to eliminate after being on a vegetarian diet for a while. It is amazing what can come out of the bodies of those who have been on the cleanest of diets! Your body is an amazingly efficient storage container. Deep-tissue cleansing can bring up strong odors from drug or other chemical deposits that have settled in the tissues for years.

Many people after or during a deep-cleansing fast taste or smell ammonia, get a metallic taste in their mouth, or have boils erupt, exposing dark pungent gooey materials. The most common eliminations, however, are mucus and parasites in the stool.

Veggie Soup for the Soul

Therapeutic fasting is for those who want deeper cellular cleansing than can be obtained through a clean diet. Some serious illnesses have been overcome by supervised fasting along with other natural therapies, which can help facilitate the removal of toxic debris in the tissues from the deepest levels. Sometimes healing crises from long fasts can be incapacitating as boils appear and burst, eyes, ears, or sweat glands ooze malodorous substances, uric acid crystals pierce the skin while exiting, and fever runs high to burn off the latent bacteria being released for elimination.

Why Fast Anyway?

So what's so great about fasting? Well, it can take a load off your digestive system, and that allows more energy for other things. The absence of food going through the system allows the body to work on the repair or restoration of other nagging ailments.

Sprouts of Info

The time it takes to break a craving permanently varies with the addiction; for instance, sugar cravings can be overcome fairly quickly, whereas bread cravings can take months to overcome. This is because the gluten from bread can linger in your intestinal tract for months or even years, and cravings don't stop until the final remnants of the food are completely cleansed from your system.

Fasting can put you in touch with your body and mind, and your thoughts about food. When I fast for one day, all I can think about is food. It makes me realize how much food can take control of your life. I find that periodic fasting keeps me in control over the food.

In addition, fasting can create a host of uncomfortable symptoms, like a healing crisis. Your specific symptoms can give you clues to the areas in your body that are toxic or that need special care. Let's take a look at some clues about what's going on inside your body when you fast or undereat:

➤ When you fast or undereat, do you get a headache, especially at the back of your head? This is a good indication that you are addicted to a food that is toxic to your system.

➤ When you fast, do you have a particular craving for a certain food or beverage? This might reveal an addiction to that food. (Sugar cravings are particularly common during the first few days of fasting.) Your body will usually make you very uncomfortable until one of two things happens: You give in to your "demons" and eat or drink the item or you refrain for several days from the food, by which time it leaves your body completely, freeing you from the craving.

➤ The morning after a fast, before you do anything else, go directly to the mirror, stick out your tongue, and observe its color. Does it appear to have a white or yellowish coating? The tongue is an indicator of the condition of the muscles and tissues inside the body, and its coating is an indication of how much mucus you have to clear from your system. When the tongue is anything but clear and pink after fasting, it means that mucus and pus are beginning to be released and your body is certainly in need of tissue cleansing.

➤ Do you experience subtle or not-so-subtle aches and pains in any area during a fast? During fasting, or sometimes while refraining from a certain food you have been unknowingly addicted to, your body has the chance to release toxic buildup from areas where the substance has accumulated. If your system is strong enough, your body will begin to eliminate debris from these areas. You might feel the elimination as a cramping, pulling sensations, jabbing type pains, or nausea as the toxins are allowed to leave the spot and flush into your blood stream for elimination.

Steer Clear

Fasting and constipation are a dangerous combination because the toxins from your tissues are being released in quantity and need to be eliminated from your system as soon as possible.

It is imperative that you keep your elimination channels open while fasting in order to allow the toxins a way out of the body. When you abstain from food, the digestive tract is not stimulated to move, and constipation can easily set in. Here are some suggestions to help each eliminative channel stay clear:

➤ **Skin and lymph system.** Dry skin brushing followed by a sauna, lymphatic massage. Avoid applying lotion, allow skin to breath, wear less clothing if appropriate, and wear loose clothing or at the very least natural, breathable fibers.

➤ **Kidneys.** Drink plenty of pure or distilled water and try herbs that flush the kidneys, including parsley, juniper berries, cornsilk, dandelion, or hydrangea. Skin brushing also aids the kidneys. Don't resist the call of nature and avoid becoming dehydrated.

➤ **Intestines.** Use colonics, enemas, or colonemas. Herbs that stimulate the intestines and liver include cascara sagrada, yellow dock, aloe vera juice, turkey rhubarb, licorice root. Try reflexology, acupuncture, and some light exercise like walking. Avoid constipation!

➤ **Respiratory system.** Deep breathing exercises can aid in the cleansing process. Don't suppress mucus discharges from the lungs and sinus cavities. Bear with the cleansing by blowing your nose when needed and allowing yourself to cough to expel mucus.

A Fast Fast

Please check with a fasting expert when attempting a serious or lengthy fast. They can let you know what to expect and can coach you through healing crises you may have. If the fasting or nutrition specialist is not a physician they will probably have you get a checkup from your physician before you begin your fast.

If not, it would still be a good idea for you to do so, just so you can discover weaknesses that will need special attention during the fast, which can be somewhat stressful on the body, depending on how long you have filled your system with unclean foods. Have I prepared you and warned you enough? I hope so. As promised, here are the steps to take if you are a healthy person and have decided to fast:

➤ **Day one,** eliminate all junk foods, including chips, sodas, greasy foods, all processed foods, caffeine, and alcohol. If you are still eating meat, eliminate that here as well.

➤ **Day two,** eliminate all animal products if you are a lacto, ovo, or any type of vegetarian other than a strict vegetarian or vegan.

➤ **Day three,** eliminate all grains (this means all breads, rice, cereals, every grain product).

➤ **Day four,** eliminate all vegetables—now you should only be eating fruits.

➤ **Day five,** eliminate all food. Continue drinking plenty of pure water to flush toxins from your system and begin taking cascara sagrada or your favorite herbal combination to keep the bowels moving. Continue this water fast for two to five days or whatever is most comfortable or advisable for you.

Sprouts of Info

Some people fast until they go through a cycle of low energy (this is when the body is focused on cleansing) followed by a boost of energy, as the body is freed from toxins. Many folks experience renewed energy on about the fourth day of a fast.

You can also choose to make your fast a vegetable or juice fast, meaning that you pick one type of fruit or vegetable to juice, and drink that juice in addition to water for the entire fast, beginning on day five. And remember, no matter what type of fast you go on, keep the elimination channels open!

➤ Break the fast on day one with nothing but liquids, soup, broth, and fruit or vegetable juices.

➤ The second day after you break the fast you can begin to include fruits in the diet and maybe a few steamed vegetables.

➤ On the third day you should add salads and other fresh produce.

➤ From day four on you can slowly add in your grains and go back to your regular eating habits, without, of course, adding back the junk.

It is best to follow up a fast with a customized, supplemental, nutritional program designed for your particular body, lifestyle, and needs. Many nutritional deficiencies can cause cravings for things that aren't healthy. Fat cravings can indicate a need for essential fatty acids (see Chapter 5, "Supplements for the Vegetarian"). Sugar cravings can mean you need chromium. And if you are totally zinc starved, you will lose your appetite completely and become anorexic. Seek someone who can help you find the nutrients you need to stay well.

The Least You Need to Know

➤ Eating more whole foods and fewer processed foods ensures that you get enzymes along with the nutrients present in whole foods. Eating whole foods is an example of living close to nature and is the most natural way to nourish your body.

➤ Food combining strives to avoid mixing starches and proteins together in one meal to help the body improve its digestive ability and therefore bring the body into a natural state of balance.

➤ Juicing fresh produce is a healthy way to get an abundance of nutrients and saves digestive energy.

➤ Fasting should be taken seriously, especially if you are very toxic or ill. Any major fast should be supervised by an expert.

Chapter 23

Making Vegetarianism Your Business

In This Chapter

➤ Discover how cheap it can be to be vegetarian

➤ Learn how to make money in the media as a vegetarian

➤ Consider starting a vegetarian food business

➤ Involve yourself with vegetarian-friendly investments

➤ Start a vegetarian retreat or counseling practice

It can be cheap to be a vegetarian, as long as you eat wholesome foods as nature provides them, and I'll illustrate just what I mean soon. Then, with all the money you'll be saving by being vegetarian, you might even want to invest in the business of vegetarianism!

Maybe you are considering what you want do for retirement. Maybe you're bored with your current occupation and are ready for a change. Why not consider a new business that's a spin on your new diet? There are a world of possibilities and plenty of opportunities to find and then fill your niche in the vegetarian realm.

As people become more conscious of protecting the environment and sustaining energy and resources and continue to strive toward healthier lifestyles, the business of vegetarianism will continue to grow, hence, job security! Who knows, maybe you'll be the world's next Betty Veggie-Crocker!

Bulking Up on Money

Before we dive into making money, let's talk about how much you can save by being vegetarian. All you need to remember is that some of the best things in life are free. Think of it: The things most critical to life and happiness are free aren't they? We need air and water, both free, and love, which is freely earned. Nature provides us with everything we need to live happy and healthy.

You don't need to be a millionaire or even part of the upper class to eat well as a vegetarian or vegan. In fact the more you eat nature's foods, the cheaper it is. When you fill yourself with wholesome foods, you will naturally be more nourished and will need less food than if you were living on processed foods.

Sprouts of Info

Preparing large quantities of your bulk and fresh foods all at once, like juicing and freezing vegetable and fruit juices or making soups and other freezable dishes, is not only more economical but also saves preparation time for busy schedules.

Let me give you an example that just saved me close to $40 at the store. I just purchased a 25-pound bag of organic carrots for juicing from my local Boise Co-op. The bag cost me $12.50. I spent an hour or two the next morning scrubbing and juicing the majority of the carrots. I filled little plastic containers with juice and packed all but one of them in the freezer for later.

I set aside a few of the carrots and chopped some, put them in a baggie, and put that in my crisper for stir-fry or other veggie dishes. I took some other carrots and chopped them into carrot sticks, which are great for dipping in various dips as snacks or to go along with a sandwich at lunch. I shredded a few carrots and put them in another baggie. Shredded carrots can be sprinkled on salads or put in a sandwich as garnish.

Juicy Savings

I wound up with approximately 225 ounces of carrot juice, plus the carrots I set aside for other uses. If I were to purchase the equivalent amount of carrot juice already juiced and frozen (which is how I got my little plastic containers in the first place, by the way), I would have spent $49 (14 bottles at about $3.50 each), and I wouldn't have had carrots for snacking or stir-fry! That's a huge savings for spending an hour or two juicing and cleaning up.

Oh, but you think a juicer is expensive? Well, my particular juicer was a gift from a family member one year, but even if I were to buy one, the money I save would pay for a reasonably priced juicer over and over!

Remember that you pay more the more food is handled, denatured, processed, packaged, advertised, and labeled. That means that bulk foods and whole foods are always more economical than are prepared, ready-to-eat, and other processed foods. Buying in bulk saves waste, too.

A Pound of Flesh

To prove that meat eating is more expensive than vegetarian eating, look at the following comparisons for a pound of animal flesh compared to some vegetarian alternatives:

➤ One pound of tofu (approximately $2.70) is about ...

> $2.30 cheaper than a pound of tuna.
>
> $3.30 cheaper than a pound of steak.
>
> $.80 cheaper than a pound of chicken breasts.

➤ One pound of pinto beans ($.60) is approximately ...

> $4.40 cheaper than a pound of tuna.
>
> $5.40 cheaper than a pound of steak.
>
> $2.90 cheaper than a pound of chicken breasts.

➤ One pound of organic brown rice ($.75) is approximately ...

> $4.25 cheaper than a pound of tuna.
>
> $5.25 cheaper than a pound of steak.
>
> $2.75 cheaper than a pound of chicken breasts.

Sprouts of Info

Generally, even the processed foods you choose to purchase, such as chips and cereals, are cheaper in bulk, or in larger sizes.

So there, you've just managed to save $10.95 buying a pound each of tofu, rice, and pinto beans rather than three pounds of steak. What are you going to do with all that extra cash? Why don't we talk next about what you entrepreneurial vegetarians might want to do with your surplus.

The Growing Vegetarian

Entrepreneurs, take note: The trend toward vegetarianism is growing quickly and strongly, and you don't have to sit by idly watching. If you are good at numbers and like wheeling and dealing, why not get in on the vegetarian trend and make money by investing in the positive changes taking place in the world?

Consider some of these recent statistics:

➤ Over 30 million Americans have explored eating a more vegetarian diet.

➤ Aging baby boomers are eating more meatless meals.

➤ About one third of U.S. teenagers think that being a vegetarian is cool.

➤ Health and taste are the top two reasons consumers are eating more meat-free meals.

➤ Consumption of beef has dropped 30 percent (that money is going somewhere).

➤ Consumption of veal has dropped 70 percent.

➤ Many fast-food chains and some major food processors now offer meatless options.

➤ Mainstream public health organizations are promoting a plant-based diet.

➤ Ninety-three percent of polled consumers oppose farm animal abuse, and 80 percent favor government regulations.

That means that a lot of change is taking place, and a lot of folks are using their consumer power, not only to find vegetarian alternatives, but to make more humane and earth-friendly choices. It is obvious there is a place for the vegetarian who wants to cater a business to these changing needs.

Investing in the Veggie Trend

The meatless craze has caught on, sales have skyrocketed, and experts predict we won't see it slow down anytime soon. The Soy Foods Association of North America, for instance, reports that the soy industry had a 45 percent increase in sales from 1998 to 1999!

Vegetarians, and especially vegans, like to know they are making a difference with their choices. You can help them make a difference in the world by helping them invest their money in stocks and trends that all have to do with vegan, vegetarian, and environmental causes, or in companies that are putting forth the effort to make positive changes by investing in sustainable development and other environmentally positive technologies.

If you are considering investing your money for profit while keeping your investments in line with your social and moral beliefs, check out a few of the following investment companies, considered "Earth-friendly":

Steer Clear

All else being equal, consumers will purchase an environmentally friendly product over a product that has no benefit or that might be toxic to the environment.

➤ **Eco Deposits**
1-888-ECO-BANK
www.eco-bank.com

➤ **Green Century Funds**
1-800-93-GREEN
www.greencentury.com

➤ **Natural Business Communications**
303-442-8983
www.naturalbiz.com

➤ **Pax World Fund**
1-800-767-1729
www.paxfund.com

➤ **New Alternatives Fund**
610-239-4600
www.newalternativesfund.com

➤ **The Women's Equity Mutual Fund**
1-888-552-WEMF
www.womens-equity.com/

Although the preceding companies all might not invest on purely vegan principles, you can get a prospectus from each and see what they have to offer. If you can't find a completely vegan investment group, maybe you have just found your niche in the investment world!

Sprouts of Info

If you are good with stocks and bonds, why not consider becoming a broker to help your clients invest in companies that you and they can morally support and believe in, like veggie-burger makers or organic farms?

Always a Rebel

Your choices and investments certainly save animals' lives and Earth's resources and reduce pollution. Major trends mean changes in the big picture. Boycotting products that harm the world, along with your support of products that make better use of the land and provide safer, more natural foods will change things whether you set out to do it or not. The impact of your choices changes the way politics and the economy circulate.

Consider Frances Moore Lappé, author of the famous book *Diet for a Small Planet,* and the social awareness she has created by speaking out against a meat-based diet. Her book tells us that she used the money she earned for writing one of her books to co-found Food First, a nonprofit public education and documentation organization. She also cofounded the Institute for the Arts of Democracy. She created her own career based on her thoughts about food!

Veggie Soup for the Soul

Here's a classified ad for you:

Farm animals and the resources it takes to raise animals for human consumption are depleting and do nothing to help sustain earth's resources. Wanted: An ingenious inventor to come up with new materials or better ways to use them that will help in the sustainability of the Earth's resources.

Down to Earth

Are you down to earth? Is there nothing you like better than to be out in nature, digging in the dirt, taking in the fresh air and sunshine? Have you ever considered growing an organic garden? Not only does organic gardening save you money at the grocery store, it feeds the soul for many who love tilling the soil.

Many people feel nurtured themselves when they nurture a fertile piece of earth. Maybe you love to garden, but you are so busy with your office job that you don't have time for it. Maybe it's time for a change?

How about starting an organic farm? Why not? You can do what you love, work the soil, learn tons, feed people good, wholesome, nourishing foods, and save the earth. Wow, sounds like noble work to me!

How does your garden grow? Organically, I hope. Here's a list of organizations you can contact for more information on organic growing:

➤ **Alternative Energy Resources Organization (AERO)**
44 North Last Chance Gulch
Helena, Montana, USA 59601

AERO is a nonprofit organization dedicated to the development of sustainable agriculture, energy technologies based on renewable resources and conservation, and vital rural communities.

➤ **Canadian Organic Growers, Inc. (COG)**
Box 6408, Station J
Ottawa, Ontario K2A 3Y6
www.gks.com/cog

COG is a Canada-wide, nonprofit, voluntary association devoted to all aspects of sustainable agriculture. It provides a quarterly magazine to members.

➤ **Ecological Agriculture Projects (EAP)**
P.O. Box 191, MacDonald College,
21-111 Lakeshore Road,
Ste-Anne de Bellevue, PQ H9X 1CO

This group has a sizeable collection of information on ecological farming. It publishes numerous papers and offers courses on eco-farming. Write for a publications list.

➤ **Northern Plains Sustainable Agricultural Society (NPSAS)**
RR#1, Box 73,
Windsor, ND, USA 58424

Sprouts of Info

Food scientist and vegetarian John Harvey Kellogg practically created an empire with his vegetarian ways—just look at what the Kellogg cereal company has become. It's much more than Special K!

NPSAS is a nonprofit educational organization. NPSAS members work with the Carrington Research Station on research projects and hold field days in the summer.

➤ **Organic Food Producers Association of North America (OFPANA)**
P.O. Box 664,
Lehigh Valley, PA, USA 18001

OFPANA is a continent-wide trade association representing the major organic food processors, distributors, private companies, organic farm organizations, and consultants. In 1985 OFPANA drafted guidelines for the organic food industry. This group encourages common certification standards.

Is Food Your Business?

Okay, so maybe you're not an earth person, but you love to eat. You can take that taste for quality vegetarian food, put together a stellar business plan, and open a vegetarian restaurant, vegetarian health food store, or how about a veggie-food vending business?

How many vendors do you see selling hot dogs, pretzels, or ice cream in the city or even outside Home Depots and other busy stores? Plenty! Have you seen any of those vendors selling tofu hot dogs, veggie burgers, and veggie burritos? I doubt it, and I think it would be a grand idea.

Do you not only love food, but the water, too? Why not consider a floating veggie vending service where you serve veggie snacks, freshly juiced juices, and plenty of bottled water right on the lake? Folks can boat up and order a pita wrap while they catch some rays. Speaking of that, why not sell cruelty-free sunscreen and recycled natural-fiber beach towels?

Making It All Up

If you have a flair for cooking, being a good vegetarian chef can serve you well, especially now that restaurants are seeing more demands for vegetarian items. Why not start a business selling pre-made vegetarian sandwiches to health food stores? How about rounding up an enthusiastic clientele in your local business park and visiting them at lunchtime to deliver your special veggie wraps to their offices?

If you are the inventive type there is always room for a new and tasty prepackaged veggie item. Take a look at how fast the Gardenburger company

Sprouts of Info

The catering business is another way you can work with food and help others enjoy vegetarian meals. I attended a catered vegan wedding, and the caterers did a splendid job, even down to the tofu wedding cake!

grew—you can find Gardenburgers almost everywhere these days! As the trend continues, folks will seek more and more interesting food and taste ideas.

Although there are many meat alternatives, some vegans and health-conscious people are having a hard time getting pure vegan *and* healthy in the same item. Products such as hydrogenated oils are showing up in some of the vegan products, which the health-conscious shun. Think taste, but think health-conscious, too, and you'll be sure to come up with a big hit!

Put Your Money Where Your Mouth Is

There are so many ways to make money being a vegetarian in the media that they are probably obvious to you, but let's brainstorm together anyway. Take this book, for starters. I'm a vegetarian, and I got paid to write about it for you—ta da!

The media includes all forms of communication, including the printed word, TV, and radio. Also consider public speaking to groups as well as creating videos and audiotapes to spread the word about the wonderful world of vegetarianism.

Veggie Soup for the Soul

Consider Susan Havala, a licensed, registered dietitian (among other qualifications) who wrote the first edition of *The Complete Idiot's Guide to Being Vegetarian*. She is a vegetarian dynamo when it comes to spreading the word about vegetarian nutrition. She frequently gives lectures, writes articles online and in magazines, works with the American Dietetic Association, and has appeared on television and made videos. (Phew, I need a protein shake just thinking about all she does!) She and others like her show how great a demand there is for people working in the business of vegetarianism.

If you are a writer, study your vegetarian niche, and get your articles out there to the vegetarian and natural health magazines. Write books and send them to the publishers who are hungry for your information. If you've been sitting on piles of wonderful vegetarian recipes, compile them in a cookbook and market it to all the health food stores. Why not become famous? Your work will help others and yourself, and that's always a nice balance.

Do you think you have some innovative ways of cooking or preparing vegetarian foods? How about a video on what you have to offer? Why not produce your own cable vegetarian cooking show? It can be done. There is also a hungry audience out there that would love to listen to your vegetarian or vegan radio show (remember to call me if you start it— I make a great radio guest!).

The number of vegetarians is growing, and so is the need for information on vegetarian dishes, vegetarian restaurants, products, books, groups, investments, and creative, tasty foods. As a thriving, creative, healthy vegetarian, you have lots of information that others would love to have. The media is an excellent way to share what you know.

The possibilities for media-based vegetarian businesses are endless. It takes only a little creativity, the right contacts, and a little faith in your personal perspective and uniqueness as a vegetarian, and before you know it, you won't be able to imagine you ever had a boring job.

Sprouts of Info

Are you a cartoonist? Remember how funny Gary Larson's *The Far Side* cartoons that picked on vegetarianism were? Why not start your own satirical vegetarian comic strip—we could all stand to laugh at ourselves, and being in the business of making others laugh can't be bad karma!

The Business of Helping Others

Of course, if you are a dietitian, nutritionist, holistic health practitioner, herbalist, chiropractor, doctor, naturopathic physician, traditional naturopath, yoga instructor, physical therapist, or any type of vegetarian in the health care field, you have a unique opportunity to serve as an example of what proper vegetarian nutrition can do for your health.

If you are in the nutritional consulting business you can specialize in helping others transition into a vegetarian diet properly with the nutritional supplements they might need, helping them create vegetarian dishes that they enjoy, or creating weight-loss programs for the new vegetarian or for those who do not eat as well as they should.

If you are in the resort business, you can specialize in catering to vegetarians. Or open a travel agency that specializes in vegetarian resorts, bed and breakfasts, and events. For inspiration, look up various holistic and vegetarian retreats and centers such as Moinhos Velhos, a retreat center in Portugal that offers a two-week holistic fasting cleanse in the countryside (find it on the Internet at www.moinhos-velhos.com).

Finally, if you are vegetarian because of your compassion for animals, did you know that there are organizations that give grants for starting your own refuge for farm or other animals? There are also some funds that grant money to grassroots organizations to promote animal welfare and vegetarian diets. Wonderful, isn't it? Here are some organizations to contact if this is something that interests you:

➤ **Regina Bauer-Frankenberg Foundation for Animal Welfare**
Attn: Uwe Lindner, Vice President, Private Banking
Chemical Bank
270 Park Ave.
New York, NY 10017-2070

➤ **The Sabina Fund**
(A grant given to grassroots projects that promote a plant-based diet)
301-530-1737
www.farmusa.org/grant.html

➤ **Bernice Barbour Foundation**
(Interested in funding "hands-on" animal care projects)
Attn: Eve Lloyd Thompson, Treas. & Secy.
130 Main St.
Hackensack, NJ 07601
301-972-8883

➤ **Summerlee Foundation**
c/o Melanie Roberts
5956 Sherry Ln., Ste. 1414
Dallas, TX 75225-8025
214-363-9000
Fax: 214-363-1941

There are so many things you can do to make vegetarianism your business that I could go on for several more pages. If nothing else, I hope I have helped you appreciate all those hard-working vegetarians out there. Maybe I even lit the spark of a new idea that you will take and run with. I wish you prosperity in your endeavors.

The Least You Need to Know

➤ It is more economical to be a vegetarian than a meat–eater, especially if you choose natural foods over processed or prepared foods.

➤ Vegetarians and vegans can choose to support environmental and ethical causes through their investments.

➤ The growing number of vegetarians increases the need for vegetarian businesses. Some provide food, some provide products and services, and some provide information.

➤ The market for businesses based on a vegetarian diet and philosophy is practically endless.

Part 6

Your Choice Affects the World

*Well, believe it or not, I still haven't told you all of the reasons many choose a vege-
tarian diet. You've learned about all the health and nutritional aspects associated
with your diet, but how about the ecological, political, ethical, and social aspects that
will affect you, and you them, when you choose to be a vegetarian? Whatever issues
you find most compelling, I'm sure you'll be pleased to discover how much excess
water consumption, land waste, pollution, and hunger you will not contribute to simply by eliminating meat from your life!*

*In this part, I'll also share the disturbing facts about how most farm animals raised
for slaughter are treated. Although this might come as a shock to some, the conditions
are real, and because you are a vegetarian, you should be able to read this chapter
and rest easy knowing you are not contributing to the atrocities. The information contained in this section will help to deepen your commitment to being a vegetarian, and
make you aware of how your choices can change the world.*

Chapter 24

Saving Planet Earth

In This Chapter

➤ Learn how your vegetarian diet saves water

➤ See why meatless means cleaner air

➤ Discover why the vegetarian diet makes better sense for land usage

➤ Understand the environmental effects of meat eating

Every choice you make has a consequence. But did you realize that what you choose to eat has effects that reach far beyond just you and your personal health? Your diet has great consequences. We've already looked at what those consequences are for your health and beauty. In this chapter I'll show just how the food we choose affects the health of the planet.

Water Use: Raising the Steaks

It seems ironic that the majority of the Earth's surface is made of water but that fresh, clean water is something that has to be highly managed, maintained, and controlled to supply everyone with enough for their needs. People put a heavy demand on the water supply.

Just think of how many times each day you use water for drinking, bathing, flushing, washing, cooking, brewing drinks, or making ice. Then of course you water your indoor plants, possibly a lawn, your pets, and fill the bird baths! Water is a precious resource that should not be taken for granted, although most of us do at times.

Just like the regular meat-eater doesn't think about how the neatly packaged animal parts came to be, we don't think about the true source of our water. Because tap water is supplied to most homes in abundance, we can forget how much effort goes in to bringing us that water, and where the true source of the water is.

Water, Water, Everywhere?

Fresh water comes mainly from what the earth's atmosphere provides us through rain and snow, which adds to our reservoirs, lakes, streams, rivers, and underground aquifers, known as groundwater. In fact about 90 percent of our drinking water comes from groundwater. From there it is collected for use by digging wells, treated with chemicals, and sent through the city water system to your tap. The faster groundwater is used up, the more resources it takes to bring new water to the surface. These resources take more energy (which pollutes the Earth) and more chemicals (which also pollute the Earth).

Water tables are dropping across the United States, and according to author Frances Lappé in *Diet for a Small Planet* (Ballantine Books, 1991) water tables are dropping from six inches to six feet per year in some places in the United States. Some land is sinking by as much as 29 feet as the groundwater is drawn out in some areas of California.

What are we doing to ourselves? When we deplete the Earth's natural resources we are biting the hand that feeds us. Humans cannot live for more than a few days without water. A 10 to 20 percent loss of your body water content can result in death if not replenished immediately.

But it seems as if we are practically dehydrating Mother Earth! The earth is also a living organism. We need to be aware of the tremendous waste that takes place with our water both on a consumer level and on a larger scale so that we can make choices that can help sustain the health of the planet for our children's future.

Draining Us Dry

As a vegetarian you are certainly doing a lot of good for the Earth's water resources because you are not contributing to the demand for meat, which takes a tremendous toll on the water supply. How? Farmers need plenty of water to raise agricultural crops for human consumption, but they actually use *more* water to raise crops that are grown and harvested for animal feed!

This is due to the rise of feedlots for cattle, pigs, and other farm animals raised for slaughter. About 50 percent of the water consumed in the United States is being used to grow crops used for grain-fed animals, where only about 35 percent of water used for irrigation is for food crops meant for humans. It is estimated that it takes about 2,500 gallons of water to produce a 1-pound beef steak. That's about 15 times the amount of water needed to produce the same amount of protein from plant sources.

It doesn't take such enormous amounts of water to produce fruits and vegetables. For example it takes only about 23 gallons of water to produce 1 pound of tomatoes, 25 gallons of water to produce a pound of carrots, and 33 gallons to produce a pound of wheat! So when you eat a plant-based diet you use water much more efficiently and conserve a precious resource.

Sprouts of Info

Agricultural wastes are more and more often being detected in local water supplies. This means more chemicals must be used to clean the water, which uses up even more resources just to manage drinking water supplies, fueling the vicious cycle of chasing symptoms with more poisons.

The amount of water required to fill your plate with a beautiful vegetable stir-fry is significantly less than eating a puny piece of meat. Besides that, meat is a concentrated food, whereas a stir-fry is high in water-saturated foods. Not only do you save the Earth's resources, you also get some of that water back in the foods you eat.

Dirty Business

The vegetarian diet conserves water directly, and it also lessens water pollution due to agricultural waste products. Animals living in the wild who are free to roam excrete their wastes over a large area. These waste products return to the soil and are properly recycled by the earth's natural processes. In modern industrial farming, animals are smashed into feedlots or forced to live under other crowded conditions that produce an overwhelming amount of manure concentrated in one area. Nature can't absorb these wastes back into the land safely. That leaves the excess to wash off or soak in and pollute rivers and streams.

Pig factories, for example, use an enormous amount of water just to flush pig manure into pits surrounding the area. This factory runoff pollutes surface and ground water. Wastes from both pig and poultry factories serve as a catalyst for Pfiesteria outbreaks, a toxic form of algae. This toxin has killed billions of fish and causes memory loss in humans who come in contact with it.

Pig waste also creates ammonia, which evaporates into the air and contributes to acid rain, again polluting the water and soil. If nothing else the vegetarian lessens the demand for these factory farms, which are so unnatural that they actually wound the earth and pollute the environment.

Air Pollution and Cattle

We know that clean drinking water is precious to life because you can survive only a few days without it. Now consider how precious clean air is to your life. How long can you last? Thirty, 60, maybe 90 seconds without air? My advice is not to test yourself on that one, but do realize how important this free resource is.

Realize as well that when your air is dirty and polluted your body must work harder to filter particles. When it is too polluted, illness sets in. Because you cannot replace your lungs and bronchioles like you can the air filters on your vehicle, you need to help keep your respiratory system healthy and clean by protecting yourself, especially when you are in a polluted environment.

Here are a few tips on filtering air before your respiratory system has to:

➤ Air filters, ionizers, essential oil diffusers, and duct filters for the home or office are all ways to cut down on airborne particles.

➤ Wear proper masks when working with any dust-producing materials. This includes natural materials like wood. Breathing in sawdust particles is hard on your own filtering system.

➤ Choose to exercise in nonpolluted environments. If your health club is remodeling, find another place to exercise until all the dust has settled. If you are a runner or bike rider, choose the countryside and parks to get your exercise rather than city streets where carbon dioxide, asbestos, and other pollutants are abundant.

➤ Spend some time out in the country regularly, or anywhere with plenty of trees (plants filter the air) and breathe deeply to bring fresh air into your lungs and blood stream.

➤ Don't smoke or stay in smoky environments. With each puff of a cigarette you suck in at least 2,000 chemicals. From there they go into your blood stream for a ride to your liver and kidneys, which must filter out these damaging toxins. The sticky tar from cigarettes sticks to your lungs and creates a great environment for bacteria and fungus to propagate, making you much more susceptible to bronchitis, pneumonia, and other lung infections.

All these are simple things you can do personally to take a load off your lungs. And just being a vegetarian helps to reduce air pollution on a global level because it reduces the pollution created by factory farming.

Waste Deep in Pollutants

Remember that the only reason humans can survive is because the Earth's atmosphere surrounds our globe. You can think of the atmosphere as an invisible skin around the planet. Every time you use a toxic chemical, the fumes never completely leave. They remain somewhere, in some form, inside the skin of our atmosphere.

Although these fumes dissipate so you cannot smell or see them anymore, many of them have an effect on the Earth as an organism. Naturally occurring chemicals can be just as bad as the manufactured kind. Farm animals produce quite a few of them; in fact they account for about 10 times more waste than the human population.

Steer Clear

The atmosphere is Mother Earth's respiratory system. Just like you could not live without your respiratory system, life on Earth would die out if we were to lose the atmosphere. To protect our atmosphere we cannot continue to poison it.

➤ Cattle naturally produce methane gas. Methane gas makes up 9 percent of the gasses that are creating the greenhouse effect. The greenhouse effect is directly linked to global warming.

➤ Livestock, and especially cattle, also produce waste that is high in nitrous oxide, another greenhouse gas. Animal waste is the second largest source of emissions of this gas; cattle waste makes up 95 percent of it.

➤ Deforestation of the rain forests for the purpose of raising cattle contributes to the greenhouse effect and global warming, and throws the Earth's natural climate control out of whack.

➤ Runoff from manure and dairy-house milk wash contains high amounts of nitrogen, phosphorous, pathogens, and detergents. These can flow directly into waterways, creating ideal conditions for the rapid growth of algae. Algae eat up significant amounts of oxygen and, in turn, can suffocate and damage fish habitats.

➤ Slaughterhouses are not pleasant smelling areas to live near.

➤ Transportation of cattle and swine to slaughterhouses via semi trucks contributes to diesel fuel emissions.

Is It Getting Hot Down Here?

Some might think that the warmer planet that global warming will create won't be so bad—especially those of us who live with long northern winters. But the sad truth is that the rapid unbalancing of our earth's atmosphere causes other deleterious effects, some that you might not have thought about. Let's take a look at some of these things:

➤ Melting of the polar ice caps raises sea levels, causing seawater to contaminate drinking water sources.

➤ Increased heat causes dry conditions, making food production more difficult.

➤ Hotter conditions lead to a greater need for air conditioning; air conditioners release greenhouse gasses and add to the problem.

➤ Greenhouse gasses deplete the ozone layer, which shields us from harmful sun-rays, leading to more skin cancer.

➤ Displacement of animals and plants due to strange weather patterns damages nature's balance and causes plants and animals that cannot adapt quickly to become extinct.

These are all good reasons not only to pass up the meat, but to go "green" in other products you use.

Agricultural Land Use

You might wonder, like I did, how all this imbalance got started? Let me just give you a little bit of background. First of all, some land is not appropriate for planting crops, nor does the land naturally grow food suitable for human consumption. Cattlemen could therefore allow their cattle to graze on these ranges (and of course some do), and the cattle would eat the natural vegetation.

The animal is then slaughtered and provided to people as a source of protein. The logic here is that if there is no proper land for crops, the alternative is to convert the land to grazing. This way you use the land to efficiently raise food, turning the inedible vegetation into edible meat.

So why are farmers putting cattle, swine, and other livestock in crowded *feedlots* and boiler rooms anyway? Why not let them graze in the open on otherwise inedible vegetation and then bring them in for slaughter when they're good and fat? The bottom line is the bottom dollar.

Lettuce Explain

A **feedlot** is a place where cattle and other livestock are kept penned in and crowded together. They are fed grain and soy products, and usually injected with hormones and antibiotics as well. These feedlots are for the purpose of fattening the animal before slaughter.

Feedlot Economics

Farmers must compete fiercely to stay in business. Cattle that are allowed to graze on the range gain weight more slowly than animals fattened in feedlots. And because of the extra exercise free-ranging animals get, they are generally leaner than those fed high-protein, high-grain diets in a feedlot. And cattle are sold by the pound, so the heavier the better, and the more money earned.

We already talked about how much water is used to grow the grains for grain-fed livestock. The land use, water consumption, and energy spent in fossil fuels to raise meat in feedlots far exceeds that used for free-ranging livestock.

Currently even cattle that graze the free range for a short time are still passed through feedlots, where they are fed about 22 pounds of soybean and grain products daily (up to 2,500 total pounds). They also are given hundreds of gallons of water, not to mention antibiotics and hormones, before they reach the slaughterhouse.

Logical Land Use

Raising grain for livestock to produce meat on cropland is an inefficient use of this land. Why not just eat the soy burger (made from soybeans raised for livestock feed) with an ear of corn (a grain raised for livestock feed) on a whole-wheat bun (another grain used for feeding cattle) to get your supply of protein? Wouldn't this be more efficient than waiting for that steer to be fattened up on practically the same foods and then eating one pound of the animal's body?

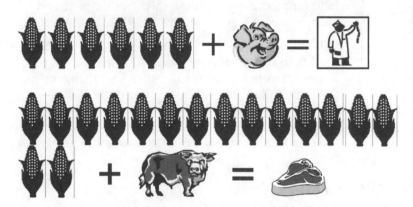

It takes six pounds of grain crops to produce one pound of pork. It takes 16 pounds of grain crops to produce 1 pound of steak.

(Clipart images compliments of Microsoft)

A vegetarian diet is a more efficient use of the land. Just think of what we could do with all that extra grain if folks cut down on meat consumption. Grain is significantly cheaper than meat, and you get much more food when you focus your diet around grains rather than meats. If everyone was a vegetarian, there would be a whole lot more food to go around!

Many believe that the land used to raise grains for livestock feed could be put to better use for both the farmer and the community. Think of the water, fossil fuels, and air pollution that would be saved if the majority of people cut out grain-fed meat from their diet. Of course these things require a great deal of change and won't happen overnight, but simply by being vegetarian, you contribute to a slow shift for the better.

Clear-Cut Reasons for Change

What about the rain forests? Are they really chopping down a tree in the tropical rain forest for every burger you consume? Well, North America's eating habits do have an effect on the rain forests. In Central America in particular, rain forests are clear cut for cattle grazing, and most of those cattle are raised for export to the United States.

In fact most of the cattle raised in poorer countries are exported, because their own people are too poor to afford meat. So, unfortunately, yes, according to researchers Christopher Uhl and Geoffrey Parker, one hamburger can represent about 55 square feet of rain forest destruction.

Making Way for Beef

Here's a simplified version of how this clear cutting for beef comes about. In an effort to pay off foreign loans the governments of the poor countries that own the rain forests offer pieces of it to developers. The government offers these lands for almost nothing on the condition that the developer makes use of the land for production of some sort. The simplest and least expensive way to develop this land is to clear cut it and raise cattle for export.

Another way this land is developed is for the raising of soy products harvested for livestock feed that gets exported to the United States. So even if the United States didn't import a huge number of foreign cattle, the cattle raised in feedlots in the States would still be responsible for some of the clear cutting of rain forests.

Steer Clear

As long as the demand for beef continues, the clear cutting of rain forests will go on. Concerned individuals can do their part by healing the source of the problem, which is meat consumption.

Who Needs Rain Forests?

Why worry about the rain forests? You don't have to be an environmentalist or even give a rat's tail about the health of the Earth to have a reason to do your part in saving these forests. Rain forests are special habitats that are an integral part of our climate control. They are also among the only places in the world where certain medicinal herbs can be found and certain animal and bug species thrive.

There are literally volumes of information that would fill several encyclopedias still waiting to be discovered about the rain forests, but these places are being destroyed faster than we can study them. Clear cutting for raising livestock or livestock feed plays a big role in the deforestation.

Here are some major reasons for saving the rain forests, both for your own personal good and for the big picture:

➤ **Global warming.** Remember how plant life cleans our air? Dense tropical rain forests serve as a holding tank for carbon dioxide, a major contributor to greenhouse gas. When these plants are destroyed, the carbon dioxide is again released in great amounts back into the atmosphere.

➤ **Medicinal herbs.** Some great healing herbs are harvested from the rain forests. Maybe the cure for a disease you are enduring will be discovered in these incredible places; maybe you are already using herbs that are now being sustainably harvested from these areas. Clear cutting means these healing substances will no longer be available to you.

➤ **Animal, insect, and plant habitats are being destroyed,** forcing thousands of species into extinction.

➤ **Rapid land erosion** causes flooding, which reduces the ability of local populations to take care of themselves, which further increases the need for assistance from more developed countries.

Isn't it amazing how interconnected everything is? Your every action and choice can have an effect on things around the globe! You can certainly sleep easier knowing that your choice of a vegetarian diet will have a positive impact on the planet. Now you have even more reason to smile while eating your tofu loaf!

The Least You Need to Know

➤ A vegetarian diet uses about 15 times less water than a meat-based diet, which helps conserve one of Earth's natural resources.

➤ The raising and production of meat leads to air pollution and increases greenhouse gases, which could be reduced if more people were to follow a vegetarian diet.

➤ It takes an enormous amount of grain-fed cattle to produce a small amount of meat, making a meat-based diet less efficient for agricultural land use than a vegetarian diet.

➤ Clear cutting rain forests for raising cattle and cattle feed damages our atmosphere, destroys a valuable source of medicinal plants, drives species to extinction, and has a host of other terrible consequences, some yet to be discovered.

Chapter 25

A Higher Purpose

In This Chapter

➤ Learn about some religions that restrict meat eating

➤ Help your child develop a reverence for life

➤ Learn the underlying philosophy of the breatharian

➤ See how vegetarianism can nourish the humanist in you

Many of us don't even think about how society came to follow certain common practices, rituals, and traditional behaviors that are today still carried out and considered common sense. When you discover the reasons behind the dietary restrictions that some religions follow, it can deepen your understanding and give you further reasons to eliminate meat from your life. Adding depth to a decision strengthens your conviction and helps you remain a vegetarian for life.

For those who wonder where meat, ethics, and religion fall together, I'm going to serve up a dish consisting of at least a serving of each. Right now you might be wondering if this chapter is an example of poor subject combining! However, the mental vegetarian stew that you will wind up with by the end of the chapter will, I hope, taste quite good. So grab a bowl, tuck in your napkin, and I'll serve up some inspirational grub!

The Long Arm of the Religious Law

The earliest laws and regulations probably came about through trial and error and from human observations of nature and animals. We learned plenty about food from observant people who watched and who got ill or died and noted what they had eaten that might have caused it. This information was then shared by those who passed along the people's knowledge. These were often religious leaders, and so this information became part of their collective wisdom and eventually part of religious law.

You have to remember that people's knowledge of disease was scant until as recently as a couple of hundred years ago. Humans knew neither about bacteria and viruses nor what caused, cured, or prevented them from causing harm. We didn't understand how wastes could carry contaminants or that refrigeration keeps food from spoiling. All these things had to be learned. Religious laws and regulations helped transmit and reinforce this knowledge and turn common-sense habits into common law.

It's for Your Own Good

Many religious dietary laws came into being this way. For example, Jewish life is enriched by *kosher* dietary laws, which may have kept devotees from food-borne illness in ancient times and which today serve to keep modern devout Jews safe from the "evils" that foods like bacon or shellfish can do to the body!

Lettuce Explain

Kosher is a Hebrew term that means "proper" or "fit." The term is used especially for foods that orthodox Jews are allowed to eat according to Jewish law.

It can be empowering to gain insight into why a particular religion would restrict certain flesh foods. Let's touch on a few of the religions that incorporate some dietary restrictions and attempt to uncover their initial reasoning.

Some who question why they should follow ancient dietary practices when we now have the use of refrigeration, pasteurization, and other food-safety technology have been told by their spiritual leaders that they should follow the laws for the sake of honoring their religion. Keeping faith in traditional practices, even when they do not necessarily serve you at the moment, is a demonstration of your respect for your ancient roots and the wise people who passed on these guidelines in good faith.

The Divine Meal Plan

I have heard a priest explain that it doesn't matter what man comes up with that justifies circumventing God's laws. There is no way to get around God's pearly gates if they are locked, for all truth is revealed in the end. I guess he was saying that if we try to live beyond what is meant to be right for us, it will catch up with us in the end. That holds true for diet just as much as anything else.

If our bodies are not meant to handle meat on a consistent basis, then this should be taken into consideration. Maybe we need to consider the implications of eating a meat-centered diet and compare it to using the wrong type of tool for a job. For instance you could use a blender to chop vegetables, but the blender isn't going to do as effective a job as chopping your food by hand or using a food processor.

Eventually, the blender, which is predominately designed to blend liquids, will break down, and sooner than it would if it were not used to chop vegetables. Man did not create the blender for chopping vegetables, just as the Creator did not create humans to eat meat on a regular basis.

The Judeo-Christian Food Ethic

Although vegetarian diets are relatively new to North America, they are common practice for many Americans whose religions advocate a vegetarian diet. Let's talk about a few of the popular religions and the dietary restrictions they observe.

References to dietary restrictions are abundant in the Old Testament of the Bible. Here are a few of the forbidden animals. Check out Chapter 11 in Leviticus for a complete list.

➤ Rabbit

➤ Camel

➤ Pig

➤ Any seafood that does not have fins and scales (this would include shellfish)

➤ Eagle

➤ Vulture

➤ Owl

➤ Stork

➤ Flying insects that swarm (darn, I guess I'll cancel that order for chocolate-covered mosquitoes!)

Sprouts of Info

Today Roman Catholic Trappist monks still practice vegetarianism to fulfill their vows of austerity and self-sacrifice.

Overall, the Bible does not forbid humans to eat animals, but it does restrict the types of animals. The laws found in the Bible are clear that only animals that are herbivores (vegetarians!) should be eaten, and of them, only those that have cloven hoofs *and* chew their cud are acceptable. With regard to fish, only those with fins and scales are acceptable.

Looking back at what we've learned about the tapeworm's affinity for pork and the affinity of shrimp and other shellfish for human sewage can make you wary of eating those types of animals anyway. Pigs are notorious for eating slop and waste materials as food. Bugs in general feast on wastes, as do shellfish. Maybe ancient people saw that creatures who work as nature's undertakers should not be intercepted by humans for consumption, just as you wouldn't make a meal from your garbage disposal or compost pile.

Some Christian vegetarians believe that, although it might be lawful to eat animals not on the forbidden list, to eat meat everyday is gluttonous, just as wine is accepted

but drunkenness is unholy. Still others believe that God's words in Genesis 1:29 sum it up: "Behold, I have given you every herb-bearing seed which is upon the face of all the earth, and every tree ... to you it shall be for meat."

Sprouts of Info

Christians who are interested in the theological view of vegetarianism can read *Christianity and the Rights of Animals,* by Andrew Linzey (Crossroad Publishing, 1987).

Seventh-day Adventists, Vegetarians Seven Days a Week

Seventh-day Adventists are members of an evangelical church that originated in New England in the mid-nineteenth century. One of its main beliefs is that the body is a temple for the Holy Spirit and must not be defiled. For many strict Adventists, smoking, drinking alcohol, and consuming caffeine are condemned, and vegetarian diets are encouraged.

Seventh-day Adventists restrict meat in their diets largely because meat is stimulating to the body, as are tobacco, alcohol, and caffeine. I have met other religious folks, including Jehovah's Witnesses, Latter-Day Saints, Mennonites, and Amish people who follow these same dietary restrictions because of the physically stimulating nature of meat.

Veggie Soup for the Soul

The Journal of American College of Nutrition (volume 17, no. 5, and volume 18, no. 2) describes the results of a study comparing certain health factors in vegetarian Seventh-day Adventists and Catholics in Denver, Colorado. Of all subjects tested, the vegetarian Adventists came out with better blood lipid numbers, lower blood pressure, and lower risk for Type 2 diabetes than the nonvegetarian Catholics.

Is That Kosher?

The Jewish religion has some of the best-known dietary restrictions—go back to Leviticus if you need to check on your favorites (no eating weasels!). It is most famous for banning pork and shellfish: pigs because they are a cloven-hoofed animal that doesn't chew the cud, and shellfish because it has no fins. Products such as milk and cheese from any forbidden animal are also off limits. The Jews might also have been the first to practice food combining, since the dietary laws forbid mixing meat and milk. That is why a kosher kitchen will have two sets of dishes—one for cooking and serving meat, and one for dairy (reminds me of some veggie-carnivore kitchens I know). Jewish law also has strict rules about the humane slaughter of animals.

What would a kosher vegetarian meal consist of? Nothing different than a vegetarian meal. How the meal is prepared would be of more concern if you were cooking for a traditional Jew. Here are some tips on preparing a kosher vegetarian meal for your Jewish friends:

➤ Dishes and cooking utensils that were used for meat cannot be used for preparing and serving dairy products.

➤ During Passover, no leavened bread is to be eaten.

➤ Don't serve your traditional Jewish friends a meal using any utensils or dishes that have been used to prepare any nonkosher item.

These laws have the effect of avoiding cross-contamination between animal products and other foods, just as the food safety guidelines of recent times suggest that you use separate utensils and cutting boards for raw meat.

When purchasing processed kosher foods, you'll need to learn how to read your food labels and symbols. Here's a rundown of some symbols to look for as a kosher vegetarian:

Lettuce Explain

Cloven hoof literally means divided hoof and includes animals like cattle, deer, sheep, and antelope that have two toes on each hoof.

Sprouts of Info

For more information, read Richard H. Schwartz's *Judaism and Vegetarianism* (Micah Publications, 1988). And please feel free to send me input if you are an Orthodox Jew who follows a vegetarian diet. I'll make sure I include your perspective in future editions of this book.

➤ Look for a "*K*" on the label, which means the food is kosher.

➤ A "*P*" on the label means Parve, which means the product contains no meat or dairy, but it *might* contain fish or eggs. Read your ingredients to be sure.

➤ "*Kosher D*" means the product either does contain dairy or could have been made with dairy machinery.

Read your labels carefully and contact your rabbi for specifics if you have questions. Another good source of info is the Orthodox Union at 212-563-4000. Remember, if you are a vegetarian, at least you won't have to worry about finding kosher meat.

Hinduism—Ya'll Come Back Now

Some religions, such as Hinduism and Buddhism, abstain from meat partly because of a belief in reincarnation. Certain sects believe that all life is sacred and that our souls continue to come back to Earth (reincarnate) to learn lessons. Because any human's departed soul might come back in the body of an animal, animals should be shown respect. Consuming animal flesh is therefore off limits.

Sprouts of Info

A book that gives a Buddhist perspective on vegetarianism is *To Cherish All Life: A Buddhist View of Animal Slaughter and Meat Eating,* by Philip Kapleau (Rochester Zen Center, 1981).

According to Vedic scriptures, it is considered sinful to kill cows or eat their flesh. The scriptures warn that the sinful human who eats the flesh of cows will be reborn and killed as many times as there are hairs on the body of the slaughtered animal. The Vedic scripture also explains that wars are a direct consequence of the slaughter and eating of innocent animals.

Overall, Buddhists and Hindus show reverence for all life. As the Christian's follow the commandment "Love thy neighbor," the Hindu's Unity of Life Doctrine would add to that precept "Love thy neighbor, and every living creature is thy neighbor."

Spiritual Connections

There are many spiritual and philosophical belief systems that include vegetarian or other food-related precepts. I would like to share a few of the more interesting ones I've come across.

Many people have a vision of a utopia where all is peaceful. There is no pollution, fighting, violence, impure thoughts, or killing. I see happy people eating lots of fruit, and lions and tigers living together peacefully while sharing tofu with the antelope. Wouldn't that be something?

I don't think we'll ever quite paint that picture here on Earth, although it is a peaceful vision to work toward! Even so, it is no bad thing to live as though your personal actions will change the entire world in your lifetime. No matter what, every action you take adds to the evolution of the planet, so eating and living cruelty-free only add to the positive changes.

Lighten/Enlighten

Various groups that are working toward spiritual enlightenment see eating, especially heavier foods such as red meat, as a distraction from the true goal of the soul. They believe that the lighter and more alive the foods they eat are, the less dense the physical body becomes, leading them toward higher states of consciousness and enabling them to become closer to God.

Because the strict vegetarian and vegan eat less dense and heavy foods, their bodies are usually lighter or cleaner on the inside, if you will. A clean body is generally more sensitive to toxins such as chemicals and prescription drugs; heavy, greasy, fat-laden foods; and other stimulants such as alcohol and caffeine. The physical change these toxins cause can lead the emotions or behavior astray. Sticking to a clean vegetarian diet helps these folks stay clear and make the best choices.

Clean and Quiet

Along with the physical sensitivity that comes with a clean diet, the vegetarian can become more psychically sensitive as well. Eventually, negativity, pollution, loud noises, chaos, or violence can terribly disturb a clean vegetarian's psyche.

Sprouts of Info

Various religions have certain days for fasting or giving up of certain foods for a period of time. This helps take the focus away from the physical body and lets the person focus on spiritual issues.

Overall, a clean vegan or strict vegetarian has a greater need for peace and periods of solitude, more so than do folks who live on meat. This need for a peaceful life can spur the vegetarian to work toward a more peaceful world for everyone through prayer, ritual, or even activism.

Of course, vegetarianism is not for everyone, for these very reasons. Those who live a hussle-bussle, fast-paced, chaotic life might not be able to handle the pure vegetarian diet, although almost everyone can benefit from eating less or no meat. But in general, those who can live in a relaxed and peaceful environment will more likely thrive on the pureness of a pure vegetarian diet—at least until we build our vegetarian utopia and there is no violence or pollution in the inner or outer worlds.

All I Need Is the Air I Breathe

Breatharianism is a philosophy that says when a person reaches a perfect state of health and a totally natural state of being, he or she will be in perfect harmony with the Creator and require no food or water. As a result, breatharians believe, the aging process will be slowed dramatically. Now I do not advocate the idea of living on air (talk about a restrictive diet!), but the philosophy is interesting and is wonderfully idealistic in its teachings.

The reason I mention it is to illuminate how food can control your life without you even being conscious of it. You will see this clearly if you ever fast—it's unbelievable how many times a day you think about food!

Although I don't really believe in breatharianism, I do believe that when you eat to live instead of live to eat, your mind and body have more freedom to put forth good work, thoughts, and ideas, either through your work, your children, your students, or

your prayers. Just think of Albert Einstein and all that he gave in his work—he was a vegetarian!

Breatharianism is an extreme example of moving all of your energies away from your addictions to food to attain not only higher levels of health, but higher levels of consciousness.

Would Gandhi Steer You Wrong?

Great social philosophers who were also vegetarians include Mahatma Gandhi and George Bernard Shaw, both of whom professed the philosophical side of vegetarianism. Their cruelty-free diets supported their nonviolent messages by extending their belief systems to their dinner plates.

Every decision you make has a consequence. Although most meat-eaters are not killing any animals personally, their choice to eat meat means that they have contributed to the taking of a life to satisfy their tastes. If you sincerely believe the commandment "Thou shall not kill," then you ought to consider whether you need to take the commandment literally. Maybe we should not only not kill, but not make choices that contribute to the killing of another being.

With all this said, I still feel it's important to remember that vegetarianism, just like religion and spirituality, is a personal choice. I'd like to sum it up with an excerpt from the Bible:

> "The man who eats everything must not look down on him who does not, and the man who does not eat everything must not condemn the man who does, for God has accepted him." (Romans 14:3)

Teach Your Children Well

Most parents find it important to teach their children how to be gentle and compassionate toward animals, not just for the animals' sake, but to foster gentleness and an understanding of the sanctity of life.

Have you ever seen parents with their children at a petting zoo filled with baby farm animals? The parents instruct their children to be nice to the animals, not to hit or pull, but to touch or pat the animal gently. The children are always thrilled to be around the animals. You see giggles, laughter, and utter fascination.

Veggie Soup for the Soul

Modern vegetarianism in the West is actually a fairly recent phenomenon, which entered the public consciousness in the mid–1800s when a British organization, the Vegetarian Society, coined the term "vegetarian." Since then vegetarianism has been promoted worldwide by an international nonprofit group called the International Vegetarian Union.

What does it mean to that child when the parent then stops at a restaurant on the way home for a meal that consists of animal flesh? How can we be nice to an animal when it is alive and then close our eyes to what happens behind the scenes when we order that hot dog or plate full of chicken nuggets?

Respect for Life

The respect we teach our young to show for all life in general has a profound psychological impact throughout their lives. If we teach them (by example or otherwise) that it is okay to blatantly or without reverence use animals for pleasure or satisfaction, to satisfy a perceived (but not real) need, to disregard the animal's life, then what precedent are we setting for that child?

Could we be showing our children by extension that it is acceptable to be arrogantly judgmental toward people who might be at a disadvantage in their eyes? Could it foster the philosophy, "I get what I want as long as I am stronger than you, no matter what the consequences are to anyone else"? Or might it inflate their ability to see the power they have over others who are weaker, especially another person who might not have a voice to speak up for his or her rights?

I don't know the answers, but I truly believe that every action has an effect on our psyche and our world. I would suspect that if a child is taught from the beginning that every life is sacred, then even if the child chooses to eat meat, he or she will have learned a lesson in how to be grateful. A deep-seated philosophy of life without compassion or reverence for other creatures can lead to dangerous and ruthless acts. Surveys generally indicate that those who feel grateful for the things they have are happier people overall. So if nothing else, a child who can be grateful might have a happier life.

Denying the Truth

Humans also have a great capacity for denial. Most of us want to believe that the source of all meat is the grocery store, neatly packaged, no eyes, nose, hair, mouth, or face to stare at, letting us remain in comfortable denial about what these "foods" really are. We cannot contribute to the deception that our chicken nuggets, hamburgers, and hot dogs are not the body parts of slaughtered animals and expect our children to not live in denial.

Denial can get us into trouble, lead to personality disorders, and keep us from personal growth and self-actualization. If we want our children to see life's whole picture we need to inform them about the impact of their simplest choices. Educating them about one of their most simple daily choices—food— will help them think holistically and can deepen their understanding of life processes.

Sprouts of Info

"A man of my spiritual intensity does not eat corpses."

—George Bernard Shaw (attrib.)

If given the chance to decide for themselves, I bet that 80 to 90 percent of all children would be vegetarians naturally. I am writing this to you on my laptop computer as I watch a five-year-old girl across the way pick the pepperoni off of her pizza and eat the pizza plain. I've heard it said that children are closer to representing God because of their newness in the world. And the clean, undeveloped tastes of most of the children I see demonstrate to me something that I heed—we really don't need so much meat!

The Least You Need to Know

➤ Many religions restrict the eating of some types of animals, and some prohibit meat altogether.

➤ Some philosophical and spiritual teachings say that eating lighter foods brings you closer to your Creator by freeing up your physical energies, which enables you to center your mind on a higher, more spiritual purpose.

➤ Eating lighter and more natural foods can cause an individual to become more sensitive physically and psychically, creating the need for a peaceful and less polluted environment and lifestyle.

➤ Teaching children reverence for life and the consequences behind their choices can be a healthy way to instill gratefulness and prevent denial in a child, whether or not they choose to be vegetarians.

Chapter 26

Enlightened Appetites

In This Chapter

➤ Learn about the irradiation of foods

➤ Get an update on Mad Cow disease

➤ Understand what there is in meat that you didn't bargain for

➤ Find out what happens to damaged animals

➤ Take a quick look at meat inspection practices

Have you heard that your foods are being bombarded with radioactive rays to kill bacteria? I'll give you some valuable information about this that can help vegetarians and occasional meat-eaters make a wise decision about whether or not to eat these foods. This chapter discusses the philosophy of following nature's laws and how some of our modern agricultural practices seem to be taking us away from anything natural, and where this is leading.

Here you'll read the latest on Mad Cow disease, find out what happens to animals that literally can't stand up for themselves, and learn about things found in meat that the meat-eater might not have bargained for! This chapter is meant to enlighten you about what goes on behind the scenes in the food business, and how your vegetarian choices can help support the farmers who are more in touch with natural laws.

X-Rated Meat?

Did you know that the food you are eating might have been purposely blasted with radiation? The FDA has approved the irradiation of red meat, but other foods, such as poultry and even fresh produce and spices, are already being bombarded with this radiation. First of all, let me explain what irradiated foods are and how the process is done. *Irradiation* kills organisms such as salmonella, listera, and E. coli that cause food poisoning without harming the food, says the FDA. The foods are placed in a secure irradiation chamber and blasted with a powerful electron beam that scans the food and breaks the DNA bonds of bacteria that could be lurking on it.

Food irradiation is not new—in fact, the patent that paved the way with an x-ray process to treat meat was granted in 1921. This form of discharging kiloGrays (lethal to humans) onto foods is expected to be used more frequently in the future, especially as food-borne illness scares increase.

Lettuce Explain

Irradiation is a process that showers foods with powerful radiation after the foods are placed inside a secure chamber. The purpose is to burst apart the DNA molecules of any food-borne bacteria that could cause food poisoning.

Just Like Pasteurization?

Today food irradiation is being used in over 40 countries. Foods such as poultry, potatoes, fresh fruits, and some spices are being regularly zapped to control sprouting and ripening and to prolong shelf life, not to mention kill bacteria.

Some proponents compare the use of irradiation to the pasteurization of cow's milk. Many restaurant owners are ecstatic over the use of irradiation because, as one chef explained, it serves as his cheapest insurance to protect the public from food poisoning. This could be a life-saving benefit. The FDA claims it's safe, and producers say there is no harm to the foods that are irradiated. Taste tests show that no one can tell the difference between irradiated and untreated foods. And some say it will help reduce the use of pesticides.

These are all valid arguments, and I'm not saying irradiation is always bad in all cases. But I do have a different perspective on the issue. Let's take a look at some of the questions that arise over all this radiation business, and see what its opponents are saying.

First, let's take a look at what "no harm to the food" really means. No harm obviously doesn't mean that the food has not been altered in some way. Even when we microwave food it destroys and changes certain enzymes and naturally occurring components in the food.

The following table shows the known effects that irradiation has on food and gives some thoughts to ponder.

What Irradiation Does to Foods and Some Thoughts to Ponder

Fact	Commentary
Irradiation produces about the same amount of nutrient loss in foods as other processing methods, such as canning.	Whole, live, enzyme-rich foods direct from nature nourish your body. If irradiating fresh produce makes the food equivalent to a canned or otherwise processed food, why bother with the fresh produce?
Irradiated strawberries and other fresh fruits last significantly longer than produce that has not been irradiated without rotting or molding, and potatoes are stunted and can therefore be stored longer.	If we get life from the foods we eat, why would we want to purchase fresh produce that has effectively been embalmed?
Irradiation causes the skins of some fruits to soften.	Could this be anything like what radioactive fallout does to human skin?
Irradiation causes undesirable flavors change in cheese, milk, and other dairy products.	Pew!
Irradiated meat tends to have a darker color and smell different, described as smelling "off."	Your nose knows!

A Few More "What Ifs"

Just a few more philosophical questions to think about when it comes to irradiation:

➤ If irradiation kills the bacteria on produce, wouldn't it also kill off the good bacteria that naturally occur on the skins of fruits? Just as humans have a balance of good and bad bacteria, so do fruits and vegetables. We know what the overuse of antibiotics has done to our immune systems, not to mention producing drug-resistant strains of bacteria. Does it seem like a good idea to do the same thing to produce?

➤ Don't you think nature intended for you to receive the good bacteria that naturally occurs on fruits and veggies, not to mention all their other components?

➤ Why and how have humans been able to eat all sorts of fresh foods for hundreds of years, and suddenly we are bombarded with epidemic outbreaks of food-borne illness? What is going on? Could it be that our immune systems are now so weakened due to poor nutritional habits, chemical-laden foods, pesticides, stress, lower nutritional contents in foods, and widespread antibiotic use that we are more susceptible to these food-borne illnesses? Is attempting to chase away the bugs the best strategy for overall health? Or would building up our own immune systems by giving our bodies what they need to function optimally be a better strategy?

Steer Clear

Irradiating meat and produce does not mean that the food can't be contaminated at a later date. In other words, the same food safety precautions need to be followed when handling irradiated foods as nonirradiated foods. Do not cross contaminate, be sure to wash your hands, wipe surfaces clean, and use other sensible hygiene when handling all food.

➤ What are the long-term effects of eating irradiated foods? And is it getting to the real source of the problem? Sources say that the mass irradiation of foods can be an alternative to pesticide use. Granted, almost anything we can do to stop using so many harmful chemicals is a positive step, but what about the farmers who have organic and pesticide-free farms? They've already figured it out without the use of irradiation.

➤ Irradiation of red meat has been pushed to protect the consumer from the deadly acid-loving E. coli bacteria. However, a recent Cornell U. study showed that you could reduce the bacteria to harmless levels by feeding the cattle grass or hay for just five days prior to slaughter. This changed the pH of the cow's intestine, ridding it of most of the deadly E. coli. Isn't this a better way to protect the consumer than trucking nuclear waste through our communities to irradiation facilities?

I'm not necessarily saying that no foods should be irradiated, nor am I saying to shut down those who offer irradiated products. What I am trying to do is give you some information to think about so that you can decide for yourself where you want your energy to go. Do you want to support taking care of the symptoms, or would you rather help correct the source of the problem? I see irradiation as working on the symptom and doing nothing to force agribusiness to create better farming practices that would lessen the food-borne problems that stem from factory farm filth.

You can work at the source of the problem in two ways. First work on becoming healthier and stronger by eating and living well. Eliminate those foods that attract sickness to your body, such as meat, sugar, and refined carbohydrates. Clean your system and nourish it by giving it fresh, live, whole foods from nature.

And second, support the groups, organizations, and farmers who value providing whole, unadulterated, organic, clean foods. Doing both will benefit your health and the state of the world.

Veggie Soup for the Soul

Notice how more and more antibacterial soaps are being advertised these days. Do they seem to be effective at preventing bacterial illness, or do you continue to hear about more bacterial outbreaks? These soaps are another demonstration of the overuse of antibiotics. Wouldn't you rather take common, sensible, hygienic precautions and build a strong body rather than rely on stronger antibiotic creams, lotions, soaps, sprays, and radiation to kill naturally occurring bugs for you?

The Case for Clean Food

There are a few things you need to know no matter which side of the fence you are on about irradiation. If it makes you feel safer to eat irradiated foods or if you would like to avoid these foods entirely, you should look for the following symbol in the figure when grocery shopping.

Since 1986, all irradiated products sold in stores must carry this international symbol, the radura.

This symbol is required to be posted near or on irradiated foods. Although you can seek or steer clear of foods with this symbol at your grocery store, restaurants and hospitals are not required to disclose this information when the foods are served. Because irradiation sterilizes foods, hospitals have been serving radiated foods to AIDS patients and other patients with compromised immune systems for some time.

Unfortunately, our food chain is horribly complex, with its multitude of handlers and subjection to more bacteria and other problems. Food irradiation might serve to protect people from food-borne illness, especially those people who regularly live on processed foods and mass-produced agriculture.

Choosing Clean Food to Begin With

However, choosing foods that need to be irradiated because they are harboring so much bacteria is not getting us any closer to living as nature intended. It doesn't bring us any closer to balancing our body's natural needs. It doesn't particularly nourish us or give us a longer life. The job of the FDA is not to make sure that FDA-approved items are good for you. Its job is to make sure that approved products or procedures are not going to kill you, at least right away.

Only nature can provide you with what your body really needs to be well naturally. An absence of disease doesn't necessarily equal vibrant health, just as a fruit or vegetable that has been hybridized to make it sterile; sprayed with chemicals to keep the bugs away; genetically altered so it doesn't squash too easily; grown with chemical fertilizers to make up for the minerally depleted soil it was planted in; picked green so it can get to you before it rots; and irradiated to kill bacteria isn't necessarily going to provide you with complete nourishment!

Lettuce Explain

The **radura** symbol is the flower-like, green, international symbol that is required by law to be posted where irradiated foods are sold, either near by or directly on the foods themselves. It is not required to be posted where these foods are served, however, such as in hospitals or restaurants. There is currently industry pressure to eliminate the radura symbol from packaging and to shrink the warning label to the font size of the ingredient list.

Demand a Healthy Food Supply

There are no easy solutions to the complicated chain of problems involved in agribusiness. However, to eat as well as you can, supporting the farmers who have your best interests at heart can at least make a small impact.

Demand will always run the show, so as a vegetarian your buying power can facilitate change. You'll want to keep your eye out for trends that continue to take us farther away from the natural ways in life. The farther we stray from nature's laws, the farther from health we go. Nature's balance is way out of kilter.

Irradiation might be necessary for protecting the masses, but vegetarians (unfortunately) are not the masses. Dan Glickman, Agriculture Secretary of the United States, stated in an article that the complexity of the food chain these days is totally different than it used to be. Parts of a chicken that were originally processed in one state might end up in 700 different fast-food restaurants across the country within three days!

Sprouts of Info

I think it will be the vegetarians and organic farmers who help make way for positive changes in our agricultural system. Maybe we can even find a way for family farmers to compete with agribusiness. It would sure beat this endless chase to produce more and more for less and less.

The FDA now allows irradiation of beef to kill bacteria.

(Drawing by artist Glenn Beckmann, Kenai, Alaska)

The food industry is working hard through the media to convince you to accept the safety of food irradiation. My advice is to research the facts from all sides, not just from that of the food industry, and make sure you protect yourself from the possible health effects by choosing foods that are closer to nature whenever they are available.

How Now Mad Cow

Most of you have probably heard plenty about *Mad Cow disease,* technically termed bovine spongiform encephalopathy (BSE), which is a disease of the brain primarily affecting cattle. The British Health Secretary announced in 1996 that research shows that BSE can be transmitted to humans who ingest flesh or other parts of an animal afflicted with the disease.

The disease was first discovered between 1985 and 1986 in cows in Britain and was not thought at first to be a widespread threat to humans. Unfortunately, that wasn't the case. Another brain affliction very similar to BSE is Creutzfeldt-Jakob (CJD), which humans may contract when eating an animal affected with BSE. The incidence of CJD has doubled in the last decade.

These diseases eat away at the nervous system and destroy the brain, basically turning it into a sponge. Unfortunately this is not the same thing as figuratively having a sponge for a brain to soak up information. This disease is terrible. Victims suffer confusion, speech, sight, and hearing loss, dementia, convulsions, coma, and death.

Lettuce Explain

Mad Cow disease, also called bovine spongiform encephalopathy (BSE) and in humans Creutzfeldt-Jakob (CJD), is a fatal affliction of the nervous system. The disease is contracted by consuming meat or other products of an animal afflicted with BSE.

There is no treatment besides prevention, and even prevention is complicated because the disease is caused not by an ordinary organism like bacteria but by a mutant protein that is unaffected by antibiotics, sterilization, and irradiation.

Of course, the threat of this disease has scared many people away from red meat. Some McDonald's hamburger chains in Britain announced that they would not sell hamburgers until an acceptable non-British source of beef could be found. Beef was removed from school lunches in Britain, while Germany, France, and Belgium restricted imports of British beef. Millions of Britain's cattle were slaughtered as a safety precaution. No cases of either of these diseases have been reported in the United States.

Too Little, Too Late

Major restrictions went in to place worldwide to protect people from Mad Cow disease. Because the disease can be spread from animal to animal, the FDA placed bans on feeding livestock feeds that contain animal slaughter by-products to help prevent the disease here in the United States.

Lettuce Explain

Ruminants are hoofed animals that chew their cud, including cattle, sheep, goats, deer, and elk. **Rendering** is the process of separating fat from meat and other animal remains by the process of slow heating.

However, the FDA only prohibited the feeding of *ruminants* (ground-up pieces of cattle, basically) and mink parts to cattle. (Mink are included in the ban because they can spread a disease similar to Mad Cow disease.) This means that the FDA still allows the feeding of pig parts, blood, and gelatin obtained from *rendering* plants to cattle and other ruminant animals.

Man has not only turned naturally vegetarian animals into meat-eaters by mixing slaughterhouse by-products into their own feed, we have effectively turned these animals into cannibals! Could the terrible diseases that result from eating their own species be another consequence of our throwing off nature's fine balance?

Mad Cow Supplements

Even if a person has not eaten the meat of an infected cow, other ingredients can find their way into a vegetarian kitchen, including supplements containing glandulars, growth hormones, or any other supplemental products that are derived from cattle or other animals.

For instance, melatonin is a supplement used by many to restore youth and regulate sleep. Melatonin is manufactured by the pineal gland, which is in the brain. Responsible manufacturers use a synthetic form of the hormone for supplementation instead of getting their source from the pineal glands of livestock or rats.

My advice is that you not take melatonin from any animal source. Because a manufacturer is not required to disclose its source on the label, if the label doesn't state the source clearly, find out before you take it.

Always read your labels and make sure you can trust the manufacturer for your supplements—that goes for all supplements. For guidelines on what to look for in a reputable herbal and supplement manufacturer, see my book *The Complete Idiot's Guide to Herbal Remedies* (Alpha Books, 1999).

What Is Being Done

If you are an occasional meat-eater, it might ease your mind to know that The European Union ruled that British beef was again safe for import, although France has maintained its ban. New, faster tests have recently been developed that improve the previous testing procedures for Mad Cow disease. This new test can check up to about 1,000 beef carcasses each day, and the developers believe it is a world breakthrough for testing.

Rarely Well Done

Don't rest too easy yet, though. As I write today, a case of Mad Cow disease was discovered in Denmark in a four-year-old cow. With such strict measures put into place to stop the spread of the disease, this report is baffling to those involved. However, Mad Cow disease can take about five years to appear. In humans exposed to contaminated human growth hormone it can take 20 years to appear.

Even more terrifying are recent reports of new variants of CJD cropping up. At least seven new moms at a hospital in England recently might have been infected with a new variant of CJD by the surgical instruments used to perform caesarian sections. The new variant is believed to survive the sterilization of surgical instruments! At least one of the moms gave birth to a baby who suffers from neurological damage, indicating that the CJD may be transmitted from mother to child!

So what is a vegetarian to do? Keep eating your clean vegetarian diet, avoid meat and supplements that contain animal products, and hope that more people will go vegetarian and lessen the demand for meat so the cattle farmers will be forced to try new, safer alternatives to raising beef, such as organic ranching. Let's hope that our refusal to add to the imbalance of nature, reinforced by positive support for the farmers who support natural practices, can help restore a little bit of balance to our seemingly upside-down world!

The FDA Recommended Allowances

As you've learned, the FDA, USDA, and other food-related governmental agencies are not in place to take over responsibility for your health or your family's health. Nor are these agencies set up to tell you what is healthful, wholesome, or nutritious for your body. You're responsible for investigating on your own and seeking help from others who are in the business of helping you be and become well nutritionally.

However, the FDA and other regulatory agencies are in business to try to protect you from obviously harmful and life-threatening contaminants sold to the public. We rely on it for a certain amount of food-safety insurance so we can relax and enjoy our meals!

It does try to police all aspects of the food industry to help limit the occurrences of widespread food-borne illnesses. But no one is perfect, and certainly no system is perfect, nor can we expect it to be. This is where you need to be enlightened and take responsibility for your food purchases and food handling.

Look Me Over

The majority (about 65 percent) of the USDA's inspection workforce are dedicated to slaughterhouse inspection. These inspectors examine carcasses of animals by smell, sight, and touch to look for obviously diseased flesh. This system works pretty well.

Unfortunately, however, the biggest problem linked with food-borne illness in meats is the harmful bacteria lurking on the carcasses. Bacteria cannot be inspected for because you cannot see them. Irradiation kills these bacteria, but you must then weigh the pros and cons of irradiation.

No problem for the vegetarian, but for those who are still eating meat sometimes and are looking to secure long-term health, I strongly suggest you purchase organic, hormone-free, free-range, nonirradiated meat, obtained as fresh as possible.

Steer Clear

The U.S. authorities suspended shipments of beef from hormone-fed cattle from the United States voluntarily last year until improved monitoring and control procedures were put in place. The EU believes some hormones might have carcinogenic effects.

Yummy Hormones

Another thing to bear in mind is that when the FDA sets safe limits for various additives to animal feed, it doesn't take into account the potential accumulated buildup of hormones, pesticides, and other additives that come through our foods.

Five hormones are approved for use in the United States. Two are synthetically derived compounds not found naturally in humans, but they are allowable in animal products for human consumption.

These hormones are considered Generally Recognized As Safe (GRAS) by the FDA, but so are many chemical and unnatural substances added to our foods that you are better off avoiding. Other additives in the GRAS category include 200 food dyes and over 2,100 food flavorings.

Not Even Fit for Slaughter

On their way to the meat-packing plant farm animals are often shipped in overly crowded conditions without food, water, proper ventilation, or proper temperature control. Due to these stressful conditions some animals collapse, get trampled, become ill, or otherwise break down or die. All of these animals, including pigs, cows, chickens, horses, and sheep, alive or not, are classified as *downers*.

Due to public safety concerns any dead animal, and those unable to walk on their own, must be disposed of. In the States there are about 280 rendering plants where these animals are taken and basically boiled and ground down into a grainy powder, which is sold as feed for cattle, pigs, chickens, and domestic pets.

It is estimated that about 100,000 cows each year die of unknown causes. About 1 percent of beef cows are downers. Road kill may also be disposed of in rendering facilities.

Lettuce Explain

Downers are animals like farm animals or road kill that die for unknown reasons or that have collapsed or been crippled or otherwise incapacitated due to horrendous conditions when being shipped to slaughter. These animals are "processed" at rendering facilities and sold as animal food.

Just a Dumb Animal?

You are fooling yourself if you believe that animals are stupid and cannot sense death, experience fear, or feel pain. According to a livestock-handling consultant in Colorado, cattle that act normally on the range or at the ranch can begin to act wildly when on their way to slaughter and especially after they get to a meat-packing plant.

It seems the female cattle are more likely to express their fears. One observer reported that cattle go so wild that they panic, "beat their brains out," tear their hooves off in gates, and generally cause chaos during unloading or in preslaughter facilities. Why would this be if the animal didn't sense its impending doom?

Obviously animals in such a severe state of distress are pumping out a tremendous amount of hormones, adrenaline in particular, which has been nicknamed the fight-or-flight hormone. The hormone is released from the adrenal glands and circulated throughout the blood stream when a person or animal feels threatened.

This hormone saturates the animal's body tissues. The remnants of these hormones are eventually passed on to the consumer when he or she eats the animal's flesh. Cattle that panic in this manner produce dark-cutting meat, which is bad for packers and beef merchandisers.

Support Your Local Organic Farmer

Some farmers and field workers do have a special affinity for nature. They see how nature works and understand the gifts that the earth provides. Talk to some of them, and you will see. The farmer who is in touch with nature is usually a good man or woman. Support these people with your pocketbook by purchasing their foods.

Wouldn't you rather support the good-old-fashioned farmer who works with the earth to bring you wholesome, nourishing, unadulterated, nonhybrid, pesticide-free, nonwaxed, vine-ripened food? Ahh, utopia!

The Least You Need to Know

➤ There are arguments for and against the irradiation of meat and produce. Investigate the issue for yourself, and look for the radura symbol when you purchase food.

➤ Remember that even if you choose to buy irradiated foods, you still need to follow the same food safety measures that you would with nonirradiated foods.

➤ Vegetarians don't need to worry about Mad Cow disease but should be careful to choose supplements that do not contain animal products.

➤ Vegetarians should work toward making positive change by supporting organic farmers and those who work more closely with nature. These farmers help keep balance in a very unbalanced industry.

➤ Governmental agencies do not have the job of ensuring your health but are in place to ensure that you are not poisoned by outright dangerous substances. The responsibility of working toward health is up to you.

Chapter 27

The Joy of Being Humane

In This Chapter

➤ Understand factory farming

➤ Learn about the atrocities farm animals endure

➤ Find out why many ovo vegetarians avoid factory-farmed eggs

➤ Discover why veal is a cruel meal

➤ Take a quick look at the life of a farm animal

This chapter was not only the hardest one in the book for me to write, but might be the hardest one for you to read. Its contents are what compelled me to become a vegetarian in the first place. To any person with a compassionate bone in his or her body the realities of slaughterhouses and factory farming are easily enough to drive a person to give up meat for good.

Instead of trying to tug at your compassionate heartstrings by painting mental pictures of sad, doe-eyed, human-like farm animals in your mind's eye, I have to assume you are already a compassionate being, and that as a person considering a vegetarian diet you are going to be opposed to the outright abuse and suffering of another living being, human animal or nonhuman animal. Therefore, I am going to tell it like it is, without too much commentary, because the facts speak for themselves. If you are interested in seeing some of the atrocities for yourself, I'll list some sources where you can get an eyeful.

Although I presented you with enough information in this book to compel you to go veg for your own health, to help the environment, or for spiritual and ethical reasons, most people won't go to any extreme unless they feel a deep emotional need to do so. The vegetarians I've known who stay vegetarians are people who abhor cruelty to animals. They are simply unable to eat the flesh of an animal, knowing what they know about the conditions the animal had to bear before it showed up as meat on a plate.

If you want to continue to shut your eyes to the reality of factory farming, close this book now. Because after your eyes are opened you might feel fooled or become angry or deeply upset. I hope that by taking in this information you will become more secure in your decision not only to eliminate meat but to continue to do so for the rest of your life—and you'll join those who are vegetarians for *all* the right reasons. Believe it or not you can change the world, one bite at a time.

Bottom Line Is by the Pound

Hog, cattle, and poultry farmers raise animals for profit. This means that animals that are not used for their by-products, such as sheep for wool, dairy cows for milk, and birds for their eggs, are sold by the pound for their weight in flesh. Unlike raising a pet, a person who raises something strictly for weight does not need to be concerned over how well-adjusted the animal is, what diseases it might be susceptible to, and what stresses and other suffering it has to withstand. Generally as long as the animal is plump and standing it is enough to bring its seller a decent price.

Farmers around the world are beginning to understand that animals feel discomfort, stress, terror, and pain and are affected psychologically by their environment and their treatment by their caretakers. They see how animal-rights proponents, activist organizations, and groups of compassionate individuals abhor the inhumane treatment of animals in general.

Sprouts of Info

Research done by Meat Stinks (www.meatstinks.com) tells that over 91 million pigs were slaughtered and more than 17 billion pounds of pig flesh were produced in the United States in 1997. Americans consumed 62.8 pounds of pig flesh per capita.

Farmers are realizing that animals that are treated just a little more kindly have a better reproduction rate, which means a better bottom-line profit for the farmer. But don't let this make you believe that farmers feel kindly toward the animals they raise for slaughter. The bottom line is that agribusiness is a business, not a walk in the park with a loyal dog, a warm snuggle with your new fluffy kitten, or a moment of synchronistic connectness between you and your horse.

Nothing is done to help farm animals cope, be comfortable, or even be satisfied with the conditions under which they are raised, unless of course the effort is rewarded with a substantial return on the bottom dollar at the marketplace. Even if an individual in this business wanted to care, the way today's agribusiness works it would be almost impossible to give any mass-produced, factory-farmed animal a comfortable, stress-free, pain-free life before or during their terrifying trip to the slaughterhouse and continue to stay in business.

This Little Piggy Went to Slaughter

Pigs are the most intelligent of all animals raised for food. Although their brains are small, pigs are actually as smart as or smarter than dogs. They are easily trained, and can be thoughtful, interesting animals. Left on their own, we find that pigs socialize, build community places to sleep together, forage for food in the woods, eliminate away from their community nests, and are quite active and even playful.

When sows (female pigs) are ready to give birth, or *farrow*, they dig a little birthing area and fill it with hay and twigs, staying with their new piglets for a week or so until the babies are ready to join the pig group.

Pigs raised in factory farms have no ability to play, socialize, exercise, run, walk, eliminate away from their beds, or otherwise do anything that can allow them to stay psychologically healthy or balanced.

Most pigs raised in factory farms are raised in total confinement in factories where they might never even see the light of day until they are hustled into trucks for slaughter. Pregnant sows are confined to concrete-floored pens, void of soft grass or hay (as they would have if they had the freedom to roam). These pens equal just about the size of their own bodies, so small it barely allows them room to lay down, let alone move freely.

Lettuce Explain

Farrow means to give birth and is the term used to describe the birthing process for a female pig (sow).

Stir Crazy

Pigs demonstrate the negative effects of their confinement, boredom, and unnatural habitat in their behavior. Most pigs raised in these pens chew relentlessly on the bars of their pens. Still others bite each other, especially the tails of other pigs, and some even resort to stress-induced cannibalism, demonstrating their stir craziness.

Because of this habit of tail biting in pig factories, farmers are encouraged to *dock* (chop off) the pigs' tails close to the pig's body, using side-cutting pliers or another blunt instrument, because the crushing action helps control the gushing blood when the tail is cut.

Lettuce Explain

Docking is the procedure of chopping off a pig's tail with the crushing force of a blunt instrument, such as pliers. Docking is done to confined pigs that, because of stressful living conditions, chew on each other's tails.

Talk about treating the symptom! Instead of giving the pigs more room and allowing them to return to normal behavior for stress relief, pig farmers find that the cost of space is too expensive and resort to docking the pigs' tails rather than coughing up the dough to pay for more humane conditions.

Suffering the Consequences

Here's a sad summary of the cruel conditions and suffering that factory-farmed pigs endure:

➤ Concrete or slated floors designed for ease of manure disposal creates foot disorders and eventually deformity, although as noted by one factory farmer, most pigs are slaughtered before gross deformity is obvious.

➤ Sows give birth and their piglets are taken from them early so that they can begin the gestation cycle again sooner and produce more offspring. One manager in the meat business summed up this practice succinctly when he described these sows as "sausage machines."

➤ Confinement that not only keeps pigs fat due to a lack of exercise and movement, but contributes to an enormous amount of boredom, frustration, and psychological stress. Pigs develop porcine stress syndrome (PSS) from living under these terrible conditions.

➤ Poor-air quality from inhaling their own excrement because of the confining conditions, poor nutrition, overcrowding, and big temperature swings make pigs susceptible to porcine respiratory disease complex (PRDC). Symptoms of this disease are coughing, respiratory distress, poor weight gain (notable to the farmer), and fever.

➤ Living in darkness deprives the animal of the sunshine nutrient, which should be free to every creature in my opinion. Remember that sunshine serves as a mild immune stimulant and is antibacterial.

These unnatural living conditions are not only cruel to the animals, but also create a breeding ground for filth that leads to diseased pigs swarming with bacteria and viruses.

Hosts of Pathogens

Here's just a sampling of the bacteria, pathogens, and viruses found in the blood and meat of pigs, as well as diseases they suffer not previously mentioned:

➤ **Anemia:** slow growth rate, labored breathing, pale skin

➤ **Agalactia:** inadequate milk supply, weakness, fever, rapid breathing

➤ **Atrophic rhinitis:** inflammation of the lining of the nasal cavity, difficulty in breathing, death

➤ **Brucellosis:** reproductive failure, possible threat to human health

➤ **Dysentery:** bloody diarrhea, dehydration, weight loss

➤ **Foot-and-mouth disease:** fever, blisters on feet, snout, mouth, and tongue, and death

➤ **Hemophilus parasuis:** blood and nervous system disorder

➤ **Hemophilus pleuropneumoniae (HPP):** death with a bloody froth from the mouth

➤ **Histopathology lesions:** skin lesions from diseased tissue caused by microscopic bacteria

➤ **Infectious arthritis:** abdominal pain, labored breathing, fever, inflamed testicles, lameness

➤ **Leptospirosis:** bacterial disease that can cause stillbirth, spontaneous abortion, and weakness

➤ **Mastitis:** inflammation of the udder

➤ **Metritis:** inflammation of the uterus

➤ **Mycoplasma:** coughing, labored breathing, slow growth, lung lesions, death

➤ **Parasites:** lice, mange, worms

➤ **Pasteurella multocida type** A: labored breathing, coughing, listlessness, sudden death

➤ **Pneumonia:** persistent cough, labored breathing, lung lesions, high temperature, death

➤ **Pseudorabies:** mouth frothing, teeth grinding, spasms of the esophagus, shaking, convulsions, coma, death

➤ **Salmonella:** diarrhea, stunted growth, leads to pneumonia, death

➤ **Swine fever:** infections, fatal viral disease characterized by high fever, hemorrhages in skin, spleen, and other internal organs

➤ **Transmissible gastroenteritis (TGE):** vomiting, diarrhea, severe dehydration

To prevent the diseases caused by their filthy living conditions, hog farmers use mass vaccination programs and put large quantities of medications in the animals' feed. No wonder irradiation of meat has come into play! I'm sticking to soy sausage patties, thank you very much.

Chicken, Chicken, Run and Hide

The atrocities that chickens and other poultry endure, whether they are being raised for slaughter, egg production, or both, were alarming to me when I first researched what is involved in mass-producing eggs. No wonder many vegetarians refuse to eat eggs at all.

Steer Clear

Many vegetarians do not eat or use any items that take an animal's life. However, some feel that the life a chicken lives to produce eggs might be worse than if the chicken were put to death. Many ovo vegetarians consume eggs only from free-range chickens or from small local farms.

Lettuce Explain

Debeaking is the searing off of chicks beaks with a hot-bladed instrument. The rapid pace in which this procedure is normally carried out (about 10 to 15 chicks per minute), can result in careless work leading to blisters, burned nostrils, and severe mutilations of the chicks.

Here's a quick overview of the factory-farmed chicken's life.

First an egg is hatched in a hatchery (actually the numbers are more like 10,000 to 50,000 at a time) and a new baby chick emerges into the world. Then all the chicks are *debeaked,* a painful process of searing off the baby chicks' beaks, similar to pigs having their tails docked.

Debeaking is done to prevent chickens from pecking each other while forced to live in overcrowded, stressful conditions. Chickens naturally have a pecking order, an internal instinct that keeps them in balance in normal environments. Farmers who have free-ranging chickens on old-fashioned farms have no need to debeak chicks. But chickens that cannot get away from each other in crowded conditions can peck each other to death. Debeaking is another example of treating the symptoms.

A Short and Horrible Life and Death

Chicks are then divided into two groups, broilers and layers. The broilers live for about seven weeks in horrendously crowded, windowless sheds, with the conditions environmentally manipulated for accelerated, premature growth. They are fed automatically, and the room is usually not cleaned until they are removed for slaughter.

This means the birds breathe in their own filth, like any confined animals are forced to do. Farmers are warned to wear respirators when they enter the broiler sheds because microorganisms and air-borne bacteria fill the air. These young animals are manipulated by artificial lighting to make them mature faster and to control their moods.

After sitting in their own excrement for weeks, many of these birds suffer from blisters on their chests, hock burns, and ulcerated feet. Finally, at the end of these seven weeks, the doors fling open, the birds are grabbed by their feet, smashed into crates, and carried off to the slaughterhouse.

There they wait their turn to be strung up by their legs and carried upside down by metal shackles to an area where their heads are submerged in an electrified tank of water, which stuns the birds. Some are rendered unconscious, some are not. This is not monitored. From there, still conscious or not, the birds are passed through an area where their throats are slashed by a mechanical blade.

Not all birds are killed by the blade, however, because the mechanical process is not 100 percent accurate. Nevertheless, the birds are submerged in a tank of boiling water, and those who missed the blade are boiled alive. This is so common that the poultry industry has its own name for these birds; it calls them redskins.

A Slow and Painful Life and Death

The layer chicks have a different fate. First, after the chicks are hatched, the males are separated from the females. Different farmers have their own practices for the disposal of male chicks. Generally they are considered garbage and most are stuffed into plastic bags where they crush each other and eventually suffocate. Some are gassed. Others are ground up (dead or alive) to be processed into chicken feed and then fed to their egg-laying sisters.

When the females are ready to lay eggs they are usually debeaked again before being jammed into wire battery cages, piled into barns and deprived of sunlight, fed hormones and antibiotics, and sometimes manipulated by artificial lighting. Hen's toes frequently become caught in the wire floor of their cages; their flesh sometimes grows completely around the wires.

Here they live their life, sick and stressed, forced to lay eggs until they can lay no more. Retired egg-layers are not sold as whole chickens because of the poor condition of their bruised and abscessed bodies. They are sold as parts for chicken potpies, chicken soup, or pet food.

These unnatural conditions create birds that are highly susceptible to disease (stress lowers the immune system in both humans and nonhumans). High levels of antibiotics are fed to these birds just to keep diseases and infections from completely taking over.

And, of course, a certain number of the hen's offspring get sent to hatcheries for incubation, where the process begins all over again.

Steer Clear

Ninety percent of all commercially sold eggs come from chickens raised on factory farms, so if you are a concerned ovo vegetarian, be sure to seek eggs from free-ranging chickens from old-fashioned farms.

Veggie Soup for the Soul

In the 1920s the role of vitamins A and D in bone development was discovered, and it was found that chickens did not need sunshine and exercise in order to utilize calcium for proper bone development if the synthetic version of these vitamins could be added to their feed. This is how the factory farm boiler rooms came about. Chicken and egg production once belonged to farm wives, who were the main suppliers of this industry. Soon the factory farm took over.

Foie Gras *Is a Faux Pas*

Chickens aren't the only birds that suffer under factory farming. In fact some of the cruelty is so appalling that investigations in New York have prompted a new bill prohibiting the cruel feeding methods used on ducks and geese at *foie gras* farms.

Ducks and geese raised for pâté (a spread made of ground-up duck and goose livers) are force-fed. An inflexible tube is forced down their throats, causing what must be painful lacerations to the animal. Pounds of feed are pumped directly into the animal's stomach. This gross amount of food distends the animal's abdomen so severely that it can barely wobble away from the force-feeding area.

Lettuce Explain

Foie gras is a goose or duck's liver swollen from force-feeding on corn. When the birds are slaughtered their livers are removed and ground up, and sold as pâté, a fancy party food dip for nonvegetarian humans.

Force feeding makes proper digestion almost impossible and therefore causes the animal's liver to become swollen, which brings more pâté to the table. Just think about how uncomfortable you have been if you have ever overeaten or stuffed yourself at a meal. These animals are subjected to this routine daily.

In the U.K. and Germany foie gras production is illegal. New York is one of the last states where foie gras production is still allowed.

Don't Gobble a Turkey, Either

Turkeys are a big commodity, especially during holidays like the American Thanksgiving. They are more popular now that consumers are eating less red meat and more poultry. But turkeys are not exempt from the cruelty and horrendous conditions found on factory farms. In addition to being subjected to debeaking, turkeys sometimes have to endure having their toes chopped off. None of these procedures are done with any kind of anesthesia.

Commercially farmed turkeys also are genetically manipulated to be bigger and heavier, with larger breasts. Many are artificially inseminated because their bodies have been bred to become so large that their skeletal system can't keep up, and their legs can barely support them. This makes it difficult or impossible for the male to mount a female to reproduce naturally.

Veal, a Cruel Meal

Even many staunch meat-eaters refuse to touch veal, and you don't see it on restaurant menus so often anymore. Veal is meat from an anemic baby male calf. Many people ban veal from their diets on principle. Here's why:

Lettuce Explain

Bob veal is meat from calves that are slaughtered at about two to three days old, versus regular veal, which is the meat from an anemic calf about 14 to 16 weeks old. Bob veal is cheaper meat and is usually sold for processed foods like TV dinners.

➤ Dairy cows give birth to a newborn calf. If it is male it will be raised either as beef or veal. Some calves are taken from the mother immediately and slaughtered for *bob veal*, or infant calf meat.

➤ Those not slaughtered almost immediately are chained or put into veal crates where they are immobilized and kept in completely darkened, solitary conditions until they become anemic and their muscles atrophy. This is not done to save money on space, but to keep the animal from any movement. Lack of sunlight keeps the calf's muscles from developing, keeps his bones weakened (lack of vitamin D), and keeps his blood count low. Why? This treatment is what promotes soft, tender, gourmet veal meat.

➤ During this time the calf is deprived of its mother's milk (they leave that for human consumption) and is instead fed formula deliberately stripped of iron (which would reverse their anemia).

➤ Starved for iron, these calves lick the metallic parts of their crate and lick urine-saturated slats if they can, attracted to the minerals in these materials. They are also frequently dehydrated so that they will drink larger quantities of their liquid feed.

Needless to say, these pitiful dilapidated creatures are subject to every illness that might come their way due to their weakened, sickly condition. Therefore, they must be constantly pumped up with antibiotics to keep them alive during their brief existence.

These baby cattle are slaughtered at about 14 to 16 weeks of age, most of them too crippled and weak to even walk or stand. Many die on the way to slaughter.

333

The Makings of a Burger

And last, but certainly not least, we have beef cattle. The animals raised for beef are usually hauled long distances before they reach you as steak or hamburger. You've

Lettuce Explain

Waddling is another identification technique used in addition to or in place of branding. Waddling is a procedure that entails cutting chunks out of the animal's hide in the area under the neck, making it large enough so that ranchers can identify their cattle from a distance.

Sprouts of Info

Vegetarians should be happy to know that the Farm Animal Reform Movement (FARM, www.farmusa.org), the Farm Sanctuary, and similar organizations are fighting to improve these situations. They work to pass laws to protect downers and to raise funds and help people adopt these downed animals and allow them to live out the rest of their lives without abuse.

learned what happens to some of their little brothers, who are processed as veal. And you've learned how they are fed in feedlots, in cramped conditions, and how they panic when they get to the slaughterhouse.

But we can't forget some of the other horrors connected with being raised for slaughter. Beef cows have their testicles ripped off, their horns removed, and are branded with a searing piece of hot iron, or marked by *waddling*, which involves cutting out a chunk of flesh under the neck, all, of course, without the use of anesthetics.

From the Range to You

During the long-distance transport from where cattle are born to where they are fed to where they are slaughtered, they are crowded into metal trucks where they suffer from temperature extremes, lack of food and water, loud noises, fear, and stress.

Then, finally, away to the slaughterhouse they go. After being unloaded from trucks they are strung up by their hind legs on metal conveyer belts (much like chickens) and slaughtered at a rate of about 250 per hour. Although the animals are supposed to be stunned by a blow to the head, as with any rushed high-volume procedures, especially when dealing with panicking animals, these stuns are not 100 percent accurate, leaving conscious animals kicking and struggling while hanging upside down, forcing the slaughterhouse worker to struggle to kill or stun the animal.

What a Downer

As farm animals are unloaded at the processing plants some inevitably fall onto the ground instead of landing on the assembly line conveyor belt. Slaughterhouse workers don't have the time or the inclination to save individual animals that fall through the cracks. Sometimes the birds, cattle, sheep, or pigs die after being crushed by machinery or vehicles operating near the unloading area. Still others die of starvation or exposure after being abandoned. Some find these suffering animals easy pickings for pet food and use tractors, forklifts, winches, or chains to drag large downed animals to the slaughterhouse to be processed. These methods tend to break bones, tear limbs, and otherwise maim the already damaged animal.

Veggie Soup for the Soul

Many beef cattle who live on the range, foraging and fending for themselves, might be no better off than those born to the dairy cows. These cattle are not adequately protected against inclement weather, and some die of dehydration while others may freeze to death. And who will protect them from UFO abductions? (Just kidding, sorry.) Injured, ill, or otherwise ailing animals might not receive necessary veterinary attention. One common malady afflicting beef cattle is called "cancer eye." Left untreated the cancer eats away at the animal's eye and face, eventually producing a crater in the side of the animal's head.

Unfortunately, although it is hard to believe, these animals are not protected by the animal welfare act. Sometimes these animals are dumped alive into the garbage or onto piles of dead animals. Sometimes they are completely abandoned and left out in the elements to starve to death.

E.I.E.I. Ouch!

Simply put, the factory farming system of modern agribusiness is designed to produce the maximum amount of meat, milk, and eggs as quickly and cheaply as possible, and in the least amount of space.

Cows, calves, pigs, chickens, sheep, goats, turkeys, ducks, geese, rabbits, and other animals raised in factory farms are kept in the smallest areas possible, often restricting their movement so they are not even able to turn around.

These farm animals are deprived of exercise, sunshine, and any sort of natural environment so that all of their bodies' energy goes toward producing flesh, eggs, or milk for human consumption.

They are fed growth hormones to fatten them faster and are genetically altered to grow larger or to produce more milk or eggs than nature intended. They are loaded with antibiotics and other drugs to keep them from being taken over by bacteria and viruses. They live a life of suffering from the beginning to the end.

A vegetarian diet does not add to these horrors. Lacto ovo vegetarians who do eat animal products should consider purchasing their eggs and dairy products only from farmers who employ more humane practices. And if you can still stomach meat after reading this chapter, please look for organic free-range options. Your local co-op is a good place to start.

The Least You Need to Know

➤ Animal factory farming manipulates and interferes with natural processes to produce more animal products at the expense of the animals' welfare.

➤ Pigs are intelligent creatures that suffer when raised in filthy, unnatural conditions. These conditions create a breeding ground for a number of viruses, parasites, and dangerous bacteria.

➤ Chickens and other birds, whether raised for eggs or as poultry, are subjected to crowded, putrid, inhumane conditions.

➤ Veal is the flesh of a baby calf taken from a milking cow days after its birth, raised in horrific conditions, and slaughtered at 14 weeks old.

➤ Lacto ovo vegetarians or occasional meat-eaters who are concerned about the humane treatment of animals should try to obtain their animal products from farms where the animals are not subjected to inhumane conditions.

Chapter 28

A Passion for Compassion

In This Chapter

➤ Find out how to live and shop cruelty-free

➤ Discover how to help protect farm animals

➤ Learn how you can help companion animals, and other animals, too

➤ Join up with some animal advocacy organizations

➤ Learn to enjoy a compassionate, healthy, balanced life and lead by example

Now that you know the reality of a meat-based diet, I want to empower you to do something about it. You can make a big difference simply by going vegetarian, but if the last chapter made you want to become involved in a more focused and direct way this chapter is for you.

Unfortunately, animal abuse is found in almost all areas of society, including entertainment, agriculture, cosmetics testing, medical and scientific laboratory testing, and the fur industries. We find abuse of companion animals, destruction of wildlife, and the use of animals in schools for dissection.

We can all do our personal part to help end animal abuse and suffering, with or without being an activist, but if you do want to become an activist you can get a taste of it here. This chapter gives some contacts and information you can use to help gain protection for all animals.

Cruelty-Free Living

One of the greatest powers we have is our buying power. Money runs the economy, and your money contributes to the demand for certain products. It drives what kinds of items are manufactured and made available. A good example is the meat alternative market, which has soared to new heights in the last few years because of increasing demand.

American consumers in particular have helped that market to expand and grow, and we are being rewarded with more delicious alternatives. Most of us can now find at least five types of meat substitute in our stores. You've asked for it with your purchases and now you have more choices, and more are on the horizon!

This same rule of supply and demand holds true for other consumer goods, from the obviously cruel products like fur to the not-so-obviously cruel products like many hairsprays, cosmetics, and household items.

Most people already know not to drink shampoo, eat a tube of toothpaste, or flush their eyes with toilet bowl cleaner! However, some companies continue to force-feed these substances to rabbits, rats, mice, dogs, cats, guinea pigs, and other animals just so they can put a label on the product that reads "Keep away from children" or "Not intended for internal use."

Needless Cruelty

The truth is that the FDA does not require animal testing for beauty products. It only requires that each ingredient in a cosmetic product be adequately substantiated for safety. These safety tests can be done without the use of animals. Millions of animals suffer terribly and are killed in the name of testing products despite the lack of requirements to use animals.

In addition, the makers of household items, such as cleaning formulas and the like, are also not required by their governing body, the Consumer Product Safety Commission (CPSC), to test their products on animals, but many manufacturers do it anyway.

Manufacturers determine testing methods. Companies like the idea that their products were tested on animals because they feel it is a good defense in the face of possible consumer lawsuits. Others believe that testing on animals helps them compete in the marketplace because consumers demand products with exciting new ingredients, and animal tests are often considered the easiest and cheapest way to prove that new ingredients are safe. The reality is that animal tests are not necessarily the best, cheapest, or most accurate.

Let's look at some of the animal experiments used to test many beauty and household products.

Eye for an Eye

The eye irritancy test is commonly used to test hairsprays and other beauty products. During this test a liquid, flake, granule, or powdered substance is dropped into the eye(s) of a group of restrained albino rabbits. The animals are immobilized in apparatuses from which only their heads protrude.

Sprouts of Info

The results of eye irritancy tests are not 100 percent accurate because the results vary from laboratory to laboratory and even from rabbit to rabbit.

These devices keep them from being able to rub their eyes with a paw or otherwise remove the burning substance from their eyes. In addition to being restrained the rabbits' eyelids are held open with clips. When painful substances are placed in their eyes many animals break their own necks during their struggle to escape. They usually receive no anesthesia during the tests.

Testing lasts for an average of 72 hours while the lab technician periodically records the damage done. Reactions to the substances include swollen eyelids, inflamed irises, ulceration, bleeding, massive deterioration, and blindness.

Eye irritancy tests are generally done on rabbits because rabbit eyes have no tear ducts and so cannot wash away the painful substances. Humans' eyes do tear, so eye irritancy tests only show what might happen if a person got a splash of shampoo in his or her eye and then refrained from blinking or tearing for three days.

Does that make sense to you? Even placing a drop of harmless saline eye drops into your eye without your eyes watering is simply impossible. How do these tests help protect the consumer?

Why would you purchase a product to use on your skin, your face, your hair, or any area near your eyes that is capable of burning a hole in your eye? I like to use products with natural ingredients that are recognizable to my body. All you have to do is smell a product before you purchase it to see if you want to put it in or on your body! Just because the product was tested on animals does not prove its safety.

Acute Toxicity Tests—Not So Cute

Acute toxicity tests, also called lethal dose or poisoning tests, determine the amount of a substance it takes to kill a group of test animals. In these tests the substance being tested is force-fed to an animal via a tube inserted into the animal's stomach or through holes cut directly into the animal's throat.

Other ways the substance is administered include

➤ Injection under the skin

➤ Injection into a vein

339

Steer Clear

How many new substances must man continue to create in order to help the consumers get a better hold on their hairdo or a whiter toilet bowl? Why must manufacturers insist on doing their own tests on ingredients that have already been tested by other manufacturers? Companies that do not test on animals use compiled information collected from past tests to create new products.

Sprouts of Info

A survey conducted in the United States by the AMA showed that the majority of Americans are against using animals to test cosmetics.

➤ Injection into the lining of the abdomen

➤ Added to the animals feed

➤ Inhaled through a gas mask

➤ Placed directly into the eyes

➤ Inserted into the rectum or vagina of the animal

During acute toxicity tests experimenters observe and record the animals' reactions, such as convulsions, labored breathing, diarrhea, constipation, emaciation, skin eruptions, abnormal posture, and bleeding from the eyes, nose, or mouth, and eventually death.

In a similar test called the LD50 (Lethal dose 50) test the animals can sometimes take up to four weeks to die. The LD50 test is used to determine how much of a substance it takes to kill at least 50 percent of the animals being tested.

These cruel testing methods have always been the norm, but things are changing due to consumers' awareness. Now researchers have come up with nonanimal alternatives to test potentially fatal substances.

Researchers who seek to use alternatives to animal tests must first prove the reliability of the existing animal tests in order to prove that the nonanimal test method is just as reliable. This forces the researchers to admit that the traditional animal test results vary widely!

Animal Test Alternatives

There are hundreds of manufacturers of household and beauty products who refuse to engage in animal testing. Manufacturers who do not use animals can substitute cell and tissue cultures, corneas donated from eye banks, and sophisticated mathematical models and computer programs to determine the safety of products. (After all, we are living in the age of computers—why should our testing methods stay in the Dark Ages?)

These manufacturers tend to choose ingredients for their products that already have proven track records. These companies maintain and use databases that show ingredient and formula information they've gathered from other companies that have already performed safety tests in vitro, in human clinical studies, or both. Many of these companies do not use toxic or dangerous ingredients in their products and instead take advantage of the many safe ingredient alternatives available, even fruits, vegetables, and grains!

Veggie Soup for the Soul

Tom's of Maine is the manufacturer of a line of natural cruelty-free products, including deodorant, toothpaste, mouthwash, and other great items. Until now toothpaste companies had to conduct lethal animal testing in order to get the ADA to approve their toothpaste with fluoride. For seven years Tom's petitioned the American Dental Association to give its toothpaste the ADA seal of approval without Tom's having to use lethal animal testing. Tom's worked diligently with researchers to develop other means of testing the effects of fluoride. Finally, the ADA accepted the results of these alternative studies and gave Tom's its approval. Good going, Tom's of Maine!

I see animal testing alternatives just as I see meat alternatives! They are easy, available, and less harmful to animals, the environment, and ultimately our bodies. As more and more of us live cruelty-free, the manufactures that are still animal testing will begin to see that they are losing more and more customers. Those who choose alternative methods will gain more support, and therefore prosper. Once again consumers will create a new norm.

Don't Be Cruel, Buy Cruelty-Free

Public opinion plays a big role on how things are done. The European Union (EU) proposed banning cosmetic testing on animals due to public outcry just a few years back. And many companies across the world have responded to the public's wishes.

There are some things you can do to be sure you don't contribute to the needless suffering of animals used in product testing. For starters, patronize companies that do not test on animals. PETA can give you a complete list of such companies. Contact them at:

> **PETA (People for the Ethical Treatment of Animals)**
> 501 Front St.
> Norfolk, VA 23510
> Phone: 757-622-PETA (7382)
> Fax: 757-622-0457
> E-mail: info@peta-online.org

Look for the Logo

Although switching to all nonanimal tested (cruelty-free) products can be a tedious process at first, the work is over after you find your favorite brands. It is unlikely that any company with a no-testing-on-animals policy would suddenly decide to switch to animal testing.

➤ Look for the cruelty-free logo on cosmetic and household products, shown here. This new international logo can only be used on packaging and advertising by manufacturers that sign the Corporate Standard of Compassion for Animals, a strong pledge stating that they do not conduct or commission animal tests for their products, nor do they use ingredients or formulations that are tested on animals. In addition, once the logo is licensed they agree to an independently commissioned audit to verify their compliance with the Standard. The CCIC logo is the international symbol used by manufacturers of cosmetic and household products that comply with the Corporate Standard of Compassion for Animals. The logo program is supported by a unique coalition of more than 50 animal advocacy organizations worldwide, and was launched during the winter of 1998.

The international cruelty-free logo used by manufacturers of cosmetic and household products that do not test on animals.

(Logo used here with permission from the Coalition for Consumer Information on Cosmetics)

Veggie Soup for the Soul

The Coalition for Consumer Information on Cosmetics (CCIC) will work to ensure that companies using their logo do not conduct or commission animal testing. Most products manufactured with compassion may be safer for the earth and safer for you, anyway, since these products tend to be more natural, environmentally friendly, and less toxic overall.

➤ If you find that you use some products that are not cruelty-free that you just cannot live without, write the company to tell it you will boycott unless it comes up with alternatives to animal testing. This consumer feedback works! Many companies who once tested on animals have switched to other methods. At the least you will get a response telling you where the company stands on the issue, and you can decide from there if you can continue to support it with your patronage.

After you get the swing of it, you'll see that cruelty-free is an easy way to live, eat, and shop.

Who'll Protect Babe?

If you're already a vegetarian you are already doing your part to lower the numbers of animals (approximately eight billion annually) who suffer and are killed for meat, dairy products, and eggs. But, you say, your activist blood compels you to do more? Let's take a look at some of the ways you can help.

Here are some organizations to contact to work for the betterment of farm animals:

➤ **Council for Agricultural Science and Technology**
4420 West Lincoln Way
Ames, IA 50014-3447
Phone: 515-292-2125
Fax: 515-292-4512
E-mail: cast@cast-science.org

➤ **ARM (Farm Animal Reform Movement)**
P.O. BOX 30654
Bethesda, MD 20824
Phone: 301-530-1737
E-mail: farm@farmusa.org

➤ **Farm Sanctuary**
P.O. BOX 150
Watkins Glen, NY 14891
Fax 607-583-2041
Web site: www.farmsanctuary.org/join/joinform.htm

➤ **Humane Farming Association**
P.O. Box 3577
San Rafael, CA 94912
Phone: 415-771-CALF
Fax: 415-485-0106
E-mail: hfa@hfa.org
Web site: www.hfa.org/

Steer Clear

Most of the states in the United States have anticruelty legislation to prohibit gross mistreatment of animals. However many states' legislation excludes farm animals from these laws, as if to say, "Well, of course you can't be kind to an animal raised for slaughter!" To top it off, no federal legislation exists that protects farm animal's well-being.

Sprouts of Info

The Humane Farming Association includes over 125,000 members, making it the largest organization dedicated to the protection of farm animals in the United States.

Sprouts of Info

Since 1987, six states have enacted laws that establish a student's right to refuse to dissect animals in the classroom. If you want more information contact the Dissection Hotline through PETA at 1-800-922-FROG (1-800-922-3764) or e-mail education@peta-online.org.

➤ **Compassion in World Farming**
Charles House, 5A Charles Street
Petersfield, Hampshire
GU32 3EH, England
Phone: +44 (0)1730 264208 / 268863
Fax: +44 (0)1730 260791
E-mail: compassion@ciwf.co.uk

Here are some more personal things you can do as an activist to protect farm animals from abuse:

➤ Become a strict vegetarian or vegan.

➤ Boycott restaurants that serve veal and let them know why.

➤ Fill out comment cards in restaurants requesting more vegetarian items on the menu.

➤ Ask your state legislators to sponsor bills that would prohibit the use of veal crates.

➤ If you do choose to eat meat or other animal products occasionally, buy organic, free-range products when possible.

Lead by Example

If you choose to become an activist to protect animals, many people will look at you and your lifestyle scrupulously to learn what a vegetarian or vegan activist is all about. It would be unwise for you to speak up loudly about your beliefs and then not carry your actions through at home. If you are going to work toward making changes in animal welfare, be sure you have done your homework first by living as a vegan or vegetarian and choosing cruelty-free products.

Although many vegetarians strive toward the vegan ideal by not eating or wearing any obvious animal products and by using cruelty-free products, our society is saturated with animal by-products. Pobody's nerfect, but if you are doing your best to avoid animal products your efforts are admirable. At least you know that you are not contributing to the reasons animals are processed in the first place.

Here's a sampling of some hidden animal ingredients and their vegan alternatives. For more on ingredients in food and cosmetics, consult *A Consumer's Dictionary of Cosmetic Ingredients,* by Ruth Winter (Three Rivers Press, 1999) and *A Consumer's Dictionary of Food Additives,* by Ruth Winter (Three Rivers Press, 1999).

Ingredient	What It Is	What It's Used In	Vegan Alternative
Adrenaline	From adrenal glands of animals	Medicine	Synthetics
Allantoin	Uric acid from cows	Creams and lotions	Comfrey root extract, synthetics
Carmine, Cochineal, or Carminic Acid	Red pigment from crushed female cochineal insect	Used to color items red; commonly found in lollipops, red apple sauce, shampoos, cosmetics	Beet juice
Egg protein	Poultry eggs	Shampoos, skin care items	Plant proteins
Keratin	Protein from ground-up animal horns, hooves, feathers, and hair	Shampoos, permanent wave solutions, hair rinses	Soy protein, almond oil, rosemary

No Need to Kill

I think those who try to tell you that you wouldn't have film processing, red lollipops, perfume, glue, or other items if we didn't kill animals might not be thinking the whole process through. Currently, animal by-products are cheap and easy to use because they are the end result of the bigger industry.

Most animal ingredients used for things such as film processing or fertilizers are used because they are waste products or leftovers from processing animals for consumption. If no one ate meat I believe inventors would come up with more synthetic or plant-based products for these uses. Remember, they used to use horses for glue and whales for soap! Now we know we have options, and these animals are not so commonly killed to make these products.

Dissecting the Question

Cruelty to animals extends beyond testing labs and the food industry, though, and a classic example is found someplace you might not have thought of: our schools. How do vegetarian

Sprouts of Info

Nowadays, dissection can be handled in more humane ways as more alternatives such as 3-D computer models become available to kids, schools, and teachers who oppose the use of animals for this purpose.

students handle the requirement to dissect animals in class? I like to share the story of a high school girl who refused to dissect a frog in her science class several years back.

Although this girl was a very good student, the school was prepared to issue her a low grade for her science class if she refused the dissection assignment. The school probably assumed that if it let this girl "get away with" not doing her assignment on the grounds of individual ethics, it might open a Pandora's box for students who want to avoid other types of assignments. Rules are rules, and the school held its ground … for a while.

The case went to court, and it was revealed that this girl actually lived out her ethics in other areas of her life. They found that the girl and her family were vegetarians. None of the cosmetics or beauty products in their home were tested on animals and were not derived from animals. The cleaning products were even cruelty-free. The final verdict was that the girl had a genuine ethical commitment to her beliefs, and they worked out an alternative to the dissection. Her courageous actions paved the way for alternatives for future students and teachers.

I thought that was a fantastic test for a 16-year-old to take on. She not only stood up for what she believed in, but showed the way for other students to follow a cruelty-free lifestyle and to refuse to take part in activities that are in opposition to their ethics, even when these activities are mandatory in school. I guess it's true when they say "everything's negotiable."

Nobody's Companion

Companion animals are put down (euthanized) literally by the tons each year. Each year homeless pets and unwanted, abandoned, and stray cats, dogs, kittens, and puppies are picked up by or delivered to pounds. Here they live until they either get adopted, are sent to medical testing labs for atrocious experiments (via pound seizure), or are euthanized.

The dead bodies are disposed of, usually through rendering plants where they are processed and sold as ingredients in consumer or manufacturing products.

Compassion for all animals is healthy, but many tend to have a softer spot for companion pets like dogs and cats. You can do your part to prevent the needless suffering and death of thousands of companion animals yearly.

Here are a few things you can do:

➤ Get all your companion animals spayed or neutered. This reduces the massive number of unwanted animals. Fixing your pet generally makes the animal better behaved, curbs or ends its need to run away, and can prevent dogs from fighting, cats from spraying, and other nasty but natural hormonally driven behaviors.

➤ Adopt your pets from the pound to save a life.

➤ Do not support breeders. Adoption helps save lives, whereas purchasing from a breeder adds to the demand for more animals. For every bred animal that gets a home, several die in a pound. Many pure-breds, sweet, healthy, loving animals, can be found at the pound. You can find adult animals, baby animals, and all ages in between.

➤ Do not support pet stores that sell animals. Pet stores get their animals from puppy farms, places with generally horrendous conditions where puppies are bred for profit. The horrors are too deep to go into here, but take my word for it: If you are looking for a pet, go to the pound.

Steer Clear

Pet stores are places that can easily spread disease from animal to animal.

Profiting from Pets

The only animal I ever purchased was a kitten from a pet store in a mall in Colorado. (This was before I knew anything about animal rights, of course.) To make a long story short, the kitten was infected with a fatal and highly contagious disease, feline leukemia, and died before she ever had a chance to grow up, which broke my heart, as well as my pocketbook in vet bills.

When I notified the pet store that the other kittens that were in the same pen as mine were probably affected as well, it took *no* action. It continued to sell the rest of the kittens, who were probably infected, contributing to the spread of the disease, not to mention breaking new owners' hearts! I've never patronized a pet store since, but have adopted many healthy, wonderful, long-time companion animals from the Dumb Friend's League and other humane societies.

How to Help

Here are a couple of organizations to contact for information on how you can do more to help:

➤ **In Defense of Animals**
131 Camino Alto, Suite E
Mill Valley, CA 94941
Phone: 415-388 9641
Fax: 415-388 0388
General inquiries and correspondence e-mail: ida@idausa.org

➤ **Animal Protection Institute**
P.O. BOX 22505
Sacramento, CA 95822
Phone: 916-731-5521
Web site: www.api4animals.org/

Note that all of the organizations listed on these pages are nonprofit and take donations that you can use as a tax deduction. If you have no time to put into the welfare of animals, donate money to a favorite organization that will do the work for you.

Animals for Profit

Farm animals, companion animals, and animals used in cosmetic and household product testing are just the tip of the iceberg when it comes to animal abuse and victimization. We haven't even discussed animals used in scientific experiments, animals used and abused for entertainment in circuses, zoos, theme parks, and other show businesses, nor have we touched on the subject of fur, trapping, and poaching.

I believe it is fairly safe to say that the use of animals for any type of income usually exploits the animals involved. Even if there is no specific abuse or neglect to the animal by a person directly, such as beatings, withholding of food or water, poor shelter, and exposure to extreme conditions, animals exploited for profits certainly lose their God-given rights to freedom.

Steer Clear

Most animals used for entertainment purposes are exploited and their needs are met with minimal attention—many times just enough to make sure they can perform well enough to get you to pay for the show, similar to how RDA is the minimum amount of nutrients you need to fend off disease. Both are far from ideal. If you are a compassionate consumer, consider getting your entertainment elsewhere.

Animals captured and trained or held in a manmade environment strictly for show are denied their natural habitat and freedom to roam and live their lives while encountering all the experiences, good and bad, they would in the wild. It removes them from nature's finely balanced food chain. Man as a predator is interfering with nature's balance by removing animals from natural environments.

Making Your Tail Wag Again

I don't want to leave you on a sad note, though, with your tail tucked between your legs. I'm certain that those of you who care and are touched by the plight of animals will do your part *not* to contribute to animal suffering. But try not to let the issue consume you. Personally speaking, I used to be a mad animal rights activist, marching, posting signs, writing daily letters, boycotting, petitioning, "veganising" everything, and chastising those who ate veal and other cruelty-filled meals.

A lot of the efforts I and other activists made really helped make progress for animal rights, and I can see the changes today: many of the companies I sent letters to no longer test on animals, the use of the steel leg-hold trap has been banned in many areas, and the wearing of fur is generally a faux pas these days. But I had to let up on the intensity of my actions because I realized I was living angrily, and I lost my opportunity to inspire those around me at the time to become vegetarians.

Leading by Example

After I calmed my boisterous protests and started living by example, I was surprised how others tuned in to my vegetarian lifestyle and then followed my lead. Leading by example was much more effective for my animal-rights recruiting campaign.

Although I still do my part by buying cruelty-free products, spaying or neutering my pets, and being a vegetarian, I realize that I cannot save all the animals. I won't be able to completely heal the source of the problem of animal suffering no matter how many protests I attend. I am comforted by the fact that living the way I do helps, and I am happy with that.

Have a Healthy Happy Life!

By now you are probably ready to cross the street to avoid a meat-eater. Remember, though, that it's not right to expect everyone to be a vegetarian—maybe not even yourself! As a nutritional consultant I have discovered that pure vegetarianism is not for everyone, so my goal is to help each person get the best nutrition possible, with the best balance of diet and supplements for their needs.

That said, it remains true that humans are not designed to eat a meat-centered diet. Therefore, I suggest that everyone limit the amount of meat they eat by shifting to a more creative plant-based diet. I also suggest that people who do eat meat obtain organic, free-range products. These two things alone contribute greatly to your health and that of the environment, and aid in the balance of all things.

I hope you will not only become more of a vegetarian in your eating habits and food choices, but that you will use the information I have shared with you in this book to make your diet more healthful, interesting, fun, and nourishing. My wish is that you gain joy from knowing that your diet not only helps you feel and look better, but that being vegetarian helps make the world a better place.

So until we meet up again in the next book, enjoy your veggies!

The Least You Need to Know

➤ Just by being a vegetarian you are helping to better your own health, the health of the earth, and the welfare of animals in general.

➤ Using cruelty-free products ensures that you do not contribute to unnecessary testing of cosmetics and household products.

➤ Many organizations exist that you can join to work for the welfare of animals. If you don't want to be an activist you can contribute to an organization that will work for you to protect animal welfare.

➤ Although strict vegetarianism might not be for everyone, eating a plant-based diet and using animal products that are organic and come from free-range animals can contribute to a person's health, the well-being of the earth and the animals, and the farmers who offer these products.

A Veggie Vocabulary

autointoxication   A condition caused by a constipated bowel in which bowel toxins are harbored and circulated throughout the rest of the body by the blood stream.

beans   A plant with edible pods and seeds eaten cooked as a vegetable.

bioflavonoids   Nutrients found mainly in the rinds of citrus fruits and in the edible skins of most fruits, such as grapes and apples. They play a role in strengthening capillary fragility and permeability and serve as antioxidants.

bob veal   Infant calf meat, slaughtered at about two to three days old. Regular veal is the anemic meat from a calf about 14 to 16 weeks old. Bob veal is cheap meat usually sold for processed foods such as TV dinners.

breatharianism   The philosophy that teaches that when a person reaches a perfect state of health and a natural state of being, he or she will be in perfect harmony with the Creator and require no foods or water. Because of this, the aging process will be slowed dramatically.

carob (also called **locust bean**)   A tree used for its bittersweet leathery beans. The tree is native to the Mediterranean area and other warm climates. Carob is frequently used as a chocolate substitute.

casein (also **caseinate, sodium caseinate**)   A milk protein that is used as an additive in some "nondairy" replacers. Read your labels if you are eliminating all animal products from your diet.

ciguatera poisoning   Occurs mostly in reef-dwelling fish from tropical and subtropical climates; the toxin becomes more concentrated as it moves up the food chain. Commercially harvested red snapper and barracuda have been found to contain this toxin, but hundreds of other species have been implicated. Symptoms of ciguatera poisoning include diarrhea, vomiting, burning sensations in your mouth and throat, and numbness. It can affect the nervous system, heart, and respiratory system.

circulatory system   The body system that pertains to your entire blood transportation system and consists of the heart, veins, arteries, capillaries, and blood vessels.

complete protein   Contains all essential amino acids and is found in animal products and in some plant foods such as soybeans.

concentrated foods   Most starchy and heavy protein foods such as animal products, baked potatoes, grains, nuts, and seeds. When food combining, eat only one concentrated food per meal. Concentrated foods are, for the most part, devoid of water content.

cruelty-free, or **manufactured with compassion**   Terms that describe any product, such as household cleaners, solvents, dish detergents, cosmetics, toothpastes, beauty aids, mouthwash, and so on, that have not been tested on animals or made with animal derivatives.

curry   A pungent mixture containing up to 20 spices, herbs, and seeds. Curry originated in India and is used to flavor many Asian foods. A chief ingredient is turmeric; other ingredients can include sesame seeds, cloves, cardamom, fennel, nutmeg, red pepper, black pepper, coriander, saffron, and pimento. Curry is generally found in powder form, but pastes and liquids are also available.

cyanocobalamin   The usable part of the B_{12} vitamin. Other forms of B_{12} are called analogs, and scientists believe that the analogs could interfere with the useful cyanocobalamin, leading to a deficiency.

dairy   Any milk-based product such as cheese, milk, yogurt, and butter.

debeaking   The process of searing off the beaks of factory-farmed baby chicks with a hot-bladed instrument. The rapid pace in which this procedure is normally carried out (10 to 15 chicks per minute) can result in careless work, leading to blisters, burned nostrils, and severe mutilations of the chicks.

dendrites   Branched extensions of nerve cells that receive electrical signals from other neurons and act as conductors for signals to the cell body. Any new, repeated behavior creates new dendrites, making pathways for the new behavior.

diverticulitis   A condition in which abnormal protrusions of the lining of the colon become inflamed, causing severe abdominal pain, often accompanied by fever and constipation.

docking   The procedure of chopping off a pig's tail with the crushing force of a blunt instrument, such as pliers. Docking is done to confined pigs who, because of stressful confined living conditions, chew on each other's tails.

downers   Animals such as farm animals or road kill that die for unknown reasons or that have collapsed, been crippled, or otherwise incapacitated due to horrendous conditions when being shipped to slaughter. These animals are "processed" at rendering facilities and sold as animal food.

essential amino acids   Amino acids that cannot be manufactured by the body and that need to be supplied in the diet. These eight amino acids are lysine, isolecine, leucine, methionine, phenylalanine, thereonine, tryptophan, and valine.

essential fatty acids   Fatty acids that are not manufactured by the body but that are essential to proper functioning of the body. Essential fatty acids are the building blocks for hormones, cell membranes, and other chemical messengers.

ethics   A system of moral standards or principles.

eye teeth (also referred to as the **canines**)   In adults these are teeth numbers 11, 6, 22, and 27 on dental charts, and C, H, M, and R in children.

farrow   To give birth; the term used to describe the birthing process for a female pig (sow).

feedlot   A place where cattle and other livestock are kept to be fed grain and soy products and often to be injected with hormones and antibiotics as well. These feed-lots exist to fatten animals before slaughter.

foie gras   A food made from duck or goose livers swollen by the force-feeding of corn. When the birds are slaughtered their livers are removed, ground up, and sold as pâté, a fancy party spread for nonvegetarians.

free radicals   Unstable and destructive oxygen atoms. They are created by the body's natural processes, and therefore everyone lives with an undisruptive amount at all times. However, when excess free radicals are created by exposure to toxins in the air, water, and diet, or by constipation and stress, the damage they do increases and can cause cancer, premature aging, and other degenerative conditions.

gelatin   The boiled bones and hooves of animals, often used to make capsules for supplements.

halitosis   Bad breath. Can be caused by constipation, which can result from eating animal flesh and dairy products.

haustras   The bulbous pouches that make up the large intestine. The haustras work by peristaltic action to move food material back and forth inside the intestinal walls for final processing before elimination.

healing crisis   A positive, natural, detoxification process that the body performs when given the opportunity to release toxins. Symptoms are similar to illness and vary per individual, but usually are involved with the body's elimination channels. Symptoms of a healing crisis can include fever, diarrhea, nausea, headaches, boils, and foul or mucus discharges via the skin, bowels, respiratory system, and urinary system.

incomplete protein   A protein that lacks one or more of the essential amino acids. Most incomplete proteins are found in plants, but eating a variety of foods ensures an adequate consumption of complete proteins.

irradiation   A process of showering foods with powerful radiation after the foods are placed in an irradiation chamber. The purpose of irradiation is to burst apart the DNA molecules of food-borne bacteria that might be in the foods and cause food poisoning. Irradiated foods must be clearly marked in markets, but no regulations are in place for restaurants or hospitals.

kosher   A Hebrew term for "proper" or "fit." The term is used especially for foods that Orthodox Jews are allowed to eat according to Jewish law.

lacto ovo vegetarian   A person who eats no animal flesh, but who does eat eggs and dairy.

lacto vegetarian   A person who eats no animal flesh or eggs, but who does eat dairy.

legumes   A plant that has pods as fruits and roots that contain nitrogen-fixing bacteria. The word "legume" comes from French *légume* and from Latin *legumen,* which means "bean of unknown origin."

lipemia   A condition in which dietary fat is accumulated in the blood. This condition lasts for about four hours after you consume fat as the liver attempts to break it down and eliminate it from the body.

listeria monocytogenes   A bacteria that can be found in and on dairy products, poultry, and eggs. Listeria poisoning is termed listeriosis; symptoms include headache, nausea, fever, and vomiting. It can be potentially deadly to those with weak immune systems such as the elderly, those with immune system diseases, and young children.

macrobiotic diet   Based on an Asian philosophy of yin and yang—both life force energies. Different foods are categorized as more yin or more yang as are different conditions of the body. The idea is that you can help your body back to balance by feeding it more yin- or more yang-type foods. When the body is harmonized it is free of disease.

Mad Cow disease, also referred to as **bovine spongiform encephalopathy (BSE)** and **Creutzfeldt-Jakob (CJD)**   A fatal affliction of the nervous system. The disease is contracted by consuming the meat or other products of an animal afflicted with BSE.

meat   The term used throughout this book to define foods made of the flesh of animals.

metabolism   The ongoing interrelated chemical processes taking place in your body that provide the energy and nutrients to sustain life. Your metabolism is controlled by glandular activities in your thyroid, adrenals, and pituitary glands, and can be slowed or sped up depending on how your glands perceive the needs of the body. A slow metabolism can be linked to weight gain.

Murphy bag   A container of food snacks that you can put together and use while traveling to supplement your meal or serve as a backup when you are stuck somewhere without vegetarian food. Make your Murphy bag to suit your specific travel needs. It comes in handy when Murphy's Law strikes!

nutrient   Any substance that provides nourishment; for example, the minerals a plant takes from the soil or the constituents in food that keep a human body healthy and help it grow, maintain, and rebuild tissue.

nut   The fruit of a plant that usually has a hard shell.

ovo vegetarian   A person who eats no animal flesh or dairy, but does eat eggs.

peristalsis or **peristaltic action**   The wavelike contractions of the intestinal tract that move partially digested food through the digestive tract.

pescatarian, also referred to as **pesco vegetarian**   A person who eats a primarily plant-based diet, but who also eats fish or sea life. *Pesco* is Spanish for fish.

prostaglandins   Hormone-like substances that are made by fatty acids and have functions that include controlling smooth muscle contractions and regulating body temperature and inflammatory responses. They also play a role in controlling blood pressure, blood clotting, and water retention. Their balance is important in preventing PMS.

pyruvate   A naturally occurring substance in the human body that also is found in apples, red wine, and cheese.

radura   International, green, flower-like symbol that is required by law to be posted where irradiated foods are sold, either nearby or directly on the foods themselves. This symbol is not required in places where these foods are served, however, such as in hospitals or restaurants.

refined grains   Grains considered less nutritious than grains in their whole state because of the grinding and high heating process. Examples of refined grain products are rolled oats and flours.

rendering   The process of separating fat from meat and other animal remains by the process of slow heating.

ruminants   Hoofed animals that chew their cud, including cattle, sheep, goats, deer, and elk.

salmonella   A bacteria that is commonly found in and on eggs, and in and on poultry products such as chicken. Three types exist. The two common strains cause food poisoning called salmonella gastroenteritis, which creates acute symptoms such as diarrhea, cramps, fever, and vomiting and can be fatal for immunosuppressed individuals. A third type is responsible for typhoid fever.

scombroid poisoning   Occurs from eating fish that has not been properly refrigerated and that has had the chance to begin decomposing. Proper cooking of fish does not eliminate this toxin. Symptoms of scombroid poisoning include allergic-type reactions, headache, diarrhea, dizziness, irregular heartbeat, itching, shortness of breath, flushing, muscle weakness, and may include a peppery taste in the mouth.

seafood   Term used in this book to refer to the fish and other animal life from the sea.

seeds   Contain the embryo of a new plant. You can think of them as the eggs of the plant kingdom.

seitan   A brown, slick-textured, high-protein, low-fat form of wheat gluten found in health food stores, generally near the tofu. It is made from whole-wheat flour and is used in sandwiches and stir-fry and as a meat substitute.

stevia   An herb used as a replacement for sugar that is even used by diabetics, although there is much political debate over its use. Stevia contains the following nutrients: phosphorus, magnesium, potassium, selenium, silicon, sodium, manganese, as well as small amounts of calcium, iron, and zinc.

stomach teeth   Molars. In adults these teeth are teeth numbers 3, 2, 14, 15, 30, 31, 18, 19, and 1, 16, 17, and 32 (the wisdom teeth, which may or may not come in). In children these teeth are letters S, L, I, and B, which usually come in first, indicating the child is able to chew and digest solid foods. They are followed by A, J, T, and K.

tamari   A less salty version of soy sauce; a dark, salty liquid made from fermented soybeans, used as a flavoring agent, especially in oriental foods.

testa   The protective coating on the outside of a seed that keeps it from germinating until conditions are right. The testa serves as an enzyme inhibitor, which can inhibit our digestion as well. Therefore, it is best to eat seeds that are well-ground or chewed thoroughly.

vegetarian   A plant-based diet of vegetables and fruits, nuts, seeds, and grains, and the people who follow this diet. Vegetarians do not eat meat.

waddling   A type of identification marking used in addition to or in place of branding. Is a procedure that entails cutting chunks out of the animal's hide in the area under the neck, making it large enough so that ranchers can identify cattle from a distance.

whole foods   Foods that are created by nature and that are eaten in their unaltered, unprocessed state, such as raw fruits and vegetables.

whole grains   The most nutritious grains. Contain many vitamins and minerals, and when cooked correctly can provide natural enzymes. A whole grain is in its unprocessed state.

Vegetarian Cookbooks

Cooking with Meat Substitutes

Cooking with Seitan: The Complete Vegetarian 'Wheat-Meat' Cookbook, by Leonard Jacobs and Barbara Jacobs, 185 pages. This cookbook is a must for anyone new or wishing to try seitan.

Fabulous Beans, by Barb Bloomfield, 143 pages. Beans have many benefits. They are a great source of protein, fiber, vitamins, and minerals, not to mention being extremely affordable! Use them often in place of meat—this cookbook gives you over 100 vegan recipes to show you how!

Soyfoods Cookery, by Louise Hagler, 112 pages. This book focuses on all soy foods, their benefits, and easy ways to add soy to your diet.

The Tempeh Cookbook, by Dorothy R. Bates, 96 pages. Don't get stuck in a rut using tempeh only as a burger replacement or in stir-fry. With this cookbook you can learn fun, easy, and healthful ways to cook delicious tempeh.

The TVP Cookbook: Using the Quick-Cooking Meat Substitute, by Dorothy R. Bates, 96 pages. Rated five stars by readers, this book is fun and easy to understand. Learn how to make TVP work for you as a meat substitute in a variety of dishes.

Tofu Cookery, by Louise Hagler, 160 pages. This beautifully photographed cookbook entices you with glossy 8 × 10 photos of the finished product and then shows you how to turn tofu into almost any dish, including main courses, appetizers, condiments, and even dessert. (One of my personal favorites for tofu creativity.)

Tofu Quick and Easy, by Louise Hagler, 96 pages. Filled with quick and easy menu tips for preparing over 120 delicious tofu dishes.

Low–Fat/Low–Cholesterol Vegetarian

Most vegetarian (especially vegan) diets are low fat anyway, but for those who are giving up meat for their heart health, try these great cookbooks to facilitate a faster recovery.

The Almost No-Fat Cookbook: Everyday Vegetarian Recipes, by Bryanna Clark Grogan, 192 pages. Grogan is wise in understanding how what we eat is deeply engrained in our psyche. Her recipes are for "comfort" foods such as low-fat chocolate cake, low-fat homemade ice cream, and even low-fat fries. All are dairy-free and healthy, but are still able to feed the psychological need.

Lighten Up! Tasty, Low-fat, Low-Calorie Vegetarian Cuisine, by Louise Hagler, 160 pages. Here Louise shares her delicious and filling recipes that will help you trim the fat, calories, and cholesterol from your diet while adding fiber. Over 130 easy recipes.

Fat-Free and Easy: Great Meals in Minutes! by Jennifer Raymond 152 pages. Inspired by the requirements of Dr. Dean Ornish's "Open Your Heart Program," the author, a nutrition specialist and guest chef with Dr. Ornish, supplies quick, easy vegan meals sure to delight you and keep your heart healthy.

The Vegetarian No-Cholesterol Family-Style Cookbook, by Kate Schumann and Virginia Messina, M.P.H., R.D., 147 pages. Wonderfully creative and delicious recipes geared toward homestyle cooking but with a new twist, and all low in fat!

Meatless Cooking

Classic Vegetarian Recipes, by Sue Ashworth, Carole Handslip, Kathryn Hawkins, Cara Hobday, Jenny Stacey, Rosemary Wadey, and Pamela Westland. 256 brightly photographed pages. This book was a recent find. The book is absolutely packed with close-up photographs of beautiful veggie dishes, along with the recipes, of course— I like to have the photos to see what "looks good" to cook. So far, everything made from this one has tasted as good as it looks!

The American Vegetarian Cookbook from the Fit for Life Kitchen, by Marilyn Diamond, 422 pages. Many readers give this cookbook five stars! Fantastic life-changing cookbook helps you prepare vegetarian meals with proper food combining. Learn to eat well and stay fit. Gives the inside information about what occurs in your body when you eat various foods. Interesting and empowering information, a good choice.

The Higher Taste, A Guide to Gourmet Vegetarian Cooking and a Karma Free Diet, 161 pages. Contains some of my favorite recipes for Indian, Mexican, Italian, Asian, and a variety of other delicious meatless dishes. Contains photos and text that shows why we can all be vegetarian. Instructs you on how to make your own ghee and curd. (This book might not be available in book stores. You can get a copy through ITV 3764 Watseka Avenue, Los Angeles, California 90034, 213-559-7670.) The book contains a complete list of Govinda's restaurants (vegetarian Krishna restaurants) around the world.

GardenCuisine, by Paul Wenner, 386 pages. The author is the creator of the famous Gardenburger and GardenVegan and not only shares over 150 delicious recipes but also tells how to heal yourself and the planet through meatless eating. Inspirational and motivational reading and cooking.

Diet for a Small Planet, by Frances Moore Lappé, 479 pages. The first half makes a strong political case for not eating meat; the last half contains recipes for a variety of meatless meals. Well researched.

Vegetarian Cooking for Everyone, by Deborah Madison, 742 pages. Described as the most comprehensive primer for vegetarian cooking ever published, a beautiful volume featuring 1,400 diverse gourmet recipes from the founding chef of the Greens restaurant in San Francisco. (The majority of the recipes are vegan.)

Meatless Meals for Working People, by Debra Wasserman and Charles Stahler, 96 pages. A great book for busy or hectic lifestyles, great tips for where and how to eat as a nonmeat-eater. Also includes nutritional information.

Cooking Vegetarian: Healthy, Delicious, and Easy Vegetarian Cuisine, Vesanto Melina, R.D., and Joseph Forest, 239 pages. Not only serves up a rich variety of vegetarian dishes but includes nutrient analysis, shopping and simplifying tips, and information for creating full-flavored vegetarian meals.

Moosewood Restaurant Cooks at Home, Fast and Easy Recipes for Any Day, by The Moosewood Collective, 416 pages. Contains a huge variety sure to please all tastes, also includes low-fat vegan kids' foods and time-saving tips.

Vegan Cookbooks

The Single Vegan, by Leah Leneman, 127 pages. So many of my single friends tell me, "I'd eat better, maybe even vegetarian, if I wasn't cooking for just myself." This book is the answer. Great ideas for recipes and even shopping lists and vegan stables to have on hand to make it easy.

Cooking with PETA: Great Vegan Recipes for a Compassionate Kitchen, by the staff at PETA, 223 pages. This fun book includes 200 favorite compassionate (animal-free) recipes and explains sources of vegan ingredients.

Nonna's Italian Kitchen, by Bryanna Clark Grogan, 255 pages. (*Nonna* is Italian for grandma). So you can't figure out how to make cheesy tasting Italian dishes without the cheese? This author makes vegan Italian look and taste *delicióso!*

The Uncheese Cookbook: Creating Amazing Dairy-Free Cheese Substitutes and Classic 'Uncheese' Dishes, by Joanne Stepaniak, 192 pages. This book is a hit with cheese lovers who want (or need) to go vegan. Turn nuts and other nondairy foods into your own dairyless brie or uncheesecake!

Table for Two: Meat-and-Dairy-Free Recipes for Two, by Joanne Stepaniak, 192 pages. This is a much-needed vegan cookbook for couples. The author helps you create simple, tasty recipes for two requiring less than 30 minutes to prepare.

The Millennium Cookbook: Extraordinary Vegetarian Cuisine, by Eric Tucker and John Westerdahl, 258 pages. The Millennium Restaurant has been praised for its fabulous and innovative approach to vegetarian cuisine. Provides gourmet vegan recipes that are delicious, beautiful, and have an international flair.

Vegan Vittles: Recipes Inspired by the Critters of Farm Sanctuary, by Joanne Stepaniak, Suzanne Havala (Contributor), 176 pages. Cited by readers as the best of the best vegan cookbooks. Some turn from vegetarian to vegan after making these delicious mouth-watering recipes. You can't pass this one up!

Special-Needs Cooking

Vegetarian Cooking for People with Diabetes, by Patricia Le Shane, 144 pages. Over 100 low-fat vegetarian recipes that will help you manage diabetes while still enjoying tasty foods.

Vegetarian Cooking for People with Allergies, by Raphael Rettner, D.C., 128 pages. Includes many vegan recipes that are free of common allergy-causing foods. A great way for the allergy suffer to go veg.

CalciYum! Calcium-Rich, Dairy-Free Vegetarian Recipes, by David and Rachelle Bronfman, 192 pages. Worried about getting your calcium when you give up dairy? Worry no more. These 120 delicious, dairy-free, calcium-rich recipes show you the way to get calcium from breakfast to dessert. Great recipes to consider for helping you build better structural system health.

Eat Right, Live Longer, by Neal D. Barnard, M.D., 336 pages. Want to eat not only for longer life, but to live healthy longer? Find out how foods can slow and reverse some aspects of aging and can play a role in weight, menopause, hypertension, diabetes, arthritis, and a host of other "age" related illnesses. Healthful vegetarian recipes by Jennifer Raymond are included.

American Heart Association Kids' Cookbook, by the American Heart Association, edited by Mary Winston, Ed.D., R.D., with additions by James H. Moller, M.D. A cookbook for kids, the 34 recipes included are mostly vegetarian and 9 are vegan. Older kids can use this on their own while younger ones will need some supervision.

150 Easy Meatless Vegetarian Times Low-Fat and Fast Recipes, by the editors of *Vegetarian Times* magazine, 288 pages. Includes 175 tempting recipes using a variety of grains such as quiona, couscous, pastas, Asian noodles, and fresh vegetables.

Better Than Peanut Butter & Jelly: Quick Vegetarian Meals Your Kids Will Love! by Wendy Muldawer and Marty Mattare, 176 pages. The title tells all! This cookbook includes 150 low-fat, low-sugar, kid-tested recipes.

Veggie-Related Videos and Posters

Healthy, Wealthy, and Wise, a video based on the book *The Higher Taste,* based on the teachings of His Divine Grace A.C. Bhaktivedanta Swami Prabhupda, can be found where *The Higher Taste* is found.

The New Four Food Groups Posters, The Choose Health! versions from Physician's Committee for Responsible Medicine. These 22 × 17-inch posters use brilliant color photos along with serving recommendations for getting your nutrition without cholesterol or fat. Purchase via PCRM's Web site (www.pcrm.org) or at online bookstores.

Cooking with Kurma: Gourmet Vegetarian, video. Kurma presents a vegetarian cookery video that has exciting tasty recipes. For those who like to follow along with a video instead of reading, what a fun way to learn to cook tasty veg! Great Indian-style foods.

A Diet for All Reasons, video by Michael Klaper, M.D. A videotaped presentation of the reasons for going vegetarian. Dr. Klaper shows surgical footage of a hard string of cholesterol being removed from a heavy meat-eater's artery. A great visual for giving up animal products for heart health. Overall a very informative and entertaining presentation. Order by contacting Paulette Eisen Nutritional Services, 4900 Overland Ave. #234, Culver City, California 90230, 310-289-4173.

Web Sites for the Meatless

Vegetarian and Vegan Organizations

I've listed a handful of popular vegetarian sites to get you started. Most of these sites offer vegetarian recipes, lists of vegetarian restaurants, vegetarian news, the latest vegetarian and vegan books and cookbooks, answers to common questions, and many other links to help you get into the veg scene!

➤ **Worldwide Vegetarian URL Collection.** www.quanyin.com/eng/article/vegurl.html

This one offers URL's from vegetarian organizations all over the world and is a great place to start.

➤ **The Vegetarian Resource Group.** www.vrg.org

➤ **The Vegetarian Society of the United Kingdom.** www.vegsoc.org

➤ **The Virtual Vegetarian.** www.vegetariantimes.com

➤ **Vegetarian Pages.** www.veg.org

➤ **Physicians Committee for Responsible Medicine.** www.pcrm.org

➤ **North American Vegetarian Society.** navs-online.org/

➤ **Evergreen Healthy Vegetarian Association.** ehva.tripod.com/index.html

This Web site is available in Chinese and English.

Veggie Recipes Online

These are a handful of recipe sites that offer a collection of delicious and varied vegetarian and vegan dishes. If you're not hungry now, you will be once you start reading what's for dinner at these sites!

➤ **Veggies Unite.** www.vegweb.com

Offers everything from meat substitute meals to suggestions for holiday meals.

➤ **The Low Fat Vegetarian Recipes Archive.** www.fatfree.com

Contains over 3,000 low-fat vegetarian recipes. Includes a USDA nutrient database for all foods.

➤ **John's Vegetarian Recipes and Information.**
www.interlog.com/~john13/recipes/

Offers recipes in four languages (English, Spanish, French, and German)!

➤ **Indian Vegetarian Cooking.** members.tripod.com/~epicure/home.htm

Offers a variety of traditional Indian vegetarian recipes.

➤ **Vitalita Culinary Group (VCG).** www.vitalita.com/cookbooks.html

Graciously offers a free, vegan, whole-food cookbook online; most recipes are gluten-free, too. Book includes photos and a variety of delicious-sounding recipes. (See how some of the best things in life are free?)

➤ **Even Sven's Vegetarian Recipe Exchange.**
members.tripod.com/%7Eevensven/vegrecipes.html

Specializes in swapping and collecting recipes that are quick, easy, meatless, and cheap! A great site for students and those who aren't into cooking fancy, just great-tasting veggie meals.

➤ **Healing Feats Holistic Health Services.** www.healingfeats.com/recipes.htm

This one is my holistic information site, but I have a collection of some favorite dishes listed here.

➤ **Your Environment, Your Health.** www.fortunecity.com/boozers/austral/375/recipie.html

Includes hundreds of vegetarian recipes, updated frequently.

➤ **Quaker Bonnet.** www.quakerbonnet.com/veg.htm

Offering a variety of vegetarian and vegan recipes from around the world—Asian vegetarian, Indian vegetarian, and even a Buddhist casserole!

Sites for the Vegetarian or Vegan Pet Owner

➤ **WOW BOW Distributors LTD.** www.wow-bow.com

This company offers 13 vegetarian pet foods, meatless gourmet health treats, and the most humane meat-based foods on the market. Its motto is "healthy alternatives toward a cruelty-free world." Call 1-800-326-0230 or check our the Web site for its free pet health care catalog.

➤ **Harbingers of a New Age.** www.tradeshows-online.com/vegepet/
Specializing in vegetarian dog and cat food.

➤ **Natural Life Pet Products, Inc.** www.sament.com/natlife

➤ **AltVetMed.** www.altvetmed.com/index1.html

This site is a *must* for any pet owner who wants to know how to take care of his or her pets using more natural methods. It includes a guide to holistic veterinarians, natural flea control, a list of natural pet food suppliers (including many who are not online), acupuncture and chiropractic care for pets, and much more!

➤ **Wysong.** www.wysong.net

➤ **Abundant Earth.** www.abundantearth.com

➤ **Nature's Pet.com.** www.naturespet.com

Offers Noah's Kindom Dogfood premix, a vegetarian and herb-based, premixed pet food to which you add your own protein. Now that you know which foods are protein-rich, you know you can add lentils, tofu, or other meat substitutes.

➤ **Reptile House and Bird.** www.reptilehouseandbirds.com

Vegetarian food for your reptilian pets! Look for Monster Munch!

➤ **Dr.Goodpet.** www.goodpet.com

➤ **F&O Pet Products.** wegancats.safeshopper.com/

Offers a wide variety of vegetarian cat and dog products, including starter packs.

Index

W–X–Y–Z

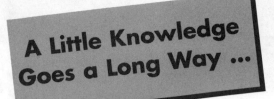
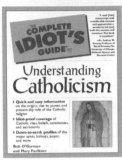

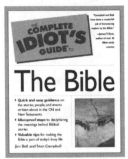

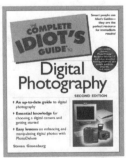
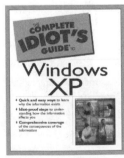